'The depth and range of Milton Lodge's contributions to political psychology are highlighted by the distinction of the authors contributing to this volume. Its broad focus encompasses motivated reasoning, transfer of affect, and the problem of wobbly citizen civic expertise, among other topics.'
—*David O. Sears, Distinguished Professor of Psychology and Political Science, UCLA*

'This is an important book. It demonstrates the powerful and far reaching influence that Milton Lodge has had on the development of political psychology. Not only has his personal research had a singular influence on the field but his example has demonstrated how political psychologists should conduct their work to meet the highest academic and scholarly standards.'
—*Edward G. Carmines, Distinguished Professor, Warner O. Chapman Professor of Political Science, and Rudy Professor, Indiana University*

'This is a book to prize. It is above all a book of ideas — most centrally, the ideas of the preeminent researcher in the field, Milton Lodge, but additionally, as a bonus, the ideas of many who have had the good fortune of learning from him by working along side of him.'
—*Paul M. Sniderman, Fairleigh S. Dickinson Jr. Professor of Public Policy, Stanford University*

THE FEELING, THINKING CITIZEN

This book is an appreciation of the long and illustrious career of Milton Lodge. Having begun his academic life as a Kremlinologist in the 1960s, Milton Lodge radically shifted gears to become one of the most influential scholars of the past half century working at the intersection of psychology and political science. In borrowing and refashioning concepts from cognitive psychology, social cognition and neuroscience, his work has led to wholesale transformations in the way political scientists understand the mass political mind, as well as the nature and quality of democratic citizenship.

In this collection, Lodge's collaborators and colleagues describe how his work has influenced their own careers, and how his insights have been synthesized into the bloodstream of contemporary political psychology. The volume includes personal reflections from Lodge's long-standing collaborators as well as original research papers from leading figures in political psychology who have drawn inspiration from the Lodgean oeuvre. Reflecting on his multi-faceted contribution to the study of political psychology, *The Feeling, Thinking Citizen* illustrates the centrality of Lodge's work in constructing a psychologically plausible model of the democratic citizen.

Howard Lavine is Arleen C. Carlson Professor of Political Science and Psychology at the University of Minnesota and Director of the Center for the Study of Political Psychology. He is author of *Open versus Closed: Personality, Identity and the Politics of Redistribution* (2017) and *The Ambivalent Partisan: How Critical Loyalty Promotes Democracy* (2012), which won the Robert E. Lane and David O. Sears Book Awards. He is editor of *Advances in Political Psychology*.

Charles S. Taber is Professor of Political Science and Dean of the Graduate School at Stony Brook University. He received his PhD from the University of Illinois, Urbana-Champaign in 1991, and works in the fields of political psychology and computational modeling. Taber has contributed to the growing literature on the psychological mechanisms that drive public opinion, and his 2013 book, *The Rationalizing Voter*, coauthored with Milton Lodge, won the Robert E. Lane Book Award and the Book of the Year Awards from the Experimental Politics and Migration and Citizenship Sections of the American Political Science Association.

Routledge Studies in Political Psychology
Edited by Howard Lavine, *University of Minnesota*

Advisory Board: Ted Brader, *University of Michigan;* Eugene Borgida, *University of Minnesota;* Marc Ross, Bryn Mawr College and Linda Skitka, *University of Illinois, Chicago*

Routledge Studies in Political Psychology was developed to publish books representing the widest range of theoretical, methodological and epistemological approaches in political psychology. The series is intended to expand awareness of the creative application of psychological theory within the domain of politics and foster deeper appreciation of the psychological roots of political behavior.

1 **The Many Faces of Tolerance**
   Attitudes towards Diversity in Poland
   Ewa A. Golebiowska

2 **Emotions in Conflict**
   Inhibitors and Facilitators of Peace Making
   Eran Halperin

3 **Fox News and American Politics**
   How Television News Shapes Political Views and Behaviors
   Dan Cassino

4 **The Political Psychology of Women in U.S. Politics**
   Edited by Angela L. Bos and Monica C. Schneider

5 **The Feeling, Thinking Citizen**
   Essays in Honor of Milton Lodge
   Edited by Howard Lavine and Charles S. Taber

THE FEELING, THINKING CITIZEN

Essays in Honor of Milton Lodge

Edited by Howard Lavine and Charles S. Taber

NEW YORK AND LONDON

First published 2018
by Routledge
711 Third Avenue, New York, NY 10017

and by Routledge
2 Park Square, Milton Park, Abingdon, Oxon, OX14 4RN

Routledge is an imprint of the Taylor & Francis Group, an informa business

© 2018 Taylor & Francis

The right of Howard Lavine and Charles S. Taber to be identified as the authors of the editorial material, and of the authors for their individual chapters, has been asserted in accordance with sections 77 and 78 of the Copyright, Designs and Patents Act 1988.

All rights reserved. No part of this book may be reprinted or reproduced or utilised in any form or by any electronic, mechanical, or other means, now known or hereafter invented, including photocopying and recording, or in any information storage or retrieval system, without permission in writing from the publishers.

Trademark notice: Product or corporate names may be trademarks or registered trademarks, and are used only for identification and explanation without intent to infringe.

Library of Congress Cataloging-in-Publication Data
A catalog record for this book has been requested

ISBN: 978-0-8153-7939-3 (hbk)
ISBN: 978-0-8153-7940-9 (pbk)
ISBN: 978-1-351-21594-7 (ebk)

Typeset in Bembo
by Apex CoVantage, LLC

CONTENTS

List of Figures   ix
List of Tables   x
List of Contributors   xii
Foreword by Jeffrey A. Segal   xiv

1. A *Festschrift* for a Friend   1
   Howard Lavine and Charles S. Taber

2. Conversations About *The Rationalizing Voter*   11
   Charles S. Taber

3. Inside the Black Box With Milt, and Other Lessons Learned   29
   Kathleen M. McGraw

4. Citizens, Politics, and Process: The Extensive Reach
   of Milton Lodge   47
   Robert Huckfeldt

5. The Paradox of Political Knowledge   65
   Jennifer Jerit and Caitlin Davies

6. Political Expertise and Open-Minded Cognition   81
   Victor Ottati, Chase Wilson, Erika Price, and Nathanael
   Sumaktoyo

7 Belief Change: A Bayesian Perspective   99
   Marco R. Steenbergen and Howard Lavine

8 Motivated Responses to Political Communications:
   Framing, Party Cues, and Science Information   125
   James N. Druckman, Thomas J. Leeper, and Rune Slothuus

9 The Effects of First Impressions on Subsequent
   Information Search and Evaluation   151
   David P. Redlawsk and Douglas R. Pierce

10 Racially Motivated Reasoning   171
   Stanley Feldman and Leonie Huddy

11 All in the Eye of the Beholder: Asymmetry in Ideological
   Accountability   195
   Gaurav Sood and Shanto Iyengar

12 (Working Toward) Affective Transfer in the Real World   229
   Tessa M. Ditonto and Richard R. Lau

Index   *253*

FIGURES

7.1	Experimental Sequence	107
7.2	Observed and Bayesian Posteriors	115
9.1	Dynamic Information Board	156
9.2	Dynamic Information Board Item Detail	157
10.1	The Final Standardized Factor Loadings for the Two-Factor Model	180
10.2	The Smoothed Distribution of Motivated Reasoning	182
10.3	Most White Americans Believe Whites Are Treated More Fairly	183
10.4	The Predicted Probability of Answering at Least Two of the Questions Correctly	189
11.1	Relationship Between Ideology and Approval by Whether or Not Respondent and Representative's Party Match	200
11.2a	Relationship Between Actual Ideological Distance and Approval	203
11.2b	Relationship Between Actual Ideological Distance and Approval	204
11.3	Perceived Ideological Location of Democratic and Republican Senators by Party of Respondent	206
11.E4	Screenshot of the Survey Experiment	227

TABLES

7.1	Sample Evidence on the Effectiveness of Capital Punishment	109
7.2	Sample Evidence on the Fairness of Capital Punishment	109
7.3	Group Differences in Log(k)	112
7.4	Determinants of the Accuracy of Log(k)	114
7.5	Predicted Probabilities of Accuracy	114
7.6	Predicting the Observed Posteriors	116
7.7	Discrepancies Between Predicted and Observed Posteriors	116
7.8	Attitudinal Effects of Belief Change	118
9.1	Impression Type by Candidate	160
9.2	Evaluation by Impression Type	161
9.3	Vote Propensity by Impression Type	162
9.4	Candidate Information Search by Impression Type	163
9.5	Liking and Disliking Information by Impression Type	163
9.6	Effect of Subsequent Information Search on Feeling Thermometer Scores	165
10.1	Racially Motivated Reasoning Scale	178
10.2	Determinants of Motivated Reasoning	185
10.3	Frequencies for Historical Discrimination Items	187
10.4	Determinants of Historical Knowledge	187
11.1	Approval of Senator as a Function of Ideology (DW-Nominate)	201
11.2	Approval of Candidate as a Function of Actual Ideological Distance	204
11.3	Approval of Candidate as a Function of Absolute Distance	207
11.4	Approval of Candidate by Candidate Position on the Issues	209
11.A1	Approval of Senators as a Function of Ideology (CF-Scores)	218
11.A2	Approval of Senators as a Function of Ideological Extremity (DW-Nominate)	219

11.A3	Approval of Senators as a Function of Ideology (DW-Nominate) With Random Effects of States	220
11.C1	Relationship Between Approval and Ideology	222
11.D1	Approval of Candidate as a Function of Perceived Ideological Distance	224
12.1	Ratings of In-Party Candidates, by Partisans	236
12.2	Multivariate Analysis of Candidate Evaluation, Interactions With Party Identification	238
12.3	Multivariate Analysis of Candidate Evaluation, Interactions With Ethnicity, Race, and Gender	245
12.A1	(MTurk) Subject Characteristics	251

CONTRIBUTORS

Caitlin Davies, PhD candidate in Political Science, Stony Brook University

Tessa M. Ditonto, Assistant Professor of Political Science, Iowa State University

James N. Druckman, Payson S. Wild Professor of Political Science and Faculty Fellow at the Institute for Policy Research at Northwestern University

Stanley Feldman, Professor of Political Science, Stony Brook University

Robert Huckfeldt, Distinguished Professor of Political Science and Communication, University of California, Davis

Leonie Huddy, Professor of Political Science, Stony Brook University

Shanto Iyengar, Harry & Norman Chandler Professor of Communication and Professor of Political Science, Stanford University

Jennifer Jerit, Professor of Political Science, Stony Brook University

Richard R. Lau, Professor of Political Science, Rutgers University

Howard Lavine, Arleen C. Carlson Professor of Political Science and Psychology and Director of the Center for the Study of Political Psychology, University of Minnesota

Thomas J. Leeper, Associate Professor in Political Behaviour, London School of Economics and Political Science

Contributors **xiii**

Kathleen M. McGraw, Professor of Political Science, Ohio State University

Victor Ottati, Professor of Psychology, Loyola University Chicago

Douglas R. Pierce, Lecturer, California Polytechnic University

Erika Price, Senior Lecturer and Postdoctoral Research Associate in Psychology, Loyola University Chicago

David P. Redlawsk, James R. Soles Professor and Chair of Political Science, University of Delaware

Rune Slothuus, Professor of Political Science, Aarhus University

Gaurav Sood, Principal Data Scientist, Defense Advanced Research Projects Agency

Marco R. Steenbergen, Professor of Political Science, University of Zurich

Nathanael Sumaktoyo, PhD Candidate in Political Science, University of Notre Dame

Charles S. Taber, Professor of Political Science and Dean of the Graduate School, Stony Brook University

Chase Wilson, PhD Candidate in Psychology, Loyola University Chicago

FOREWORD

I write this introduction not to review an aspect of Milton Lodge's career, but as someone who is not a political psychologist who has nevertheless been influenced enormously by Milt. He is a colleague, a friend, a mentor, but most of all, a role model in terms of what an academic researcher should be. Milt was so dedicated to his research that he avoided administrative positions at all costs. And when he did on occasion get roped into administrative positions he bragged that he would purposefully mess them up so he wouldn't be asked again. This was one piece of advice that I never took. As these positions all preceded my 1982 arrival, I have no evidence if Milt was as bad as he claimed. I know first-hand that Milt did a very good job as President of the Midwest Political Science Association, so it's possible that his scholarly self-image motivated him to perceive his administrative work as worse than it actually was. And speaking about motivated reasoning, Milt always held that scientists should be working on peer-reviewed journal articles rather than books, at least until Milt decided to write his book on motivated reasoning.

After I received tenure my office moved next to Milt's. Milt and I are both part of what I refer to as "Old Men Eating Lunch" in the political science faculty lounge (Howie: we miss you!). Milt though, would be so caught up in his work that I would have to remind him that it was lunchtime. Milt is retired now, by which he means retired from teaching. He still comes into the office nearly every day and though my office is no longer next to his, I still get him around 12:30 or so every day. Milt's quip as to why he's in the office every day even though he's retired is that Janet, his utterly charming wife, told him, "I married you for better or worse, but not for lunch."

Everyone who has met Milt knows his quick wit and infectious laugh make him a memorable character. I still recall meeting only three faculty members from my interview at Stony Brook in 1982 and Milt was one of them (the other two were the acting chair and an assistant professor who, to put it charitably, had "issues"). Milt and Janet now live in a senior community, and Milt once invited me for dinner and a talk there. It was no surprise to me that Milt had quickly become one of the social centers of the community.

I noted above that I while Milt and I are not in the same fields, he has had a substantial impact on my career. It started early when my first article submission got an R&R from the *American Political Science Review*. Milt had happened to pass along an article to me (I believe by Jim Gibson) that helped me formulate my response to the one negative review. The *Review* did eventually publish the article and I always believed that the happenstance of receiving Gibson's article from Milt played a large role.

While that first publication was mainline judicial politics, my work has drifted into political psychology on more than one occasion, and Milt has been the main influence on these works. Let me start with "Supreme Court Justices as Human Decision Makers," published in the 1986 *Journal of Politics*. In that article I argued that the justices on the Supreme Court, like all human decision makers, are subject to cognitive limitations that lead to Simon-style satisficing. Looking back on that article today, it is not as clear to me now as it must have been then that I was demonstrating my argument with the observational data that I used. Nevertheless, Milt's influence was clearly there.

In the winter/spring of 1993, my PhD student Valerie Hoekstra was working on the first project from her dissertation about the influence of the Supreme Court decisions on public opinion in the locale from which the case originated. Valerie wanted to compare the Court's influence in the immediate location from the surrounding areas. For reasons that I do not recall, I helped Valerie gather the before and after survey data for *Lamb's Chapel v. Center Moriches Union Free School District*. To our surprise, we found greater impact in the surrounding community than in Center Moriches. Milt explained that, based on the Elaboration Likelihood Model, this is exactly what we should have expected. Indeed, Valerie found similar results in all of her other studies.

While I was working on the *Lamb's Chapel* paper with Valerie, rational-choice theory began making deep inroads into judicial politics. Scholars such as John Ferejohn, William Eskridge, Pablo Spiller and others argued in the so-called Separation of Powers (SoP) models, that the Supreme Court was significantly constrained by Congress and the President in its statutory decision-making, because an overturned decision would leave the Court worse off than if it simply placed policy at the point closest to its ideal point that was within the set of irreversible decisions. Perhaps due to the influence of Milt and the political psychology program at Stony Brook I was deeply suspicious that the Court would have the knowledge to know when Congress was likely to overrule it and where it should place the policy in equilibrium. Of course the "as if" answer can readily be used to answer the knowledge questions if we find behavior consistent with the model. My large n empirical analyses, initially flawed and later corrected, did not find

Supreme Court behavior consistent with the model. I cannot rerun history and know whether I would have had the same suspicions about the SoP models but for my professional dealings with Milt, but I did have those suspicions and Milt is their most likely source.

I can draw clearer connections to Milt from three of my most recent projects. First, for many years I have heard Milt note that "the correlation between attitudes and behavior is 0.3." Like most social scientists, I have been well aware of the replication crisis plaguing psychology and other behavioral sciences. On the other hand, I have spent decades measuring the attitudes/ideology of Supreme Court nominees and correlating those attitudes with their voting behavior once they began service on the Court. My original finding of a 0.80 correlation between their attitudes and behavior in civil liberties cases has been replicated a variety of times. For the justices on the Court at the start of the 2016–2017 term, I now find a correlation of 0.94 between their perceived ideology when they joined the Court and their voting behavior in all cases.

My next two projects involve attempts to triangulate experimental findings on law-related phenomena with observational data from real judges. Both projects rely on motivated reasoning. The first one, with Avani Sood and Benjamin Woodson, looks at Court of Appeal decisions in Fourth Amendment exclusionary rule decisions. As most people know, the Supreme Court requires that evidence gathered in violation of the Fourth Amendment's prohibition on unreasonable searches and seizures may not be used at trial (*Mapp v. Ohio*, 1961). The U.S. Supreme Court has explicitly declared that the egregiousness of the crime does not influence whether the evidence should be excluded or not (*Flippo v. West Virginia*, 1999). Nevertheless, it would be unreasonable to expect human judges to apply the same Fourth Amendment standards to a brutal homicide investigation that they do to cases involving possession of marijuana. We find that they don't, and triangulating with Sood's experimental work (2015), have reason to believe that subconscious motivated reasoning is at work.

Finally, a current project with Lee Epstein and Chris Parker looks at the Supreme Court's First Amendment free speech decisions. Judicial scholars have long considered support for First Amendment values to be the province of liberal justices. Given recent Court decisions, however, law professors have been arguing that conservative justices are more likely to support First Amendment values (for an explanation as to why and how issues on the Supreme Court flip ideological polarity, see Baum, 2017). With motivated reasoning as the mechanism and in-group bias as the theory, we contend that that neither liberals nor conservatives inherently support First Amendment values; rather, liberals support liberal speech (e.g., "Bong hits 4 Jesus," see *Morse v. Frederick*, 2007) and oppose conservative speech, such as campaign spending by corporations (*Citizens United v. Federal Election Commission*, 2010).

Milt grew up as a working class kid from Brooklyn, including a stint in construction on the Verrazano Narrows Bridge, connecting Brooklyn and Staten

Island. He enlisted in the army, served in Germany, came home and went to college on the G.I. Bill, and then graduate school at Michigan. He started his academic career at the University of Iowa before Joseph Tanenhaus pulled him to Stony Brook. I have followed Milt's footsteps in terms of the Presidency of the Midwest and election into the American Academy of Arts and Sciences. Ever the mentor, Milt had a significant role in both. Let me conclude by stating that Milt's focus has always been on his research. When he retired (again, "from teaching") he would not let us have a dinner or throw a party for him. Given that the core of a *festschrift* is on research, he should be happy. It is entirely fitting for his illustrious career.

Jeffrey A. Segal

References

Baum, Lawrence. (2017). *Ideology in the Supreme Court*. Princeton, NJ: Princeton University Press.
Citizens United v. Federal Election Commission, 558 U.S. 310 (2010).
Flippo v. West Virginia, 528 US 11 (1999).
Lamb's Chapel v. Center Moriches Union Free School District, 508 U.S. 384 (1993).
Mapp v. Ohio, 367 U.S. 643 (1961).
Morse v. Frederick, 551 U.S. 393 (2007).
Sood, Avani Mehta. (2015). Cognitive cleansing: Experimental psychology and the exclusionary rule. *Georgetown Law Journal*, 103, 1543–1608.

1
A *FESTSCHRIFT* FOR A FRIEND

Howard Lavine and Charles S. Taber

This book is an appreciation of the long and illustrious career of Milton Lodge. Having begun his academic life as a Kremlinologist in the 1960s, Milt radically shifted gears to become one of the most influential scholars of the past half century working at the intersection of psychology and political science. In borrowing and refashioning concepts from cognitive psychology, social cognition and neuroscience, Milt's work has led to wholesale transformations in the way political scientists understand the mass political mind, and therefore the nature and quality of democratic citizenship (e.g., Lodge & Hamill, 1986; Lodge & McGraw, 1995; Lodge, McGraw, & Stroh, 1989; Lodge, Steenbergen, & Brau, 1995; Lodge & Taber, 2013; Taber & Lodge, 2006). The field of political psychology has grown substantially over the course of Milt's career at Stony Brook, and there are now political psychologists scattered across the globe. We don't think it would constitute too severe a case of motivated reasoning to claim that Milton Lodge has been a vital impetus to that growth.

In putting these chapters together, we asked Milt's closest peers to reflect on his work, to describe how it has influenced their own careers, and to trace out how Milt's insights have been synthesized into the bloodstream of contemporary political psychology. Some of Milt's friends tackled this task by writing novel research papers or by reviewing a body of their own work. Others wrote more personal reflections. We found the essays delightful to read, and we oversaw this project with joy. Milton, however, is not likely to be as happy about it. We didn't warn him that we were doing this (much less ask his permission), mainly because we think he would have vetoed it (we *know* he would have). He'd have said it was a waste of our time and that anyway this sort of thing would only embarrass him. But we asked Janet, and she was enthusiastic and gave us a green light. So, we're sorry for this Milt; we hope you're not too mad. We disregard because we love.

Many of the friends in this volume arrived at Stony Brook as young scholars, some with backgrounds in social psychology, others with degrees in political science. We felt like we had a grasp on something, perhaps without being quite sure where we were headed. Luckily, we entered into regular and sustained conversation with Milton. For one of us, this resulted in a 25-year collaboration involving the co-authorship of several articles and an award-winning book. For another, there was daily conversation, collaboration on articles, and sharing a room for 20 years (and running) at the Palmer House. For all of us, there was the opportunity to kick back in Milt's office—or, of course, in the lunchroom, where only very serious topics were ever discussed—and talk about whatever it was we were trying to figure out. It was, and for those still down the hall, continues to be, an experience to savor. Milt's door is always open, he's never too busy to listen to your problems, professional and otherwise, and you nearly always walk out better than you walked in.

A key aspect of Milt's vision in building political psychology at Stony Brook was the hiring of psychology PhDs fresh out of graduate school. This reflected his belief that explicating the rhyme and reason of the mass political mind required a deep understanding of basic psychological theory. It never seemed to bother him that upon arrival, none of these individuals—with the exception of Leonie Huddy—knew much about political science (see Kathleen McGraw's humorous discussion of this point in this volume). By contrast, we (psychologists) were pretty anxious about the road that lay ahead. We were armed with experimental methods and theories of social cognition, attitude change, intergroup relations, and evolutionary psychology, but whether and how any of this could be marshaled to publish an article in a political science journal we knew not. Thankfully, our colleagues were patient, and gave us plenty of breathing room. Milton was central in this regard. He took each of us under his wing, assured us that we had the right stuff, and pointed us to what he thought were the most promising questions. He also read our work, and gave thoughtful consideration to how we might insert ourselves into debates in political science. As invaluable as he was as a mentor, what really inspired us was seeing Milton *do* political psychology. As we will elaborate below, he showed us that to succeed in the discipline with a psychological orientation, you needed to apply your expertise to the big questions that animate political scientists (e.g., how can people act rationally in politics given how little they know about it?). We witnessed Milt rise to this challenge over and over again. He made it look easy.

Despite his pleasure in seeing young psychologists succeed in making the transition to political science, Milt seemed a tad remorseful about it, too. He rather hoped we would retain our identities and intellectual focus as psychologists, as he himself was steeped in the latest offerings in *Psychological Review*, *Journal of Personality and Social Psychology*, and *Psychological Science*. As far as back as the 1990s, Milt had largely given up on believing that citizens could provide useful information about their political views through self-report (a conclusion that strongly resonates with four decades of work in social psychology, e.g., "The Unbearable Automaticity of Being," Bargh & Chartrand, 1999; "Telling More Than We Can Know," Nisbett & Wilson, 1977). What Milt took away from his deep dive into the psychological literature—especially that pertaining to motivated bias, the automaticity of affect and its judgmental consequences—was strongly at odds with leading theories of reasoning and choice in political science. His primary intellectual agenda over the next 20 years, which resulted in his coauthored magnum opus, *The Rationalizing Voter*, would be to explore the implications for democratic citizenship of basic features of human cognition. It was during this period in the late 1990s that the two of us began to collaborate with Milt on studies of automatic affect and cognition (e.g., Lavine, Lodge, Polichak, & Taber, 2002; Lodge & Taber, 2000, 2005).

The friends in this volume present different perspectives on how Milt's work is central to constructing a psychologically plausible model of the democratic citizen. Here, we would like to reflect on what we see as Milt's unique vantage point. To begin, we view political psychology (within political science) as structured in three concentric circles. The outermost ring of the circle is composed of scholars who study individual-level political behavior, but who neither cite psychological literature nor have much interest in identifying the psychological mechanisms by which their findings are mediated. For these scholars, "preferences are like 'tastes,' for which, as the saying goes, there is no accounting, thus rendering them not merely non-economic but non-analyzable" (Wildavsky, 1987, p. 5). From where we sit, this is a shrinking part of the political psychology pie. Contemporary scholarship in political behavior increasingly raises questions about *how* and *why*, not because political scientists have come to regard them as intrinsically interesting (as psychologists do), but because our colleagues increasingly believe that getting the *politics* right requires understanding the underlying *psychology*. As we will illustrate in more detail below, this is a key component of the Lodgean approach, and a core feature of the gradual acceptance of psychological approaches among mainstream political behaviorists over the past 40 years.

Next comes the middle ring of the circle. This is where most of us most comfortably reside; it includes a broad swath of scholars who readily identify as political psychologists, many of whom were trained by individuals with interdisciplinary research agendas. Scholars in this ring consume and draw inspiration from the primary source literature in psychology, and apply it to shed light on specific topics in political science. Finally, we come to the innermost ring of the circle. This is the rarified region where the application of psychological theory moves the tectonic plates of political science. In this zone, the interdisciplinary conversation occurs at a highly general and abstract level, permeating debates across multiple substantive topics (for an excellent example, see Zaller & Feldman, 1992). Work in this inner ring also typically comes with strong normative implications, which broaden the conversation to include those who study democratic theory. This is the region that Milt inhabits.

Having spent the better part of two decades reacting to Converse's essay on citizen incompetence (for a review of this work, see Kinder & Sears, 1985), political psychologists took a cognitive turn in the 1980s to examine how information is acquired, organized in memory and retrieved in making political judgments. Milt's research was at the forefront of this new era. As Lodge et al. (1995, p. 309) noted, "fifty years of survey data portray a rather bleak picture of the American citizen as one who is not nearly as aware as our models suppose and less informed than normative theories prescribe." Lodge and colleagues also acknowledge that citizens cannot recall much detail from election campaigns or national issue contests. But, they ask: do these limitations necessarily imply that ordinary citizens are unresponsive to elite debates? That all the give and take of highly salient presidential campaigns simply fails to register in citizens' minds as they form their own judgments?

We believe this is how most political scientists viewed the matter up until the breakthrough *APSR* paper of Lodge et al. (1989). The problem with this standard knowledge-based view, as Lodge and colleagues point out, is that it is predicated on the assumption that citizens' conscious recollections of information mediate their political judgments (This was precisely what John Zaller would argue just three years later!). In this view, political judgment is constrained by *memory*—by citizens' capacity to recall what they like and dislike about political issues and candidates as they enter the voting booth or when they are asked to express an opinion in a survey. When it turned out that most citizens' memory dumps were depressingly meager, it stood to reason that they were guilty as charged of being inattentive and ignorant, their judgments lacking responsiveness and rationality. Lodge and colleagues' (1989) remarkable contribution was to show that these conclusions were flawed because the primary assumption underlying them—the implicit psychological model of information acquisition and integration—was wrong. Instead, Lodge and colleagues demonstrated that people extract the evaluative implications of political information in real time, integrate them into an ongoing running tally, and then proceed to forget the non-gist descriptive details. In this more adaptive view, political judgments are *not* constrained by the pros and cons citizens can subsequently recall. To express an opinion, they need only to retrieve the current value of the updated online tally, a tally that *reflects* the information to which they were exposed. This process-focused model forcefully challenged the long-standing assumption that rational choice flows from information holding and ideological awareness. It also communicated the general message that psychological approaches could be used within political science to provide new—and in this case, radically different—conclusions about the democratic capabilities and proclivities of ordinary citizens. Lodge et al. (1995, p. 310) expressed this point eloquently:

> Thus it may well be that the citizen's inability to recall basic political facts reflects limitations of the human mind rather than unsophistication of the

democratic citizen. Our criticism, then, is not just directed against memory-based models of the vote choice but, more broadly, challenges the memory-based assumption underlying contemporary analyses of political behavior in general and, still more broadly, the negative normative conclusions routinely drawn from the citizenry's failure to recall campaign events.

Lodge and colleagues' conclusions strongly suggested that Americans aren't empty-headed and unresponsive after all. They simply failed to retain the information on which their political evaluations were (rationally) built, a feature of the way the mind works, not a shortcoming of the democratic citizen. This led many of our colleagues to reevaluate their pessimistic view of the nature and quality of citizen competence.

In the mid-1990s, Milton pivoted away from the online model, as he and Chuck Taber initiated their long-running project on motivated reasoning and the automatic activation of affect (Bargh & Chartrand, 1999; Kahneman, 2011). In 1990, Ziva Kunda published what was to become one of the most influential articles in modern social psychology ("The Case for Motivated Reasoning"). Kunda reviewed a wide range of studies of attitude and belief change, and argued that all social reasoning occurs in the service of both accuracy goals (i.e., the desire to form beliefs that align with the facts or the preponderance of the evidence) and directional goals (i.e., the desire to arrive at particular conclusions). In pondering the relevance of Kunda's concept of motivated reasoning for mass *political* reasoning, Lodge and Taber ignited something close to a paradigm shift in how political psychologists study and understand the mass political mind. From Converse's (1964) devastating claim of citizen incompetence up until work on the online model, the discipline grappled with the question of whether the mass public possessed the interest and ability to form stable, meaningful political beliefs and opinions (e.g., Delli Carpini & Keeter, 1996). Lodge and Taber presented a very different characterization of *J.Q. Public*; it wasn't so much that she was ignorant and detached; rather, she was hopelessly *biased*.

In their widely cited paper "Motivated Skepticism in the Evaluation of Political Beliefs," Taber and Lodge (2006) write that citizens are confronted daily with arguments designed to either bolster their opinions or challenge their prior beliefs. The question for political scientists who study mass behavior is how people adjudicate between conflicting claims. Are they fair and balanced, adjusting their beliefs upward or downward as the evidence dictates? That is, are they typically motivated by accuracy? In a word, Taber and Lodge find, no. Rather than reasoning from the bottom up in an attempt to draw conclusions that respect the facts, they find that reasoning typically proceeds from the top down in an attempt to draw prefabricated conclusions designed to uphold standing political commitments. They note that from a normative perspective, the interpretation and evaluation of new information should be kept independent of one's priors. It appears, however, that people often do otherwise. Taber and Lodge find that citizens selectively seek out information that validates their attitudes while actively avoiding information that challenges them, and that they critically scrutinize and counterargue incongruent information while accepting congenial information at face value. Although maintaining discredited beliefs can be costly to both the individual and society at large, psychologists have argued that protective information-processing strategies are a form of implicit affect regulation serving to maintain psychological equanimity (Festinger, 1957; Sherman & Cohen, 2002). In this respect, Taber and Lodge's findings dovetail with the primary conclusion of the influential "New Look" in social perception from the 1940s (Bruner & Goodman, 1947), that "perception and cognition are obedient to goals, needs, and fears and at times are more subservient to these inner states than to the constraints of reality" (Markus & Zajonc, 1985, p. 140).

Consistent with Kunda's original formulation, however, Taber and Lodge do not claim that ordinary citizens are consciously motivated to be biased. The human brain is not akin to Fox News. Rather, they argue that people are "typically unable to control their preconceptions, even when encouraged to be objective." That this is indeed the case, and what it means for the nature and quality of mass political attitudes, is the major topic taken up in *The Rationalizing Voter*. In brief, Lodge and Taber (2013) demonstrate in numerous carefully designed experiments that most political concepts are "hot" for most people, meaning that they evoke an instantaneous experience of positive or negative affect, or in psychological language, they come automatically to mind, without effort, intention, or the ability to disrupt. It is the implications of these basic features of human cognition that Lodge and Taber build into a new theory of mass politics.

The central conclusion of *The Rationalizing Voter* is that our basic neurocognitive architecture facilitates judgmental biases on the basis of prior attitudes and unnoticed affective cues (some of which are irrelevant to politics). As Lodge and Taber write "at the moment an object is registered, an evaluative tally is automatically called up, triggering a series of largely unconscious, often somatically embodied processes that drive the perception and evaluation of events in the defense of one's prior attitudes" (p. 206). Their theory produces a fundamental insight about the nature of mass political reasoning: that it is not really reasoning at all; rather, it is *rationalization*. At least it is rationalization in the sense that conscious considerations used to construct a political judgment are biased—severely so—by the automatically activated affective tally. This is very nearly the conclusion reached by Jonathan Haidt (2012) in *The Righteous Mind*, who referred to the idea that people engage in deliberative reasoning to reach their judgments as "the rationalist delusion." In both Lodge and Taber and Haidt's formulation, reasoning is post hoc; it is merely the servant of the automatically activated affective tally.

One might respond to the arguments in *The Rationalizing Voter* along the lines that what Lodge and Taber have observed is characteristic of unsophisticated citizens—those who rely principally on emotion in forming their political judgments (Sniderman, Brody, & Tetlock, 1991)—but that sophisticates think more deeply and evenhandedly. Perhaps they are more capable; almost by definition they are. But it's not how sophisticates typically behave. In fact, the opposite appears to be the case: the biases and rationalizations uncovered by Lodge and Taber are stronger and more reliable among more active and knowledgeable citizens. This, they argue, is a simple function of having stronger prior attitudes and a more sophisticated set of defensive beliefs and strategies. However, the implications are profound: sophisticates were praised by Converse (1964) as the good citizens (they're ideological; they hold stable attitudes). Yes, they're more ideological and hold more stable opinions. But we think the normative value of those facts depends on the process through which they were produced. If it occurs through the automatic activation of affect followed by biased reasoning (i.e., rationalization), they seem much less praiseworthy.

Though this volume is an unplanned city, its boulevards and buildings have emerged with a certain internal logic, attributable no doubt to the theoretical focus of its subject, Milton Lodge. We begin with personal reflections from Chuck Taber and Kathleen McGraw on their overlapping but distinct collaborations with Milton. Bob Huckfeldt then describes how his own path breaking research on the influence of social context and networks on citizen behavior was affected by a year at Stony Brook. Jennifer Jerit then tackles one of the central paradoxes raised by Milt's work on motivated reasoning: the normative value of knowledge. Continuing this theme, Victor Ottati, Chase Wilson, Erika Price, and Nathanael Sumaktoyo examine the relationship between political expertise and open-mindedness. Persistence and persuasion have been the yin and yang of political attitude research and a central theme of work on the rationalizing voter, so it is no surprise that several chapters in this volume focus on belief change. Marco Steenbergen and Howie Lavine take a Bayesian approach to belief updating, finding several important moderators for motivated biases, including ambivalence. Jamie Druckman, Thomas Leeper, and Rune Slothuus then report research on the connections between motivated reasoning and framing theory in the context of beliefs about science. The sequence of information is central to belief updating, and Dave Redlawsk and Douglas Pierce examine how first impressions are formed for new candidates and then become the priors that may bias subsequent information processing. Motivated reasoning is an important source of defensive racial attitudes for both individualists and egalitarians, find Stanley Feldman and Leonie Huddy, who argue that "racially motivated reasoning" can help unravel complex perceptions of the pervasiveness of racial discrimination. In an increasingly polarized environment, how do parties keep the support of relatively moderate rank and file voters? Gaurav Sood and Shanto Iyengar find that motivated perceptions of the policy positions and voting records of public officials help to maintain party support. The last chapter in the volume, by Tessa Ditonto and Rick Lau, examines boundary conditions for affect transfer, as shown for example in the controversial "smiley face" studies in *The Rationalizing Voter*. Ditonto and Lau do find support for the transfer of feelings from an unnoticed prime to an object of thought (a political candidate), but their results are generally weaker and more contingent than what Lodge and Taber found.

There is no ceremony with Milt; no hierarchy and no seniority. It is all about the ideas and the friendship and the camaraderie. He does it with humility. If this book is a surprise party, it is a good bet that Milt will be that guest of honor who smiles uncomfortably at the attention. We hope he will come to appreciate the love and respect that stand behind the surprise, and that this is a necessary party because his profound influence on us and on our discipline cannot go unremarked.

References

Bargh, John A. & Chartrand, Tanya L. (1999). The unbearable automaticity of being. *American Psychologist*, 54(7), 462–479.

Bruner, Jerome S. & Goodman, Cecile C. (1947). Value and need as organizing factors in perception. *Journal of Abnormal and Social Psychology*, 42, 33–44.

Converse, Philip E. (1964). The nature of belief systems in mass publics. In David Apter (Ed.), *Ideology and discontent* (pp. 206–260). New York: The Free Press.

Delli Carpini, Michael X., & Keeter, Scott. (1996). *What Americans know about politics and why it matters*. New Haven, CT: Yale University Press.

Festinger, Leon. (1957). *A theory of cognitive dissonance*. Stanford, CA: Stanford University Press.

Haidt, Jonathan. (2012). *The righteous mind*. New York: Pantheon Books.

Kahneman, Daniel. (2011). *Thinking, fast and slow*. New York: Farrar, Straus, and Giroux.

Kinder, Donald R. & Sears, David O. (1985). Public opinion and political action. In Gardner Lindzey & Elliot Aronson (Eds.), *The handbook of social psychology* (3rd ed., pp. 659–741). New York: Random House.

Kunda, Ziva. (1990). The case for motivated reasoning. *Psychological Bulletin*, 108(3), 480–498.

Lavine, Howard, Lodge, Milton, Polichak, James, & Taber, Charles S. (2002). Explicating the black box through experimentation: Studies of authoritarianism and threat. *Political Analysis*, 10(4), 343–361.

Lodge, Milton & Hamill, Ruth. (1986). A partisan schema for political information processing. *American Political Science Review*, 80, 505–520.

Lodge, Milton & McGraw, Kathleen M. (Eds.) (1995). *Political judgment: Structure and process*. Ann Arbor, MI: University of Michigan Press.

Lodge, Milton, McGraw, Kathleen M., & Stroh, Patrick. (1989). An impression-driven model of candidate evaluation. *American Political Science Review*, 83, 399–420.

Lodge, Milton, Steenbergen, Marco, & Brau, Shawn. (1995). The responsive voter: Campaign information and the dynamics of candidate evaluation. *American Political Science Review*, 89(2), 309–326.

Lodge, Milton & Taber, Charles S. (2000). Three steps toward a theory of motivated political reasoning. In Arthur Lupia, Mathew McCubbins, & Samuel Popkin (Eds.), *Elements of reason: Cognition, choice, and the bounds of rationality* (pp. 183–213). New York: Cambridge University Press.

Lodge, Milton & Taber, Charles S. (2005). The automaticity of affect for political leaders, groups, and issues: An experimental test of the hot cognition hypothesis. *Political Psychology*, 26(3), 455–482.

Lodge, Milton & Taber, Charles S. (2013). *The rationalizing voter.* Cambridge: Cambridge University Press.

Markus, Hazel & Zajonc, Robert B. (1985). The cognitive perspective in social psychology. In Gardner Lindzey & Elliot Aronson (Eds.), *The handbook of social psychology* (3rd ed., pp. 137–230). New York: Random House.

Nisbett, Richard E. & Wilson, Timothy DeCamp (1977). Telling more than we can know: Verbal reports on mental processes. *Psychological Review,* 84(3), 231–259.

Sherman, David K. & Cohen, Geoffrey L. (2002). Accepting threatening information: Self-affirmation and the reduction of defensive biases. *Current Directions in Psychological Science,* 11, 119–123.

Sniderman, Paul M., Brody, Richard A., & Tetlock, Philip E. (1991). *Reasoning and choice: Explorations in political psychology.* Cambridge: Cambridge University Press.

Taber, Charles S. & Lodge, Milton. (2006). Motivated skepticism in the evaluation of political beliefs. *American Journal of Political Science,* 50(3), 755–769.

Wildavsky, Aaron. (1987). Choosing preferences by constructing institutions: A cultural theory of preference formation. *The American Political Science Review,* 81(1), 3–22.

Zaller, John & Feldman, Stanley. (1992). A simple theory of survey response: Answering questions versus revealing preferences. *American Journal of Political Science,* 36(3), 579–616.

2

CONVERSATIONS ABOUT *THE RATIONALIZING VOTER*

Charles S. Taber

With all due respect to hockey, Milton Lodge's team sport of choice is theoretical speculation. This is why each of Milt's significant contributions to the field of political psychology—measurement of attitudes (1970s), knowledge structures (1980s), online processing (1990s), motivated reasoning (2000s), and automaticity (2010s)—was coauthored, and indeed his career can be seen as a series of conversational partnerships with colleagues and students. My own long research program with Milt, which culminated in the 2013 book, *The Rationalizing Voter*, was fueled by endless hours of freewheeling brainstorming, and I have never had more (academic) fun or been more productive.

I met Milton Lodge in 1989, when Stony Brook's political science department hired me to teach undergraduate courses in international relations and graduate courses in computational modeling. I was attracted to Stony Brook because of my fairly unusual intersection of interests, which included political cognition in addition to foreign policy decision-making and international conflict processes. I suspect Milton played an important role in the decision to hire me, and he certainly played a determinative role in my subsequent migration toward political psychology and applications in American politics, a shift which took more than a decade to realize but which began with our first conversation in August 1989. But let me step back for a moment to acknowledge the various influences at the University of Illinois, where I did my doctoral work, which undoubtedly made me an appropriately odd job candidate for Milton and Stony Brook.

Trained as a mathematical modeler in international relations at the Merriam Laboratory for Analytic Political Research, where I was advised by Dina Zinnes, I was particularly interested in formal models of decision-making. I also discovered the field of political psychology at the University of Illinois from Betty Glad, Bob Wyer, and especially Jim Kuklinski. It was Jim and later Bob Boynton,

12   Charles S. Taber

a visiting scholar from Iowa, who introduced me to political cognition and got me thinking about the processes of political thinking. As a result, my theoretical interests became less and less approachable through mathematical modeling, and I gravitated toward computational methods to formally represent process models of elite decision-making, culminating in the development of the POLI model of U.S. foreign policy belief systems in my dissertation (Taber, 1992). This interest in computational methods and cognitive science ended up outlasting my work in international relations and foreign policy decision-making and became an important foundation of my collaborations with Milton. I was primed to think about the causes of political behavior in process terms, and I had technical skills and theoretical knowledge that augmented Milt's own understanding of political cognition. But I did not know this yet in the fall of 1989.

My first research conversation with Milton occurred while I was unpacking boxes in my new office at Stony Brook, and it was during that first encounter that I was recruited to help Milt think about process models of voter decision-making. I did not think I was at all interested in "the American voter," but I did know I was interested in more conversation with Milton.

When I arrived at Stony Brook, Milton was already deeply engaged in one of his most productive conversational partnerships, with Kathleen McGraw, whose breadth and depth of knowledge of social psychology and (in particular) experimental design were like rocket fuel to my own crude ideas about political cognition. The three of us met frequently during my early years at Stony Brook, and these discussions truly became the basis of all that followed. Most importantly, I found that "the American voter" was in fact a useful foil for my growing interest in human cognition.

Opening Pandora's Black Box

In 1990, Lodge, Stroh, and Wahlke wrote that "political science models of vote choice are black-box models: They are silent about how voters actually go about interpreting information and integrating the 'evidence' into a summary evaluation of the candidates" (p. 5). This was the fundamental research puzzle that energized Milton during the first decade of my collaboration with him. With Kathleen and their students, Milton was already working from structure (schemas) toward process (online models of candidate evaluation). This work culminated in several seminal articles (Lodge, McGraw, & Stroh, 1989; Lodge, Steenbergen, & Brau, 1995) and an important edited book, *Political Judgment: Structure and Process* (Lodge & McGraw, 1995). Marco Steenbergen, then a Stony Brook graduate student, and I had a chapter in that volume in which we explored formal models of voter decision-making in a series of "computational experiments" (Taber & Steenbergen, 1995). Milton's chapter in this book is notable for its theoretical precision, including process flowcharts and formal representations of memory. These two chapters and a 1993 paper by Boynton and Lodge anticipated the approach we took in the later development of our theory of political information processing (Lodge & Taber, 2013).

A grant proposal to the National Science Foundation from this period put our approach thus:

> The aim of this grant was to develop a computer program that would realistically mimic the processes citizens go through when forming and revising their evaluations of political candidates. The research is progressing in servo fashion as we move from laboratory experimentation (where we manipulate the content and context of candidate messages) to our model of the process (which is instantiated as a computer program) and back again into the laboratory to test the theory's predictions on vote choice and preference.
>
> *(Lodge, Steenbergen, & Taber, 1993, p. 1)*

As we theorized about processes within the black box of political cognition, three broad hypotheses motivated our computational and experimental work:

1. Citizens are active information processors; human cognition is sequential in nature, and existing knowledge affects the way people interpret and integrate environmental information.
2. Citizens face severe limitations in information-processing capacity; as a result, they are boundedly rational at best.
3. Citizens are less interested in politics than in their daily lives; under normal circumstances, voters will not engage in effortful and elaborate decision-making processes, but will use more simplified heuristics to make political decisions.

Taber and Steenbergen (1995), for example, developed and tested a set of formal voter decision rules (e.g., weighted additive, lexicographic, prospect theory) by casting these rules as computational models and then comparing the behavior of these "electoral robots" with the behavior of human subjects in experimentally controlled elections. In this way, we could determine whether complex, information-rich models (e.g., weighted additive) behave more or less like human voters in varying information environments than did simpler voter models (e.g., lexicographic). Among other things, we found that heuristic rules did better than demanding rules under high information load (many candidates with many attributes) as we had hypothesized.

This interest in formal theorizing through computational models characterized my early conversations and projects with Milton as we grappled with how to open the black box of political information processing, but after this early flurry we entered a period of focus on behavioral research in our Laboratory for Experimental Research in Political Behavior.

Motivated Reasoning

From my first exposure, I was critical of the simplistic debate between online (OL) and memory-based (MB) models of political information processing which dominated discussion at Stony Brook in the 1990s, and this view was reinforced by the 1998 arrival to Stony Brook of Howie Lavine, who quickly became another key conversational partner. Like Kathleen, Howie was trained as a social psychologist, and his knowledge and insights were critical to the development of our thinking on motivated reasoning, hot cognition, and automaticity. While the OL model, which claims that information is processed for evaluative implications at the time of exposure rather than at the time of decision, was an important insight into an affective heuristic that enables "high information rationality" at relatively low cognitive cost, it seemed clear to me that MB processing was also necessary to make sense of the findings. As I put it in my 2003 *Handbook of Political Psychology* chapter,

> These two models are often presented as competing or even incompatible—with memory-based processes being seen as more applicable to complex, ambivalent attitude objects (issues) and online processes as more applicable to simpler, univalent objects (candidates). But the "debate" is an unproductive one, driven by extreme interpretations nobody really believes. The online model cannot mean that all details are forgotten; such an organism would not have in [long term memory] the ingredients necessary to discern the evaluative implications of new information at the time of exposure. And the memory-based approach cannot mean that people refrain from all evaluation of information at the time of exposure; such an organism would have no ability to resist persuasion or otherwise maintain beliefs through time.
>
> *(Taber, 2003, pp. 528–529)*

The sequential nature of information processing and the interaction between OL evaluation and MB processes led us to an interest in how prior feelings and knowledge about political candidates, groups, and ideas might motivate and bias the evaluation of new information. That is, considerations stored in memory (prior beliefs) should have significant impact on how information is interpreted at the time of exposure and therefore should influence the OL evaluation process; similarly, feelings toward political persons, groups, and ideas should influence the retrieval of considerations from memory. MB and OL processes conspire to produce motivated reasoning. In taking this direction we were very influenced by Ziva Kunda's 1990 article, "The Case for Motivated Reasoning."

Following Kunda, we argued that citizens are motivated both to be accurate and to be right. That is, there is pressure to perceive the environment as it actually is (accuracy motivation) and to perceive the environment as validating one's prior beliefs and feelings (partisan motivation), and these pressures often come into tension. Partisan or directional motivations, which we conceive more broadly than political party preferences, lead to both confirmation and disconfirmation biases, which in our conversations circa 2000 were a product of three psychological mechanisms (Lodge & Taber, 2000; Taber, Lodge, & Glather, 2001):

1. Hot cognition claims that all social concepts that have been evaluated in the past are now "affectively charged," positively or negatively tagged, with the affective charge linked directly to the concept in memory (Abelson, 1963; Bargh, 1997; Fazio, Sanbonmatsu, Powell, & Kardes, 1986).
2. Online processing holds that every time you learn something new about an object (person, group, or idea) you update your impression, incrementing for positive information and decrementing for negative (Anderson & Hubert, 1963; Lodge et al., 1995).
3. The "How-Do-I-Feel" affect heuristic provides the critical mechanism whereby the OL tally becomes information in subsequent processing. When a citizen encounters a political object, the relevant OL tally comes automatically to mind (Clore & Isbell, 2001), coloring perceptions of new information. One cannot think of "gun control" or "affirmative action," for example, without bringing to mind judgments made in the past.

Two experimental papers from this period explored the "dark side" of motivated reasoning about political issues (Taber & Lodge, 2006; Taber, Cann, & Kucsova, 2009). We found that it is not reasonable to expect ardent proponents of affirmative action, gun control, or legalization of marijuana, for example, to weigh the evidence on the issues evenhandedly. The same evidence is taken as support for contradictory issue positions or opposing candidates in the real political world, by spin doctors and citizens alike (not to mention scholars and scientists). When political operatives do it, we call it framing the narrative. Our findings suggest that people, especially that small but critically important subset of the population who care and know the most about things political, are by default not evenhanded.

To summarize, we found that people simply feel that the information they agree with is stronger, more compelling evidence than the information that they disagree with (the prior attitude effect); when processing pro and con information on an issue, people actively denigrate the information with which they disagree while accepting compatible information almost at face value (the disconfirmation bias); when given some control over the source of information, people seek out confirmatory information and avoid that which they expect might challenge their priors (the confirmation bias); all three of these biases provide pro-attitudinal information to the online impression updating process, such that attitudes become more extreme (polarization); the result is that the same stream of balanced pro and con information leads partisans to diverge in their attitudes; and finally, all of these biases are particularly pronounced for citizens with knowledge and strong prior attitudes, the very folks on whom normative democratic theory relies most heavily.

Hot Cognition

A central claim of our theory of motivated political reasoning is that the primary trigger for partisan bias is the valence affect one experiences automatically on exposure to a political object that has been evaluated in the past. We have tested the hot cognition hypothesis in several ways over the years (e.g., Morris, Squires, Taber, & Lodge, 2003; Kim, Taber, & Lodge, 2010), but the most direct behavioral test was reported in our 2005 *Political Psychology* article. This was our first major work that used reaction time (RT) experimental methods to tease out the structures and processes of thought, an approach we relied on heavily in our later work on automaticity (Burdein, Lodge, & Taber, 2006; Lodge & Taber, 2013). In an associative network model of memory, hot cognition can be seen as the result of spreading activation across links between concept and affect memory nodes. When a concept (e.g., Trump) is primed in an experimental study, this should spread activation to the OL tally linked to Trump that carries the given subject's evaluation of Trump, based on past information processing. For example, if a person has a positive attitude toward Donald Trump (positive OL tally), then presentation of the prime Trump should facilitate retrieval of positive affect. In the sequential attitude priming paradigm we adopted, this facilitation can be measured by the speed with which the subject indicates that an unrelated target word is positively valenced. In short, the positivity aroused by the Trump prime would facilitate responses to positive target words (e.g., rainbow) and inhibit responses to negative target words (cancer).

These experiments documented hot cognition across a broad range of political objects, including political leaders, groups, and issues. Moreover, we found that automatic affective responses were especially strong among those with the strongest attitudes, for non-ambivalent primes, and for the most knowledgeable respondents.

But why is this important? Of what possible significance can that first split second of information processing be? We see three fundamental implications of this research for political science. First, the hot cognition postulate promises an answer to a puzzle that has long engaged political scientists—the problem of rational action by citizens in a democracy. Second, the temporal primacy of affect in the first 200 ms kick-starts motivated biases when citizens encounter attitudinally contrary information (Ditto & Lopez, 1992; Lord, Ross, & Lepper, 1979; Munro et al., 2002; Taber et al., 2001). And last but assuredly not least is what we see as an important revision in how we political scientists conceptualize and measure attitudes.

Citizens, we know from decades of survey research, are "not so *sapiens.*" In fact, their ignorance about and apathy toward politics is axiomatic in political behavior research. And yet, we also know that citizens can be rationally responsive to new information (for evidence on the "paradox of the dysfunctional citizen," see Taber, 2003; Taber & Young, 2013). Several resolutions have been offered for this dilemma, including the "magic of aggregation" (Kinder, 1998), in which individual foibles cancel out in the broad electorate. It is also likely that citizens overcome some of their limitations through the judicious use of simplifying heuristics, like party identifications or group endorsement cues (Kuklinski & Quirk, 2000), leading to "low information rationality" (Popkin, 1991). But our research conversations from this period were most animated by the prospect of *high information rationality* for citizens, whose evaluative feelings toward candidates, groups, and ideas may be completely responsive to the information stream. At least in theory, hot cognition coupled with online processing provides the most robust and optimistic solution to the paradox of the limited but rational citizen.

But we also know that this reliance on hot cognition as a distillation of information comes with a heavy price. Motivated biases, as described above, are triggered in the first few milliseconds of exposure to a political object, and they are triggered by hot cognition. So, while the prospect of high information rationality is exciting, the reality of motivated reasoning tempers this theoretical path to rational democratic action.

The study of political attitudes has gone through several important phases, in particular moving from a "file drawer" view of memory storage and retrieval to a model in which attitudes are constructed from more or less ambivalent considerations at the time of expression (Zaller & Feldman, 1992). While attitude measurement is relatively straightforward in the file drawer model, it is more complex under the constructivist model, where the expression of attitudes will be influenced by many contextual factors including question wording, interviewer characteristics, and broader environmental priming. This distinction is of course related to the OL vs. MB processing debate discussed above, but hot cognition offers a synthetic integration of these two views of the conceptualization and measurement of attitudes. Simply put, evaluative feelings about political objects anchor the retrieval and expression of attitudes toward those objects, inducing greater coherence and constraint than would be expected by a pure MB processing model, but less than would be expected by simple retrieval of a formed attitude from a file drawer. Sadly, in my view, this important consequence of hot cognition has largely been unexplored in the recent literature on attitudes and memory processes.

Automaticity

Sometime in the mid-1990s, I sat through Milton's graduate seminar on Political Cognition, which broadened and deepened my understanding of cognitive psychology. Automaticity provided the central organizing principle for Milton's treatment, and our research conversations also began to focus on fundamental theoretical and normative questions of automaticity and control.

In John Bargh's (1994) useful formulation, conscious control requires *awareness*, *intentionality*, *self-regulation*, and *cognitive effort*, and the absence of any of these introduces degrees of automaticity. Much of political thinking by average citizens as well as political elites, in our view, is unaware, unintentional, uncontrolled, and relatively effortless, and we began to be more and more persuaded that our discipline's overriding focus on conscious thinking was incomplete at best, and likely highly misleading. Our neurobiological systems are built by evolution to be capable of rapid and automatic response when warranted by environmental threat or fleeting opportunity. It is a key human "superpower" that we can respond to large quantities of information in complex environments through rapid, parallel, cognitive processing. As Kahneman (2011) has famously put it, we can Think Fast. And yet, our conscious control processes are debilitated by the limited capacity of working memory, the slow, serial nature of conscious mental processes, and our relatively low motivation to exercise control over the automatic "cognitive monster" (Bargh, 1999). Given motivation, mental capacity, and time, Kahneman is correct that we *can* productively Think Slow, and fully rational behavior requires us to think both fast and slow, but much of the time we do not go beyond thinking fast. This primacy of automaticity and affect over slow conscious cognitive control is the primary claim of *The Rationalizing Voter* (2013).

Smiley Faces and *John Q. Public*

Milton and I have been fortunate to have had a succession of outstanding graduate students through our long research collaboration. I have already mentioned Pat Stroh and Marco Steenbergen, who collaborated on early projects, and we also had valuable partnerships with a number of later students. I want to highlight two projects that were particularly important to the development of our research program in its later, automaticity phase.

Most work on automaticity, the bulk of our own included, focuses on the immediate cuing effects of a stimulus or context on momentary feelings, thoughts, and behaviors. Snap judgments of people, for example, are known to be influenced by affective or cognitive primes. But what about the downstream consequences of unconscious processing? What about the influence of primes or context on the stream of information processing over longer than instantaneous periods of time? What about what we have called "affective contagion," where early primes or processing events provide an affective direction to memory retrieval, altering the conscious contents of thought so that controlled deliberation is influenced by prior unconscious feelings? We tackled these questions with the help of Cengiz Erisen, whose dissertation reported a series of experiments designed to test affective contagion (Erisen, Lodge, & Taber, 2014; Lodge & Taber, 2013). To my knowledge, these experiments were the first to explore the impact of unnoticed cues on policy attitudes as mediated through their influence on the contents of conscious considerations.

In the Erisen, Lodge, and Taber experiments, we manipulated exposure in the lab to simple affective cues while student subjects were asked to think explicitly about a political issue (immigration or energy security). These primes were subliminally presented images of cartoon smiley, frowny, or neutral faces. The results across these experiments supported our expectations that fleeting affective images would alter the balance of conscious thoughts about an unrelated policy. In fact, the effect sizes were far larger than either Milt or I really expected, which led us to require several replications under different experimental procedures before we were comfortable publishing the results (Erisen et al., 2014). Most important, we observed in these experiments a substantial impact of smiley or frowny face primes on subsequent attitudes on the political issues, supporting a path model in which incidental primes alter the contents of thought, which then mediate an indirect effect on ultimate policy attitudes reported at least 30 minutes after exposure to the primes. We think this is an astonishing result from a conventional point of view, and it supports one of our most controversial claims, that millisecond impacts of affective primes have measurable downstream effects on political thinking. This is the most critical answer to the fundamental "who cares?" question about the relevance of cognitive processing on a millisecond scale.

From our very earliest conversations, Milton and I saw great value in formalizing theory, though our work on political cognition has never been amenable to simple mathematical representations. There has always been a computational element to our thinking, even during the period when we focused almost exclusively on experiments, and we always treated our underlying theory as a descriptive process model of political cognition. We were delighted when our student, Sung-youn Kim, became interested in developing our theory as a fully working computational model for his dissertation (Kim et al., 2010; Lodge & Taber, 2013).

John Q. Public (JQP) is an affect-driven, dual-process model of information processing designed to capture both Fast and Slow Thinking (Lodge & Taber, 2013). It is dual process in that JQP distinguishes between two modes of information processing, automatic and controlled, though these modes interact in producing thinking and behavior, and it is affect-driven in that positive and/or negative feelings are integral to the processing of information, providing motivation, direction, and information to both conscious and unconscious thought.

The fundamental assumption driving our model is that affective and cognitive reactions to external and internal events are first triggered unconsciously, followed spontaneously by the spreading of activation through associative pathways that link thoughts to feelings to intentions to behavior, so that very early events, even those that are invisible to later conscious awareness, set the direction for all subsequent processing. We become consciously aware of the cascade of thoughts and feelings very late in this stream of processing, though our conscious subjective experience *feels* like controlled thinking, reasoning, and acting (Custers & Aarts, 2010; Libet, 1985; Lodge & Taber, 2013). This subjective sense of conscious control is often, perhaps usually, illusory.

JQP represents cognitive and affective structures and processes formally within a single computational framework (Kim et al., 2010; Lodge & Taber, 2013): (1) long-term memory (LTM) is represented as an associative network, formally as a node-link structure; (2) activation and decay mechanisms in LTM govern accessibility and retrieval into conscious working memory (WM); (3) attitudes are constructed from accessible memory objects; and (4) cognitive and affective associations (considerations and attitudes) are updated through operations on LTM. All theoretical processes are explicitly represented as mathematical operations on the node-link structure of LTM.

In a test of the overall theoretical model (as opposed to narrower tests of hypotheses derived from this theoretical structure), artificial agents, constructed to behave according to our theoretical processes of fast and slow, feeling and thinking, closely tracked the behavioral trajectories of real citizens in the 2000 presidential campaign. The set of artificial agents, initialized to represent real respondents to the 2000 National Annenberg Election Study (Romer, Kenski, Waldman, Adasiewicz, & Jamieson, 2003) at the start of the 2000 presidential campaign, "read" the campaign news coverage, processed this information according to our theory, and formed new beliefs and attitudes about the major presidential candidates. The trajectories of the artificial agents' attitudes through the election campaign mirrored the trajectories of their human counterparts. In fact, *JQP* significantly outperformed a Bayesian updating model based on Gerber and Green's formulation (1998), which we attribute to the presence of motivated reasoning biases triggered by hot cognitions about the candidates. *JQP* was able to replicate the responsiveness to new information, persistence of underlying attitudes, and polarization over time that were observed in the NAES data, while the Bayesian model struggled to track combination of responsiveness and persistence seen in the data. Further work using *JQP* agents to simulate experimental participants has also been successful, and the model has also been used to explore particular hypotheses like the relationship between OL and MB processing (Lodge & Taber, 2013).

Implications and Critical Conversations

Over the years Milton and I have made a number of controversial claims, and our work on *The Rationalizing Voter* has implications that are difficult to explain within conventional approaches to political behavior. Most centrally, our work challenges our discipline's theoretical and empirical focus on conscious thinking. It is a fact that the bulk of human cognition occurs out of view of conscious reflection; we claim that this underlying stream of unconscious thinking, based on rapid, parallel memory processing along affective and cognitive currents is consequential for, even determinative of political behavior. And yet, measurement strategies for political beliefs and attitudes rely almost entirely on verbal self-reports. Surveys and experiments alike ask people to tell us through conscious introspection what they think, feel, expect, or intend. From our perspective, these questions or prompts in context should be viewed as complex primes, causing some thoughts, feelings, goals, and behaviors to become more accessible, and responses are a joint function of the prior contents of LTM and these complex primes. Even the most sophisticated measurement models do not incorporate what we now know about how people process complex cues to produce responses. In most cases, these responses are still viewed as simply revealing underlying beliefs, attitudes, and intentions.

Even more fundamental, we are very skeptical that people can reliably and accurately report their feelings, beliefs, emotions, expectation, intentions, or behaviors. Most of our experience occurs outside of conscious awareness, so we cannot in many cases report the actual causes of our thoughts and behaviors. Moreover, as recollections fade from memory, motivated beliefs will tend to replace actual memories. Rationalizing citizens often cannot tell us why they think or do what they do. We must design research to uncover these automatic processes, and at least so far such research is both expensive and intensive. It is far easier to continue to pretend that survey responses reveal full and accurate causal processes.

In 2013, the journal *Critical Review* (Friedman, 2012) published a symposium on our work on motivated reasoning. Several leading political psychologists, in fact an embarrassingly eminent panel of judges, commented on Taber and Lodge (2006). These were decidedly friendly critiques, but there were some very useful challenges to our theoretical argument. Milton and I found three questions particularly worthy of further discussion and research (Taber & Lodge, 2012). First, what are the actual motivations that exist in the "political wild"? Do real citizens experience greater motivation to be accurate than our research suggests or than our experimental designs manipulate? There is research, for example, showing that monetary incentives for experimental subjects reduce motivated biases, at least for "factual questions" (Bullock, Gerber, Hill, & Huber, 2015; Prior, Sood, & Khanna, 2015). Perhaps this incentivized approach better captures the "real world" than our own experiments. This is a very interesting point, and Milton and I agreed (Taber & Lodge, 2013) that stronger accuracy motivations could reduce biases. But does the real world supply strong accuracy motivations, akin to actual monetary rewards, for citizens in a democracy? Our own experience and observation suggests that it is very unlikely that most citizens experience incentives like a pay raise for the accurate processing of political information, though this is an empirical question that deserves study. As an aside, it would be useful if some of these tests of incentivized reasoning replicated the kind of policy biases we have studied as opposed to biases in perceptions of simple factual questions.

A second interesting challenge from this symposium asked how we reconcile our findings of sticky beliefs and attitudes with the findings of the persuasion and framing literatures that public opinion can be moved, sometimes quite easily. This issue cuts to the core of why our *JQP* theory can provide a synthesis of seemingly contradictory findings that other approaches (e.g., a Bayesian model) struggle to explain. Because of its incorporation of motivated reasoning processes along with OL processing mechanisms, our model can account for both persistence and persuasion and it can predict when we should expect one or the other. Citizens are more responsive to arguments and information when prior feelings are weak, when they have little personal knowledge about the issue, and when the persuasive appeals are presented outside of awareness. By contrast, persistence is most likely when prior feelings are strong, when people are knowledgeable, and when the appeals are consciously perceived.

Milton and I claim that belief perseverance is fueled by strong prior feelings, but a third challenge from the *Critical Review* symposium argues that perseverance stems not from affect itself, but rather from confidence in the accuracy or truth value of one's priors. Our fundamental response to this point is that the distinction posed between the affect one feels and the conviction one thinks is suspect. There is a tendency in the literature to conflate accuracy motivation, controlled processing, and cognition on one side of the dual-processing framework, with directional motivation, automatic processing, and affect on the other side. Milton and I do not see dual-processing theories in this way. Affect and cognition, accuracy and directional motivations, operate at both fast and slow speeds and through both central and peripheral routes. Beliefs in the truth of one's priors are strongly related to and likely are a consequence of feelings and desires and often become drivers of motivated bias. Moreover, conscious processing can be quite biased in its own right, and it is always the product of earlier unconscious processing (as we demonstrated in the smiley face experiments).

I would like to conclude this section on challenges and controversies with a brief note on external validity and the importance of replication. The evidentiary basis for most of the research that Milt and I have done rests on laboratory experiments, in which we test hypotheses derived from our theory in controlled settings using student samples. How should this evidence be viewed by political psychologists and political scientists more broadly?

In almost all cases, our experiments have been intended to test hypotheses about basic human information processes rather than the actual contents or products of thought. While there may be some domain differences in information processing, in general we assume that memory processes (storage and concept integration, spreading activation, retrieval) and judgment processes (evaluation, confidence or likelihood estimation) are fairly uniform across decision domains, so that preferences over political candidates, groups, or ideas will be formed in the same fundamental ways as preferences over apartments, movies, or romantic partners. If this assumption is correct, then our hypotheses and tests should be about *how* people think rather than *what* they think, and well-designed studies of process should generalize to most other objects of thought.

It is fair to say that Milton and I have been less concerned with external than internal validity, not because we don't care about generalization of findings but because we care more about whether we have valid findings to generalize. There is a premium paid for realism in our discipline, sometimes at the expense of internal coherence, control, and causal inference. Moreover, the assumptions that underlie claims of realism often go unexamined. Are monetary incentives for accuracy in motivated reasoning studies really more externally valid than the social incentives used in our research? Does a subject in a 60 minute dynamic information board study really have a more comparable experience to the typical citizen in an election campaign than if she were in a static decision study? I am not so sure. I am sure that these added complications reduce experimental control and therefore internal validity.

We have a "replication crisis" in psychology, I am told, and the reputational damage as evidenced by Twitter wars and public hand wringing has extended broadly to experimental research throughout the social sciences. It seems to me that we have lost sight of the purpose of replication in science. It has always been commonplace that results from one study may not replicate in subsequent studies, especially for cutting-edge research. A 2016 survey of scientists across many fields published in *Nature* (Baker, 2016) found that 70% reported failing to replicate another researcher's work and 50% reported failing to replicate their own published work. These "replication failures" appeared in print without consternation as normal science and they are treated as additional information (along with the original findings). So why is it a moral collapse if some social science findings are not supported in subsequent research? Given our relative scientific immaturity, I would think we would expect that. It is also clear to me that some of the "gotcha police" currently scouring for failures and implying research malfeasance in social psychology do not understand the differences between direct and conceptual replication or the evidentiary value of a replication failure. I fear that the real effect of this crisis in psychology will be to drive researchers away from important but risky research topics. In political science, I believe we are already seeing a backlash away from experimental research, which will be disastrous for our field. The increasing number and sophistication of experiments in political science have been very important to our progress as a scientific discipline because we have begun to tackle fundamental process hypotheses about political behavior rather than being content with mere description or weak causal inference from survey data.

Throughout our collaboration, Milton and I have followed the practice common in psychology of designing programs of multiple experiments, designed to tell a theoretical and empirical story or test a hypothesis from several directions. In some sense, each of our publications contains a set of conceptual replications. However, most of our experiments were conducted by our research team in our laboratory using Stony Brook undergraduate student subjects, so they are not independent replications. Some of our work fits into larger bodies of research and so there are many findings that bear on these hypotheses. Motivated reasoning, for example, should be viewed as a well-established finding in the literature, given the large number of consonant findings across multiple labs, designs, and samples. I think both OL and MB judgment processes are solid, though how they interact needs further research. Hot cognition fits into decades of work from psychology, but updating processes are still weakly understood. Both affect transfer and especially affect contagion need further study. Direct replication of the smiley face study would be valuable because these findings have been controversial and there is not a body of independent research supporting the hypothesized process. And of course, for all of our work, I welcome tests of limits, moderation, competing causal processes.

A Concluding Note on Conversational Partnerships

The findings from our 25-year *Rationalizing Voter* project have important implications for the theory and practice of democracy, but it is worth noting that these normative implications were never of paramount interest to Milton or me. The extensive normative discussion in the conclusion to our 2006 paper, for example, was largely added to please reviewers and conference discussants. I am glad that we were pushed to think about these larger questions, but it never came naturally and it was never part of the theoretical or research design conversations that drove the work. And yet the normative implications are the reason our research has had impact. Milton's work has always had an uncanny relevance for the "big questions" of political science. Perhaps he harbors an unconscious affection for political philosophy. Certainly his curiosity about human limitations and human rationality provide a laser focus to all of his many research projects.

Our research always starts and ends with conversation, and I think that simple fact is important. There is a romantic and largely false notion of great ideas arising from within a single great thinker's head. Modern science occurs explicitly in teams. Even those few intellectual hermits credited with great breakthroughs had their ideas within the web of scientific thought of their day. Science progresses in communities. My own experience over the past quarter century strongly supports the notion that communication is at the core of productive research. It seems fitting that I conclude my retrospections about my conversational partnership with Milton Lodge by commenting on the value of collaboration, even though the solo-authored journal article remains the prime credential for tenure in much of our discipline.

I have experienced a number of important benefits from collaboration. More heads are better than one when the task is generating ideas. This is why we commonly come together with others to "brainstorm." A small research community has developed showing the benefits of diversity of ideas in groups for creative decision-making (Page, 2008). If creativity is the process of making novel connections among ideas, then the odds of this happening increase as the diversity of ideas and people increase. In our partnership, the ideas came from Milton, from me, from our colleagues, from students, from anonymous reviewers and avowed critics. Forming these ideas into research designs and our broader research program was not easy, but it did come naturally. To this day, Milton and I neither know nor care who first came up with the main ideas. Fertility of ideas without the constraints of ownership is one of the great benefits of our collaboration.

Conversation also provides a gentle filter on ideas that can be very useful. A productive partnership requires sufficient trust to share partially formed ideas, knowing that real clunkers will probably not stand the test of discussion. Over time, partners, teams, communities winnow out bad ideas. The best research conversations follow a pattern in which early thoughts are free and open, accepting of risky or seemingly untenable ideas, while later discussion is more focused and challenging.

Most important, collaboration is fun! Who wants to dine alone when the alternative is brilliant company? Everything about research, even the credit, is best when shared. The Eureka moment is not truly experienced until the insight is shared. The grind of planning and running the experiment, the frustration of the analysis, the strategizing about presentation, the negotiation over write up, and then the response to reviewers and critics can only be fully appreciated when shared. It has been my great fortune to share my research career with Milton Lodge.

References

Abelson, Robert. (1963). Computer simulation of "hot" cognition. In Silvan Tomkins & Samuel Messick (Eds.), *Computer simulation of personality, frontier of psychological theory* (pp. 277–298). New York: John Wiley and Sons, Inc.

Anderson, Norman & Hubert, Stephen. (1963). Effects of concomitant verbal recall on order effects in personality impression formation. *Journal of Verbal Learning and Verbal Behavior*, 2, 379–391.

Baker, Monya. (2016). 1,500 scientists lift the lid on reproducibility, *Nature*, 533, 452–454.

Bargh, John. (1994). The four horseman of automaticity: Awareness, intention, efficiency, and control in social cognition. In Robert Wyer & Thomas Srull (Eds.), *Handbook of social cognition: Basic processes* (pp. 1–40). Hillsdale, NY: Erlbaum.

Bargh, John. (1997). The automaticity of everyday life. In Robert Wyer (Ed.), *Advances in social cognition* (pp. 1–61). Mahwah, NJ: Erlbaum.

Bargh, John. (1999). The cognitive monster: The case against controllability of automatic stereotype effects. In Shelly Chaiken & Yaacov Trope (Eds.), *Dual process theories in social psychology* (pp. 361–382). New York: Guilford Press.

Bullock, John G., Gerber, Alan S., Hill, Seth J., & Huber, Gregory A. (2015). Partisan bias in factual beliefs about politics. *Quarterly Journal of Political Science*, 10, 519–578.

Burdein, Inna, Lodge, Milton, & Taber, Charles S. (2006). Experiments on the automaticity of political beliefs and attitudes. *Political Psychology*, 27(3), 359–371.

Clore, Gerald & Isbell, Linda. (2001). Emotion and virtue and vice. In James Kuklinski (Ed.), *Political psychology in practice* (pp. 103–123). New York: Cambridge University Press.

Custers, Ruud & Aarts, Henk. (2010). The unconscious will: How the pursuit of goals operates outside of conscious awareness. *Science*, 329(5987), 47–50.

Ditto, Peter & Lopez, David. (1992). Motivated skepticism: Use of differential decision criteria for preferred and nonpreferred conclusions. *Journal of Personality and Social Psychology*, 63(4), 568–584.

Erisen, Cengiz, Lodge, Milton, & Taber, Charles S. (2014). Affective contagion in effortful political thinking. *Political Psychology*, 35(2), 187–206.

Fazio, Russell, Sanbonmatsu, David, Powell, Martha, & Kardes, Frank. (1986). On the automatic activation of attitudes. *Journal of Personality and Social Psychology*, 50(2), 229–238.

Friedman, Jeffrey. (Ed.) (2012). Political dogmatism [Special issue]. *Critical Review*, 24(2).

Gerber, Alan & Green, Donald. (1998). Rational learning and partisan attitudes. *American Journal of Political Science*, 42(3), 794–818.

Kahneman, Daniel. (2011). *Thinking, fast and slow*. New York: Farrar, Straus, and Giroux.

Kim, Sung-youn, Taber, Charles S., & Lodge, Milton. (2010). A computational model of the citizen as motivated reasoner: Modeling the dynamics of the 2000 presidential election. *Political Behavior*, 32(1), 1–28.

Kinder, Donald R. (1998). Opinion and action in the realm of politics. In Daniel T. Gilbert, Susan T. Fiske, & Gardner Lindzey (Eds.), *The handbook of social psychology* (pp. 778–867). New York: McGraw-Hill.

Kuklinski, James & Quirk, Paul. (2000). Reconsidering the rational public: Cognition, heuristics, and mass opinion. In Arthur Lupia, Mathew McCubbins, & Samuel Popkin (Eds.), *Elements of reason: Cognition, choice, and the bounds of rationality* (pp. 154–187). Cambridge: Cambridge University Press.

Kunda, Ziva. (1990). The case for motivated reasoning. *Psychological Bulletin*, 108(3), 480–498.

Libet, Benjamin. (1985). Unconscious cerebral initiative and the role of conscious will in voluntary action. *Behavioral and Brain Science*, 8(4), 529–539.

Lodge, Milton & McGraw, Kathleen. (Eds.) (1995). *Political judgment: Structure and process*. Ann Arbor, MI: University of Michigan Press.

Lodge, Milton, McGraw, Kathleen, & Stroh, Patrick. (1989). An impression driven model of candidate evaluation. *American Political Science Review*, 83(2), 399–420.

Lodge, Milton, Steenbergen, Marco, & Brau, Shawn. (1995). The responsive voter: Campaign information and the dynamics of candidate evaluation. *American Political Science Review*, 89(2), 309–326.

Lodge, Milton, Steenbergen, Marco, & Taber, Charles S. (1993). Computational experiments in candidate evaluation and vote choice, National Science Foundation Grant Proposal (NSF Grant SES-9310351).

Lodge, Milton, Stroh, Patrick, & Wahlke, John. (1990). Black-box models of candidate evaluation. *Political Behavior*, 12(1), 5–18.

Lodge, Milton & Taber, Charles S. (2000). Three steps toward a theory of motivated political reasoning. In Arthur Lupia, Mathew McCubbins, & Samuel Popkin (Eds.), *Elements of reason: Cognition, choice, and the bounds of rationality* (pp. 183–213). New York: Cambridge University Press.

Lodge, Milton & Taber, Charles S. (2005). The automaticity of affect for political leaders, groups, and issues: An experimental test of the hot cognition hypothesis. *Political Psychology*, 26(3), 455–482.

Lodge, Milton & Taber, Charles S. (2013). *The rationalizing voter*. Cambridge: Cambridge University Press.

Lord, Charles, Ross, Lee, & Lepper, Mark. (1979). Biased assimilation and attitude polarization: The effects of prior theories on subsequently considered evidence. *Journal of Personality and Social Psychology*, 37(11), 2098–2109.

Morris, James, Squires, Nancy, Taber, Charles S., & Lodge, Milton. (2003). Activation of political attitudes: A psychophysiological examination of the hot cognition hypothesis. *Political Psychology*, 24(4), 727–745.

Munro, Geoffrey, Ditto, Peter, Lockhart, Lisa, Fagerlin, Angela, Gready, Michael, & Peterson, Elizabeth. (2002). Biased assimilation of sociopolitical arguments: Evaluating the 1996 U.S. presidential debate. *Basic and Applied Social Psychology*, 24(1), 15–26.

Page, Scott E. (2008). *The difference: How the power of diversity creates better groups, firms, schools, and societies.* Princeton, NJ: Princeton University Press.

Popkin, Samuel L. (1991). *The reasoning voter: Communication and persuasion in presidential campaigns.* Chicago, IL: University of Chicago Press.

Prior, Marcus, Sood, Gaurav, & Khanna, Kabir. (2015). You cannot be serious: The impact of accuracy incentives on partisan bias in reports of economic perceptions. *Quarterly Journal of Political Science,* 10, 489–518.

Romer, Daniel, Kenski, Kate, Waldman, Paul, Adasiewicz, Christopher, & Jamieson, Kathleen Hall. (2003). *Capturing campaign dynamics: The National Annenberg Election Survey.* New York: Oxford University Press.

Taber, Charles S. (1992). POLI: An expert system model of U.S. foreign policy belief systems. *American Political Science Review,* 86(4), 888–904.

Taber, Charles S. (2003). Information processing and public opinion. In David O. Sears, Leonie Huddy, & Robert L. Jervis (Eds.), *Handbook of political psychology* (pp. 433–476). London: Oxford University Press.

Taber, Charles S., Cann, Damon, & Kucsova, Simona. (2009). The motivated processing of political arguments. *Political Behavior,* 31(2), 137–155.

Taber, Charles S. & Lodge, Milton. (2006). Motivated skepticism in the evaluation of political beliefs. *American Journal of Political Science,* 50(3), 755–769.

Taber, Charles S. & Lodge, Milton. (2012). The scope and generality of automatic affective biases in political thinking: A reply to the symposium. *Critical Review,* 24(2), 247–268.

Taber, Charles S., Lodge, Milton, & Glather, Jill. (2001). The motivated construction of political judgments. In James H. Kuklinski (Ed.), *Citizens and politics: Perspectives from political psychology* (pp. 198–226). London: Cambridge University Press.

Taber, Charles S. & Steenbergen, Marco. (1995). Computational experiments in electoral behavior. In Milton Lodge & Kathleen McGraw (Eds.), *Political judgment: Structure and process* (pp. 141–178). Ann Arbor, MI: University of Michigan Press.

Taber, Charles S. & Young, Everett. (2013). Political information processing. In Leonie Huddy, David O. Sears, & Jack Levy (Eds.), *The Oxford handbook of political psychology* (pp. 525–558). Oxford: Oxford University Press.

Zaller, John & Feldman, Stanley. (1992). A simple theory of survey response: Answering questions versus revealing preferences. *American Journal of Political Science,* 36(3), 579–616.

3

INSIDE THE BLACK BOX WITH MILT, AND OTHER LESSONS LEARNED

Kathleen M. McGraw

Introduction

Howie Lavine and Chuck Taber asked the contributors to this project to discuss their own programs of research while reflecting on Milt's influence. My immediate reaction to this invitation was a simple one: I honestly do not believe I would have had a successful academic career as a political scientist if I had not had the opportunity to work with, and learn from, Milt Lodge.

I completed my PhD in Social Psychology at Northwestern University in 1985, and was hired by the State University of New York at Stony Brook (as it was then known) as an Assistant Professor of Political Science in 1986. It was a position for which I was in many ways unprepared, never having taken a political science course as a graduate student, and perhaps as an undergraduate. I certainly had never planned on working in an academic field other than social psychology. My independent research program while a graduate student had largely focused on attributions of responsibility and moral reasoning, devoid of focus within a specific domain, such as politics (McGraw, 1985; McGraw & Bloomfield, 1987; McGraw, 1987a; McGraw, 1987b; McGraw, 1987c).

I was fortunate that my training at Northwestern involved not only a deep submersion in social psychology, but also the opportunity to study and work with four highly regarded social psychologists who combined their rigorous theoretical interests with a healthy appreciation for the applied implications of those theories: Jenny Crocker, with her interests in intergroup dynamics and self-esteem (e.g., Crocker & McGraw, 1984; Crocker, Thompson, McGraw & Ingerman, 1987); Tom Tyler, with his interests in the impact of self-interest and procedural justice in legal, political, and organizational settings (e.g., Tyler & McGraw, 1983; Tyler, Rasinski, & McGraw, 1985; Tyler & McGraw, 1986; McGraw & Tyler,

1986); Reid Hastie, who provided state-of-the-art training in social cognitive psychology and behavioral decision-making, linked to his work on jury decision-making; and Tom Cook, a founder of the field of program evaluation and applying social science methodology to social issues. Crocker, Tyler, Hastie, and Cook served as tremendous mentors and role models, and the example of their sustained attention to applied matters facilitated my transition to the discipline of political science.

Nonetheless, I felt woefully ill-equipped to be a political scientist. Of course, the Stony Brook Department of Political Science has had a long-standing commitment to political psychology, manifested in part by a strategy of hiring social psychologists with meager political science credentials. The faculty members in the department were accustomed to nurturing and mentoring these hires, and that certainly was my experience; I have nothing but fond memories of the Stony Brook faculty and my interactions with them.[1] The transition to political science was made easier by the addition of similarly focused colleagues: by the late 1980s, a vibrant political psychology community existed at Stony Brook, including Stanley Feldman, Leonie Huddy, Victor Ottati, Chuck Taber, and me. Milt was the force that shaped this group and the glue that held it together.

From the outset, Milt took it upon himself to further my professional development as a political scientist.[2] We met often to discuss our mutual interests. I have on occasion shared this anecdote with graduate students to illustrate the depths of my ignorance in those early days:

Setting: Milt and Kathleen in his office, discussing the political implications of social psychological theories and research on schemas (i.e., organized knowledge structure):

MILT: Well, you know what Converse would say about that?
KATHLEEN: Converse? Who is that?
MILT: *The Nature of Belief Systems in Mass Publics? The American Voter?*
KATHLEEN: What? What? (having never encountered any of this)
MILT: (having retrieved a folder with the Converse chapter from his file cabinet): Why don't you read this before we meet again?

And so my education in political science proceeded. In addition to lively discussions about the intersection of social psychology and political science, Milt made sure that I was integrated into the growing national network of political psychologists, by securing invitations for me to participate in academic conferences and book projects.

Two final general observations. The first is that Milt's professional generosity and kindness was more than matched by his personal generosity and kindness. I was a regular guest in his and his lovely wife Janet's home, spending many holidays with them. The Lodges' hospitality has been experienced by a countless number of Stony Brook faculty members and graduate students. The second is that Milt has a marvelous sense of humor: I never laughed as much or as often as I did with him, often about non-academic matters too ribald to detail here.

I now turn to more substantive matters. I begin with a discussion of Milt's early days at Stony Brook, to provide the context for understanding how the "Stony Brook School" (Rahn, Sullivan, & Rudolph, 2002) of political psychology emerged in the 1980s. I then discuss the genesis and evolution of our collaborative research on the online processing model, as well as other research projects that foreshadowed his motivated reasoning project with Chuck Taber. A brief discussion of my independent research program on accountability and elite rhetoric follows.

Milt's Intellectual Evolution and the Origins of Stony Brook Political Psychology

Stony Brook is a young university, founded in 1962. One consequence of this is that the Department of Political Science was established in the midst of the discipline's behavioral revolution, with an explicit directive to specialize in behavioral research and, in particular, experimental methods (Iyengar, 2011). The department chairs during this formative period, in particular Joe Tanenhaus and Bernie Tursky,[3] were deeply committed to experimental laboratory research. At a time when sophisticated experimental laboratories were non-existent in the discipline, Tanenhaus, Tursky, Milt, and John Wahlke built an extensive state-of-the-art suite of facilities that included psychophysiology labs (modeled after Tursky's Harvard labs), computer labs for tracking cognitive functions, and social psychology labs (modeled after Stanley Schacter's labs at Columbia) that included rooms with one-way mirrors and advanced video editing systems.

After earning his PhD at the University of Michigan in 1967, Milt took a position at the University of Iowa. As many readers probably know, he began his political science career as an expert in Soviet politics, with a focus on the attitudes of political elites in the post-Stalin period (Lodge, 1968a, 1968b, 1969). He was only at Iowa for four years (although promoted to Associate Professor in that short time span). I regret that I don't know precisely what led Milt to shift intellectual gears, although clearly his friendship with John Wahlke at Iowa and their mutual dissatisfaction with standard techniques for measuring attitudes were pivotal. In 1972, Milt and John published an article titled "Psychophysiological Measures of Political Attitudes and Behavior" (Wahlke & Lodge, 1972). This was the first article Milt published after the work on Soviet elites. It is notable not only because it foreshadowed the focus of the first wave of the Stony Brook behavioral research program but also because it articulates the two standards that served as guiding principles for the remainder of Milt's research career, namely the values of interdisciplinary scholarship and experimentation:

> what is urgently called for is not merely an multiple-indicator approach in the design and conduct of research but, even more important, a multi-disciplinary

conception of the subject matter to be researched.... Only properly controlled experiments can adequately test properly formulated generalizations of the kind of political behavior research must tackle.

(Wahlke & Lodge, 1972, pp. 529–530)[4]

Milt moved to Stony Brook in 1972, and he and his colleagues embarked on a well-funded and productive research program aimed at demonstrating the value of psychophysiological and psychophysical (e.g., magnitude scaling) methods to measure political attitudes. He and his colleagues published more than a dozen articles, several chapters, and the book *Magnitude Scaling of Social Psychological Judgments* (Lodge, 1982) in his first decade at Stony Brook. While much of this work was published in the discipline's most prominent outlets (e.g., *APSR* and *AJPS*), the measurement research program ultimately did not have much impact on political science research, for at least two reasons. The first is attributable to difficulties in terms of time and expense in implementing the psychophysical and psychophysiological measurement procedures. The second explanation lies in the cognitive revolution that took place in social psychology in the 1970s and early 1980s. This was a seismic intellectual shift that unavoidably shaped the direction that political psychology would take, a direction that Milt and the Stony Brook Political Psychology program (which was started in 1977) were well-positioned to influence.

The psychophysiological and psychophysical scaling research was unified by a central psychological theme, namely the valid and reliable measurement of attitudes. However, the research was not characterized by much in the way of explicit consideration of cognitive psychological principles; rather, the focus was primarily on measurement. Milt and his colleagues' interest shifted to explicitly cognitive psychological principles in the late 1970s. The zeitgeist of the cognitive revolution, and Milt's voracious intellectual appetite for new developments in the social sciences, made this development inevitable. It would also seem that Joe Tanenhaus played an important role in moving the focus of the Stony Brook behavioral research program toward cognitive psychology. Milt shared this in a memorial tribute to Joe Tanenhaus:

> It soon became clear—to him first, the rest of us later—that the problem of how to measure strength of opinion accurately was within reach. What next? Joe wasn't much interested in working at the second decimal place. His son, Michael, was completing his dissertation in cognitive psychology and introduced Joe to contemporary models of human information processing and experimental procedures for determining the meaning of concepts. Joe's recommendation to us was to focus on the stimulus side; to determine the meaning of the words used in questionnaires to refer to political objects and processes.... His work on political cognition will,

I think, be seen as pushing the behavioral persuasion in political science beyond its present boundaries.

(Lodge & Tursky, 1981, p. 139)

Sadly, Joe Tanenhaus died too soon in 1980, and it was Milt's vision and efforts, in collaboration with his colleagues and students, that transported the cognitive revolution to political science.

Political Cognition: Structure and Process

Milt's initial investigations into political cognition displayed a distinct change in theoretical focus, as he and his colleagues began to draw explicitly upon contemporary cognitive psychological models of the content and structure of concepts and knowledge structures to understand the meaning of partisan and ideological concepts (Bastedo & Lodge, 1980; Lodge & Wahlke, 1982; Sharp & Lodge, 1985). While the papers with Bastedo and Sharp continued to make use of magnitude scaling, the Lodge and Wahlke (1982) article is notable for a significant shift in measurement strategy: this is the first of Milt's published articles to utilize the standard cognitive psychological measurement tools of reaction times, recall, and recognition to draw inferences about cognitive structures, or schemas.

These initial studies of the meaning, content, and structure of political concepts laid the groundwork for Milt's significant collaborative research with Ruth Hamill in the early 1980s on political schemas (Hamill & Lodge, 1986; Hamill, Lodge, & Blake, 1985; Lodge & Hamill, 1986). Ruth was a 1980 University of Michigan social psychology PhD, whose dissertation was on self-schemas (i.e., knowledge structures about the self). The Lodge and Hamill studies were wide-ranging investigations of several questions: the content and structure of political knowledge structures, the consequences of political schemas for the processing of political information, and the characteristics of "schematic" and "aschematic" citizens.

The Lodge and Hamill research on political schemas was perhaps the most prominent manifestation of political psychology's embrace of "schema theory" in the early 1980s (many of the leading scholars contributed chapters to Lau and Sears's [1986]) edited volume, *Political Cognition*). Kuklinski, Luskin, and Bolland (1991) characterized this era in their thoughtful 1991 *APSR* critique, "Schema theory is decided 'in'" (p. 1341). Milt and I contributed a response to the Kuklinski et al. "Where Is the Schema" (1991) critique, as did Pam Conover, Stanley Feldman, and Art Miller (Lodge, McGraw, Conover, Feldman, & Miller, 1991).

I reference this *APSR* exchange on the utility and measurement of schemas for two reasons. The first is that I found the Lodge and McGraw response to Kuklinski and others (1991) to be unsatisfying. In that article, we developed a hypothetical schema of an imaginary reader. The example was psychologically sound, and we made our points effectively, but at the end of the day, it was a made-up knowledge structure. I became interested in better understanding different methods used to assess the content and structure of associative networks (the term "schema" having given way to "associate networks" as the currency of choice in social scientific investigations of knowledge structures; McGraw & Lodge, 1995). Along with Neil Pinney and Marco Steenbergen, I conducted several studies on the structure of memory for political actors, making use of the adjusted ratio of clustering (ARC) measure (Roenker, Thompson, & Brown, 1971). The ARC is a measure of categorical clustering in free recall that provides a means for inferring the categories used to organize memory. In our studies, we focused on the extent to which memory for political actors was organized along evaluative (positive and negative) versus substantive (issue and personal) dimensions, concluding that impressions of political actors were largely organized along the substantive dimension (McGraw, Pinney, & Neumann, 1991; McGraw & Steenbergen, 1995).

The Lodge and McGraw response to Kuklinski et al. (1991) is also of note because our analysis was representative of an important transition in Milt's political psychological priorities at this time, away from understanding the content of political knowledge structures per se to explication of dynamic procedural models that explain political evaluation processes. Soon after the *APSR* schema exchange, we published an edited volume, *Political Judgment: Structure and Process* (Lodge & McGraw, 1995), bringing together contributions from some of the leading scholars working in the field of political cognition. While the "structure versus process" organization of the volume is somewhat artificial, it is noteworthy that Milt's independent contribution, titled "Toward a Procedural Model of Candidate Evaluation" (Lodge, 1995), is squarely focused on cognitive processes and dynamics, rather than structure.

The Online Processing Model

Our initial study on online processing and candidate evaluation (Lodge, McGraw, & Stroh, 1989) is perhaps the most prominent indicator of Milt's embrace of cognitive process models. The cognitive revolution in social psychology in the 1970s and 1980s shifted the field to an information-processing perspective, with a focus on three fundamental questions (McGraw, 2000). First, how is social information stored and organized in memory? Second, how does information that is stored in memory affect the processing and interpretation of new information, as well as subsequent judgments, choices, and behaviors? Third, how are mental representations changed by new information, experiences, reflection, and other processes?

One of the most influential contributions to the social cognition literature was Hastie and Park's (1986) *Psychological Review* article that introduced the distinction between online and memory-based processing. Both models are fundamentally concerned with how information that is stored in memory affects opinions; the key differences lie in the nature of the memory input or evidence used to produce the opinion, as well as the timing of opinion construction. Simply, when memory-based processing occurs, opinions are constructed at the time the judgment is expressed, by retrieving specific pieces of information stored in long-term memory and combining the evaluative implications of the retrieved information to compute an opinion. In contrast, under online processing, people integrate the evaluative implications of new information relevant to the target of judgment by continuously updating an online tally of the summary judgment as the information is encountered. When it is necessary to express an opinion, the summary tally is retrieved from memory, not the specific pieces of information that contributed to it.

While I fully believe the principles of online and memory-based processing would have made their way into Milt's research agenda at some point, my connections to the Hastie and Park research program no doubt hastened the time line. Both Hastie and Park were my close friends at Northwestern (and Hastie my dissertation advisor), and so naturally I had in-depth knowledge of their studies and theoretical arguments. One of the first conversations Milt and I had at Stony Brook involved a discussion of recent developments in social cognition, where I described Hastie and Park's (then) forthcoming paper. Milt was intrigued, and suggested we conduct a study, along with Pat Stroh, to investigate these processes as they apply to evaluations of political actors. The Lodge and colleagues' (1989) experiment was for the most part a straightforward adoption of the Hastie and Park (1986) principles and research paradigm: participants learned information (i.e., policy positions) about a hypothetical Republican congressman; global evaluations of the congressman were provided; and surprise recall and recognition tests[5] of the policy positions were given. The participants' information-processing goal was experimentally manipulated, because the goal of forming an impression/summary judgment is the critical determinant of online processing (Hastie & Park, 1986). The crucial empirical test for determining which type of processing characterizes opinion formation involves a comparison of the impact of two "tallies" on the judgment of interest: a summary measure of the participants' evaluative ratings of all of the information they encountered, to capture online processing; and a summary measure of their evaluative ratings of the policy information they remembered, to capture memory-based processing. Consistent with Hastie and Park (1986), Lodge and colleagues (1989) found no relationship between memory and judgment when an impression formation goal was activated (rather, the online tally was the significant determinant of evaluations of the congressman); in contrast, when the impression formation goal was inhibited, the relationship between memory and judgment was significant, indicative of memory-based processing.

Those familiar with the social psychological literature may have very likely reacted to the Lodge and colleagues' (1989) study by saying, "How could it be otherwise?" I confess that was part of my first reaction, too, and I was initially surprised by the attention that the study received. Milt, on the other hand, saw from the beginning the contribution the study would make, namely by challenging reigning assumptions in political sciences that citizens evaluate political candidates in a memory-based fashion (e.g., Kelley & Mirer, 1974) and so forcing a disciplinary reconsideration of the cognitive processes underlying candidate evaluation, vote choice, and opinion formation (Zaller & Feldman, 1992).

The most important follow-up to Lodge et al. (1989) is Lodge and Steenbergen's (1995) *APSR* article, a significant accomplishment because of its methodological ambition and its strong statement of the normative implications at stake. My more modest research contributions to the online model were designed to extend the propositions of the model in several ways. The first (McGraw, Lodge, & Stroh, 1990) was a study conducted with Milt and Pat Stroh immediately after Lodge et al. (1989). This was the first study to consider the role that individual differences in political sophistication (i.e., interest in, and knowledge about politics) play in moderating candidate evaluation processes. Because of their greater interest in politics, sophisticates should be more likely to spontaneously approach political targets, especially candidates, with the goal of forming an impression, which is necessary for efficient online processing to occur. As expected, we found that sophisticates were significantly more likely to engage in online processing, while the less sophisticated were more likely to rely on the information immediately available in memory to form an opinion of the candidate. Similar sophistication-based processing differences are reported in McGraw and Pinney (1990); McGraw, Hasecke, and Conger (2003); and McGraw and Dolan (2007). These results, along with Milt and Chuck Taber's compelling evidence of enhanced motivated reasoning among sophisticates (Taber & Lodge, 2006; Lodge & Taber, 2013), support the indisputable conclusion that individual differences in political sophistication play a fundamental role in how citizens process information in the political domain.

The McGraw et al. (1990) experiment was also designed to investigate the extent to which the order of information is encountered, as well as the subjective importance of information, influence the weight accorded to evidence in online processing. Here, too, sophistication differences emerged. Sophisticates were characterized by a primacy effect, with information encountered early on contributing more weight to the online tally, while the less sophisticated exhibited a recency effect, with information encountered later contributing more weight. Information that was subjectively important also contributed the greatest weight to the online tally for both sophisticates and nonsophisticates, although the former were influenced by all the information they encountered (important or not), while the latter were only influenced by information they personally felt was important. This evidence of weighting differences attributable to information order and subjective importance remains underappreciated, as virtually no subsequent research on online and memory-based processing (my own included) has considered the extent to which different types of information affect the weighting of the two tallies.[6]

Investigations of online and memory-based processing have operationalized the tallies as unidimensional, lying along a bipolar (negative to positive) continuum. This is entirely consistent with traditional psychological treatments of attitudes. The 1990s saw a rise in social and political psychology scholarship arguing this unidimensional view of attitudes is incomplete, with researchers arguing that attitudes can also be characterized as two-dimensional, or rooted in separate positive and negative components. This perspective argues that ambivalence, or "the coexistence of both positive and negative evaluations" (Lavine, Thomsen, Zanna, & Borgida, 1998, p. 401) is critical to understanding attitudes and opinions. The McGraw et al. (2003) experiment was designed to explore the implications of ambivalence for online processing. In addition to the standard unidimensional online and memory-based tallies, a second set of tallies was created to capture the extent to which the information encountered and recalled about a political candidate was characterized by ambivalence (this study used the widely used objective formula of ambivalence proposed by Thompson, Zanna, & Griffin, 1995). While the results reported in McGraw, Lodge, and Jones (2002) could be crisper and more compelling, they do suggest that online ambivalence contributes an independent and negative impact on candidate evaluations, above and beyond the effects attributable to the unidimensional online tally (with those results largely limited to participants higher in political sophistication).

My final published extension of the online processing model (McGraw & Dolan, 2007) involved a shift to a perhaps surprising domain, namely attitudes about nation-states.[7] While the online and memory-based processing models were developed by Hastie and Park (1986) to account for evaluations of people, the models have been applied more generally to the formation of attitudes about a wide variety of targets. As a general principle, social psychological research suggests that attitudes about social groups and collectives tend to be formed in a memory-based fashion (Hamilton & Sherman, 1996), and so we expected attitudes about an unknown nation-state in most circumstances to be the result of memory-based processes. But we also theorized that an important exception might exist. The key insight of the McGraw and Dolan (2007) study was the recognition that states can be represented, or embodied, in various ways, such as through a national leader, abstract symbols, institutional processes, etc. We hypothesized, and found, that when a state was personified[8] through pictures and repeated references to its leader, attitudes about the state resulted from online processes; when the state was not personified (i.e., represented in impersonal ways), memory-based processing dominated. In short, the online processing of information that characterizes evaluations of people transfers to the formation of attitudes about states (and, we would predict, other collectives) when the state is personified.

Research investigating online and memory-based opinion formation processes, conducted by the Stony Brook scholars and by others, has largely been a statistical battle of regression coefficients: which tally better predicts the outcome judgment? In these empirical tests and subsequent discussion, scholars have largely taken an "either-or" approach (i.e., this judgment results from online processes, this other judgment stems from memory-based processes). While this approach is understandable and even desirable from the perspective of theory development, it also flies in the face of the fact that most scholars working in this tradition believe a hybrid model, incorporating both online and memory-based components, is more psychologically realistic (Hastie & Pennington, 1989, were the first to articulate this perspective). In theory, the hybrid model is almost certainly correct. It is disappointing that political and social psychologists have not made more progress in specifying how empirical investigations of such a hybrid model would proceed.

Whither Motivation?

Milt has had a long-standing interest in incorporating motivational processes into political models of judgment and decision-making, even during the height of the cognitive revolution in the 1980s. I simply do not recall if we ever seriously discussed extending the online processing model to incorporate motivation. This "opportunity-not-taken" (on my part) probably is the result of my stubborn failure to embrace the "hot cognition" revolution, as well as the fact that by the mid-1990s, I knew that my time at Stony Brook was coming to an end. Rather, the important project of synthesizing online processing and motivational mechanisms was undertaken by Milt and Chuck Taber, and I will leave it to Chuck to describe how that research program developed.

Milt and I did collaborate on two projects examining motivational processes. These were very much one-shot studies, and they can be seen as expressions of Milt's core interest in motivation, shaped by my beliefs about relevant social psychological principles that might inform our research questions. The first set of studies, conducted in collaboration with Mark Fischle and Karen Stenner (McGraw, Fischle, Stenner, & Lodge, 1996), were investigations of bias in trait descriptions of political leaders. Personality traits can be characterized along multiple dimensions, including breadth, which involves the number of distinct behaviors a given trait subsumes (e.g., "good" is a broad trait, whereas "charitable" is a narrower trait). The trait breadth attribution bias (John, Hampson, & Goldberg, 1991) refers to the impact of prior attitudes towards an individual on the breadth of trait attributions. Simply, people tend to select broad positive traits and narrower negative traits to describe people they like. Conversely, they tend to choose broad negative traits and narrower positive traits for people they dislike. This asymmetry in trait attribution is motivated by the desire to maintain existing impressions of the target. In two studies, we demonstrated the existence of the trait breadth attribution bias in judgments of contemporary political leaders.[9]

The second motivation-themed project with Milt was conducted in collaboration with Jeff Jones (McGraw et al., 2002). Milt often raised the question, "why do people continue to believe what they want to believe?", and we had several discussions of how we might approach the problem. We never reached an answer that was mutually satisfying, and the eventual design of the McGraw et al. (2002) study strayed pretty far from what Milt would have preferred.[10] At the time, I was quite taken with Jacobs and Shapiro's (2000) book, *Politicians Don't Pander*, and their provocative arguments shaped the direction this study took, which focused on the development of suspicion about elite policy positions when those positions are articulated in a situation suggestive of pandering to audience preferences. The social psychological literature suggests that the psychological state of suspicion is "relatively sophisticated, . . . characterized by active, careful consideration of the potential motives" (Fein, 1996, p. 1167). However, this heightened cognitive activity is anathema to many or most citizens, suggesting that suspicion is a state that most would prefer to avoid. Our proposed solution to this paradox, supported by the results reported in McGraw et al. (2002), is that agreement with the stated policy position plays a critical role: people who agree with the message accept at face value the validity of the stated position, and so are not suspicious, even in circumstances strongly suggesting of pandering, while those who disagree with the message are more likely to express suspicion. In other words, evaluative reactions to a message determine whether suspicion is aroused. This is a reasonable psychological response that plays right into the hands of the strategically self-interested politician, because inherent to the decision to pander to audience views is the rational selection of a consensual policy position with which the majority of an audience is likely to agree.

Accountability and Elite Rhetoric

As noted earlier, my research as a graduate student at Northwestern focused on attributions of responsibility and moral reasoning, with a specific focus on the causal reasoning processes that gives rise to judgments of responsibility and blame. I naturally wanted to continue this line of investigation as a political scientist, focusing on understanding attributions of responsibility for political outcomes, in particular outcomes that might be regarded as "predicaments," that is, situations that are politically difficult, unpleasant and/or embarrassing. I began by designing a study that would have been a straightforward application of key principles from social psychological attribution theory (i.e., manipulating the severity of the political predicament and the partisan similarity of the politician; Berger, 1981). That design felt frustratingly inadequate, because it failed to capture what anyone familiar with the political world would take to be self-evident: namely, when politicians find themselves in a predicament, they are not passive bystanders but rather take an active role in trying to shape audience reactions by engaging in various rhetorical strategies. Accordingly, I refocused my interests in political responsibility by emphasizing the impact of political explanations, or accounts.

I discussed these ideas with Milt, as well as with Shanto Iyengar and other colleagues, although the specifics of those conversations are long forgotten. They pointed me to the relevant classics in political science that provided the much-needed normative and political foundations for the subsequent studies. For example, Fenno's *Home Style* emphasized the centrality of explanations to theories of representation: "theories of representation will always be incomplete without theories that explain explaining" (1978, p. 162). Pitkin (1967) emphasized that explanation is a key manifestation of accountability in a representative democracy: representation implies "acting in the interest of the represented, in a manner responsive to them. . . . The representative must act in such a way that there is no conflict, or if it occurs, an explanation is called for" (pp. 209–210). While political scientists, especially congressional scholars, have long recognized the importance of "explaining the vote" (Bianco, 1994; Fenno, 1978; Kingdon, 1973; Mayhew, 1974), there was little systematic empirical work on the antecedents and consequences of political explanations. Similarly, while there were rich psychological and sociological literatures on accounts, they did not provide much in the way of theoretical guidelines as to the psychological process mechanisms or conditions under which accounts would have an impact on public opinion.

I sought to remedy these gaps in the literature by creating a 2x2 typology of four different types of political accounts (excuses, justifications, concessions, and denials) and by developing a theoretical framework that specified the unique impact of the different types of accounts on specific political judgments, such as attributions of responsibility, trait inferences and global evaluations of political actors, and policy opinions (for details, see McGraw, 1990, 1991, 2001, 2003, 2011). It is clear that satisfactory accounts boost evaluations of politicians, whereas unsatisfactory accounts have damaging evaluative consequences, raising the question of what makes for a satisfactory political explanation. Some broad generalizations exist. First, explanations that are more common in political rhetoric are generally more satisfactory, in line with the argument that the public responds more favorably to political rhetoric that is familiar (Bennett, 1980; Edelman, 1988; McGraw, 1991). Second, all else equal, individual characteristics matter, with more trusting and less sophisticated citizens expressing satisfaction with political accounts (McGraw & Hubbard, 1996). Existing attitudes about the politician or the policy decision that is explained serve as an anchor (McGraw, Best, & Timpone, 1995), with people more satisfied with explanations provided by politicians they like or for decisions of which they approve. Fenno pointed to the importance of consistency between established reputations and explanatory style (1978), and laboratory evidence provides support for this intuition (McGraw, Timpone, & Bruck, 1993). Finally, at least in the political realm, justifications appealing to normative principles (especially ethical standards like fairness and moral conscience) are consistently among the most satisfactory explanations, whereas excuses involving a diffusion of responsibility are among the least satisfactory (McGraw, 1998).

Concluding Thoughts

I began by stating that I doubt that I would have had a successful academic career without Milt's influence. The more significant counterfactual is this: it is hard to imagine how the field of political psychology would have evolved without Milt's sustained emphasis on theoretically motivated and rigorous experimental investigations of the cognitive psychological foundations of political thought, judgment, and reasoning. Of course, the field of political psychology surely would have developed and even flourished, but arguably it would be a very different scholarly enterprise without Milt's (and his Stony Brook colleagues, past and present) pioneering efforts to incorporate cognitive psychological principles into the discipline of political science.

I left Stony Brook for Ohio State in 1998, largely for family reasons. Upon reflection, it strikes me as incredible that I have spent a larger portion of my career at OSU. It's been said that academic administrative responsibilities will find you unless active steps are taken to avoid them. While Milt Lodge was the quintessential good departmental citizen, he always maintained a healthy aversion to higher level administrative responsibilities. He frequently offered advice on how to cultivate an academic career without significant administrative commitments. This was a lesson that I failed to absorb (as apparently, did Chuck Taber), as I spent much of my time at OSU in departmental and college administrative positions. While I have no regrets, perhaps if there had been a Milt-like colleague in Columbus, a different career trajectory would have resulted.

Thanks for everything, Milt!

Notes

1. The culture of the Stony Brook department was very collegial. The faculty members ate lunch together daily as a group. We had regular poker nights, and enjoyed the occasional adult beverage together. When I was hired in 1986, I was the only woman in the department, and I was soon approached by several well-meaning female faculty members from other departments in the university who worried that I might be feeling lonely and isolated. I told them that nothing could be further from the truth: that the department had been entirely welcoming and inclusive towards me.
2. Obviously, I was not unique in receiving this attention from Milt, as several other contributors to this volume have similar stories to tell.
3. The department's penchant for hiring scholars with non-traditional credentials began with Tursky. He did not hold a PhD in any discipline but rather was a technical engineer who built and directed a psychophysiology laboratory in the Department of Social Relations at Harvard in the 1960s. Milt attended a training program in psychophysiology at Harvard in the early 1970s, met Bernie, and convinced him to come to Stony Brook to head the behavioral research laboratory there. Tursky was appointed a Professor of Political Science and quickly became chair, a position he held until 1985 (Jamner, 2014).
4. Political scientists who came of age in the late 20th and early 21st centuries probably cannot fully appreciate the boldness of this call for an experimental political science in the early 1970s. More than a decade later in 1986, I was advised by several scholars—political scientists and social psychologists—that I could not possibly succeed in the discipline as an experimentalist. Milt told me to ignore that advice, for which I am grateful. I was pleased to be able to be an early advocate for experimental methods in political science (McGraw & Hoekstra, 1994; McGraw, 1996).
5. Hastie and Park (1986) relied entirely on free recall data. In contrast, Lodge et al. (1989) relied entirely on the recognition data, to investigate both the content of memory in the first part of the paper and the memory-judgment relationship in the second.

6. A related measurement observation: there is effectively no consensus on how the online and memory-based tallies should be operationalized (setting aside the questions of weighting). Although all researchers take into account positive and negative reactions to information encountered and remembered, some have made use of percentage measures, others averages, and still others difference measures. There has been too little consideration of the psychological processing assumptions underlying these various operationalizations of the tallies, or their statistical properties (Redlawsk, 2001 and McGraw & Dolan, 2007, Footnote # 8, are beginnings).
7. At the time, Tom Dolan was an OSU graduate student majoring in International Relations, and the starting point of the research question was the subject of a final paper he wrote for my graduate Political Psychology seminar.
8. This study provided information about a real country and leader (Moldova and its then-President Voronin), about which our undergraduate research participants knew virtually nothing. While nearly all political psychological research on online processing has relied on hypothetical political candidates to insure that the research participants do not have prior knowledge or attitudes about the target, and so that the researcher has full control over the information to which the research participants are exposed (Lodge & Steenbergen, 1995), McGraw and Dolan (2007), as well as McGraw and Pinney (1990) and Rahn, Krosnick, and Breuning (1994) suggest designs in which greater realism can be introduced.
9. A concrete example from the McGraw et al. (1996) paper: Those with a positive attitude towards Ronald Reagan described him as "kind" (a broad positive trait) whereas those with a negative attitude granted that he was "compassionate" (a narrower trait). Conversely, those with negative attitudes judged Reagan to be "unintelligent" (a broad negative trait) whereas those with a positive attitude conceded he was "naïve" (a narrower trait). The breadth of the traits used in these studies was established from Hampson, Goldberg and John's (1987) scaling of more than 500 trait terms.
10. It goes without saying that Milt and Chuck Taber answered this question in a much more comprehensive and compelling fashion in their motivated reasoning project (Lodge & Taber, 2013).

References

Bastedo, Ralph W. & Lodge, Milton. (1980). The meaning of party labels. *Political Behavior*, 2, 287–308.

Bennett, W. L. (1980). The paradox of public discourse: A framework for the analysis of political accounts. *Journal of Politics*, 42, 792–817.

Berger, Jerry M. (1981). Motivational biases in the attribution of responsibility for an accident: A meta-analysis of the defensive attribution hypothesis. *Psychological Bulletin*, 90, 496–512.

Bianco, William T. (1994). *Trust: Representatives and constituents.* Ann Arbor, MI: University of Michigan Press.

Crocker, Jennifer & McGraw, Kathleen M. (1984). What's good for the goose is not good for the gander: Solo status as an obstacle to occupational achievement for males and females. *American Behavioral Scientist*, 27, 357–369.

Crocker, Jennifer, Thompson, Leigh L., McGraw, Kathleen M., & Ingerman, Cynthia. (1987). Downward comparison, prejudice, and evaluations: The effects of self-esteem and threat. *Journal of Personality and Social Psychology*, 52, 907–916.

Edelman, Murray. (1988). *Political language: Words that succeed and policies that fail.* New York: Academic Press.

Fein, Steven. (1996). Effects of suspicion on attributional thinking and the correspondence bias. *Journal of Personality and Social Psychology*, 70, 1164–1184.

Fenno, Richard E. (1978). *Home style: House members in their districts*. Boston, MA: Little Brown.

Hamill, Ruth & Lodge, Milton. (1986. Cognitive consequences of political sophistication. In Richard R. Lau & David O. Sears (Eds.), *Political cognition* (pp. 69–93). Hillsdale, NJ: Lawrence Erlbaum.

Hamill, Ruth, Lodge, Milton, & Blake, Frederick. (1985).The breadth, depth, and utility of class, partisan, and ideological schemata. *American Journal of Political Science*, 29, 850–870.

Hamilton, David L. & Sherman, Steven J. (1996). Perceiving persons and groups. *Psychological Review*, 103, 336–355.

Hampson, Sara E., Goldberg, Lewis R., & John, Oliver P. (1987). Category-breadth and social-desirability values for 573 personality terms. *European Journal of Personality*, 1, 241–258.

Hastie, Reid & Park, Bernadette. (1986). The relationship between memory and judgment depends on whether the task is memory-based or on-line. *Psychological Review*, 93, 258–268.

Hastie, Reid & Pennington, Nancy. (1989). Notes on the distinction between memory-based versus on-line judgments. In John M. Bassili (Ed.), *On-line cognition in person perception* (pp. 1–17). Hillsdale, NJ: Erlbaum.

Iyengar, Shanto. (2011). Laboratory experiments in political science. In James N. Druckman, Donald P. Green, James H. Kuklinski, & Arthur Lupia. (Eds.), *Cambridge handbook of experimental political science* (pp. 73–88). New York: Cambridge University Press.

Jacobs, Lawrence R. & Shapiro, Robert Y. (2000). *Politicians don't pander: Political manipulation and the loss of democratic responsiveness*. Chicago, IL: University of Chicago Press.

Jamner, Larry D. (2014). In memoriam: Bernard Tursky (1918–2012). *Psychophysiology*, 51, 1059–1060.

John, Oliver P., Hampson, Sarah E., & Goldberg, Lewis R. (1991).The basic level in personality-trait hierarchies: Studies of trait use and accessibility in different contexts. *Journal of Personality and Social Psychology*, 60, 348–361.

Kelley, Stanley & Mirer, Thadeus. (1974). The simple act of voting. *American Political Science Review*, 61, 572–591.

Kingdon, John W. (1973). *Congressmen's voting decisions*. New York: Harper and Row.

Kuklinski, James H., Luskin, Robert C., & Bolland, John. (1991).Where is the schema? Going beyond the 's' word in political psychology. *American Political Science Review*, 85, 1341–1356.

Lau, Richard R. & Sears, David O. (1986). *Political cognition*. Hillsdale, NJ: Lawrence Erlbaum.

Lavine, Howard, Thomsen, Cynthia J., Zanna, Mark P., & Borgida, Eugene. (1998). On the primacy of affect in the determination of attitudes and behavior: The moderating influence of affective-cognitive ambivalence. *Journal of Experimental Social Psychology*, 34, 398–421.

Lodge, Milton. (1968a). Soviet elite participatory attitudes in the post Stalin period. *American Political Science Review*, 62, 827–839.

Lodge, Milton. (1968b). Groupism in the post Stalin period. *American Journal of Political Science*, 12, 330–351.

Lodge, Milton. (1969). *Soviet elite attitudes since Stalin*. New York: Charles E. Merrill.

Lodge, Milton. (1982). *Magnitude scaling of social psychological judgments*. Beverly Hills, CA: Sage.

Lodge, Milton. (1995). Toward a procedural model of candidate evaluation. In Milton Lodge & Kathleen M. McGraw (Eds.), *Political judgment: Structure and process* (pp. 111–139). Ann Arbor, MI: University of Michigan Press.

Lodge, Milton & Hamill, Ruth. (1986). A partisan schema for political information processing. *American Political Science Review*, 80, 505–520.
Lodge, Milton & McGraw, Kathleen M. (1991). Where is the schema? Critique. *American Political Science Review*, 85, 1357–1364.
Lodge, Milton & McGraw, Kathleen M. (Eds.) (1995). *Political judgment: Structure and process.* Ann Arbor, MI: University of Michigan Press.
Lodge, Milton, McGraw, Kathleen M., Conover, Pamela Johnston, Feldman, Stanley, & Miller, Arthur H. (1991). Where is the schema? Critiques. *American Political Science Review*, 85, 1357–1380.
Lodge, Milton, McGraw, Kathleen M., & Stroh, Patrick. (1989). An impression-driven model of candidate evaluation. *American Political Science Review*, 83, 399–420.
Lodge, Milton & Steenbergen, Marco. (1995). The responsive voter: Campaign information and the dynamics of candidate evaluation. *American Political Science Review*, 89, 309–326.
Lodge, Milton & Taber, Charles S. (2013). *The rationalizing voter.* New York: Cambridge University Press.
Lodge, Milton & Tursky, Bernard. (1981). Joseph Tanenhaus. *PS*, 14, 138–139.
Lodge, Milton & Wahlke, John. (1982). Politicos, apoliticos, and the processing of political information. *International Political Science Review*, 16, 131–150.
Mayhew, David. (1974). *Congress: The electoral connection.* New Haven, CT: Yale University Press.
McGraw, Kathleen M. (1985). Subjective probabilities and moral judgments. *Journal of Experimental Social Psychology*, 21, 501–518.
McGraw, Kathleen M. (1987a). Guilt following transgression: An attribution of responsibility approach. *Journal of Personality and Social Psychology*, 53, 247–256.
McGraw, Kathleen M. (1987b). The influence of base-rate information on moral judgments. *Social Cognition*, 5, 58–75.
McGraw, Kathleen M. (1987c). Conditions for assigning blame: The impact of necessity and sufficiency. *British Journal of Social Psychology*, 26, 109–117.
McGraw, Kathleen M. (1990). Avoiding blame: An experimental investigation of political excuses and justifications. *British Journal of Political Science*, 20, 119–132.
McGraw, Kathleen M. (1991). Managing blame: An experimental test of the effects of political accounts. *American Political Science Review*, 85, 1133–1158.
McGraw, Kathleen M. (1996). Political methodology: Research design and experimental methods. In Robert E. Goodin & Hans-Dieter Klingemann (Eds.), *A new handbook of political science* (pp. 1–19). New York: Oxford University Press.
McGraw, Kathleen M. (1998). Manipulating public opinion with moral justification. *The Annals of the American Academy of Political and Social Science*, 560, 127–140.
McGraw, Kathleen M. (2000). Contributions of the cognitive approach to political psychology. *Political Psychology*, 21, 805–832.
McGraw, Kathleen M. (2001). Political accounts and attribution processes. In James Kuklinski (Ed.), *Citizens and politics: Perspectives from political psychology* (pp. 160–180). New York: Cambridge University Press.
McGraw, Kathleen M. (2003). Political impressions: Formation and management. In David Sears, Leonie Huddy, & Robert Jervis (Eds.), *Oxford handbook of political psychology* (pp. 394–432). New York: Oxford University Press.
McGraw, Kathleen M. (2011). Candidate impressions and evaluations. In James N. Druckman, Donald P. Green, James H. Kuklinski, & Arthur Lupia (Eds.), *Handbook of experimental political science* (pp. 186–200). New York: Cambridge University Press.

McGraw, Kathleen M., Best, Samuel, & Timpone, Richard. (1995). "What they say or what they do?" The impact of elite explanation and policy outcomes on public opinion. *American Journal of Political Science*, 39, 53–74.

McGraw, Kathleen M. & Bloomfield, Jeremy. (1987). Social influence on group moral decisions: The interactive effects of moral reasoning and sex role orientation. *Journal of Personality and Social Psychology*, 53, 1080–1087.

McGraw, Kathleen M. & Dolan, Thomas. (2007). Personifying the state: Consequences for attitude formation. *Political Psychology*, 28, 299–328.

McGraw, Kathleen M., Fischle, Mark, Stenner, Karen, & Lodge, Milton. (1996). What's in a word? Bias in trait attributions of political leaders. *Political Behavior*, 18, 263–281.

McGraw, Kathleen M., Hasecke, Edward, & Conger, Kimberly. (2003). Ambivalence, uncertainty, and processes of candidate evaluation. *Political Psychology*, 24, 421–448.

McGraw, Kathleen M. & Hoekstra, Valerie. (1994). Experimentation in political science: Historical trends and future directions. In Michael X. Delli Carpini, Leonie Huddy, & Robert Y. Shapiro (Eds.), *Research in micropolitics* (Vol. 4, pp. 3–29). Stamford, CT: JAI Press.

McGraw, Kathleen M. & Hubbard, Clark. (1996). Some of the people some of the time: Individual differences in acceptance of political accounts. In Diana C. Mutz, Paul Sniderman, & Richard Brody (Eds.), *Political persuasion and attitude change* (pp. 145–170). Ann Arbor, MI: University of Michigan Press.

McGraw, Kathleen M. & Lodge, Milton. (1995). Introduction. In Milton Lodge & Kathleen M. McGraw (Eds.), *Political judgment: Structure and process* (pp. 1–14). Ann Arbor, MI: University of Michigan Press.

McGraw, Kathleen M., Lodge, Milton, & Jones, Jeffrey. (2002). The pandering politicians of suspicious minds. *Journal of Politics*, 64, 362–383.

McGraw, Kathleen M., Lodge, Milton, & Stroh, Patrick. (1990). On-line processing in candidate evaluation: The effects of issue order, issue salience, and sophistication. *Political Behavior*, 12, 41–58.

McGraw, Kathleen M. & Pinney, Neil. (1990). The effects of general and domain-specific expertise on political memory and judgment processes. *Social Cognition*, 8, 9–30.

McGraw, Kathleen M., Pinney, Neil, & Neumann, David. (1991). Memory for political actors: Contrasting the use of semantic and evaluative organizational strategies. *Political Behavior*, 13, 165–189.

McGraw, Kathleen M. & Steenbergen, Marco. (1995). Pictures in the head: Memory representations of political actors. In Milton Lodge & Kathleen M. McGraw (Eds.), *Political judgment: Structure and* process (pp. 15–42). Ann Arbor, MI: University of Michigan Press.

McGraw, Kathleen M., Timpone, Richard, & Bruck, Gabor. (1993). Justifying controversial political decisions: *Home style* in the laboratory. *Political Behavior*, 15, 289–308.

McGraw, Kathleen M. & Tyler, Tom R. (1986). The threat of nuclear war and psychological well-being. *International Journal of Mental Health*, 15, 172–188.

Pitkin, Hannah F. (1967). *The concept of representation*. Berkeley: University of California Press.

Rahn, Wendy M., Krosnick, Jon A., & Breuning, Marijke. (1994). Rationalization and derivation processes in survey studies of political candidate evaluation. *American Journal of Political Science*, 38, 582–600.

Rahn, Wendy M., Sullivan, John L., & Rudolph, Thomas J. (2002). Political psychology and political science. In James H. Kuklinski (Ed.), *Thinking about political psychology* (pp. 155–186). New York: Cambridge University Press.

Redlawsk, David. (2001). You must remember this: A test of the on-line model of voting. *Journal of Politics*, 63, 29–58.

Roenker, Daniel L., Thompson, Charles P., & Brown, Sam C. (1971). Comparisons of measures for the estimation of clustering in free recall. *Psychological Bulletin*, 76, 45–48.

Sharp, Carol & Lodge, Milton. (1985). Partisan and ideological belief systems: Do they differ? *Political Behavior*, 7, 147–166.

Taber, Charles S. & Lodge, Milton. (2006). Motivated skepticism in the evaluation of political beliefs. *American Journal of Political Science*, 50, 755–769.

Thompson, Megan M., Zanna, Mark P., & Griffin, Dale W. (1995). Let's not be indifferent about (attitudinal) ambivalence. In Richard E. Petty & Jon A. Krosnick (Eds.), *Attitude strength: Antecedents and consequences* (pp. 361–386). Mahwah, NJ: Erlbaum.

Tyler, Tom R. & McGraw, Kathleen M. (1983). The threat of nuclear war: Risk interpretation and behavioral response. *Journal of Social Issues*, 39, 25–40.

Tyler, Tom R. & McGraw, Kathleen M. (1986). Ideology and the interpretation of personal experience: Procedural justice and political quiescence. *Journal of Social Issues*, 42, 115–128.

Tyler, Tom R., Rasinski, Kenneth, & McGraw, Kathleen M. (1985). The influence of perceived injustice on the endorsement of political leaders. *Journal of Applied Social Psychology*, 15, 700–725.

Wahlke, John C. & Lodge, Milton G. (1972). Psychophysiological measures of political attitudes and behavior. *American Journal of Political Science*, 16, 505–537.

Zaller, John R. & Feldman, Stanley. (1992). A simple theory of the survey response: Answering questions versus revealing preferences. *American Journal of Political Science*, 36, 579–616.

4

CITIZENS, POLITICS, AND PROCESS

The Extensive Reach of Milton Lodge

Robert Huckfeldt

> [M]ost thinking occurs outside of awareness, available to neither introspection nor direct observation. Humans are designed to process rapidly and implicitly enormous quantities of environmental and internal data. But our ability to focus explicit thought is severely limited. By and large, the social sciences are not well prepared to understand this duality of cognition, and political science is no exception.
>
> (Lodge & Taber, 2013, p. 1)

The work of Milton Lodge and his collaborators has enormous influence within both political science and political psychology. His work has also generated important implications for the particular areas of concern that I have pursued with my collaborators—sources of influence on individual and group behavior that are contingent on individual location within social networks and contexts. This paper addresses some of the ways in which Milton has influenced our work. His contributions have not only provided guidance going forward, but they have also altered the ways in which we view our own earlier efforts.

I had the good fortune to spend the 1994–1995 academic year in the Department of Political Science at the State University of New York at Stony Brook. I came to Stony Brook fully intending to spend the rest of my career on Long Island, but the Fates intervened, and my stay lasted only a single year. While the entire episode might appear from the outside to have been a mistake in judgment, the year in Stony Brook turned out to be an extraordinarily productive year, and my Long Island colleagues were incredibly gracious. Indeed, the year on Long Island provided the mid-career equivalent of a postdoctoral fellowship. With little anticipation on my own part, the exposure to Milton's work produced some particularly dramatic changes in the way I came to understand my own research program.

As I arrived at Stony Brook, John Sprague and I were just finishing a book based on our 1984 South Bend election study—the book was published mid-year with SUNY-Stony Brook as my institutional affiliation (Huckfeldt & Sprague, 1995). While neither of us fully realized it at the time, we were getting ready to launch a new project, the 1996 Indianapolis–St. Louis election study, an undertaking that would reflect Milton's influence, as well as serving as a pivot point in our own efforts.

The year at Stony Brook was crucial, and Milton's influence was especially important. I had not anticipated being influenced in any particular way. After all, Milton is a political psychologist with a focus on political cognition. I saw myself as a sociological political scientist, and my own work turned on the implications of political communication and interdependence among political actors. He was reading psychology journals, while I was reading sociology journals.

By the end of the year, I had begun to think about the social networks connecting citizens to one another in new and complementary ways. Just as the connections (edges) among individuals represented in a network graph are crucial to political outcomes, so are the individuals (nodes) within those graphs. One part of the story is about the ways in which communication and interdependence among individuals produce political change at both the micro and macro levels, but another equally important story is how these connections among citizens are profoundly imbedded within processes of social and political cognition.

This view occasionally makes me an outlier in the meetings and rituals of my friends and colleagues of the Political Networks Section of the American Political Science Association. At the same time, giving nodes their due by taking account of cognition produces transformative consequences for the dynamics of interdependent actors, for the social dynamics of politics, and hence for studies of contexts and networks.

The Heart of the Problem: Citizens in Context

What are we to think when residents of Democratic neighborhoods in South Bend are more likely to vote for Democratic candidates in the 1960s, regardless of their own partisan orientations (Huckfeldt, 1983)? What are we to think when the same residents are more likely to be imbedded within friendship networks populated by other Democratic voters, once again regardless of their own partisan orientations?

One response to these questions is to assert that individuals exercise lock grip control over a series of associational choices. Even though they may not be Democrats, perhaps they select neighborhoods for reasons that co-vary with partisan composition, and perhaps there are similar criteria, once again correlated with partisanship, that come into play when they form patterns of association. Perhaps, but what are we to think when many of these same individuals believe their associates vote for Democrats, even when they actually support Republicans?

An alternative response to these questions is to consider the possibility that not only thinking, but also social interaction and communication occur outside the boundaries of individual control (Huckfeldt and Sprague, 1987). Hence the many life choices that lead to an individual's location within neighborhoods, schools, universities, workplaces, and marriages might be viewed as a probabilistic throw of the dice rather than a determinate outcome of individually imposed selection criteria. To paraphrase John Sprague, many people choose a neighborhood because of its great local schools, but how often do they consider the implications for the likely partisanship of their future neighbors?

Our argument is that politics and political communication involve activities imbedded within structured patterns of social interaction (Huckfeldt, 1983; Huckfeldt & Sprague, 1995; Huckfeldt, Johnson, & Sprague, 2004; Ahn, Huckfeldt, & Ryan, 2014). Hence political information is transmitted through social interaction, but the issue that arises is the extent to which political preferences control the flow of incoming information, and the extent to which the flow of information affects the formation of preferences. Lodge forces us to take both alternatives seriously.

My collaborators and I have undertaken a series of analyses and studies where a primary concern is the flow of information transmitted among individuals through a variety of vehicles—earnest conversations, casual remarks, bumper stickers, yard signs, and more. Some of these conversations and interactions clearly reflect partisan purpose, while others transmit only vaguely and inadvertently conveyed messages and signals.

The important point is that socially conveyed information does not carry determinate consequences for the recipient, and neither is it based on the *de novo* consideration of the message in a fair-minded vacuum. Rather, the political consequence of any single communication is contextually contingent, where the context is defined relative to the ongoing stream of communication. Indeed, what the recipient brings to the communication synapse is just as important as what the messenger conveys. Most importantly, the effect of any message within the information stream is contingent on the rest of the stream. Hence, if you are the only one of ten friends who told me I should for Donald Trump instead of Hillary Clinton, you are likely to have been less influential than if you are one of two.

Returning to the quotation from Lodge and Taber with which we began, many of the context and network effects arising on individual political cognition occur beyond the boundaries of human awareness, and most are rapidly forgotten. I am likely to forget the bumper stickers, yard signs, and conversations quite rapidly after I become conscious of them. That does not, however, mean that they are lacking in influence with enduring consequence.

Political Cognition as Social Cognition: Subtle and Automatic

During my year at Stony Brook, I was exposed to new (for me) literatures on social and political cognition, and these literatures and their insights led us in new directions. Somewhere along the way, either Milton or Kathleen McGraw introduced me to the work of Ziva Kunda (1990) on social cognition. The lesson for political scientists is that the exercise of citizenship is rooted in political cognition, and political cognition is one dimension of social cognition. In Kunda's words (1999, p. 3), social cognition refers broadly to the integration of cognition, motivation, and affect as "aspects of making sense of our social world," or in political terms, as the factors that impinge on all of us when we try to make sense of democratic politics.

Equally important, Milton introduced me to the work of Russ Fazio—a colleague who was at the time located in Department of Psychology at Indiana, and whose office in Bloomington was less than a half mile from my own. (The astute reader will notice the inherent limits of contextual propinquity.) After returning to Indiana and receiving NSF funding to undertake the Indianapolis–St. Louis study with John Sprague, I took Russ to lunch, along with Jeff Levine—our invaluable graduate student and collaborator. Jeff also spent the year in Stony Brook, and he too took away insights relevant to our joint endeavor. Indeed he became the study director for the Indianapolis–St. Louis study at the Indiana Center for Survey Research.

This lunch was certainly the most professionally valuable I have ever funded. I was aware of Russ's work on automaticity and attitude strength, but he filled in the details, gave us a bibliography, and pointed us in the direction of his own work (Fazio, 1995; Fazio & Williams, 1986) as well as toward John Bassili's (1993) implementation of latency measures (response times) in survey research. Just as important, Russ lent his moral support to our effort.

As a consequence, and thanks to the collaborative efforts of John Kennedy who was the director of the Indiana Center for Survey Research, we undertook a large-scale study of political communication in the context of the 1996 election campaign. For nearly a year, we interviewed approximately 20 new main respondents each week, as well as 15 of the political discussants they had identified, beginning in the early part of 1996 campaign and ending at the election. After the election we interviewed a post-election sample of 839 main respondents and 639 discussants as rapidly as possible, for a total sample that consisted of 2,174 main respondents and 1,475 discussants. Finally, one year later, we went back into the field to interview smaller samples of St. Louis and Indianapolis residents in an effort to construct a post hoc baseline for levels of political discussion and activity absent the stimulus of a presidential election campaign.

In addition to a wide range of survey questions, a subset of these questions included timers that were activated by trained interviewers to measure the response times of the respondents. These interviews were conducted over the phone using a computer-assisted telephone interviewing system developed at the Center for Survey Research at the University of California, Berkeley. The timer was built into the computer keyboard operated by the interviewer. The interviewers started the clock as they finished the question and stopped the clock as soon as the respondent began to answer. Only a subset of the survey questions included this interviewer-activated timer, and many of these questions were specifically designed to make the timing effective. As much as possible, we created instrumentation that provided a brief stimulus, thus allowing the nearly instantaneous start of the clock. We also adopted a cleaning procedure to eliminate wild codes and outliers (Fazio, 1990; Huckfeldt, Levine, Morgan, & Sprague, 1999). Finally, I participated in interviewer training and field testing and was greatly reassured by the procedures that John Kennedy and his staff at the Indiana University Center for Survey Research developed.

This effort produced a unique data set that provided an opportunity to consider response latencies as measures of attitude strength, as well as latencies for a range of network measures as well. Finally, in addition to the activated timers, we automatically recorded time stamps at each and every interviewer key stroke. As it turned out, these timers produced a number of benefits and advantages as well. It became clear to us that an untapped potential was available for incorporating low cost latency measures into a wide range of interviewing techniques.

The reader might rightfully question the precision of our timing procedures for recording response latencies. Milton certainly raised this question! These procedures are at least a full step removed from the precision achieved with those that involve subjects in a laboratory whose response latencies are recorded as a function of their own actions, such hitting a key on a keyboard or a button on a mouse. Our latency measures were in hundredths of seconds, not thousandths. And we could not hope to achieve the fine-grain control over the timing of response thresholds achieved in laboratory studies. At the same time, the proof of the pudding lies in the eating, and the question thus becomes, what did we learn?

Partisan Strength vs. Partisan Extremity vs. Partisan Accessibility

One of the first papers we published out of the project had little direct bearing on networks and interdependence, but instead was focused on the partisan orientations of individual citizens (Huckfeldt et al., 1999), which seemed a good place to begin. No measure of citizen politics in the United States has had a larger impact on political science or journalism than the voters' orientations toward political parties. This orientation is typically conceived as an identification with one of the two major parties in American politics—the Democrats or the Republicans. Political scientists typically measure partisan *strength* among individual citizens in terms of the *extremity* of their partisan self-identifications, using some form of the following question: "Generally speaking, do you think of yourself as a Republican, a Democrat, an Independent, or what?" The overwhelming majority chose one of the three options, and the follow-up questions ask the self-identified Republicans and Democrats to locate themselves as strong or not-so-strong Democrats (or Republicans). The Independents are asked whether they lean toward the Democrats or the Republicans.

The result is a seven-point scale, with strong Democrats at one extreme and strong Republicans at the other. This ordinal scale is an excellent predictor of voting behavior and public opinion, but measuring strength in terms of extremity produces a problem. In particular, and as Weisberg (1980) demonstrated, it is also quite possible to be a strong or intense independent, even though such an outcome is foreclosed by this standard measurement procedure! Weisberg's solution was to introduce a second dimension of partisanship, its "intensity" measured with additional survey instrumentation.

In our own analysis we also introduce a second dimension, its "accessibility" (Fazio, 1995), measured as the response latency for the first question in the partisanship battery—the "generally speaking" prompt. The resulting analysis shows that the accessibility of partisanship serves to moderate the relationship between an individual's partisanship on the seven-point ordinal scale and the individual's evaluations regarding well-known political figures of that time—Clinton, Dole, Gore, Kemp, and Gingrich. That is, the effect of partisanship is enhanced among those individuals for whom partisan loyalty comes readily to mind.

In a similar way, we measure the accessibility of the respondents' ideological affiliations on a seven-point scale from very liberal to very conservative. Here again, the accessibility of the heuristic, in this case ideology, serves to moderate the relationship between ideology and a series of ideologically relevant policy questions. That is, the cognitive accessibility of the respondent's political orientation, measured this time in terms of ideology, enhances its effect.

Finally, we imbedded an experimental treatment within the survey to measure the extent to which individuals could be persuaded to change their minds with respect to a survey question. We asked respondents the following question:

> There has been a lot of discussion recently about three issues: the need to balance the federal budget, the need to cut federal taxes, and the need to maintain government support and benefits for elderly and disadvantaged Americans. Which of these three do you think is most important?

If the respondent thought it was most important to maintain support and benefit levels we asked the following questions:

1. "Would you favor maintaining the support and benefits even if it meant increasing taxes?"

And

2. "Would you favor maintaining the support and benefits if it meant increasing the size of the budget deficit?"

If they believed it most important to implement a tax cut, we asked:

1. "Would you favor a tax cut even if it meant increasing the size of the budget deficit?"

And

2. "Would you favor a tax cut even if it meant that many elderly and disadvantaged were no longer able to receive medical care?"

Finally, if they believed it most important to balance the budget, we asked:

1. "Would you favor balancing the budget even if it meant raising taxes?"

And

2. "Would you favor balancing the budget even if it meant that many elderly and disadvantaged were no longer able to afford medical care?"

In this way, respondents were first asked to make an initial judgment regarding the three issues, before we asked follow-up questions designed as counterarguments to measure their level of commitment (Piazza, Sniderman, & Tetlock, 1990).

We might expect that the accessibility of individuals' own ideological commitments would play an important role in sustaining their initial responses to these issues, as well as resisting attempts at persuading them to change their minds. Our analysis shows that the effect of ideology on the resistance to persuasion is conditioned by the accessibility of ideology, even after taking into account the respondents' levels of political interest and knowledge.

In short, an accessibility argument regarding the utility of partisan and ideological orientations points toward the cognitive organization of memory. Some individuals hold strong, readily accessible opinions regarding a wide range of political issues and subjects, as well as their own points of partisan and ideological orientation. These people do not need to make it up as they go along! Rather, they readily (automatically) retrieve their opinions and points of orientation from memory. In contrast, other individuals hold neither opinions nor points of partisan and ideological orientations that are readily available, and these are the people most likely to exhibit inconsistent, "top of the head" responses to survey questions (Zaller & Feldman, 1992).

Thus far we have considered the implications of preconscious processes for the nature of human responses to political objects. The role of these cognitive processes also extends to the social and political communication that occurs among and between individuals. In particular, understanding the respective roles of opinion leaders and followers is enhanced when we understand not only the resistance and vulnerability to persuasion, but also the process whereby individuals perceive the levels of political expertise among others.

Perceiving Aggregates: Yard Signs and Bumper Stickers in South Bend, Indiana

Some of our earlier work in the 1984 South Bend election study addressed the importance of the immediate social environments within which individuals were located (Huckfeldt & Sprague, 1995). The research design included a three-wave survey of approximately 100 residents in each of 16 South Bend area neighborhoods, chosen to maximize social class variation. The study also included a follow-up snowball interview with a sample of the political discussants named by the main respondents.

The main respondents were randomly selected within the neighborhoods, and thus the survey could be used both to measure the political views and characteristics of the individuals, as well as to measure the aggregate characteristics within the neighborhoods. The local county planning office had defined South Bend neighborhood boundaries, and thus 1980 census data were available for these neighborhoods. This provided an opportunity to verify survey-based neighborhood measures with reference to corresponding census-based measures, thus providing assurance that our survey-based measures corresponded to reliable census estimates. These procedures also increased our confidence in survey-based neighborhood measures *not* included in the census—individual-level survey measures that were in turn aggregated by neighborhood.

In this context, a primary question was related to the consequences of campaign activities at the neighborhood level for the perceptions of neighborhood residents. As part of the survey, we asked our respondents whether they displayed a yard sign or bumper sticker. Hence we were able to aggregate this information at the neighborhood level to consider the implications arising due to the distributions of these signs and stickers for perceptions of individuals living in the neighborhoods. Democratic neighborhoods and bumper stickers were more likely to appear in neighborhoods that voted Democratic, and Republican signs and stickers in neighborhoods that vote Republican, but did the signs and stickers register any independent effect?

Prior to the election, we also asked our respondents whom they expected to win the presidential election *in their neighborhood*—Mondale or Reagan. As one might expect, respondents who lived in Democratic neighborhoods expected Mondale to win the neighborhood vote, and people who lived in Republican neighborhoods expected Reagan to win the neighborhood vote. Less obviously, even after taking into account the actual division of the neighborhood vote in the 1984 presidential contest, the distribution of yard signs and bumper stickers registered an effect on respondents' perceptions. People in neighborhoods with more Democratic yard signs and bumper stickers were more likely to think that Mondale would do well in the neighborhood, and those in neighborhoods with more Republican signs and stickers were more likely to think that Reagan would do well in the neighborhood. Again, these perceptions persisted after taking account of the actual distribution of the vote.

Viewed through the lens of political cognition research, these analyses reveal the importance of context and setting for voter expectations. None of our respondents were likely to have undertaken a formal survey of their neighbors' car bumpers or front lawns. Yet through the naturally occurring day-to-day process of life in their neighborhoods, they developed perceptions that coincided with the distribution of yard signs and bumper stickers.

How important is this sort of information? Has a bumper sticker or a yard sign ever influenced anyone to change her vote intention? We doubt it! Rather we understand these visual indicators of partisan support within the context of an attribution bias that relates to a process of social and political cognition (Ross, 1990; Ross, Bierbrauer, & Hoffman, 1976). As the relative incidence of Republican or Democratic advertising on your neighbors' cars and lawns increases, it carries the potential to produce important implications for your own judgments regarding credible and appropriate vote choices for the people who live in your neighborhood and presumably share many of your own expectations, concerns, and interests. In short, the distribution of preferences, made visible in many neighborhoods during the campaign, may indeed provide important and relevant information through a process of social and political cognition.

Political Cognition, Perception, and Influence

An important literature in social and political psychology employs the literature on cognitive dissonance (Festinger, 1957) to suggest that disagreement seldom occurs among associates. The idea is that individuals steer clear of creating discomfort in their personal relationships by associating with people who share their preferences, by avoiding political conversation with associates who hold disagreeable political viewpoints, and by selectively misperceiving the discordant messages that slip through the first two filters. (For excellent reviews see MacKuen, 1990; Mutz, 2006.)

While we never intended to diminish the implications of cognitive dissonance regarding politics within political discussion networks, our own efforts suggest that the implications may be more subtle than expected. In the Indianapolis–St. Louis study, we employed a social network name generator that asked respondents to provide the names of their discussion partners. The subject matter of the discussion was experimentally manipulated: half the respondents were asked with whom they discussed "government, elections, and politics," and the other half were asked with whom they discussed "important matters"—a generic category incorporated within the network battery employed by the General Social Survey. The remainder of the social network battery was the same regardless of the initial prompt, allowing us to assess whether political communication was specialized within communication networks (Huckfeldt et al., 2004).

After obtaining the names of up to five discussion partners from each main respondent, the respondents were asked a series of questions regarding each discussant. In asking the main respondent to report the discussants' voting preferences, we randomly ordered the discussants to avoid an order bias, and we recorded the response time as well as asking a follow-up question regarding how difficult it was for the respondent to make a judgment regarding the discussant's voting preference. We also conducted snowball interviews with a substantial subset of discussants, and hence we are able to measure the accuracy of the respondent's expectation regarding the discussant's vote.

On this basis, we evaluate three criterion measures which indicate the quality of the communication within the dyad: the accuracy of the respondent's judgment regarding the discussant's preference, the accessibility of the respondent's judgment, and the reported confidence with which the main respondent makes the judgment. Because we interviewed a sample of the discussants, we were also able to evaluate the explanatory effect of respondent characteristics, discussant characteristics, and the relationship between the two (Huckfeldt, Sprague, & Levine, 2000).

Several results stand out. First, agreement between the main respondent and the discussant, as well as between the particular discussant and the remainder of the discussion network produces a dramatic effect on the accuracy of judgment. If the respondent does not support a candidate, and if her *other discussants* do not support a candidate, she is highly unlikely to recognize that one of her discussants *does* support the candidate. In short, there is evidence to suggest that individuals generalize on the basis of their own preferences, as well as the preferences they perceive among the other members of their discussion networks, when forming a judgment regarding any particular discussant's preference. In contrast, there is little evidence to suggest that agreement *within the dyad* has any effect on the respondent's confidence in her judgment regarding a particular discussant, or on the accessibility of the judgment.

Second, the accuracy of the respondent's judgment is increased as a consequence of the extremity of the discussant's reported preferences, both with respect to partisanship and with respect to candidate evaluations. Thus more extreme partisan discussants tend to send clear and unambiguous signals that are difficult for the respondent to ignore! In contrast, there is no evidence to suggest that more extreme partisan respondents are any more or less likely to identify a discussant's political preference incorrectly. Finally, neither the respondent's perception of the discussant's knowledge, nor the respondent's reported frequency of discussion with the discussant, nor the discussant's membership in an *explicitly defined* political network appear to have any consequence for accuracy.

In short, these results show that the social and political contexts of social interaction and political discussion are profoundly important, in several different ways. First, numerous efforts have shown that social and political networks reflect the social and political contexts of local environments. If you live in a Democratic county or a Democratic neighborhood, you are more likely to interact with Democrats regardless of your own partisan inclinations (Huckfeldt, 1983; Huckfeldt & Sprague, 1995; Huckfeldt, Beck, Dalton, & Levine, 1995; Miller, 1956; Putnam, 1966). This does *not* mean that individuals fail to exercise social and political preferences when they choose associates, but rather that their choices are constrained. The constraints come in two forms. People have multiple preferences that must be realized in a single associational choice, and a potential associate's politics may be less important than other concerns, such as an agreeable personality or even a favorite team! More importantly, the probabilities of choice are constrained by the probabilities of availability and supply (Huckfeldt, 1983)—if you are surrounded by Democrats it may be more difficult to find a Republican.

At the same time, we see strong cognitive biases in the perception of discussant preferences. In particular, respondents generalize on the basis of their own preferences and the preferences of others in their discussion networks when assessing the preferences of any single discussant. Democrats are more likely to think their discussants are Democrats if they are themselves Democrats and if their other discussants are Democrats. In short, they are operating on the basis of their own self-collected sample of individuals—a sample that is biased in a way that reflects not only their own preferences, but also the preferences of others with whom they communicate and interact. Hence they are much more likely to misperceive the views of someone within the network who does ***not*** share these dominant views!

Opinion Leaders, Expertise, and Sustained Disagreement

The earliest work on opinion leaders in the Columbia studies (Berelson, Lazarsfeld, & McPhee, 1954; Lazarsfeld, Berelson, & Gaudet, 1948) established the importance of politically knowledgeable citizens who provide guidance to their less politically involved and knowledgeable associates. The problem has been that we have had very little information to validate the flow of expert information between and among citizens. Hence in our Indianapolis–St. Louis study, we not only asked our main respondents for assessments regarding how much their discussants know about politics, we also employed a knowledge battery in the snowball interviews to obtain a direct measure of the discussants' level of political knowledge (Delli Carpini & Keeter, 1996, 1993).

This provided an opportunity to address an important question that lies close to the heart of social cognition and political influence. Do citizens recognize the experts in their midst? Or, do they assess political competence among others based on associates' levels of agreement with their own viewpoints? The results point toward the accurate recognition of expertise among others, regardless of their political preferences. Moreover, the main respondents report higher frequencies of political discussion with the discussants whom they judge to be politically expert, and these expert discussants also report higher levels of political discussion in general. Hence the influence of opinion leaders is not simply that their associates recognize their expertise, but also that these experts invest more effort and time into the discussion of politics.

At the same time, expertise is not the defining ingredient of influence, and our main respondents do not automatically adopt the preferences held by their expert discussion partners. To the contrary, they not infrequently enter into relationships with people holding disagreeable viewpoints, thereby maintaining heterogeneity within the network. In short, we do not see the patterns of political homogeneity within discussion networks that many have expected. At the same time, while heterogeneity is common, very few respondents occupy minority standing within their political discussion networks. What are the implications?

As Lodge has repeatedly demonstrated, political cognition is a dynamic process (Lodge, Steenbergen, & Brau, 1995; Lodge, McGraw, & Stroh, 1989). We have taken inspiration from these arguments, overlaying the political cognition process on a social interaction process. In this context, every message received from a discussant is implicitly or explicitly validated by previous messages from other discussants. The result is that an opinion or preference that is regularly reinforced through social interaction and discussion is likely to be durable in time. A message from a discussant that fails to receive support will, in contrast, fail to be influential. *As a consequence, we would predict that two good friends with conflicting political preferences might sustain both their friendship and their distinctive viewpoints so long as both of them receive support for their divergent views from the remainder of their own separate and non-overlapping opinion networks.* In other words, you may encounter some interesting political viewpoints at the workplace, but they might not survive the validity test at your own dinner table!

This simple model is evaluated successfully based on data taken from the Indianapolis–St. Louis study (Huckfeldt et al., 2004, Chapter 5). Moreover, the argument translates into an agent-based model that helps to explain a long-enduring problem in the study of agreement, conflict, and communication identified separately by Axelrod (1997) and Abelson (1964, 1979). Both efforts construct dynamic models that predict homogeneous outcomes in which a socially communicated opinion or trait either dies out and disappears or, alternatively comes to dominate and create homogeneity. That is, both efforts fail to create a dynamic model of diffusion that sustains heterogeneity—a model in which disagreement is maintained among individuals.

In contrast, an autoregressive model of influence based on social cognition is able to sustain a heterogeneous distribution of opinion. That is, we find that when disagreement occurs among agents, it does not necessarily disappear. The simple dynamic fix that preserves heterogeneity is the capacity of agents (and people) to make an implicit comparison of an informant's message relative to the distribution of messages previously obtained from other messengers. Similar to our respondents, the artificial agents are programmed to reject messages with a higher probability that fall beyond the believable bounds set by previous social communication. In short, the influence of any dyadic change depends on patterns of preferences within the larger communication network. Social and political cognition are imbedded within social and political contexts. And hence they can be understood as processes simultaneously involving multiple actors located within complex networks of social interaction and communication.

Reconsidering Social Influence in the Context of Bayes

Once again, the Lodge focus on dynamic process has been a guiding principle for our own efforts. In *The Rationalizing Voter*, Lodge and Taber (2013) present a significant challenge to theories of democratic politics, providing compelling evidence to suggest that citizens are frequently incapable of considering new information that might affect their political views and choices. They suggest that a correctly understood Bayesian model might, indeed, be specified to address these problems. In that context, we reconsider the political economists' de facto monopoly of Bayes and Bayesian decision-making by applying it to political cognition in context. According to the Bayesian model, individuals form a prior judgment and update the judgment based on new information, after weighting both their own prior judgment and the new information by their respective variances (Bullock, 2009; Lee, 2004, pp. 34–37).

We begin by addressing the problem of social communication within the context of a voter's judgment regarding a hypothetical candidate, based on a friend's report regarding the candidate's trustworthiness (Huckfeldt, Pietryka, & Reilly, 2014). In formal terms, the Bayes theorem suggests that:

$$P(A|B) = \frac{P(B|A)P(A)}{P(B)} = P(B|A) \times \frac{P(A)}{P(B)}$$

where:
A = an individual believes that a particular candidate is trustworthy
B = a friend reports that the candidate is trustworthy
P(A) = the base rate or the prior: the probability that the individual believes the candidate is trustworthy, absent the friend's report
P(A|B) = the conditional probability that the individual believes the candidate is trustworthy, given the friend's report
P(B) = the probability that the friend would report that the candidate is trustworthy

P(B|A) = the likelihood function, or the probability that a friend's report would allege the candidate is trustworthy, given that the individual believes the candidate is trustworthy

The likelihood function is particularly important, effectively indexing the individual's assessment regarding the friend as an information source (see Bullock, 2009). In this context, the likelihood provides the expectation that the friend's report converges with the individual's own prior belief, and for these purposes it is helpful to re-express the likelihood function in its definitional form as

$$P(B|A) = \frac{P(A \text{ and } B)}{P(A)}$$

Hence the likelihood simply indexes the probability of agreement between the individual's prior and the friend's report, relative to the individual's prior. If the likelihood function is large, it means the friend is more likely to send a signal that agrees with the friend's report.

In this particular context, does Bayesian updating imply an objective analysis of incoming information? To the contrary, the key to the influence of new information is a function of whether the recipient trusts the message, where "trust" is anchored in an expectation that the individual and the messenger (in this context, the friend) has a prior that comes from a similar probability distribution (for a similar argument see Downs, 1957, Chapter 11). The important point is that the Bayes theorem does not require that individuals give equal weight to messages coming from messengers with divergent viewpoints, thus intersecting with the work of Lodge and Taber on automaticity, motivated reasoning, and rationalizing voters (2000, 2005, 2013). While many of our colleagues in the economics profession may hesitate to endorse such a view, it would appear to coincide quite nicely with the lessons that Lodge and his colleagues have taught us.

Bayesian Processes, Dynamic Systems, and the Useful Limits on Memory

Not only does a Bayesian process incorporate a screening device on the reliability of incoming information, but it also can be adapted to take into account the necessary limits on memory in any learning process. These limits are both empirical and theoretical. While any learning process involves decay in the retention of information, any stable dynamic process *must* include decay. That is, dynamic processes absent memory decay are inherently unstable. Finally, and importantly, objects stored in long-term memory decay more slowly than objects controlled in short-term (or working) memory.

Hence, in a Bayesian process, we would expect both short-term and long-term objects to decay, but the long-term elements (the priors) should decay more slowly than the short-term objects (the incoming information). Thus at the same time that an individual's prior is being updated it is also undergoing a process of decay. In this way, a dynamic Bayesian process implies a particular structure regarding the decay of both priors and new information within the updating process.

Huckfeldt et al. (2014) construct a dynamic formulation of Bayesian updating within a series of small group experiments involving repeated interactions among subjects. The experiment demonstrates that "experts" hold strongly held beliefs (priors) that decay more slowly, but all priors, regardless of their strength, are subject to decay. Moreover, these experts send messages that are biased toward their own priors. Thus, both because they send biased communications and because their priors decay more slowly, their own individually held beliefs have more influence in the collective construction of an aggregate public opinion. In short, we argue that it is possible to employ a Bayesian model that reflects many of the arguments Lodge and his colleagues have so persuasively made: the limitations of memory, the integral role of bias, and the importance of process.

Conclusion

Quite clearly, my colleagues and I owe a substantial professional and personal debt to the work of Milton Lodge and his colleagues. Milton has made a series of profound contributions to the study of politics and political behavior: the emphasis on thinking that extends beyond awareness and direct observation; the limits of introspection; the roles of accessibility and hot cognition; the impact of motivated reasoning; the importance of memory decay; and the resulting implications for dynamic processes. Each of these emphases carry profound implications for the manner in which we understand and learn about the role of citizens in democratic politics, as well as for the ways we have come to think about citizens in networks and contexts.

Even though we are seldom able to observe the cognition process directly, theories of cognition help us understand the events we observe. These events may take place in the context of mass political behavior that we read about in the newspaper, or that occur in individual survey responses, or that unfold in laboratory settings. Lodge's contributions show us that progress in political research proceeds more rapidly, becomes more meaningful, and makes more sense when we imbed these observations within theories of political cognition.

Cognition occurs through a continuing process of interaction with the political world, and hence it can be understood within a dynamic structure. A key element within any dynamic structure is memory decay as it occurs both in terms of initial conditions and newly input events. As John Sprague taught generations of students in his introductory dynamics seminar, any process that does not forget past events is inherently unstable. In this context, political cognition sheds new light on dynamic processes that can be revealed with even simple dynamical formulations.

This is particularly true at the intersection between political cognition and various forms of social and political interaction. These interactions come in the form of reading newspapers, watching the evening news, and driving past neighbors' yard signs, as well as conversations at the water cooler and across the dinner table. The end result may be registered at the voting booth or in the opinion poll, but the process producing these outcomes occurs in countless dynamic settings of individual interaction within an informational context reflecting larger social and political environments.

References

Abelson, Robert P. (1964). Mathematical models of the distribution of attributes under controversy. In Norman Fredriksen and Harold Gulliksen (Eds.), *Contributions to mathematical psychology* (pp.142–160). New York: Holt, Rinehart, and Winston.

Abelson, Robert P. (1979). Social clusters and opinion clusters. In Paul W. Holland and Samuel Leinhardt (Eds.), *Perspectives on social network research* (pp. 239–256). New York: Academic Press.

Ahn, T. K., Huckfeldt, Robert, & Ryan, John B. (2014). *Experts, activists, and democratic politics: Are electorates self-educating?* New York: Cambridge University Press.

Axelrod, Robert. (1997). The dissemination of culture: A model with local convergence and global polarization. *Journal of Conflict Resolution*, 41, 203–226.

Bassili, John N. (1993). Response latency versus certainty as indexes of the strength of voting intentions in a CATI survey. *Public Opinion Quarterly*, 57, 54–61.

Berelson, Bernard R., Lazarsfeld, Paul F., & McPhee, William N. (1954). *Voting: A study of opinion formation in a presidential election*. Chicago, IL: University of Chicago Press.

Bullock, John G. (2009). Partisan bias and the Bayesian ideal in the study of public opinion. *Journal of Politics*, 71, 1109–1124.

Delli Carpini, Michael X. & Keeter, Scott. (1993). Measuring political knowledge: Putting first things first. *American Journal of Political Science*, 37, 1170–1206.

Delli Carpini, Michael X. & Keeter, Scott. (1996). *What Americans know about politics and why it matters*. New Haven, CT: Yale University Press.

Downs, Anthony. 1957. *An economic theory of democracy*. New York: Harper.

Fazio, Russell H. (1990). A practical guide to the use of response latency in social psychological research. In Clyde Hendrick & Margaret S. Clark (Eds.), *Research methods in personality and social psychology* (pp. 74–97). Newbury Park, CA: Sage.

Fazio, Russell H. (1995). Attitudes as object-evaluation associations: Determinants, consequences, and correlates of attitude accessibility. In R.E. Petty & J.A. Krosnick (Eds.), *Attitude strength: Antecedents and consequences* (pp. 247–282). Mahwah, NJ: Erlbaum.

Fazio, Russell H. & Williams, Carol J. (1986). Attitude accessibility as a moderator of the attitude-perception and attitude-behavior relations: An investigation of the 1984 presidential election. *Journal of Personality and Social Psychology*, 51, 505–514.

Festinger, Leon. (1957). *A theory of cognitive dissonance*. Palo Alto, CA: Stanford University Press.

Huckfeldt, Robert. (1983). Social contexts, social networks, and urban neighborhoods: Environmental constraints upon friendship choice. *American Journal of Sociology*, (November), 651–669.

Huckfeldt, Robert, Beck, Paul Allen, Dalton, Russell J., & Levine, Jeffrey. (1995). Political environments, cohesive social groups, and the communication of public opinion. *American Journal of Political Science*, 39, 1025–1054.

Huckfeldt, Robert, Johnson, Paul E., & Sprague, John. (2004). *Political disagreement: The survival of diverse opinions within communication networks*. New York: Cambridge University Press.

Huckfeldt, Robert, Levine, Jeffrey, Morgan, William, & Sprague, John. (1999). Accessibility and the political utility of partisan and ideological orientations. *American Journal of Political Science*, 43, 888–911.

Huckfeldt, Robert, Pietryka, Matthew T., & Reilly, Jack. (2014). Noise, bias, and expertise in political communication networks. *Social Networks*, 36, 110–121.

Huckfeldt, Robert & Sprague, John. (1987). Networks in context: The social flow of political information. *American Political Science Review*, 81, 1197–1216.

Huckfeldt, Robert & Sprague, John. (1995). *Citizens, politics, and social communication*. New York: Cambridge University Press.

Huckfeldt, Robert, Sprague, John, & Levine, Jeffrey. (2000). The dynamics of collective deliberation in the 1996 election: Campaign effects on accessibility, certainty, and accuracy. *American Political Science Review*, 94, 641–651.

Kunda, Ziva. (1990). The case for motivated reasoning. *Psychological Bulletin*, 108, 480–498.

Kunda, Ziva. (1999). *Social cognition: Making sense of people*. Cambridge, MA: MIT Press.

Lazarsfeld, Paul F., Berelson, Bernard, & Gaudet, Hazel. (1948). *The people's choice*. New York: Columbia University Press.

Lee, Peter M. (2004). *Bayesian statistics: An introduction* (3rd ed.). London: Arnold.

Lodge, Milton, McGraw, Kathleen, & Stroh, Patrick. (1989). An impression driven model of candidate evaluation. *American Political Science Review*, 83, 399–420.

Lodge, Milton, Steenbergen, Marco, & Brau, Shawn. (1995). The responsive voter: Campaign information and the dynamics of candidate evaluation. *American Political Science Review*, 89, 309–326.

Lodge, Milton & Taber, Charles S. (2000). Three steps toward a theory of motivated political reasoning. In Arthur Lupia, Mathew McCubbins, & Samuel Popkin (Eds.), *Elements of reason: Cognition, choice, and the bounds of rationality* (pp. 183–213). New York: Cambridge University Press.

Lodge, Milton & Taber, Charles S. (2005). The automaticity of affect for political leaders, groups, and issues: An experimental test of the hot cognition hypothesis. *Political Psychology*, 25, 455–482.

Lodge, Milton & Taber, Charles S. (2013). *The rationalizing voter*. New York: Cambridge University Press.

MacKuen, Michael B. (1990). Speaking of politics: Individual conversational choice, public opinion, and the prospects for deliberative democracy. In John A. Ferejohn & James H. Kuklinski (Eds.), *Information and democratic processes* (pp. 59–99). Urbana: University of Illinois Press.

Miller, Warren. (1956). One party politics and the voter. *American Political Science Review*, 50, 707–725.

Mutz, Diana. (2006). *Hearing the other side: Deliberative versus participatory democracy*. New York: Cambridge University Press.

Piazza, Thomas, Sniderman, Paul M., & Tetlock, Philip E. (1990). Analysis of the dynamics of political reasoning: A general purpose computer-assisted methodology. *Political Analysis*, 1, 99–120.

Putnam, Robert D. (1966). Political attitudes and the local community. *American Political Science Review*, 60, 640–654.

Ross, Lee. (1990). Recognizing the role of construal processes. In Irving Rock (Ed.), *The legacy of Solomon Asch: Essays in cognition and social psychology* (pp. 77–96). Hillsdale, NJ: Lawrence Erlbaum Associates.

Ross, Lee, Bierbrauer, Gunter, & Hoffman, Susan. (1976). The role of attribution processes in conformity and dissent. *American Psychologist*, 31, 148–157.

Weisberg, Herbert F. (1980). A multidimensional conceptualization of party identification. *Political Behavior*, 2, 33–60.

Zaller, John R. & Feldman, Stanley. (1992). A simple theory of the survey response: Answering questions versus revealing preferences. *American Journal of Political Science*, 36, 579–616.

5

THE PARADOX OF POLITICAL KNOWLEDGE[1]

Jennifer Jerit and Caitlin Davies

In contemporary representative democracies such as the United States, public opinion plays a critical role, both in the turnover of elected officials and as an input in the policy-making process. But can ordinary people fulfill their responsibilities as democratic citizens? Do they have meaningful preferences to which political elites should respond? These are not trivial questions given that our political system was designed in part to limit the direct participation of the masses. For example, in *Federalist No. 68* Alexander Hamilton justified the electoral college on the grounds that a "small number of persons, selected by their fellow citizens from the general mass, will be most likely to possess the information and discernment requisite to such complicated investigations" (Hamilton, Madison, & Jay, 1961, p. 412). Similarly, John Adams wrote: "The proposition that [the people] are the best keepers of their liberties is not true. [The people] are the worst conceivable, they are no keepers at all. They can neither act, judge, think or will" (1788, p. 7, cited in Delli Carpini & Keeter, 1996, p. 25).

The research of Milton Lodge has contributed significantly to our understanding of citizen competence through its focus on political cognition—that is, by studying *how* people form their preferences. The idea, of course, is that the manner in which citizens process political information influences the content of the political attitudes they end up holding. Yet Lodge's research raises serious questions about the ability of people to arrive at reasoned judgments and instead suggests that people are held captive to their existing views and predispositions. Through decades of clever experimentation in the area of political cognition, Lodge's research program—particularly his work on online processing and motivated reasoning—challenges the conventional wisdom regarding the effects of political knowledge.[2] Whereas political knowledge is viewed by many scholars as the foundation of representative democracy, the theory of online processing/

motivated reasoning poses several challenges to this understanding. Indeed, one of the most striking results from this research program is that people with the *highest* levels of political knowledge are the most susceptible to bias. Our essay considers this paradox and the various ways it might be resolved.

We begin by outlining the conventional view of political knowledge as a prerequisite to citizen competence. Decades of research have shown that political sophistication is among the most important political resources a person can have, especially when it comes to how people reason about politics. The next section outlines how Lodge's work challenges the conventional wisdom, resulting in what we call the "paradox of political knowledge." In particular, Lodge's distinctive focus on *mechanisms*—i.e., the chain of mental events that occur in the decision-making process—forced researchers to confront important questions about the normative status of political knowledge. In the final section of this chapter, we attempt to reconcile these diverging perspectives. One of the lasting contributions of Milton Lodge's career is the research that has been stimulated by the troubling implications of his work on political cognition.

The Conventional View: Knowledge as a Prerequisite to Citizen Competence

> For citizens who are the most informed, democracy works much as intended, while for those who are the most uninformed, democracy *is* a tragedy or farce.
> (Delli Carpini & Keeter, 1996, p. 60, emphasis original)

> The less sophisticated the public, the less alert to its interests, the less active and unswerving in pursuit of them, and the less resistant to manipulation from above—the further, in short, from the democratic ideal.
> (Luskin, 1990, p. 331)

For decades (if not centuries), theorists and researchers have argued for the importance of a factually informed citizenry. On this view, citizens need to possess some minimal level of political knowledge to partake in the "vital tasks of democratic citizenship": forming preferences about public policy issues, selecting candidates to political office, and holding accurate perceptions of political reality (Lavine, Johnston, & Steenbergen, 2012, pp. 201–202).

Even though "democratic theory has never been terribly explicit about the precise requirements of knowledge" (Neuman, 1986, p. 8), an informed citizenry has long been viewed as the pillar of a functioning democratic system (e.g., Converse, 1964). People who possess more political knowledge differ in consequential ways from those who have lower levels of political information—a finding that led to a flurry of research in the United States and abroad on the environmental determinants of political knowledge (e.g., Barabas & Jerit, 2009; Curran, Iyengar, Lund, & Salovaara-Moring, 2009; Gordon & Segura, 1997; Jerit, 2009; Jerit,

Barabas, & Bolsen, 2006; Nicholson, 2003; Strömbäck, 2016). In seeking to determine which features of the political environment were associated with higher levels of political knowledge (sophistication), this body of work shares the sentiment, elegantly stated by Delli Carpini and Keeter (1996, p. 8), that political information is the "currency of citizenship."

And the evidence regarding benefits of political knowledge is convincing. People with higher levels of political knowledge are more tolerant than those with lower levels of political knowledge, even after controlling for a person's level of education (Delli Carpini & Keeter, 1996; also see McClosky, 1964; McClosky & Zaller, 1984).[3] Because political knowledge also includes facts specifically related to the act of participating in politics (what some researchers call "mobilizing information"; Lemert, 1981), knowledge is related to higher levels of voting as well as other forms of participation. Finally, the well informed differ from the less informed in a myriad of ways relating to opinion quality:

> the well informed ... are more likely to express opinions in the first place. They are more likely to possess stable opinions—real opinions, opinions held with conviction. They are more likely to use ideological concepts correctly, to cite evidence in political discussions, and to process information sensitively. They are better at retaining new information. They are more adept in the deployment of heuristics. They vote more consistently with their political interests. Information matters.
>
> *(Kinder, 2006, p. 207)*

Moreover, differences in information become magnified in the American political system where there is a multiplicity of civic responsibilities. In addition to voting in national elections, people select representatives for local and state offices, and they often vote directly on policy issues through initiative and referenda. While some of these responsibilities entail a binary choice between fixed options—and would thus seem to require little political sophistication (e.g., Sniderman, 2000)—other tasks, such as selecting the party's candidate or voting on initiatives, are arguably more complex. Add to this the various ways a person can participate in politics (contacting elected officials, demonstrating, contributing time and/or money to a campaign) and it is clear that knowledge is a crucial political resource.

One of the most persuasive arguments regarding the importance of political knowledge comes from researchers who have studied the aggregate-level consequences of an ill-informed citizenry (e.g., Althaus, 1998, 2003; Bartels, 1996). Using American National Election Studies (ANES) data, Althaus (2003) shows that the uneven distribution of knowledge has important implications for collective opinion. This occurs because of the tendency for informed people to: (1) have higher levels of opinionation, and (2) possess preferences that are more consistent with their political predispositions. As a result of the first difference, knowledgeable people are more likely to have their voices represented in an opinion poll (i.e., they give opinions more frequently than their less-informed peers). Indeed, Althaus reports that "unequal [Don't Know/No Opinion] rates give knowledgeable respondents the equivalent of two opinions for every one given by ill-informed respondents" (2003, p. 69).

The second difference relates to variation in information processing across people with high and low levels of knowledge. The opinions of the well informed tend to disperse evenly across response categories because these individuals draw from a broader range of considerations than the less informed. In contrast, the less informed

> organize around heuristic cues or frames of reference generated by the survey instrument or around common pieces of knowledge that have been recently or frequently activated in the minds of respondents by news reports or other common sources of knowledge.
> *(Althaus, 2003, p. 90)*

The end result, Althaus concludes, is that knowledgeable people are better represented by polls than their less-informed peers. This is an important conclusion in and of itself, but Althaus's argument is useful for highlighting the differences in how people with varying levels of knowledge think about politics.

To wit, there has been an accumulation of studies documenting the information-processing advantages of the politically knowledgeable. This research shows that people with high levels of political sophistication have well-developed associative networks which translate into more accessible and better organized knowledge (compared to those with low levels of political sophistication; see Fiske, Lau, & Smith, 1990). As a result of these differences in cognitive organization, people with higher levels of knowledge can generate more thoughts in response to a political object and they are more effective at recalling relevant material. Knowledge bestows upon them "information-processing efficiency and effectiveness" (Fiske et al., 1990, p. 45).

In addition to these differences in cognitive structure, there is variation in the content and style of information processing. The politically sophisticated have belief systems that are "large, wide-ranging, and highly constrained" (Luskin, 1990, p. 861; also see Converse, 1964). They "take account of nearly everything, including the kitchen sink" (Sniderman, Glaser, & Griffin, 1990, p. 127). Consequently, people with higher levels of knowledge make more complex (i.e., distal) causal attributions (Gomez & Wilson, 2001); they are better able to distinguish credible from non-credible sources and update evaluations accordingly (Alt, Lassen, & Marshall, 2016); they are more likely to draw upon "issue-relevant values" in the opinion formation process (as opposed to party cues; see Kam, 2005); and they are better able to reconcile value tradeoffs (Jacoby, 2006). Political sophisticates are more likely to be exposed to the currents of elite debate, but they possess "cueing information" that allows them to understand the relationship between the persuasive messages they receive and their political predispositions (Clifford, Jerit, Rainey, & Motyl, 2015; Zaller, 1992). More generally, Kam observes, "the politically aware are not just citizens who happen to know more about politics, they are citizens who are *effortful* processors of politics" (2005, p. 167, emphasis added; also see Hsu & Price, 1993). On this interpretation, the politically knowledgeable are more likely to be *systematic* processors—engaging in the slow, deliberative processing that forms the basis of Kahneman's (2011) System 2.[4]

Thus, a coherent image of the politically knowledgeable citizen emerges from previous research. As we elaborate in the next section, this portrait is not compatible with the evidence from Lodge's studies of online processing and motivated reasoning. Not only does Lodge's work challenge the notion that sophisticates have a proclivity for open-minded, deliberative thinking, but it also identifies these individuals as the most susceptible to biased decision-making.

A Different Interpretation: Knowledge Facilitates Bias

> Motivated, passionate, and knowledgeable citizens are the bedrock of democracy. And yet, the very passions that motivate action drive biases and polarization.
> (Lodge & Taber, 2013, pp. 168–169)

> Sophistication (qua objective knowledge of politics) turns out to be a double-edged sword. While it facilitates political understanding, it also makes it easier for citizens to defend their political attitudes through motivated bias.
> (Lavine, Johnston, & Steenbergen, 2012, p. xiv)

People approach the political world with varying amounts of political knowledge, that much is clear. Yet the conventional wisdom tells one story about how this variation matters—i.e., more information is better (Kuklinski & Coronel, 2012, p. 192)—while Lodge's research program implies a different interpretation.

We begin with the earliest elaborations of the online model (e.g., Lodge, 1995; Lodge, McGraw, & Stroh, 1989; Lodge, Steenbergen, & Brau, 1995; Lodge, Stroh, & Wahlke, 1990) because these studies raise important questions about the value of political knowledge—and whether a person's ability to recall facts is a valid indicator of citizen competence. At this time, most public opinion research presumed a memory-based process in which there was a straightforward relationship between voter memory (e.g., candidate likes and dislikes) and candidate evaluation.[5] Lodge's experiments challenged the prevailing view because they convincingly demonstrated the fallibility of human memory. For example, in an experiment in which participants were exposed to the issue stands of two hypothetical candidates (in a "campaign fact sheet") and then asked to evaluate the candidates at a later time, the overwhelming majority could not recall a single issue stand (Lodge et al., 1995).[6] This does not mean, however, that the participants in Lodge's experiment study were unresponsive to campaign information.

Quite to the contrary, there was a strong (and statistically significant) relationship between participants' affective reaction to the issue stands and their subsequent candidate evaluations—a pattern that is consistent with online reasoning.[7] Even though the level of recall for candidate issues stands was "dismal" (Lodge et al., 1995, p. 314), participants integrated specific bits of information into a global evaluation as they encountered this information (for additional evidence see Cassino & Lodge, 2007; Coronel et al., 2012; Hastie & Park, 1986).

These findings have serious repercussions for researchers who take *observed* levels of knowledge at face value. If recall is not a valid indicator of citizen competence in the voting booth, of what worth is it to recall political facts more generally? As the following passage suggests, this question lurks beneath the surface of Lodge et al.'s (1995, p. 310) study:

> Our criticism, then, is not just directed against memory-based models of the vote choice but, more broadly, challenges the memory-based assumption underlying contemporary analyses of political behavior in general, and still more broadly, the negative normative conclusions routinely drawn from the citizenry's failure to recall [political facts].[8]

In subsequent years, other scholars would raise concerns about objective measures of political knowledge. For example, Lupia (2006, p. 223) writes: "observing that survey respondents answer questions about ideological labels or common political knowledge incorrectly means nothing more, in itself, than that the respondents cannot (instantly) recall terms that political scientists and journalists know well" (2006, p. 223; also see Graber, 1993; Boudreau & Lupia, 2011). Druckman (2012) challenges the "information holding" standard as well, though for slightly different reasons. He calls for more emphasis on *process* and the conditions under which a person is motivated by accuracy versus directional goals. Likewise, Lavine, Johnston, and Steenbergen (2013, p. 220) contend that ambivalence—rather than "decontextualized information holding per se"—prompts the type of thought praised by democratic theorists (e.g., thought that is critical, systematic, and open-minded). These critiques of political knowledge, while compelling on their face, take on even greater force when combined with Lodge's evidence regarding the limited role for recall in mediating the influence of campaign rhetoric (Lodge et al., 1995).

The challenge to the conventional wisdom regarding knowledge goes deeper, though. It is one thing to claim that people can make effective decisions without being able to recall political facts; it is quite another to argue that the people who retain more information (i.e., the politically sophisticated) are the most susceptible to decision-making biases. Yet this is the conclusion of subsequent elaborations of the online model, most notably Lodge and Taber's award-winning book, *The Rationalizing Voter*. To have an online tally for a candidate or issue is to have affect toward that object. This is the phenomenon of "hot cognition" (Abelson, 1963), whereby concepts in memory carry an affective charge (positive, for liking; negative, for disliking).[9] Bias enters through the retrieval of considerations from memory, which is influenced in the direction of initial affect (through the processes of "affective contagion" and "motivated bias"; see Lodge & Taber, 2013).[10] Thus, once an object has been evaluated, subsequent information processing, including the evaluation of facts and arguments that appear in elite discourse, will be biased in the direction of the existing online tally (the well-known confirmation and disconfirmation biases; Taber & Lodge, 2006). This is not to say that the deliberative thinking of System 2 does not take place, but it requires sufficient time, effort, and motivation to overcome the processes set in motion by hot cognition.

However, and somewhat paradoxically, being politically knowledgeable makes this *less* likely to occur. Because political sophisticates have thought about and repeatedly evaluated political objects, they are anchored by numerous evaluative tallies. (The less sophisticated, for their part, have fewer affective associations mooring them to prior opinions). Thus, the very characteristics that have been portrayed as virtues of the politically informed facilitate bias in Lodge's account: A more structured (i.e., efficient) memory enhances the effects of unconscious primes; a greater information base becomes the "ammunition" sophisticates use to counterargue incongruent facts and arguments (Lodge & Taber, 2013, p. 152; also see Taber, Cann, & Kucsova, 2009); and deliberation reinforces, rather than corrects, these pathologies, strengthening preexisting attitudes in the process.

This results in what we call the "paradox" of political knowledge. Decades of research show that knowledge is associated with a host of normatively desirable outcomes. And yet, Lodge's innovative research on political cognition reveals the politically knowledgeable to be biased information processors. Other scholars have noted, but not resolved, this contradiction. For example, Lavine, Johnston, and Steenbergen observe that "Political sophistication has complex normative implications: It increases citizens' responsiveness to diagnostic information, but it also makes it easier to defend their beliefs through motivated bias" (2012, p. 219). It seems implausible, however, that political knowledge can predict both good citizenship *and* biased reasoning.

In the remainder of this essay, we look to the existing literature to reconcile these diverging perspectives. To foreshadow the argument that follows, there are two ways in which the paradox of knowledge may be resolved. The first pertains to measures of objective knowledge and what this measure represents in the theoretical model of *The Rationalizing Voter*. A long line of research has noted the ambiguities of political knowledge scales (e.g., Barabas, Jerit, Pollock, & Rainey, 2014; Mondak, 2001; Prior & Lupia, 2008). In particular, the same operational measure has been used to represent concepts as varied as media exposure, political awareness, and political expertise, just to name a few examples (Kuklinski & Quirk, 2001). The question we pose here is whether observed levels of knowledge are the best indicator for the theoretical construct in Lodge's model—i.e., prior affect. A second line of argumentation points to the importance of the information environment, by which we mean information from the mass media. Although evidence consistent with motivated reasoning continues to accumulate (e.g., Bisgaard, 2015; Gaines, Kuklinski, Quirk, Peyton, & Verkuilen, 2007; Jerit & Barabas, 2012; Lebo & Cassino, 2007), recent scholarship suggests that the information environment can also play a corrective role.

A Paradox Resolved?

> Voters are not either motivated reasoners or rational processors. Instead . . . voters can be both depending on the information environment in which they are operating.
> (Redlawsk, Civettini, & Emmerson, 2010, p. 590)

> Neutral factual knowledge is a *consequence* of two motivations, so it cannot separate people who are motivated to support partisan or accuracy goals.
> (Parker-Stephen, 2011, p. 25, emphasis original)

One method of resolving the aforementioned paradox involves closer consideration of the role of political knowledge. In *The Rationalizing Voter*, political sophisticates are described as having "greater interest" in the political world, which leads them to evaluate political objects more frequently and to "develop attitudes for a broad range of political objects" (Lodge & Taber, 2013, p. 90). According to this account, people with the highest levels of political knowledge represent individuals who "have thought about and repeatedly evaluated most of the political leaders, groups, and issues. . . [and by implication formed affective associations in memory toward these objects]" (Lodge & Taber, 2013, p. 90). Thus, it is not knowledge-as-information-holding that contributes to bias, but the existence of a prior attitude one wants to defend—known in the literature as having a "directional" motivation (Kunda, 1990). In line with this interpretation, the facilitation effects predicted by hot cognition are *strongest* for people who have "accessible, univalent" attitudes toward an object and they are the *weakest* for those who do not—namely, people who are ambivalent. This happens, Lodge and Taber (2013, p. 91) argue, because individuals who are ambivalent about an object have "*conflicting* hot cognitions."[11]

Importantly, there is a parallel finding in Lavine, Johnston, and Steenbergen (2012) in which univalent partisans make "worse" decisions than ambivalent partisans. In the Lavine et al. (2012) study, univalent partisans were more likely than the ambivalent to follow a counter-stereotypical party cue and mistakenly support an ideologically incongruent policy. Thus, *both* Lodge and Taber (2013) and Lavine, Johnston, and Steenbergen (2012) come to the conclusion that ambivalent people make normatively more desirable decisions. Lodge and Taber report that people who were ambivalent "showed no discernable evidence of automatic hot cognition" (2013, p. 91). Lavine, Johnston, and Steenbergen (2012) find that ambivalence increases the accuracy with which people perceive political events and leads to a stronger relationship between a person's attitudes and self-interest and values, among other things. Ambivalence, by either account, contributes to citizen competence. But herein lies the rub: *previous research has shown that an important predictor of ambivalence is a person's level of political knowledge* (Rudolph & Popp, 2007).

Thus, one resolution to the paradox of political sophistication is to recognize that having high levels of objective political knowledge may not, by itself, result in biased information processing. According to the theory outlined in *The Rationalizing Voter*, the antecedent to biased information processing is prior affect—i.e., having a preexisting opinion about a political object. On this view, hot cognition— not political knowledge *per se*—sets the stage for biased processing through "affective contagion" and "motivated bias" (in which a prior attitude influences the evaluation and retrieval of considerations, respectively).[12] According to the theoretical model in *The Rationalizing Voter*, the individuals who are most prone to engage in motivated reasoning are those with strong affect (i.e., a prior opinion) towards an object. In practice, however, these individuals are identified on the basis of their performance on objective knowledge questions. Thus, political knowledge is doing the work of a similar, but nevertheless distinct, concept.

A related observation was made in an insightful paper by Parker-Stephen (2011). He argues that the typical practice of measuring sophistication with knowledge scales conflates two different kinds of people: those who are influenced by directional goals and those who are motivated by accuracy. The first type, Parker-Stephen explains, are people who "support specific candidates and issues" and are thus motivated to see the world in a way that supports their partisan predispositions (2011, p. 2). This first type knows a lot about politics, objectively speaking, but they are rooting for a specific (partisan) team. These individuals are likely to have "stronger, affectively charged links" as postulated by *The Rationalizing Voter* (Lodge & Taber, 2013, p. 116; also see Taber & Lodge, 2016). The second type of person enjoys following politics, and it is for this reason he or she has high levels of political knowledge. According to Parker-Stephen, the fact that "rooters" and "followers" both have neutral factual knowledge is problematic for tests of motivated reasoning. "The strongest test," he writes, ". . . would ask, not about perceptual differences across knowledge, but about these differences across levels of motivation" (2011, p. 4).[13]

A second way to reconcile the paradox of political sophistication relates to the nature of the information environment. Even if scholars conclude that the prevalence of good decision-making depends on individual-level motivations (Druckman, 2012), the decision-making context matters. And here, there is emerging evidence that motivated reasoning does not continue indefinitely: after a certain point, incongruent information can cause even motivated reasoners to update their attitudes (Redlawsk et al., 2010; see Barabas, 2004 for related evidence). In fact, several recent studies identify the information environment as a crucial determinant to the quality of citizen decision-making. The information environment occupies a crucial place in Lavine, Johnston, and Steenbergen's (2012) theory of partisan ambivalence, largely in the form of "exogenous shocks" (e.g., scandals, economic downturns) that cause a disjuncture between a person's long-term identification with a party and their contemporary evaluation of the party's performance. The doubt engendered by this internal conflict prompts a deliberative style of thinking in which people seek out diagnostic information and become more open-minded. Yet people would not experience ambivalence were it not for the fact that information from the "real world" causes them to question the reliability of partisan cues (and to abandon simple partisan cue taking).[14]

Thus, although there is considerable debate in the literature regarding the prevalence of partisan perceptual bias (e.g., Bisgaard, 2015; Bullock, Gerber, Hill, & Huber, 2015; Gaines et al., 2007; Jerit & Barabas, 2012; Prior, Sood, & Khanna, 2015), it seems impossible to deny the potentially corrective role of the information environment. Recent studies provide a glimpse of how correction might take place. Parker-Stephen (2013) proposes a theory of "contextual motivated reasoning" in which the information environment can facilitate or inhibit partisan rationalization (for examples in the literature on framing see Druckman, Peterson, & Slothuus, 2013; Slothuus & DeVresse, 2010). When "all the facts push in one direction," Parker-Stephen writes, it becomes difficult for motivated reasoners to deny reality. This is because even strong motivated reasoners draw their preferred conclusion "only if they can muster up the evidence necessary to support it" (Kunda, 1990, p. 483).

Parker-Stephen (2013) focuses on judgments about the economy, but another study shows that facts can matter, even in a highly politicized situation such as the lead-up to armed conflict. In their examination of the Iraq War, Feldman, Huddy, and Marcus (2015) show that Democrats and Independents were motivated to seek out and process credible critiques of the Bush administration's case for war. In what truly seems like a triumph of the information environment, the authors show that the individuals most likely to be exposed to the critical reporting of regional and non-elite newspapers were the most critical of the administration's pro-war position. Feldman, Huddy, and Marcus conclude that, "Americans can sift through complex information on foreign policy and arrive at an independent political judgment under the right conditions. . . . The most important factor is the *availability* of information" (2015, pp. 2–4, emphasis added; also see Bullock, 2011).

In the end, it seems inconceivable (to us) that possessing factual information about the political world would by itself be detrimental. We agree with Delli Carpini and Keeter that raw facts, such as

> the percentage of Americans living below the poverty line, how the line is determined, and how the percentage has changed over time provide a

foundation for deliberation about larger issues. They prevent debates from becoming disconnected from the material conditions they attempt to address.

(1996, p. 11; also see Gilens, 2001)

Lodge's research demonstrates that insofar as the politically knowledgeable possess strong (i.e., univalent) attitudes toward an issue or candidate, these individuals will also be the most prone to biased reasoning. But this is hardly a foregone conclusion, as work by Parker-Stephen (2013) and Feldman et al. (2015) reveals. Recent research in political psychology—in part stimulated by Lodge's provocative conclusions—thereby provides a glimmer of hope that people will relinquish prior beliefs in the face of compelling evidence (see, for example, Bolsen, Druckman, & Cook, 2014; Nyhan & Reifler, 2015). One important task for future scholars is to more fully elaborate the conditions under which that occurs.

Notes

1. We thank Jason Barabas, Scott Clifford, Eric Groenendyk, and Yanna Krupnikov for helpful comments on a previous version of this manuscript.
2. We employ Delli Carpini and Keeter's definition of political knowledge "as the range of factual information about politics that is stored in long term memory" (1996, p. 10), and use the terms "political knowledge," "political sophistication," and "political awareness" interchangeably (for a similar approach, see Althaus, 2003; Zaller, 1992).
3. Political knowledge usually is operationalized in terms of a person's ability to correctly answer objective knowledge questions, such as identifying the party that has a majority in the U.S. House or naming the Vice President. According to Mondak, "there is compelling evidence that political awareness is best represented with data from survey batteries that measure factual knowledge" (2001, p. 224; also see Delli Carpini & Keeter, 1996; Fiske, Lau, & Smith, 1990; Zaller, 1990).
4. "System 1" and "System 2" are two styles of processing popularized by Daniel Kahneman's *Thinking, Fast and Slow* (2011; also see Stanovich & West, 2000). System 2 involves effortful mental activities and comprises our deliberate and analytical reasoning about the world. System 1 operates automatically, with little or no effort and no sense of voluntary control. The operations of System 1 are associated with a wide range of heuristic judgments and their associated biases.
5. This view is exemplified by Kelley and Mirer's "simple act of voting" model, which states: "The voter canvasses his likes and dislikes for the leading candidates and major parties involved in an election. Weighing each like and dislike equally, he votes for the candidate whom he has the greatest number of net favorable attitudes" (1974, p. 574).
6. Roughly two-thirds of participants were unable to recall the general issue stance (called a "gist" by the authors), while an even higher percentage (80%) were unable to recall the specifics of the candidates' issue stands (a "specifier").
7. The authors do not have a direct measure of participants' online tally, so they create what seems like a reasonable proxy (see Lodge, Steenbergen, & Brau, 1995, p. 316 for discussion).
8. See Lodge, Taber, and Verhulst (2011) for a related observation regarding the emphasis on conscious, as opposed to unconscious, processing.
9. A concept that has both a positive and negative charge results in ambivalence.

10. See Lodge and Hamill (1986) for related evidence in the context of partisan schemas.
11. This is distinct from having weak or non-attitudes. In that situation a person lacks hot cognitions altogether.
12. In a study that examines how the information environment contributes to mass polarization, Leeper (2014) comes to a similar conclusion, writing that "only individuals with strong, personally important attitudes are likely to engage in attitude-defensive reasoning" (2014, p. 30).
13. Parker-Stephen (2011) and Nir (2011) are among the few studies that explicitly operationalize partisan and accuracy motivations. In addition to political knowledge, Lodge and his collaborators use other individual-difference variables (e.g., attitude strength) to identify those who are most likely to engage in motivated reasoning. Such measures would seem preferable to political knowledge for another reason: If individuals' recall is as bad as Lodge's early research suggests, it is not clear what individual-level difference political knowledge scales are capturing.
14. A similar argument is made by Groenendyk (2016) who argues that the political environment can stimulate anxiety, which in turn reduces partisan bias (also see Brader, 2006 or Redlawsk, Civettini, & Emmerson, 2010).

References

Abelson, Robert P. (1963). Computer simulation of "hot cognitions." In Silvan Tomkins & Samuel Messick (Eds.), *Computer simulation and personality: Frontier of psychological theory* (pp. 277–298). New York: Wiley-Blackwell.

Alt, James E., Lassen, David D., & Marshall, John. (2016). Credible sources and sophisticated voters: When does new information induce economic voting? *Journal of Politics*, 78(2), 382–395.

Althaus, Scott L. (1998). Information effects in collective preferences. *American Political Science Review*, 92(3), 545–558.

Althaus, Scott L. (2003). *Collective preferences in democratic politics: Opinion surveys and the will of the people*. Cambridge: Cambridge University Press.

Barabas, Jason. (2004). How deliberation affects policy opinions. *American Political Science Review*, 98(4), 687–701.

Barabas, Jason & Jerit, Jennifer. (2009). Estimating the causal effects of media coverage on policy-specific knowledge. *American Journal of Political Science*, 53(1), 79–89.

Barabas, Jason, Jerit, Jennifer, Pollock, William, & Rainey, Carlisle. (2014). The question(s) of political knowledge. *American Political Science Review*, 108(4), 840–855.

Bartels, Larry. (1996). Uninformed votes: Information effects in presidential elections. *American Journal of Political Science*, 40(1), 194–230.

Bisgaard, Martin. (2015). Bias will find a way: Economic perceptions, attributions of blame, and partisan-motivated reasoning during crisis. *Journal of Politics*, 77(3), 849–859.

Bolsen, Toby, Druckman, James N., & Cook, Fay Lomax. (2014). The influence of partisan motivated reasoning on public opinion. *Political Behavior*, 36, 235–262.

Boudreau, Cheryl & Lupia, Arthur. (2011). Political knowledge. In James Druckman, Donald P. Green, James H. Kuklinski, & Arthur Lupia (Eds.), *Handbook of experimental political science* (pp. 171–186). New York: Cambridge University Press.

Brader, Ted (2006). Striking a responsive chord: How political ads motivate and persuade voters by appealing to emotions. *American Journal of Political Science*, 49(2), 388–405.

Bullock, John G. (2011). Elite influence on public opinion in an informed electorate. *American Political Science Review*, 105(3), 496–515.

Bullock, John G., Gerber, Alan S., Hill, Seth J., & Huber, Gregory A. (2015). Partisan bias in factual beliefs about politics. *Quarterly Journal of Political Science*, 10(4), 519–578.

Cassino, Dan & Lodge, Milton. (2007). The primacy of affect in political evaluations. In Russell Neuman, George Marcus, Ann Crigler, & Michael MacKuen (Eds.), *Affect effect: Dynamics of emotion in political thinking and behavior* (pp. 101–123). Chicago, IL: University of Chicago Press.

Clifford, Scott, Jerit, Jennifer, Rainey, Carlisle, & Motyl, Matt. (2015). Moral concerns and policy attitudes: Investigating the influence of elite rhetoric. *Political Communication*, 32(2), 229–248.

Converse, Philip E. (1964). Nature of belief systems in mass publics. In D. E. Apter (Ed.), *Ideology and discontent*. New York: Free Press.

Coronel, Jason C., Duff, Melissa C., Warren, David E., Federmeier, Kara D., Gonsalves, Brian D., Tranel, Daniel, & Cohen, Neal J. (2012). Remembering and voting: Theory and evidence from amnesic patients. *American Journal of Political Science*, 56(4), 837–848.

Curran, James, Iyengar, Shanto, Lund, Anker Brink, & Salovaara-Moring, Inka. (2009). Media systems, public knowledge and democracy: A comparative study. *European Journal of Communication*, 24(1), 5–26.

Delli Carpini, Michael X. & Keeter, Scott. (1996). *What Americans know about politics and why it matters*. New Haven, CT: Yale University Press.

Druckman, James N. (2012). The politics of motivation. *Critical Review*, 24(2), 199–216.

Druckman, James N., Peterson, Erik, & Slothuus, Rune. (2013). How elite partisan polarization affects public opinion formation. *American Political Science Review*, 107(1), 57–79.

Feldman, Stanley, Huddy, Leonie, & Marcus, George. (2015). *Going to war: When citizens and the press matter*. Chicago, IL: University of Chicago Press.

Fiske, Susan, Lau, Richard R., & Smith, Richard A. (1990). On the varieties and utilities of political expertise. *Social Cognition*, 8(1), 31–48.

Gaines, Brian J., Kuklinski, James H., Quirk, Paul J., Peyton, Buddy, & Verkuilen, Jay. (2007). Same facts, different interpretations: Partisan motivation and opinion on Iraq. *Journal of Politics*, 69(4), 957–974.

Gilens, Martin. (2001). Political ignorance and collective policy preferences. *American Political Science Review*, 95(2), 379–396.

Gomez, Brad T. & Wilson, J. Matthew. (2001). Political sophistication and economic voting in the American electorate: A theory of heterogeneous attribution. *American Journal of Political Science*, 45, 899–914.

Gordon, Stacy B. & Segura, Gary M. (1997). Cross-national variation in the political sophistication of individuals: Capability or choice? *Journal of Politics*, 59, 126–147.

Graber, Doris A. (1993). *Processing the news: How people tame the information tide*. New York: Longman.

Groenendyk, Eric. (2016). The anxious and ambivalent partisan: The effect of incidental anxiety on partisan motivated recall and ambivalence. *Public Opinion Quarterly*, 80(2), 460–479.

Hamilton, Alexander, Madison, James, & Jay, John. (1961). *The federalist papers*. New York: Penguin.

Hastie, Reid & Park, Bernadette. (1986). The relationship between memory and judgment depends on whether the task is memory-based or on-line. *Psychological Review*, 93(3), 258–268.

Hsu, Mei-Ling & Price, Vincent. (1993). Political expertise and affect effects on news processing. *Communication Research*, 20(5), 671–695.
Jacoby, William G. (2006). Value choices and American public opinion. *American Journal of Political Science*, 50(3), 706–723.
Jerit, Jennifer. (2009). Understanding the knowledge gap: The role of experts and journalists. *Journal of Politics*, 71(2), 442–456.
Jerit, Jennifer & Barabas, Jason. (2012). Partisan perceptual bias and the information environment. *Journal of Politics*, 74(2), 672–684.
Jerit, Jennifer, Barabas, Jason, & Bolsen, Toby. (2006). Citizens, knowledge, and the information environment. *American Journal of Political Science*, 50(2), 266–282.
Kahneman, Daniel. (2011). *Thinking, fast and slow*. New York: Farrar, Straus and Giroux.
Kam, Cindy D. (2005). Who toes the party line? Cues, values, and individual differences. *Political Behavior*, 27(2), 163–182.
Kelley, Stanley & Mirer, Thad W. (1974). The simple act of voting. *American Political Science Review*, 68(2), 572–591.
Kinder, Donald R. (2006). Belief systems today. *Critical Review: Special Issue on Democratic Competence*, 18(1–3), 197–216.
Kuklinski, James H. & Coronel, Jason C. (2012). Political psychology at Stony Brook: A retrospective. *Critical Review*, 24(2), 185–198.
Kuklinski, James H. & Quirk, Paul J. (2001). Conceptual foundations of citizen competence. *Political Behavior*, 23(3), 285–311.
Kunda, Ziva. (1990). The case for motivated reasoning. *Psychological Bulletin*, 108(3), 480–498.
Lavine, Howard, Johnston, Christopher, & Steenbergen, Marco. (2012). *The ambivalent partisan*. New York: Oxford University Press.
Lebo, Matthew & Cassino, Daniel. (2007). The aggregate consequences of motivated reasoning and the dynamics of partisan presidential approval. *Political Psychology*, 28(6), 719–746.
Leeper, Thomas. (2014). The informational basis for mass polarization. *Public Opinion Quarterly*, 79(1), 27–46.
Lemert, James B. (1981). *Does mass communication change public opinion after all?* Chicago, IL: Nelson-Hall.
Lodge, Milton. (1995). Toward a procedural model of candidate evaluation. In Milton Lodge & Kathleen McGraw (Eds.), *Political judgment: Structure and process* (pp. 111–140). Ann Arbor, MI: University of Michigan.
Lodge, Milton & Hamill, Ruth. (1986). A partisan schema for political information processing. *American Political Science Review*, 80(2), 505–520.
Lodge, Milton, McGraw, Kathleen M., & Stroh, Patrick. (1989). An impression driven model of candidate evaluation. *American Political Science Review*, 83(2), 399–419.
Lodge, Milton, Steenbergen, Marco R., & Brau, Shawn. (1995). The responsive voter: Campaign information and the dynamics of campaign evaluation. *American Political Science Review*, 89, 309–326.
Lodge, Milton, Stroh, Patrick, & Wahlke, John. (1990). Black box models of candidate evaluation. *Political Behavior*, 12(1), 5–18.
Lodge, Milton & Taber, Charles S. (2013). *The rationalizing voter*. New York: Cambridge University Press.
Lodge, Milton, Taber, Charles S., & Verhulst, Brad. (2011). Conscious and unconscious information processing with implications for experimental political science. In James

Druckman, Donald P. Green, James H. Kuklinski, & Arthur Lupia (Eds.), *Handbook of experimental political science* (pp. 155–170). New York: Cambridge University Press.

Lupia, Arthur. (2006). How elitism undermines the study of citizen competence. *Critical Review: Special Issue on Democratic Competence*, 18(1–3), 217–232.

Luskin, Robert C. (1990). Explaining political sophistication. *Political Behavior*, 12(4), 331–361.

McCloskey, Herbert. (1964). Consensus and ideology in American politics. *American Political Science Review*, 58(2), 361–382.

McCloskey, Herbert & Zaller, John. (1984). *The American ethos: Public attitudes towards capitalism and democracy*. Cambridge, MA: Harvard University Press.

Mondak, Jeffery J. (2001). Developing valid knowledge scales. *American Journal of Political Science*, 45(1), 224–238.

Neuman, W. Russell. (1986). *The paradox of mass politics: Knowledge and opinion in the American electorate*. Cambridge, MA: Harvard University Press.

Nicholson, Stephen P. (2003). The political environment and ballot proposition awareness. *American Journal of Political Science*, 41(3), 403–410.

Nir, Lilach. (2011). Motivated reasoning and public opinion perception. *Public Opinion Quarterly*, 75(3), 504–532.

Nyhan, Brendan & Reifler, Jason. (2015). Displacing misinformation about events: An experimental test of causal corrections. *Journal of Experimental Political Science*, 2(1), 81–93.

Parker-Stephen, Evan. (2011). *Following the sport vs. rooting for the team: The multiple paths to political sophistication*. Manuscript, Texas A&M University.

Parker-Stephen, Evan. (2013). Tides of disagreement: How reality facilitates (and inhibits) partisan public opinion. *Journal of Politics*, 75(4), 1077–1088.

Prior, Markus & Lupia, Arthur. (2008). Money, time, and political knowledge: Distinguishing quick recall and political learning skills. *American Journal of Political Science*, 52(1), 168–182.

Prior, Markus, Sood, Gaurav, & Khanna, Kabir. (2015). You cannot be serious: The impact of accuracy incentives on partisan bias in reports of economic perceptions. *Quarterly Journal of Political Science*, 10(4), 489–518.

Redlawsk, David P., Civettini, Andrew J.W., & Emmerson, Karen M. (2010). The affective tipping point. *Political Psychology*, 31(4), 563–593.

Rudolph, Thomas J. & Popp, Elizabeth. (2007). An information processing theory of ambivalence. *Political Psychology*, 28(5), 563–585.

Slothuus, Rune & DeVresse, Claes H. (2010). Political parties, motivated reasoning, and issue framing effects. *Journal of Politics*, 72(3), 630–645.

Sniderman, Paul M. (2000). Taking sides: A fixed choice theory of political reasoning. In Matthew D. McCubbins, Arthur Lupia, & Samuel L. Popkin (Eds.), *Elements of reason: Understanding and expanding the limits of political rationality* (pp. 67–84). Cambridge: Cambridge University Press.

Sniderman, Paul M., Glaser, James M., & Griffin, Robert (1990). Information and electoral choice. In John A. Ferejohn & James H. Kuklinski (Eds.), *Information and democratic processes* (pp. 117–135). Urbana, IL: University of Illinois Press.

Stanovich, Keith E. & West, Richard F. (2000). Individual difference in reasoning: Implications for the rationality debate. *Behavioral and Brain Sciences*, 23, 645–726.

Strömbäck, Jesper. (2016). Does public service TV and the intensity of the political information environment matter? *Journalism Studies*, 18(1), 34–55.

Taber, Charles S., Cann, Damon, & Kucsova, Simona. (2009). The motivated processing of political arguments. *Political Behavior*, 31(2), 137–155.

Taber, Charles S. & Lodge, Milton. (2006). Motivated skepticism in the evaluation of political beliefs. *American Journal of Political Science*, 50(3), 755–769.

Taber, Charles S. & Lodge, Milton. (2016). The illusion of choice in democratic politics: The unconscious impact of motivated political reasoning. *Advances in Political Psychology*, 37(Suppl. 1), 61–85.

Zaller, John. (1990). Political awareness, elite opinion leadership, and the mass survey response. *Social Cognition*, 8, 125–153.

Zaller, John (1992). *The nature and origins of mass opinion*. New York: Cambridge University Press.

6
POLITICAL EXPERTISE AND OPEN-MINDED COGNITION[1]

Victor Ottati, Chase Wilson, Erika Price, and Nathanael Sumaktoyo

Introduction

How do individuals construe the political world? How do people represent political information in memory? How do citizens use political information when deriving political beliefs, opinions, and attitudes? Political psychologists have been exploring questions of this nature for decades. A common thread running through this literature involves the claim that political experts and novices construe, represent, and process political information differently (Fiske & Kinder, 1981; Lau & Redlawsk, 2001; Lodge & Taber, 2013; Zaller, 1992). That is, a comprehensive approach to understanding political cognition cannot simply adopt a psychological model of political information processing that presumes "one size fits all." On the contrary, it is important to develop and test models of political information processing that explicitly incorporate the role of individual differences in political expertise.

Political expertise potentially influences a variety of psychological processes when individuals engage in political reasoning. The present chapter focuses on how political expertise influences cognitive processing style. More specifically, this chapter examines the extent to which political expertise influences the tendency to process political information in a *directionally biased* or *unbiased* manner. That is, we examine the effect of political expertise on "closed-minded" versus "open-minded" cognition (Ottati, 2015; Ottati, Price, Wilson, & Sumaktoyo, 2015). "Open-Minded Cognition" is structured as a bipolar psychological continuum that ranges from closed-minded dogmatism to open-minded cognition (Price, Ottati, Wilson, & Kim, 2015). An open-minded cognitive style is *directionally unbiased*. It involves a willingness to openly consider multiple intellectual perspectives, attitudes, or opinions—including those that contradict the individual's preexisting opinions and expectations. In contrast, a closed-minded or dogmatic cognitive style is *directionally biased*. It is marked by a tendency to select, interpret, and elaborate upon information in a manner that reinforces or confirms the individual's preexisting opinions and expectations (e.g., Eagly, Chen, Chaiken, & Shaw-Barnes, 1999; Nickerson, 1998; Price et al., 2015).

In examining the effect of political expertise on open-minded cognition we consider two distinct components of this construct. The first component is emphasized in traditional conceptualizations of political expertise that focus on the role of political knowledge (e.g., Delli Carpini & Keeter, 1991; McGraw, Lodge, & Stroh, 1990). From this perspective, political experts are individuals who possess a large amount of knowledge pertaining to politics whereas political novices are individuals who possess minimal amounts of political knowledge. The second component, which is the focus of our more recent research, involves *self-perceptions* of political expertise (Ottati et al., 2015). In this case, political experts are simply individuals who *believe* they possess a large amount of political knowledge whereas political novices are individuals who *believe* they possess a minimal amount of political knowledge. Importantly, this later approach emphasizes that political experts and political novices occupy distinct social roles.

Political Expertise as Political Knowledge

Previous research has employed a variety of measures when assessing individual differences in political expertise (e.g., education, political engagement, media exposure). However, the most widely accepted approach to measuring political expertise typically involves assessment of an individual's political knowledge (e.g., Delli Carpini & Keeter, 1991; but see Krosnick, 1990). That is, individuals are given a political information test. Political knowledge scores are computed by simply computing the sum or proportion of correct answers (McGraw et al., 1990; McGraw, Pinney, & Neumann, 1991). These measures assess the amount of previously acquired political information that is represented in long-term memory, and that is accessible when individuals answer questions contained in a political information test.

Is political knowledge associated with an increase or decrease in open-minded cognition? Previous research provides a mixed answer to this question. On the one hand, a number of studies suggest that politically knowledgeable individuals possess a more accurate view of political reality, a view that is less likely to be biased by prior opinions or expectations. For example, some studies reveal that politically knowledgeable individuals process political information in a systematic manner (e.g., Goren, 1997; Hsu & Price, 1993; Tewksbury, 1999), whereas politically uninformed individuals rely on heuristic cues that can produce biased political judgments and decisions (Hart, Ottati, & Krumdick, 2011; Ottati & Isbell, 1996). When evaluating a political candidate, for example, politically uninformed individuals are more likely to report judgments that are biased by incidental affective states or physical attractiveness of the political candidate (Hart, Ottati, & Krumdick, 2011; Ottati & Isbell, 1996). Politically knowledgeable individuals have been observed to correct for biases of this nature (Hart, Ottati, & Krumdick, 2011; Ottati & Isbell, 1996), or alternatively, to employ "appropriate" forms of heuristic processing that render "correct" political decisions (i.e., decisions equivalent to those that would emerge given systematic processing; Lau & Redlawsk, 2001). These findings suggest that politically knowledgeable individuals possess the skill that is required to engage in accurate, unbiased, and open-minded forms of political reasoning.

On the other hand, an equal (if not larger) body of research suggests that political knowledge increases the likelihood that individuals will engage in directionally biased forms of political reasoning—reasoning that reinforces preexisting opinions or expectations. One reason why this might occur is that knowledgeable individuals are more likely to possess crystallized political representations (e.g., party stereotypes) that potentially bias the processing of newly acquired political information. Consistent with this assumption, research indicates that politically knowledgeable individuals are more likely to exhibit a party-congruent bias when recalling information pertaining to political candidate (Lodge & Hamill, 1986; but see Lau & Redlawsk, 2001 for a different perspective). Research also suggests that, even when processing information in a systematic manner, knowledgeable individuals may engage in directionally biased information processing. Knowledgeable individuals possess well-organized memory representations that are characterized by high levels of evaluative consistency and evaluative clustering (e.g., Fiske & Kinder, 1981; Lusk & Judd, 1988; McGraw & Pinney, 1990; but see McGraw et al., 1991). Moreover, the relation between social worldviews, ideology, and policy preferences is magnified among politically knowledgeable individuals (Federico, Hunt, & Ergun, 2009; Federico & Schneider, 2007; but see Goren, 2000). These findings suggest that political knowledge may be associated with a tendency to maintain cognitive and evaluative consistency, a tendency that might bias cognition in the direction of preexisting expectations and opinions.

More generally, directionally biased reasoning strategies are evident when individuals selectively process political information, counterargue political information, or generate inferences that reinforce preexisting political attitudes and expectations (Lavine, Borgida, & Sullivan, 2000; Ottati, Fishbein, & Middlestadt, 1988; Ottati, Wilson, & Price, 2018; Taber & Lodge, 2006; Redlawsk, 2002). Research suggests that politically knowledgeable individuals can employ these motivated reasoning strategies (Lodge & Hamill, 1986; Lodge & Taber, 2013; Lusk & Judd, 1988; Taber & Lodge, 2006). Indeed, the ability to employ these cognitive strategies may be higher among politically knowledgeable individuals (Lavine, Johnston, & Steenbergen, 2012). At least in part, this is because well-informed citizens are more likely to possess strong political attitudes that can be automatically activated when deriving political judgments and decisions (Lodge & Taber, 2013). These automatically activated attitudes can trigger selective information-processing strategies that reinforce preexisting attitudes (Taber & Lodge, 2006), as well as cognitive elaborations that serve to denigrate opposing attitudes and opinions (Lodge & Taber, 2013). Moreover, when employing motivated reasoning strategies, politically knowledgeable individuals may be more confident that they are arriving at a valid and accurate judgmental conclusion (Lavine et al., 2012).

In sum, theory and research is equivocal regarding the relation between political knowledge and open-minded cognition. Some work suggests that political knowledge is associated with decreased reliance upon cognitive heuristics that produce directionally biased political judgments, or alternatively, an increased likelihood of correcting for biases of this nature. In contrast, other research implies that political knowledge can be associated with an increase in directionally biased forms of motivated political reasoning. Interestingly, our own research indicates that political knowledge is uncorrelated with open-minded cognition (Price et al., 2015). Perhaps this is because political knowledge triggers a variety of conflicting effects on open-minded cognition that, on balance, cancel. Additional research is needed to further investigate this possibility, and to examine factors that may moderate the influence of political knowledge on open-minded cognition.

Political Expertise as a Social Role

Although most research regarding political expertise focuses on individual differences in political knowledge, some have suggested that political expertise possesses multiple components (e.g., political knowledge, attention to political messages, political interest, depth of political information processing, complexity and organization of political thought; Krosnick, 1990; Luskin, 1990). The present chapter maintains a focus on political knowledge when conceptualizing political expertise, but importantly, makes a distinction between political knowledge stored in memory and the self-perception of political knowledge. That is, whereas previous research regarding political expertise examines the effect of actual political knowledge on political information processing, the remainder of this chapter focuses on *self-perceptions* of political expertise.

It is important to emphasize that self-perception of knowledge is distinct from an individual's actual level of knowledge within a domain. When individuals estimate their performance at a task, the correlation between perceived and actual performance is often low (Dunning, Johnson, Ehrlinger, & Kruger, 2003). One reason for this finding is that individuals generally over-estimate their knowledge, talents, and abilities. As a consequence, the average person believes he or she is above average, a result that contradicts statistical logic (Alicke & Govorun, 2005; Brown & Gallagher, 1992). Interestingly, the tendency to over-estimate self-competence primarily emerges for individuals possessing relatively low levels of skill (Kruger & Dunning, 1999; Dunning et al., 2003). This occurs because unskilled individuals are "doubly cursed." Their low level of skill not only produces a low level of performance, but also an inability to accurately assess performance. As a result, unskilled individuals not only perform poorly on tests, but are also unable to discern whether their answers (or anyone else's) are right or wrong (Dunning et al., 2003). Inspired by these findings, research described in the remainder of this chapter is based upon the assumption that self-perception of political expertise is distinct from an individual's actual level of political knowledge.

The distinction between self-perceived and actual political knowledge is also evident when considering the malleable nature of self-perceptions. Research indicates self-esteem possesses a malleable component that varies across situations (i.e., "state self-esteem," Heatherton & Polivy, 1991). In an analogous fashion, we assume that self-perceptions of political expertise vary across situations. For example, self-perceptions of political expertise are presumed to be high when individuals are told they have performed well on a political information test, but relatively low when individuals are told they have failed a political information test (Ottati et al., 2015). Situational variation in self-perceived expertise also arises because self-perceptions of political expertise are relative. Consider, for example, a university undergraduate political science student who discusses politics with a group of high school students. In this situation, the undergraduate political science student will perceive him- or herself to be relatively high in political expertise. In contrast, assume this same political science student attends a political science conference populated by world-renowned political scholars who are highly published. In this later situation, the undergraduate political science student will perceive him- or herself to be relatively low in political expertise (Ottati et al., 2015). In sum, for a variety of reasons, self-perceptions of political expertise possess a malleable component that varies across situations. In contrast, knowledge of politics constitutes a more stable individual-difference characteristic, changing only when individuals endeavor to educate themselves regarding political issues and affairs. As such, it is important to regard self-perceptions of political expertise and political knowledge as distinct constructs.

It should be emphasized that self-perceptions of expertise are not simply self-ratings. They also function as a form of self-categorization. Namely, when an individual perceives him- or herself to be high in political expertise, it can be said that the individual has categorized him- or herself as occupying the social role of the political expert. As is the case with other social categories (e.g., race, gender), this social category is associated with a variety of traits and behaviors that are represented in memory. The prototype of a "political expert" presumably includes a variety of traits (e.g., "intelligent," "verbally fluent," "educated in political affairs") and behaviors (e.g., "keeps abreast of political events," "frequently talks about politics") that are commonly associated with political experts in everyday life. Importantly, social roles are also associated with social norms that prescribe certain behaviors and prohibit other behaviors (Katz & Kahn, 1978; Sarbin & Allen, 1968;

Triandis, 1972, 1980; Triandis, Marin, Hui, Lisansky, & Ottati, 1984). For example, social norms permit a teacher to enthusiastically lecture about course material, and discourage a teacher from remaining completely silent during class. Students, on the other hand, are faced with a different set of normative role expectations (e.g., raise your hand to ask a question, take notes, and quietly listen).

Although role-specific normative expectations commonly prescribe specific *behavioral* responses (e.g., raise your hand), we propose that they also prescribe specific *cognitive* response patterns (e.g., carefully think about the teacher's remarks). Consider, for example, a seminar pertaining to heart disease. Some individuals attending this seminar might occupy the role of "novice" (e.g., a layperson), whereas others might occupy the role of "expert" (e.g., a cardiology professor). Novices possess limited knowledge. As such, social norms dictate that they should listen and learn in an open-minded fashion. However, the expert possesses extensive knowledge, and therefore is entitled to adopt a more forceful and dogmatic orientation (see Triandis et al., 1984 for related effects of status). Thus, whereas dogmatic statements may be tolerated when the "expert" speaks, novices are expected to adopt a more open-minded cognitive orientation (see Kruglanski & Mayseless, 1987; Leary & Hoyle, 2015 for linkages between awareness of personal limitation and open-mindedness).

According to the Earned Dogmatism Hypothesis, a similar dynamic emerges when individuals categorize *themselves* as "political experts." That is, individuals who perceive *themselves* to be high in political expertise will adopt a cognitive style that is normatively prescribed for "political experts." Because political experts have earned the privilege of adopting forceful and dogmatic political opinions, these individuals will feel entitled to respond to political messages in a more closed-minded or dogmatic fashion. Conversely, individuals who perceive themselves to be average or low in political expertise are expected to adopt a cognitive style that is normatively prescribed for the "layperson." That is, these individuals are more likely to believe they are normatively obligated to listen to political messages in an open-minded fashion. This Earned Dogmatism Hypothesis was tested in a series of experiments that manipulated self-perceptions of expertise. Because self-perceived expertise was experimentally manipulated using random assignment, effects elicited by self-perceived expertise cannot be attributed to individual differences in political knowledge.

The Earned Dogmatism Effect

According to the Earned Dogmatism Hypothesis, individuals are more likely to respond to political messages in a closed-minded manner when they perceive themselves to be "experts." Using U.S. voting age samples that varied in terms of key voter characteristics (age, gender, race, and partisanship), this hypothesis was examined in multiple experiments.[2]

Normative Approval of a Dogmatic Expert

According to the Earned Dogmatism Hypothesis, social norms entitle political experts to respond to political messages in a more dogmatic manner than political novices. Ottati et al. (2015) tested this assumption by presenting experimental participants with a description of a target person (see Na, Choi, & Sul, 2013 for related work). In the "political expert" condition, the target person was initially described as being extremely knowledgeable with regard to political affairs, and having carefully followed politics over the course of many years. In the "political novice" condition, the target person was initially described as someone who possesses a minimal amount of political knowledge, having essentially ignored politics over the course of many years. The second portion of the description, which described the target person's *current approach to politics*, was identical in the two experimental conditions. In both conditions, the person's *current approach to politics* was described as closed-minded or dogmatic. Specifically, this portion of the description indicated that the target person "no longer has much patience for political opinions or arguments he disagrees with," "tunes out messages he disagrees with," and so on. After reading the entire description of the target person, participants rated the extent to which the target person's *current approach to politics* is "warranted," "justified," and "appropriate." A "normative approval" score was computed by simply averaging these three ratings.

As predicted, normative approval was higher in the "expert" condition than in the "novice" condition. Consistent with the Earned Dogmatism Hypothesis, social norms dictated that the target person's current dogmatic approach to politics was more warranted, justified, and appropriate when the target person was described as a political expert than when the target person was described as a political novice (Ottati et al., 2015). This indicates political expertise can be conceptualized as a social role. As with any social role (e.g., mother, teacher, lawyer), the roles of "political expert" and "political novice" contain unique and distinct sets of normative prescriptions. These normative prescriptions not only pertain to behavior, but also dictate expected and appropriate patterns of cognitive responding. In particular, the "political expert" role entitles an individual to engage in relatively closed-minded and dogmatic patterns of reasoning. In contrast, the "political novice" role dictates that an individual should feel more obligated to adopt an unbiased and open-minded style of thinking.

The Problem With Success

A second experiment was designed to test the Earned Dogmatism Hypothesis by manipulating *self*-perceptions of political expertise. In this case, the manipulation was designed to elicit a "working representation" of the self that suggested the individual occupied the role of a "political novice" or "political expert" (Ottati et al., 2015). Specifically, it was assumed that successful performance on a political test would lead individuals to construe themselves as "political experts" who were knowledgeable regarding political affairs. Conversely, it was assumed that failure on a political test would lead individuals to construe themselves as "political novices" who possessed minimal knowledge of political affairs (see Trafimow & Sniezek, 1994 for related work).

Importantly, this approach enabled us to disentangle the effect of self-perceived expertise from the effect of political knowledge. This is because individuals were *randomly assigned* to a condition that promoted either success or failure on the political information test. Thus, participants in the two experimental conditions did not differ in terms of their actual level of political knowledge. In this fashion, self-perceptions of expertise were manipulated independent of participants' actual level of political knowledge. Effects of self-perceived expertise could not be attributed to individual differences in political knowledge.

The actual experimental procedure proceeded as follows. Experimental participants initially completed a multiple choice test containing fifteen items regarding specific politicians, political procedures, and government agencies. Participants were randomly assigned to complete either an easy version (success condition) or a difficult version of this political test (failure condition). For example, one question in the easy condition asked, "Who is the current President of the United States?" An equivalent question in the difficult condition asked, "Who was Nixon's initial vice president?" After completing the test, participants in the easy test condition were told that they had scored "better than 86% of other test takers." In contrast, participants in the difficult condition were told that they had scored "*worse* than 86% of test takers." Thus, the experimental manipulation was "double-barreled." Namely, the "failure" condition was intended to elicit poor actual performance accompanied by social feedback that indicated the participant performed poorly on the test. Conversely, the "success" condition was intended to elicit a high level of actual performance accompanied by social feedback that indicated the participant performed well on the test.

After completing the political test and receiving performance feedback, all participants completed a previously validated measure of Political Open-Minded Cognition (Ottati et al., 2015; Price et al., 2015). This consisted of six survey items. Three items were worded in an "open-minded" direction (i.e., "When it comes to politics, I am open to considering other viewpoints"; "I try to reserve judgment until I have a chance to hear both sides of a political issue"; "When thinking about a political issue, I consider as many different opinions as possible"). The other three items were worded in a "closed-minded" direction (i.e., "I often 'tune out' political messages I disagree with"; "I believe it is a waste of time to pay attention to certain political ideas"; "I have no patience for political arguments I disagree with"). Participants rated the extent the extent to which they agreed with each item. After reverse scoring responses the "closed" items, responses to the six items were simply averaged to produce a summary Political Open-Minded Cognition score. Previous validation research confirms that Political

Open-Minded Cognition is a unique construct that is unrelated to individual differences in political knowledge and need for cognition; negatively associated with Dogmatism, Intolerance for Ambiguity, and American System Justification; and positively associated with a tendency to discuss politics with people who disagree with oneself (Price et al., 2015).

Before performing the main analyses, a manipulation check revealed that the experimental manipulation was only partially successful. As expected, average performance on the political test was higher among participants who completed the easy test than the difficult test. However, contrary to expectation, some of the participants in the difficult test condition answered many of the test items correctly. Not surprisingly, comments provided by a number of these participants suggested that they did not believe they scored "*worse* than 86% of test takers." Thus, the experimental manipulation was ineffective for this portion of the sample. To address this problem, the data was analyzed twice. In a "reduced sample" analysis, the data was analyzed after excluding participants who performed quite well on the difficult test (answered ten or more items correctly). This "reduced sample" analysis yielded support for the Earned Dogmatism Hypothesis. Political Open-Minded Cognition was lower in the success condition compared to the failure condition. The same pattern of mean differences emerged when performing the "full sample" analysis, although in this case, the difference between the success and failure condition failed to achieve significance.

In sum, the "reduced sample" analysis in Experiment 2 provided preliminary support for the Earned Dogmatism Hypothesis. However, the "reduced sample" analysis also possessed a notable shortcoming. Specifically, it introduced a confound between self-perceived expertise and actual political knowledge.[3] We therefore employed experimental strategies that eliminated this problem in the three experiments that follow.

Ease of Retrieving Political Information

Theory and research within social psychology documents the existence of an "ease of retrieval" effect (Schwarz, 2011; Schwarz et al., 1991). Specifically, as is the case with many feeling states (e.g., mood), individuals use the feeling of "ease of retrieval" as information when deriving social judgments. For example, individuals asked to recall twelve examples of assertive behaviors (difficult) rated themselves as less assertive than individuals asked to recall six examples of assertive behavior (easy; Schwarz et al., 1991). This effect emerges because, when individuals experience feelings of difficulty in retrieving twelve assertive behaviors, they infer that they must be relatively unassertive. In contrast, when individuals experience feelings of ease in retrieving six assertive behaviors, they infer that they must be relatively assertive. In this fashion, "ease of retrieval" influences self-perceptions.

A third experiment employed a variant of Schwarz and colleagues' (1991) "ease of retrieval" manipulation when manipulating self-perceptions of political expertise (Ottati et al., 2015). In the "easy" condition, participants were asked to name two policies implemented by President Obama. In the difficult condition, participants were asked to name ten policies implemented by President Obama. To create an intensified awareness of failure in the ten policy condition, participants who named less than ten polices were required to write "I don't know" in any remaining text boxes. Due to the relative ease of retrieving two policies, it was presumed that participants in the easy condition would infer that they knew a respectable amount about politics, leading to relatively high self-perceptions of political expertise. Due to the difficulty of retrieving ten policy positions, it was assumed that participants in the difficult condition would infer that they were uninformed about politics, leading to low self-perceptions of political expertise. Importantly, participants were *randomly* assigned to the high versus low self-perception of expertise conditions. Thus, effects of the experimental manipulation cannot be attributed to individual differences in political knowledge.

The results of this experiment supported the Earned Dogmatism Hypothesis. Namely, as predicted, participants in the difficult condition (low self-perception of political expertise) reported greater Political Open-Minded Cognition than participants in the easy condition (high self-perception of political expertise).

The Relative Nature of the Expert Role

An individual (e.g., law school student) can occupy a "high-expertise" role in some situations (e.g., providing legal advice to a psychology student) and a "low-expertise" role in other situations (e.g., obtaining legal advice from a law professor). Thus, according to role theory, perceptions of expertise are relative and can vary within the individual across situations. A fourth experiment employed an experimental manipulation that focused on the *relative* nature of political expertise. This was accomplished by varying the protagonist's relative level of political expertise within the context of three situational scenarios (Ottati et al., 2015).

In one situational scenario, the protagonist occupied a "low-expertise" role when discussing politics with a group of people who knew a lot *more* about politics than the protagonist. In a second situational scenario, the protagonist occupied a "high-expertise" role when discussing politics with a group of people who knew a lot *less* about politics than the protagonist did. Finally, in the "control scenario," the protagonist encountered a group of people who were simply described as "typical" in terms of political knowledge. Participants read each of these scenarios twice, first imagining that "John" was the protagonist and then imagining that they themselves ("you") were the protagonist. After reading each scenario, participants indicated whether the situation involved people who "know a great deal about politics," "know very little about politics," or "are pretty typical in terms of their knowledge of politics." This served both as a manipulation check and as a procedure designed to strengthen the relative expertise manipulation.

Participants provided normative entitlement ratings in each of the three social role conditions. That is, participants rated the extent to which "John" (protagonist) *should* feel entitled to respond in a closed-minded fashion in each of the three social role conditions (e.g., "In this situation John should feel entitled to reject certain ideas without seriously considering them"; "In this situation, John should feel obligated to seriously consider viewpoints he disagrees with"; reverse coded: 0 = "disagree" to 10 = "agree"). In this experiment, participants did *not* respond to the "you" scenarios, which asked them to imagine that they personally occupied the role of the protagonist. These "you" scenarios were rated in a fifth experiment that follows.

The experimental procedure employed in these last two experiments possesses many advantages. First, it provides a manipulation check to ensure the experimental manipulation effectively manipulates the individual's relative level of expertise. Second, in accordance with role theory, it enables one to document that social norms regarding open-mindedness differ *within* the individual when the individual's (relative) social role varies across situations. Third, this experiment employs a within-subject design that completely controls for the effect of individual-difference variables, including individual differences in previously acquired political knowledge. Fourth, because the experimental manipulation does not elicit feelings of success or failure, it is less likely to influence the individual's emotional state—thereby ruling out alternative interpretations that involve emotion (e.g., feelings of security, anger, sadness).[4]

Perhaps most importantly, unlike the previous experiments, these experiments included a control condition. In this condition, the participant did not occupy the role of expert or novice. This enabled us to distinguish the Earned Dogmatism Hypothesis from the Obligated Novice Hypothesis. The Earned Dogmatism Hypothesis predicts that, relative to the control condition, the "high-expertise" condition will increase normative entitlement to respond in a closed-minded manner and decrease open-minded cognition. The Obligated Novice Hypothesis predicts that, relative to the control condition, the "low-expertise" role will decrease normative entitlement to respond in a closed-minded manner and increase open-minded cognition. The results obtained in the previous experiments can be interpreted as supporting either (or both) of these hypotheses.

In the fourth experiment, analysis of the manipulation check data confirmed that the experimental manipulation was extremely effective. Indeed, nearly 100% of the participants correctly identified whether each situational scenario involved people who "know a great deal about politics," "know very little about politics," or "are pretty typical in terms of their knowledge of politics." The most interesting effects were those that emerged when predicting the normative entitlement ratings. Importantly, the Obligated Novice Hypothesis was not supported. That is, average normative entitlement ratings did *not* differ when comparing the "low-expertise" condition to the "control" condition. In contrast, the Earned Dogmatism Hypothesis was strongly supported. In comparison to the control condition, the high-expertise condition significantly increased ratings of normative entitlement (Ottati et al., 2015). Consequently, we performed a fifth experiment that exclusively focused on the Earned Dogmatism Hypothesis (i.e., the low-expertise role condition was dropped).

Switching Social Roles

Although individuals may exhibit a chronic tendency to be open- or closed-minded with regard to political affairs, they will also exhibit systematic fluctuations in open-mindedness that are associated with the different social roles they occupy in various social situations. An interesting feature of the Earned Dogmatism Hypothesis is that it accommodates variation in open-mindedness that arises when an individual occupies the role of "political expert" in one situation, but occupies a less elevated political role in another situation. Role fluctuations are prevalent in everyday life. Indeed, during the course of a single day, individuals frequently move from one social role (e.g., mother at home) to another (e.g., lawyer at work).

In examining situational fluctuations in open-mindedness, we performed a fifth experiment that focuses on predictions generated by the Earned Dogmatism Hypothesis. Because the Obligated Novice Hypothesis was not supported in the fourth experiment, the fifth experiment eliminated the "low-expertise" condition. That is, each participant was simply exposed to the "high-expertise" and "control" condition scenarios. Participants read each of these scenarios twice, first imagining that "John" was the protagonist and then imagining that they themselves ("You") were the protagonist in the scenario. After reading the "John" version, participants provided normative entitlement ratings. After reading the "You" version, participants reported their *personal* level of open-mindedness by completing the Situation-Specific Open-Minded Cognition scale. This six-item scale is virtually identical to the Political Open-Minded Cognition scale, except that the political domain phrasing is replaced with situation-specific phrasing. For example, the item "I often tune out political messages I disagree with" was changed to "In this situation, I would tune out messages I disagree with." Research confirms that Situation-Specific Open-Minded Cognition systematically varies across situations. For example, Situation-Specific Open-Minded Cognition is low when individuals encounter political viewpoints that blatantly contradict mainstream opinion, and high when individuals encounter viewpoints that fall within an acceptable range of public opinion (Ottati et al., 2018). Moreover, Situation-Specific Open-Minded Cognition is positively associated with a core manifestation of open-mindedness, a tendency to selectively attend to political information that contradicts one's preexisting political predispositions (Ottati et al., 2018).

The Earned Dogmatism Hypothesis was supported once again in Experiment 5. Normative entitlement ratings were higher in the "high-expertise" condition than control condition. Situation-Specific Open-Minded Cognition was lower in the "high-expertise" condition than control condition. Moreover, supplementary analyses confirmed that the effect of self-perceived political expertise (expert versus control) on Situation-Specific Open-Minded Cognition was partially mediated by normative entitlement. Specifically, normative entitlement was negatively associated with Situation-Specific Open-Minded Cognition. In addition, examination of the adjusted cell means revealed that the magnitude of the Self-Perceived Expertise effect on Situation-Specific Open-Minded Cognition was reduced when controlling for normative entitlement. Last, a Sobel's test confirmed that normative entitlement did indeed mediate the effect of self-perceived political expertise on Situation-Specific Open-Minded Cognition.

Earned Dogmatism: Summing Up the Empirical Evidence

Recent research regarding the determinants of Open-Minded Cognition emphasizes that open-mindedness is malleable and influenced by a variety of situational cues. According to the Situational Merit Standard Hypothesis, different situations activate different normative standards which, in turn, elicit different levels of open-mindedness (Ottati et al., 2018). The Situational Merit Standard Hypothesis has been supported in multiple studies that manipulate a variety of situational cues. Thus, for example, situations that promote morally objectionable viewpoints (e.g., ethnic cleansing) elicit lower levels of open-mindedness than situations that promote viewpoints that are compatible with mainstream values. Preliminary work also suggests individuals are more likely to listen in an open-minded manner when conversing with an open-minded conversation partner than when conversing with a dogmatic conversation partner.

The Earned Dogmatism Hypothesis can be viewed as both an instantiation and extension of the Situational Merit Standard Hypothesis. The Earned Dogmatism Hypothesis *instantiates* the Situational Merit Standard Hypothesis because it presumes that an individual can occupy a specific role in one situation but a completely different social role in another situation (Katz & Kahn, 1978; Triandis, 1972; Triandis et al., 1984). Thus, for example, a college student majoring in political science might occupy the role of "political expert" when speaking with a group of high school students, but occupy the role of "political novice" when speaking with a group of political science professors. In this fashion, these two situations activate distinct social roles associated with distinct sets of normative entitlements and obligations. Consequently, these two situations elicit different levels of open-mindedness in the political science student. Experiments 4 and 5 provide strong evidence that effects of this nature are indeed real (Ottati et al., 2015).

The Earned Dogmatism Hypothesis *extends* the Situational Merit Standard Hypothesis because it implies two individuals can occupy distinct social roles in the same situation (Katz & Kahn, 1978; Triandis, 1972; Triandis et al., 1984). Consider, for example, a political discussion that focuses on foreign policy in the Middle East. In this particular situation, a Middle East scholar occupies the role of "expert," whereas a social worker occupies the role of "novice." Consequently, in this situation, the set of normative entitlements and obligations differs for these two individuals. In particular, dogmatism is viewed as more warranted, justifiable, or appropriate when exhibited by the Middle East expert than when exhibited by the social worker.

In sum, social norms entitle experts to be more dogmatic. Consequently, conditions that promote self-perceptions of high expertise increase dogmatic processing. This Earned Dogmatism Effect was obtained in multiple experiments (Ottati et al., 2015). Specifically, it emerged when using a success (high expertise) versus failure (low expertise) manipulation of test performance to influence self-perceptions of political expertise (Experiments 2 and 3). It also emerged when examining how a participant responds to two different situations, a situation in which the participant occupies the role of "political expert" versus a situation in which the participant does not occupy an elevated social position. Importantly, these effects emerged under conditions that rule out alternative interpretations involving actual political knowledge. Thus, the current findings provide compelling evidence that supports the Earned Dogmatism Hypothesis. Self-perceptions of expertise increase normative entitlement to be closed-minded, which in turn, decrease open-minded cognition.

Conclusion

A comprehensive understanding of the relation between political expertise and open-minded cognition requires that political psychologists make a distinction between individual differences in political knowledge and self-perceptions of political expertise. There are four reasons why this is the case. First, research confirms that self-perceptions of performance often fail to strongly correlate with objective measures of performance and expertise. Second, individual differences in political knowledge are relatively stable, changing only incrementally as individuals gradually progress in their "political education." In contrast, self-perceptions of political expertise are quite malleable, varying across situations that people encounter in their everyday life. Third, self-perceptions of political expertise influence open-mindedness in the political domain even when controlling for individual differences in political knowledge. Fourth, a comparison of effects elicited by self-perceived expertise and effects elicited by actual political knowledge reveals that these two components of expertise can produce distinct and sometimes opposite effects on political open-mindedness.

Notes

1. This chapter was made possible through the support of a grant from the Fuller Theological Seminary/Thrive Center in concert with the John Templeton Foundation (IH-111). Opinions are those of the authors and do not necessarily reflect the views of the Fuller Thrive Center or the John Templeton Foundation. Address correspondence

to Victor Ottati, Department of Psychology, Loyola University of Chicago, 1032 W. Sheridan Rd., Chicago, IL, 60626, vottati@luc.edu.
2. All of the Earned Dogmatism experiments were run on MTurk. Four of the experiments employed a simple design involving a single, dichotomous independent variable. One experiment employed a design involving a single, trichotomous independent variable. Sample characteristics were similar in all five experiments. Across all five experiments; the average cell size was 20, average age was 34, average percent of females was 50%, average percent of non-whites was 21%, average percent Democrats was 56%, and the average percent Republicans was 27%. This does not constitute a formal, representative sample of the U.S. voting age public (e.g., the sample is more Democratic than the U.S. voting population). However, this sample does possess considerable variation in terms of key voter characteristics (age, gender, race, and partisanship).
3. Although the exclusion procedure eliminates participants who did not believe the false feedback, it produces another problem. By excluding participants who score high in the difficult (but not easy) condition, this procedure creates a confound between actual political knowledge and self-perceptions of expertise. Namely, the average level of political knowledge is lower in the low self-perceived expertise condition (failure) than in the high self-perceived expertise condition (success). Experiments 3–5 employ designs that completely eliminate this problem.
4. Although space constraints preclude a more detailed description of Experiments 4 and 5 here, it is important to note that explicit steps were taken to eliminate alternative interpretations in terms of other variables (i.e., state self-esteem, feelings of power, euphoria, insecurity, anger, irritability, sadness, anxiety, attitude certainty, and attitude extremity). Specifically, analysis of supplementary data revealed that most of these variables failed to differ when comparing the high-expertise condition to the control condition. Borderline differences emerged when comparing feelings of irritability, sadness, and power in these two conditions. Thus, when comparing the high-expertise condition to the control condition in Experiment 5, these variables were included as control variables (see Ottati, Price, Wilson, & Sumaktoyo, 2015 for a more detailed description).

References

Alicke, M. D. & Govorun, O. (2005). The better-than-average effect. In M. D. Alicke, D. A. Dunning, & J. Krueger (Eds.), *The self in social judgment* (pp. 85–106). New York: Taylor & Francis.

Brown, J. D. & Gallagher, F. M. (1992). Coming to terms with failure: Private self-enhancement and public self-effacement. *Journal of Experimental Social Psychology*, 28(1), 3–22.

Delli Carpini, M. X. & Keeter, S. (1991). Stability and change in the U.S. public's knowledge of politics. *Public Opinion Quarterly*, 55, 583–612.

Dunning, D., Johnson, K., Ehrlinger, J., & Kruger, J. (2003). Why people fail to recognize their own incompetence. *Current Directions in Psychological Science*, 12(3), 83–87.

Eagly, A. H., Chen, S., Chaiken, S., & Shaw-Barnes, K. (1999). The impact of attitudes on memory: An affair to remember. *Psychological Bulletin*, 125, 64–89.

Federico, C. M., Hunt, C. V., & Ergun, D. (2009). Political expertise, social worldviews, and ideology: Translating "competitive jungles" and "dangerous worlds" into ideological reality. *Social Justice Research*, 22(2–3), 259–279.

Federico, C. M. & Schneider, M. C. (2007). Political expertise and the use of ideology: Moderating effects of evaluative motivation. *Public Opinion Quarterly*, 71(2), 221–252.

Fiske, S. T. & Kinder, D. R. (1981). Involvement, expertise, and schema use: Evidence from political cognition. In N. Cantor & J. F. Kihlstrom (Eds.), *Personality, cognition, and social interaction* (pp. 171–190). Hillsdale, NJ: Lawrence Erlbaum.

Goren, P. (1997). Political expertise and issue voting in presidential elections. *Political Research Quarterly*, 50(2), 387–412.
Goren, P. (2000). Political expertise and principled political thought. *Political Research Quarterly*, 53(1), 117–136.
Hart, W., Ottati, V. C., & Krumdick, N. D. (2011). Physical attractiveness and candidate evaluation: A model of correction. *Political Psychology*, 32(2), 181–203.
Heatherton, T. F. & Polivy, J. (1991). Development and validation of a scale for measuring state self-esteem. *Journal of Personality and Social Psychology*, 60(6), 895.
Hsu, M. L. & Price, V. (1993). Political expertise and affect effects on news processing. *Communication Research*, 20(5), 671–695.
Katz, D. & Kahn, R. L. (1978). *The social psychology of organizations*. New York: Wiley-Blackwell.
Krosnick, J. A. (1990). Expertise and political psychology. *Social Cognition*, 8(1), 1–8.
Kruger, J. & Dunning, D. (1999). Unskilled and unaware of it: how difficulties in recognizing one's own incompetence lead to inflated self-assessments. *Journal of Personality and Social Psychology*, 77(6), 1121.
Kruglanski, A. W. & Mayseless, O. (1987). Motivational effects in the social comparison of opinions. *Journal of Personality and Social Psychology*, 53(5), 834.
Lau, R. R. & Redlawsk, D. P. (2001). Advantages and disadvantages of cognitive heuristics in political decision making. *American Journal of Political Science*, 951–971.
Lavine, H., Borgida, E., & Sullivan, J. L. (2000). On the relationship between attitude involvement and attitude accessibility: Toward a cognitive-motivational model of political information processing. *Political Psychology*, 21(1), 81–106. Retrieved from http://dx.doi.org/10.1111/0162-895X.00178
Lavine, H. G., Johnston, C. D., & Steenbergen, M. R. (2012). *The ambivalent partisan: How critical loyalty promotes democracy*. Oxford: Oxford University Press.
Leary, M. & Hoyle, R. (2015). *General and specific intellectual humility: Conceptualization, measurement, and validation*. Presented at the Intellectual Humility: Scientific, Philosophical, and Theological Perspectives Conference, Catalina Island, CA, May, 2015.
Lodge, M. & Hamill, R. (1986). A partisan schema for political information processing. *The American Political Science Review*, 505–520.
Lodge, M. & Taber, C. S. (2013). *The rationalizing voter*. Cambridge: Cambridge University Press.
Lusk, C. M. & Judd, C. M. (1988). Political expertise and the structural mediators of candidate evaluations. *Journal of Experimental Social Psychology*, 24(2), 105–126.
Luskin, R. C. (1990). Explaining political sophistication. *Political Behavior*, 12(4), 331–361.
McGraw, K. M., Lodge, M., & Stroh, P. (1990). On-line processing in candidate evaluation: The effects of issue order, issue importance, and sophistication. *Political Behavior*, 12(1), 41–58.
McGraw, K. M. & Pinney, N. (1990). The effects of general and domain-specific expertise on political memory and judgment. *Social Cognition*, 8(1), 9.
McGraw, K. M., Pinney, N., & Neumann, D. (1991). Memory for political actors: Contrasting the use of semantic and evaluative organizational strategies. *Political Behavior*, 13(2), 165–180.
Na, J., Choi, I., & Sul, S. (2013). I like you because you think in the "right" way: Culture and ideal thinking. *Social Cognition*, 31(3), 390–404.
Nickerson, R. S. (1998). Confirmation bias: A ubiquitous phenomenon in many guises. *Review of General Psychology*, 2(2), 175–220.
Ottati, V. (2015). *Open minded cognition: General, political, religious, and situation-specific components*. Invited Presentation at the Annual Meeting of the Midwest Psychological Association, May.

Ottati, V., Fishbein, M., & Middlestadt, S. E. (1988). Determinants of voters' beliefs about the candidates' stands on the issues: The role of evaluative bias heuristics and the candidates' expressed message. *Journal of Personality and Social Psychology*, 55(4), 517.

Ottati, V. C. & Isbell, L. M. (1996). Effects on mood during exposure to target information on subsequently reported judgments: An on-line model of misattribution and correction. *Journal of Personality and Social Psychology*, 71(1), 39.

Ottati, V., Price, E. D., Wilson, C., & Sumaktoyo, N. (2015). When self-perceptions of expertise increase closed-minded cognition: The earned dogmatism effect. *Journal of Experimental Social Psychology*, 61, 131–138.

Ottati, V., Wilson, C., & Price, E. (2018). *Situation-specific open-minded cognition.* Unpublished Manuscript.

Price, E., Ottati, V., Wilson, C., & Kim, S. (2015). Open-minded cognition. *Personality and Social Psychology Bulletin*, 41(11), 1488–1504.

Redlawsk, D. P. (2002). Hot cognition or cool consideration? Testing the effects of motivated reasoning on political decision making. *The Journal of Politics*, 64(4), 1021–1044.

Sarbin, T. R. & Allen, V. L. (1968). Role theory. In G. Lindzey & E. Aronson (Eds.), *The handbook of social psychology* (2nd ed., Vol. 1, pp. 488–567). Reading, MA: Addison-Wesley.

Schwarz, N. (2011). Feelings-as-information theory. In P. A. M. Van Lange, A. W. Kruglanski, & E. T. Higgins (Eds.), *Handbook of theories of social psychology* (Vol. 1, pp. 290–308). London: Sage.

Schwarz, N., Bless, H., Strack, F., Klumpp, G., Rittenaur-Schatka, H., & Simons, A. (1991). Ease of retrieval as information: Another look at the availability heuristic. *Journal of Personality and Social Psychology*, 61(2), 195–202.

Taber, C. S. & Lodge, M. (2006). Motivated skepticism in the evaluation of political beliefs. *American Journal of Political Science*, 50(3), 755–769. Retrieved from http://dx.doi.org/10.1111/j.1540-5907.2006.00214.x

Tewksbury, D. (1999). Differences in how we watch the news: The impact of processing goals and expertise on evaluations of political actors. *Communication Research*, 26(1), 4–29.

Trafimow, D. & Sniezek, J. A. (1994). Perceived expertise and its effect on confidence. *Organizational Behavior and Human Decision Processes*, 57, 290–302.

Triandis, H. C. (1972). *The analysis of subjective culture.* New York: Wiley-Blackwell.

Triandis, H. C. (1980). Values, attitudes, and interpersonal behavior. In H. Howe & M. Page (Eds.), *Nebraska symposium on motivation* (pp. 195–260). Lincoln: University of Nebraska Press.

Triandis, H. C., Marin, G., Hui, C. H., Lisansky, J., & Ottati, V. (1984). Role perceptions of Hispanic young adults. *Journal of Cross-Cultural Psychology*, 15, 297–320.

Zaller, J. R. (1992). *The nature and origins of mass opinion.* New York: Cambridge University Press.

7
BELIEF CHANGE
A Bayesian Perspective

Marco R. Steenbergen and Howard Lavine

The dynamics of political beliefs have been a central focus of Milton Lodge's work ever since he introduced the online model of candidate evaluation some 30 years ago. The present chapter very much fits the character of that work and, indeed, was inspired by a conversation between Lodge and the first author many years ago. The use of Bayesian ideas to understand continuity and change in political beliefs is not entirely new to political science (e.g., Gerber & Green, 1997). Yet much of the existing literature focuses on aggregate opinion shifts. In this chapter, we honor Lodge's emphasis on the micro-logic of politics and apply the Bayesian perspective to individual belief change.

The question of whether citizens are open- or closed-minded is as old as political thought. A crucial aspect of this question is the degree to which citizens are able and willing to revise their prior beliefs. This is a cornerstone of all democratic conceptions (e.g., Dewey, 2004; Galston, 1988; Habermas, 1996). In a representative democracy, for example, citizens should be able to assess performance accurately if they are going to hold elites accountable. And in a deliberative democracy, citizens are expected to yield to the "unforced force of the better argument," as Habermas (1996, p. 305) famously put it.

But what evidence do we have that people change their beliefs when faced with evidence or arguments that are inconsistent with those beliefs? There has been great disagreement about this question. Early research on framing, for example, suggested that people change their beliefs very quickly—perhaps even too quickly—(e.g., Entman, 1989). On the other hand, there is considerable evidence of resistance to belief updating even when there are important new facts. In a famous experiment which inspired the present study, Lord, Ross, and Lepper (1979) found that the provision of evidence against the death penalty resulted in attitude polarization among death penalty advocates, a response that is difficult to reconcile with belief updating. Similarly, Lodge and Taber find that citizens are remarkably persistent in their beliefs, engaging in biased processing to preserve them as much as they can (Lodge & Taber, 2013; Taber & Lodge, 2006). Similar findings have been reported by Fischle (2000) and Redlawsk (2002). The result is a series of misperceptions about the political world that seem difficult to correct (Bartels, 2002; Nyhan & Reifler, 2010). All of this is said to contribute to the much-maligned "fact-free" politics that we see today.

So, are citizens too resistant to opposite evidence and arguments, too easily manipulated, or what? To answer this question, we need a yardstick of how citizens *should* update their beliefs. Without it, we do not know whether belief revisions are too steep or too shallow. This has led to the criticism that broad-sweeping claims about the virtues and vices of belief revision have, at best, a tenuous relationship with the empirical evidence (Gerber & Green, 1999).

There is a clear need for a normative model of belief revision to which actual patterns of belief change can be compared. At the level of aggregate public opinion, Gerber and Green (1997) have invoked a Bayesian framework for this purpose. In this paper, we invoke this framework at the *individual* level, i.e., we measure the elements of Bayes's rule for each person, deriving an expected posterior belief, which then serves as the benchmark against which actual posterior beliefs can be compared.

Our choice of Bayes's rule is not arbitrary. Apart from the fact that Bayesian updating models dominate economics and political science, especially in formal theory (Von Neumann & Morgenstern, 1944), there is growing evidence that human learning can be accurately described in this manner (Gopnik, 2012; Lu, Yuille, Liljeholm, Cheng, & Holyoak, 2008; Tenenbaum, Kemp, Griffiths, & Goodman, 2011). Although Bayesianism has not yet been confirmed as a model of the mind (Eberhardt & Danks, 2011), it is plausible and, as such, provides a reasonable standard for judging belief revision.

Our goal, then, is to consider the belief updating process from a Bayesian perspective that can shed light on whether and how belief change is biased. We also consider the role of a crucial individual-difference variable, to wit ambivalence. Drawing on motivational theories in psychology, we argue that biases should be less pronounced when individuals hold conflicting beliefs about a political issue. We explore these topics using data from a study about the issue of capital punishment.

Bayesian Belief Updating

Bayes's rule provides a widely accepted normative standard for belief updating (Baron, 1994). It states a logically consistent mechanism for combining prior beliefs with empirical evidence. Here, we apply the rule to a situation in which an individual's prior beliefs are challenged by contradictory evidence.

Let H denote a *statement of belief* such as "capital punishment is an effective deterrent of violent crime." (As we shall see, we used this statement in our study.)

Further, let $\bar{H}$ $ be a second, *complementary* belief statement, e.g., "capital punishment is *not* an effective deterrent of violent crime."[1] We assume that individuals have *priors* for H and $\bar{H}$, i.e., they have an a priori sense of the truthfulness of each statement.[2] These priors may be expressed in terms of subjective probabilities (Edwards, 1954). Let Pr(H) denote the prior for H. If $0 < \Pr(H) < 0.5$, this means that an individual does not believe H to be true (e.g., he or she does not believe capital punishment to be an effective deterrent of violent crime). Lower values in this range suggest greater perceived untruthfulness of H. By contrast, if $0 < \Pr(H) < 1$, then the individual believes H to be more or less true. Higher values in this range indicate greater perceived truthfulness of H. Finally, if Pr(H) = 0.5, the individual is uncertain about the truthfulness of H: he or she believes it just as likely that H is true than that it is false. The prior for $\bar{H}$ is captured by Pr($\bar{H}$): since $\bar{H}$ is the complement of H, it follows logically that $\Pr(\bar{H}) = 1 - \Pr(H)$. This not only reflects a basic axiom of probability theory but also captures a basic psychological consistency mechanism.

Now imagine that *evidence D*, is introduced. Bayes's rule states that an individual should valuate the consistency of this evidence with both H and $\bar{H}$. Let Pr($D\backslash H$) denote the *likelihood* that the evidence would have been observed if H were true. For example, assuming capital punishment is an effective deterrent of violent crime, how likely would it be to find evidence that crime rates have increased in states that apply the death penalty? Further, let $\Pr(D \backslash \bar{H})$ denote the likelihood that the evidence would have been obtained if $\bar{H}$ were true.

Bayes's theorem now specifies how the prior beliefs and evidence should be combined to form a *posterior* belief:

$$\Pr(H|D) = \frac{\Pr(D|H)\Pr(H)}{\Pr(D|H)\Pr(H) + \Pr(D|\bar{H})\Pr(\bar{H})} \quad (1)$$

The posterior for $\bar{H}$ is given by $1-\Pr(H/D)$. These posteriors are understood to be the beliefs that individuals normatively should hold after considering the evidence.

In this chapter, as in much of the literature, we are interested in belief updating when the evidence aims to challenge an individual's priors. To see the predictions that follow from Bayes's rule in this case, we re-parameterize equation (1). Expressing the left-hand side as the ratio of the prior over the posterior, invoking the complementarity of H and $\bar{H}$, and setting $\Pr(D \backslash \bar{H}) = k\Pr(D \backslash H)$ (for $k \geq 0$), we obtain

$$\frac{\Pr(H)}{\Pr(H|D)} = (1-k)\Pr(H) + k \quad (2)$$

Against the backdrop of (2), several scenarios can unfold. For example, there will be no belief updating when Pr(H) = 1 or Pr(H) = 0. If someone already is convinced of the truth, no amount of evidence will suffice to alter that person's mind. If the prior lies between 0 and 1 then belief updating can take place. Its nature, however, depends critically on k, which may be interpreted as a likelihood ratio of sorts. First, imagine that the individual believes the information to contradict H but not $\bar{H}$. In this case, $k > 1$ and the left-hand side ratio in (2) exceeds 1; the perceived degree of truthfulness of H has declined. Second, imagine the evidence is judged to be neutral, i.e., equally consistent with H and $\bar{H}$. Now $k = 1$, as is the left-hand side of (2). There should be no belief revision because the evidence is non-diagnostic. Finally, consider a person who believes the evidence to be more consistent with H than with $\bar{H}$, so that $k < 1$. Now the left-hand side of (2) is less than 1, meaning that the posterior exceeds the prior. This constitutes a polarization effect of sorts. We now explore what may cause such an effect.

Biases in Belief Updating

Equation (2) suggests several places where biased information processing may occur. First, decision makers may show a confirmation bias in the interpretation of the evidence. Second, they may show a conservatism bias in adjusting their beliefs in response to the evidence. Both biases are in the direction of the status quo, in that they cause individuals to hold onto their existing beliefs.

A confirmation bias exists when a decision maker interprets evidence as favorable or neutral toward a prior belief when, in fact, the evidence is to some degree contradictory of the belief.[3] This may be accomplished by discounting the contradictory information, by counterarguing it, or through some other cognitive response (Petty, Ostrom, & Brock, 1981).

The political and social psychological literatures are replete with empirical examples of confirmation bias (Ditto & Lopez, 1992; Fischle, 2000; Houston & Fazio, 1989; Klein & Kunda, 1992; Koehler, 1993; Kruglanski & Freund, 1983; Kunda, 1987, 1990; Lodge & Taber, 2013; Lord et al., 1979; Pyszczynski & Greenberg, 1987; Redlawsk, 2002; Sorrentino & Higgins, 1986; Stein, 1988; Taber & Lodge, 2006). Fischle (2000) observed this bias in evaluations of a political figure. In a panel study during the Monica Lewinsky scandal, he found that supporters of President Clinton were more likely to discount and counterargue evidence about his involvement with Lewinsky. Two prominent discounting mechanisms emerged. First, Clinton supporters expressed uncertainty about the truth of allegations against the president. Second, they considered the Lewinsky affair less important. Counterarguments often took the form of conspiracy theories, whereby the scandal was attributed to a right-wing effort to unseat the president.

Confirmation bias is not limited to political person perception. In a seminal study, Lord et al. (1979) showed that people who hold strong opinions about capital punishment took supporting evidence at face value, while critically scrutinizing contradictory evidence. A similar pattern was observed by Taber and Lodge (2006) for the issues of affirmative action and gun control. They found that people who held strong opinions on those issues (and were political sophisticates) believed contradictory arguments to be weaker than supporting ones. The reading times for the contradictory arguments were also longer for these individuals, due to their cognitive efforts to counterargue the arguments. Finally, in a thought-listing task, these individuals listed more belief-congruent than incongruent thoughts. The study also found that the confirmation bias produces attitude polarization: individuals became more extreme in their attitudes than they had been before exposure to counter-attitudinal arguments.

While confirmation bias and attitude polarization are sometimes interpreted as evidence that citizens are not Bayesians (Fischle, 2000; Redlawsk, 2002), these belief phenomena are, in fact, perfectly consistent with Bayes's rule (Gerber & Green, 1999). In terms of equation (2), the confirmation bias manifests itself in the value of k, which is set to favor the prior belief. As we have shown, polarization—in the sense of a posterior belief that is stronger than the prior belief—is then a logical consequence.

A second bias that may occur is conservatism—an insufficient adjustment of the prior beliefs in the light of evidence as it is interpreted by the decision maker.[4] This is a violation of Bayes's rule because the observed posterior remains too close to the prior. That is, too little weight is given to the evidence, akin to the phenomenon of anchoring and insufficient adjustment (Tversky & Kahneman, 1974).

The conservatism bias is well established in behavioral decision theory. A classical research paradigm is the "bookbags-and-pokerchips" task of Edwards (1968). In this design, there are two bags, I and II, containing white and red poker chips. The ratio of white to red chips is 70:30 in bag I and 30:70 in bag II. One of the bags is randomly chosen, and it is the participant's task to determine which bag it is by drawing repeated samples (with replacement). A reasonable prior is that there is a 0.5 probability that bag I was selected. Imagine now that in 12 samples, a participant obtained 8 white and 4 red chips. Then the posterior belief that bag I was selected should be 0.97. However, Edwards found that the typical participant's posterior was in the 0.7–0.8 range. Similar findings have been found in numerous other studies (Lopes, 1985; Nisbett & Ross, 1980; Osherson, 1990; Peterson, Schneider, & Miller, 1965; Phillips & Edwards, 1966; Shanteau, 1972, 1975; Slovic & Lichtenstein, 1971). They indicate a tendency for decision makers to adjust their priors insufficiently in the light of evidence.

A characteristic of these studies is that the likelihood of the data can be established objectively, using frequentist probability concepts. In the political belief domain, it is much less clear that the objective likelihood of evidence can be established under all circumstances. While this may facilitate subjective evaluation and interpretation of evidence (e.g., the confirmation bias), Bayes's rule still predicts a particular pattern of belief updating that ensures the logical consistency of beliefs. If, in actuality, beliefs are not updated sufficiently compared to this rule, we may view this as a conservatism bias.

The Role of Ambivalence

An important question is whether all individuals are equally prone to these biases. In terms of the confirmation bias, much attention has been paid to the strength of prior beliefs. Taber and Lodge (2006) demonstrate that individuals who hold strong prior beliefs are more likely to discount and counterargue evidence that contradicts those beliefs (see also Pomerantz, Chaiken, & Tordesillas, 1995). The theoretical rationale for this finding is that strong convictions generate a partisan *information-processing motivation*. This prompts individual to defend their beliefs: their ego is invested in those beliefs and they will not give up on them without putting up a fight first (see also Kunda, 1987, 1990).

But a partisan motivation is not the only possible information-processing motivation. As dual-process theorists in social psychology have argued (see e.g., Chaiken, Liberman, & Eagly, 1989; Petty & Cacioppo, 1986), some people, some of the time are motivated not by partisan considerations, but by accuracy or "validity-seeking" goals in which individuals seek to hold an attitude that best squares with the available evidence. Such a goal produces an entirely different style of information processing. Rather than ignoring or discarding evidence, individuals motivated by accuracy process information evenhandedly. They do not automatically counterargue evidence that comes their way. Rather, they take the information seriously, weight its merits, and use it to inform their beliefs (see Kunda, 1987, 1990). In other words, they act much like the citizen that most democratic theorists envision.

Who would be motivated by accuracy? We believe that individuals who are ambivalent about the issue that is at stake fall into this group. Ambivalence means that an individual holds conflicting considerations about an issue. That is, some considerations lead the individual to favor a policy, while others lead to opposition of that same policy.[5] There is now a great deal of evidence suggesting that ambivalence moderates political information processing. For instance, policy attitudes marked by evaluative conflict are held with less certainty and reliability (Alvarez & Brehm, 1995, 2002), they are more difficult to retrieve from memory (Huckfeldt & Sprague, 1998; Lavine, Borgida, & Sullivan, 2000; Lodge & Taber, 2005), more vulnerable to persuasion and response effects in surveys (Bassili, 1996; Lavine, Huff, Wagner, & Sweeney, 1998; Tourangeau, Rasinski, Bradburn, & D'Andrade, 1989), and less likely to predict subsequent political behavior than relatively univalent (non-ambivalent) attitudes (Lavine, 2001; Lavine, Johnston, & Steenbergen, 2012).

Delving more deeply into the matter, two mechanisms are responsible for the prediction that ambivalence should moderate biases. First, biased processing is typically associated with hot cognition (Lodge & Taber, 2013; Redlawsk, 2002; Taber & Lodge, 2006). The hot cognition hypothesis holds that prior beliefs and attitudes come to mind automatically and subsequently color all information processing, including that of contradictory evidence. However, ambivalent attitudes—and one would assume beliefs as well—lack the quality of automaticity (Lodge & Taber, 2005) and, hence, are less prone to a biasing effect. Second, ambivalence makes it less likely that individuals reach their confidence threshold, i.e., the point at which they feel confident they have arrived at the right decision or judgment. This is an important trigger of systematic processing (Chaiken et al., 1989). While such processing is not synonymous with unbiased processing—a great deal of effort can go into producing biased perceptions—under some conditions there is likely to be a correlation. This should happen, for example, when there is a precise balance between the conflicting considerations—a sort of knife edge situation—which literally implies that the individual is a priori undecided. This is the scenario we shall consider in this paper.

The distinctive processing motivation of ambivalent individuals should thus leave a mark on belief change. We anticipate four effects that we test in this paper. First, in terms of a confirmation bias, ambivalence should moderate the effect of prior belief strength. If a person holds a policy-relevant belief strongly, this should normally motivate that person to interpret contradictory evidence in a biased manner. But this should not be the case if the person also holds a second policy-relevant belief that is inconsistent with the first belief. In this case, the evaluative direction of the evidence may contradict the first belief but it can be quite consistent with the second belief. Thus, the individual should be less biased in the interpretation of the evidence.

Second, we expect ambivalence by itself to produce a more accurate perception of the evidence, at least when the individual is placed in an evaluative information-processing mode. We put this as a condition because evaluation is essential for making ambivalent individuals aware of the conflicting considerations that they hold. Absent an evaluative goal, it is not clear that ambivalent citizens pay any more attention to the evidence and how it relates to their preexisting beliefs than non-ambivalent citizens. However, when called on to evaluate the evidence, citizens will relate the evidence to their existing beliefs. For ambivalent citizens, this means that the evidence is interpreted in light of conflicting considerations, and the awareness of this conflict should trigger evenhanded processing of the evidence. In contrast, non-ambivalent citizens will quickly realize that the evidence contradicts their beliefs and this should trigger a partisan processing motivation that facilitates a confirmation bias. Thus, we expect an interaction between ambivalence and processing mode, such that a confirmation bias is less likely when a person is ambivalent and is asked to evaluate the evidence.

Third, ambivalence should also influence conservatism in belief change. In a previous study, we found that conservatism is a second "line of defense" that comes into play only when individuals do not show a confirmation bias (Steenbergen, 2001). But the need to use this line of defense should exist only when a person is non-ambivalent. In that case, contradictory evidence, which indeed is perceived as such, threatens beliefs and a conservatism bias allows the person to still hold onto those beliefs. Ambivalent citizens should not be motivated in this way. Their concern for accuracy should cause them to give due weight to the evidence in belief updating so that they should show a smaller conservatism bias (if they show one at all).

Finally, belief change should have different attitudinal implications for ambivalent than for non-ambivalent citizens. Non-ambivalent citizens may adjust their policy attitudes along with their policy beliefs, but we would expect that their attitudes will remain strongly anchored in the attitudes that existed before the belief change. For ambivalent citizens, these existing attitudes should matter less because they are focused on contemporary information, i.e., the latest evidence. We now describe a study that was designed to test these predictions.

Methods

Participants

The participants in this study were 96 undergraduate students at the University of North Carolina (UNC) at Chapel Hill. The students were enrolled in an introductory American government course, which required their participation in a political science study. Due to the nature of this course, most of the participants were freshmen and sophomores. Around two-thirds of the participants were women, and about 85 percent were white. Forty-eight percent of the sample identified with the Republican Party versus about 40 percent Democrats. In ideological terms, the sample is about equally split between liberals (36 percent) and conservatives (39 percent).

Procedures

The experiment took place in the Political Psychology Laboratory of the Political Science Department at UNC in the spring of 2001. Groups of up to ten participants entered the lab and sat down behind a PC. After receiving detailed instructions and signing the informed consent form, each participant completed a series of practice trials on the PC. The goal of these trials was to familiarize the participants with the question format of the experiment. At the end of the practice trials, the participants had an opportunity to ask clarifying questions about the question format. Only after these questions had been answered did the actual study start. This study was entirely computerized, lasted about 25 minutes, and had three stages.

Stage 1: During the first stage of the experiment, the participants answered a series of questions concerning their level of political interest, their importance ratings of various political issues, and their positions on those issues. One of the issues presented was capital punishment, which was also the focus of the second stage of the experiment.

Stage 2: In the second stage, the participants were asked to express their prior beliefs about two aspects of capital punishment: effectiveness and fairness.[6] They were also asked to evaluate evidence relevant to these aspects and to provide posterior beliefs about them. As we discuss in detail below, an information-processing mode manipulation was implemented during this stage of the study.

Figure 7.1 outlines the experimental paradigm for the second stage of the experiment, which is similar to the procedure described by Slovic and Lichtenstein (1971, p. 671). First, the participants received a belief statement (H) concerning a particular aspect—fairness or effectiveness—of capital punishment. Next, they indicated a prior for this statement ($\Pr(H)$) and an implied prior for the complementary statement ($\Pr(\bar{H}) = 1 - \Pr(H)$). At this point, evidence (D) was introduced. The participants evaluated the consistency of this evidence with the statement that they had received and with its complement; this produced data about $\Pr(D\backslash H)$ and $\Pr(D \setminus \bar{H})$. This information suffices to compute posterior beliefs according to Bayes's rule (1). The final step in the experimental sequence

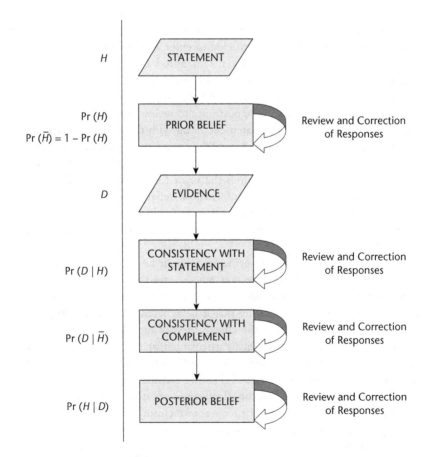

FIGURE 7.1 Experimental Sequence

was to measure the actual posterior beliefs of the participants ($\Pr(H\backslash D)$), which could then be compared with the Bayesian posteriors. Whenever the participants were asked to evaluate a statement or evidence, they were given an opportunity to review and correct their response (as indicated by the curved arrows next to the boxes in Figure 7.1).

In more detail, the participants first saw a statement about the effectiveness of capital punishment:

Capital Punishment Is an Effective Deterrent of Violent Crime

They were then asked: "In your opinion, how true is this statement? That is, how strongly do you believe this statement is true?" They indicated their belief by entering a number from 0 to 100. (This is a modified probability scale where the probabilities are multiplied by 100 to make the scale more user-friendly.) If a participant believed the statement to be untrue, he or she was instructed to enter a number from 0 to 49.99. The more untrue the participant believed the statement to be, the lower the number he or she gave. If a participant believed the statement to be true, then he or she was instructed to enter a number from 50.01 to 100. The truer the participant believed the statement to be, the higher the number he or she gave. Finally, if a participant was uncertain about the truthfulness of the statement, he or she was instructed to enter the number 50.

Next, the participants had an opportunity to review and change their answer. A feedback screen showed the statement along with the prior that the participant had entered. The screen also showed the complementary statement ("capital punishment is not an effective deterrent of violent crime") with its (implied) prior, which was equal to 100 minus the prior for the statement. The participants were asked if the displayed information reflected their beliefs correctly. If they answered "yes," then they moved onto the next step of the experimental sequence. Otherwise, they had unlimited opportunities to change and again review their answer.

The next step was to present evidence relevant to the statement. By design, the participants received evidence that ran counter to their prior belief. Thus, participants who believed that capital punishment is an effective deterrent of violent crime saw evidence suggesting that it is ineffective. In contrast, those who had indicated skepticism about the effectiveness of capital punishment received evidence about its deterrent quality. Participants that had indicated uncertainty were randomly assigned to receive evidence either affirming or denying the effectiveness of capital punishment. Table 7.1 shows examples of the evidence that the participants received concerning the effectiveness of capital punishment; Table 7.2 does the same for fairness. The evidence was taken from news reports and Internet sites of proponents and opponents of the death penalty.

The entire sequence was repeated for a second statement concerning the fairness of capital punishment. This statement read:

TABLE 7.1 Sample Evidence on the Effectiveness of Capital Punishment

Capital Punishment Is Effective

A recent scholarly report claims that states with capital punishment have violent crime rates that are 35 percent lower than states that do not apply the death penalty. This finding remains even after controlling for other differences between states.

Capital Punishment Is Ineffective

The FBI recently released a report suggesting that crime rates have actually increased by as much as 20 percent in those states that have the death penalty. This result holds even after controlling for other factors that may affect the incidence of violent crime.

TABLE 7.2 Sample Evidence on the Fairness of Capital Punishment

Capital Punishment Is Fair

According to a recent FBI report, since 1973 only 59 death row inmates have been released after exonerating evidence was brought forth. In the vast majority of cases, people who have received the death penalty are in fact guilty of the crimes of which they are accused.

Capital Punishment Is Unfair

A recent academic study found that there have been more than 350 cases in the U.S. over the last two decades in which a person was sentenced to die for a crime they did not commit. The report also states that 24 innocent people were executed during this time period.

Capital Punishment Wrongfully Executes Innocent People

Again, the participants indicated a prior belief about this statement (and about its complement, "capital punishment does not wrongfully execute innocent people"), read, and evaluated evidence that ran counter to this prior, and provided a posterior belief.

Stage 3: After completing these tasks, the third stage of the experiment started. This stage consisted of a series of political knowledge and demographic questions. In addition, the participants indicated their position on the issue of capital punishment (like they had done in stage 1). Upon completion of this stage, the participants were debriefed and thanked for their cooperation.

Experimental Manipulation

There was one critical between-subjects manipulation, namely the information-processing mode.[7] Half of the participants were randomly assigned to a memory-based condition, which prompted them to memorize the evidence. This goal was primed by the following instruction set at the beginning of stage 2 of the experiment (cf. Taber & Lodge, 2006):

> We will now ask you to evaluate a series of arguments about important political issues. We will also ask you to take a look at some evidence that is relevant to these arguments.
>
> We would like you to pay very close attention to the arguments and evidence. At the end of the study, we will ask you to write a short report outlining as accurately as possible what the evidence is and how it relates to the arguments. It is important that you try to be as accurate as you can.

The other half of the participants were asked to evaluate the evidence. This objective was primed by changing the last two sentences of the instruction set to:

> When you see the evidence, please evaluate whether you agree with it or not. To help you do this, you will have an opportunity to write down your reactions to the information as you encounter it.

In this condition, the participants could list up to three thoughts about the evidence immediately after they read it.

Ambivalence Measure

Our conception of ambivalence centers about the potential conflict between prior beliefs about the effectiveness and fairness of capital punishment. We believe such conflict to be present if some individual feels that capital punishment is effective but unfair, or if she feels that it is fair but not effective. By contrast, the absent of ambivalence is exemplified by people who believe the death penalty to be effective and fair or ineffective and unfair.

We capture ambivalence by computing a Griffin-type measure (see Thompson, Zanna, & Griffin, 1995). This type of measure has become standard in ambivalence research and it serves our purposes well. Specifically, we compute ambivalence as

$$A = \frac{|E - 50| + |F - 50|}{2} - |E - F|$$

Here, E is the person's prior about the statement that "capital punishment is an effective deterrent of violent crime" and F is his or her prior about the statement that "capital punishment executes innocent people." The first term of the formula measures the average strength of the priors, while the second term measures belief inconsistency.

Belief Change 111

Results

We present the results in three parts. First, we consider the way in which the participants evaluated the evidence they received. Next, we discuss participants' posterior beliefs. Finally, we describe the implication of belief change for attitudes about capital punishment.

Interpretation of the Evidence

According to Bayes's theorem, decision makers evaluate the consistency of the evidence they receive with all possible statements of belief. In terms of equation (2), they evaluate $k = \Pr(D \setminus \bar{H}) / \Pr(D \setminus H)$. Depending on the value of the parameter k (and on the prior), the decision maker downgrades the posterior relative to the prior, upgrades the posterior, or does not update at all.

The experiment contained data about $\Pr(D \setminus \bar{H})$ and $\Pr(D \setminus H)$, so that it is possible to compute k. To simplify interpretation and minimize the effects of outliers, we use $\log(k)$ instead of k.[8]

$\Pr(D | \bar{H})$ and about $\Pr(D | H)$, so that it is possible to compute k. To simplify interpretation and to minimize the effect of outliers, we use $\log(k)$ instead of k itself. This measure behaves as follows: (1) $\log(k) < 0$ if $\Pr(D \setminus \bar{H}) < \Pr(D \setminus H)$, i.e., the evidence is deemed more consistent with H than with $\bar{H}$; (2) $\log(k) = 0$ if $\Pr(D \setminus \bar{H}) = \Pr(D \setminus H)$, i.e., the evidence is deemed equally consistent with H and $\bar{H}$; and (3) $\log(k) > 0$ if $\Pr(D \setminus \bar{H}) > \Pr(D \setminus H)$, i.e., the evidence is considered more consistent with $\bar{H}$ than with H.

Table 7.3 displays the ranges and means of $\log(k)$ for different treatment groups. First, consider the top panel of this table, which concerns the statement "capital punishment is an effective deterrent of violent crime." Two-thirds of the sample received evidence that capital punishment is ineffective. This evidence is objectively more consistent with the complementary statement, "capital punishment is not an effective deterrent of violent crime," than with H, so one would expect $\log(k) > 0$. Looking at Table 7.3, one sees that 48.4 percent of the participants acted in accordance with this expectation (mean $\log(k) = 0.919, p < 0.01$). However, the remaining participants, which constitute a majority, did not behave this way. Indeed, 45.3 percent of the participants in this group deemed the evidence more consistent with H than with $\bar{H}$ (mean $\log(k) = -0.323, p < 0.01$). Another 6.3 percent of the participants in this group considered the evidence to be equally consistent with both hypotheses.

One third of the sample received evidence that capital punishment is an effective deterrent of violent crime. This evidence is objectively more consistent with H than with $\bar{H}$ so that one would expect $\text{Log}(k) < 0$. However, as the top panel of Table 7.3 shows, only a minority (21.9 percent) drew this conclusion (mean $\log(k) = -0.316, p < 0.01$). A majority (59.3 percent) evaluated the evidence to be more consistent with $\bar{H}$ than with H (mean $\log(k) = 0.713, p < 0.05$).

TABLE 7.3 Group Differences in Log(k)

Effectiveness of Capital Punishment (CP)

	CP is Ineffective (N=64)		CP is Effective (N=32)	
Log(k)	Percent	Mean	Percent	Mean
< 0	45.3	−.323★★	21.9	−.316★★
= 0	6.3	.000	18.8	.000
> 0	48.4	.919★★	59.3	.713
Overall		.299⁺		.354★

Fairness of Capital Punishment (CP)

	CP is Unfair (N=29)		CP is Fair (N=67)	
Log(k)	Percent	Mean	Percent	Mean
< 0	34.5	−2.529★	40.3	−1.477★★
= 0	17.2	.000	11.9	.000
> 0	48.3	.362★★	47.8	.664★★
Overall		.697⁺		−.278

Notes: ⁺ $p < -.10$, ★ $p < .05$, ★★ $p < .01$ (2-tailed).

Another 18.8 percent of the participants in this group considered the evidence to be equally consistent with both statements.

Similar results emerged for the statement "capital punishment wrongfully executes innocent people." Almost 70 percent of the participants received evidence running counter to this statement. That evidence is objectively more consistent with the complementary statement than with H so that one would expect $\log(k) > 0$. As the bottom panel of Table 7.3 shows, this expectation held true for 47.8 percent of participants that received incongruent information (mean $\log(k) = 0.664, p < 0.01$). However, a sizable portion (40.3 percent) of participants in this group evaluated the evidence to be more consistent with H than with $\bar{H}$ (mean $\log(k) = -1.477, p < 0.01)p$. In addition, 11.9 percent found the evidence to be just as consistent with H than with $\bar{H}$. Overall, $\log(k)$ was -0.278 on the average; while not statistically significant, this is in the wrong direction.

Finally, consider the group of participants who received evidence that capital punishment wrongfully executes innocent people (about 30 percent of the sample). This evidence is objectively more consistent with H than with $\bar{H}$; as a result, we would expect $\log(k) < 0$. As the bottom panel of Table 7.3 reveals, however, only a minority (34.5 percent) of participants perceived the evidence in this manner (mean $\log(k) = -2.529, p < 0.05$). Most of the participants (48.3 percent) in this group drew the opposite conclusion (mean $\log(k) = 0.362, p < 0.01$). A smaller group (17.2 percent) believed the evidence to be equally consistent with H and $\bar{H}$.

These results suggest a distinctive bias in the evaluation of the evidence. Only a minority of the participants interpreted the evidence in the way it was objectively directed. Most of the participants either deemed the evidence non-diagnostic or interpreted it opposite of its direction. Given that the evidence contradicted the prior beliefs of most of the participants, the bias can be interpreted as a confirmation bias (see Ditto & Lopez, 1992; Koehler, 1993; Lord et al., 1979; Taber & Lodge, 2006). That is, most of the participants evaluated the evidence as supportive of or neutral with respect to their prior beliefs when, in fact, the evidence ran counter to them.

To obtain a better sense of the nature of the confirmation bias, we performed an ordered logit analysis of the accuracy of the interpretation of the evidence. By accuracy we mean that a participant correctly identified the direction of the evidence. In this analysis, we combine the effectiveness and fairness dimensions. Thus, correct perception of the evidence on both dimensions yields an accuracy score of 2, correct perception on one dimension yields an accuracy score of 1, and correct perception on neither dimension yields an accuracy score of 0. As a first approximation, we predict accuracy as a function of the strength of the priors, the information-processing manipulation, and political knowledge.[9] Our expectation is that accuracy is less likely when the prior beliefs are strong and when the processing manipulation invites evaluation of the evidence. It should be more likely if political knowledge is high.

The results of this analysis are shown in Table 7.4 under the heading Model 1. As expected, the strength of the priors has a statistically significant negative effect on accuracy. While the signs on the processing manipulation and political knowledge are in the right direction, these two variables fail to attain statistical significance. Thus, the results replicate the finding of Taber and Lodge (2006) that strong prior beliefs tend to produce a confirmation bias whereby evidence is not perceived in the way it was intended.

How does ambivalence change these results? Earlier, we suggested that ambivalence should moderate the impact of the strength of priors and information-processing mode. Hence, we created appropriate interaction terms and re-estimated the model as Model 2. As the results in Table 7.4 suggest, we find support for a moderating effect in two cases: there is a significant interaction of ambivalence with the strength of the effectiveness prior and the processing mode manipulation, but not with the strength of the fairness prior. Multicollinearity and a small sample size may be partially to blame for the one failure, but overall these results are suggestive of a moderating role for ambivalence.

This becomes even clearer when we convert the results into predicted probabilities, as is done in Table 7.5. This table simulates different priors and converts them into corresponding strength and ambivalence measures. These are then translated into the probability of interpreting the evidence correctly 0, 1, or 2 times. We see that univalent beliefs trigger biased interpretation of the evidence, with an accuracy score of 0 being the mode. This tendency becomes even more pronounced when the information-processing mode is evaluative in nature. In

TABLE 7.4 Determinants of the Accuracy of Log(k)

Predictor	Model 1	Model 2
Strength of Effectiveness Prior	−.037★	.026
	(.016)	(.030)
Strength of Fairness Prior	−.035★★	−.080★★
	(.013)	(.028)
Scrutiny Goal	−.301	.977
	(.402)	(.679)
Political Sophistication	.053	−.003
	(.010)	(.112)
Ambivalence		−.092[+]
		(.054)
Ambivalence × Strength 1		.004★★
		(.001)
Ambivalence × Strength 2		−.002
		(.002)
Ambivalence × Goal		.074★
		(.031)
Threshold 1	−1.935★	−1.046
	(.860)	(1.147)
Threshold 2	−.370	.648
	(.835)	(1.136
Pseudo R^2	.069	.126

Notes: Table entries are ML ordered logit estimates with robust standard errors in parentheses.
$N = 96$.
[+] $p <.10$, ★ $p <.05$, ★★ $p <.01$ (2-tailed test).

TABLE 7.5 Predicted Probabilities of Accuracy

Scenario	0	1	2
Univalent-Memorize	.796	.146	.058
Univalent-Scrutinize	.971	.022	.007
Ambivalent-Memorize	.750	.158	.091
Ambivalent-Scrutinize	.120	.142	.738

Notes: Univalent simulations set ambivalence to the minimum value; ambivalent simulations to the maximum value.

these cases, partisan motives seem to dominate the processing of evidence that runs counter to one's prior beliefs. When the processing mode is memorization, ambivalent participants seemed to do only slightly better than univalent participants. However, we see a different pattern when the processing mode is evaluative. Now ambivalent participants seem to be quite accurate, suggesting that this condition triggered balanced information processing for those individuals.

Belief Change **115**

Posterior Beliefs

Knowing a person's prior and evaluation of the evidence, we can compute the posterior using equation (1). How do these predicted posteriors relate to the actual posteriors that the participants provided? Figure 7.2 shows the scatter plots of the observed and Bayesian posteriors for the two belief statements that the participants evaluated. In each plot, the thin gray reference line indicates where the observed posterior beliefs would be if the participants were perfect Bayesians. The thick black line gives the ordinary least squares (OLS) fit to the data. A detailed description of the regression results can be found in Table 7.6.[10] These scatter plots show a conservatism bias in belief updating (Edwards, 1968; Lopes, 1985; Nisbett & Ross, 1980; Osherson, 1990; Peterson et al., 1965; Phillips & Edwards, 1966; Shanteau, 1972, 1975; Slovic & Lichtenstein, 1971). That is, belief adjustment is insufficient in light of the evidence as it is evaluated by the participants. Thus, when Bayes's theorem implied a low posterior, the participants tended to give a posterior that was too high. Conversely, when Bayes's theorem implied a high posterior, the participants tended to give a posterior that was too low. As

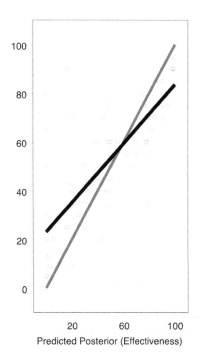 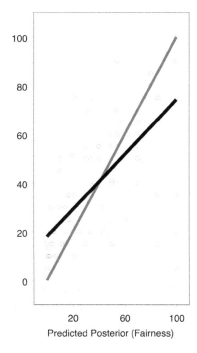

FIGURE 7.2 Observed and Bayesian Posteriors

Notes: The graph is a scatter plot of the predicted Bayesian and the observed posteriors. The thin gray lines are reference lines depicting what a one-to-one correspondence between the two posteriors would look like. The thick black lines are ordinary least squares (OLS) regression lines.

TABLE 7.6 Predicting the Observed Posteriors

Predictor	Effectiveness	Fairness
Predicted Posterior	.606**	.563**
	(.059)	(.081)
Constant	22.975**	17.948**
	(4.089)	(2.711)
R^2	.619	.46

Notes: Table entries are OLS regression coefficients with robust standard errors in parentheses.
N = 96.
** $p < .01$ (2-tailed).

TABLE 7.7 Discrepancies Between Predicted and Observed Posteriors

Predictor	Effectiveness		Fairness	
	Model 1	Model 2	Model 1	Model 2
Accuracy k	7.049*	−5.187	7.209+	−2.448
	(3.005)	(4.122)	(3.841)	(5.173)
Political Knowledge	−.075	−.151	−.658	−.182
	(.764)	(.718)	(.985)	(.988)
Ambivalence		.020		.222+
		(.082)		(.118)
Ambivalence × Accuracy		−.668**		−.570**
		(.168)		(.214)
Constant	10.847*	11.671*	17.674*	18.805**
	(5.153)	(4.756)	(6.828)	(6.671)
R^2	.036	.187	.021	.075

Notes: Table entries are OLS regression coefficients with estimated standard errors in parentheses.
N = 96.
+ $p < .10$, * $p < .05$, ** $p < .01$ (2-tailed).

a result, the observed posteriors tended to be more moderate than one would expect them to be based on Bayes's rule.

It is instructive to model the absolute discrepancies between the predicted and observed posteriors. Specifically, we can see if those who accurately perceived the evidence are also more accurate in their observed posteriors. In this analysis, we also control for political knowledge. The results are shown in Table 7.7 under the heading Model 1. This table suggests that participants who accurately perceived the direction of the evidence show greater discrepancies between the predicted and the observed posteriors. This is consistent with Steenbergen's (2001) suggestion that conservatism only occurs in the absence of a confirmation bias. That is, conservatism is a second line of defense that is used when a person is unable to redirect the interpretation of evidence in a partisan manner.

But does an accurate interpretation of the evidence always produce a conservatism bias? We would expect that it does not, since not everyone is motivated by partisan goals. If our theory is correct, then ambivalent individuals are motivated by accuracy. Such individuals should not only perceive evidence accurately, but also give it sufficient weight in the belief updating process. This suggests that we should introduce ambivalence into the model and interact it with accuracy. The sign on this interaction should be negative, as we would predict smaller discrepancies between the predicted and observed posteriors. Model 2 in Table 7.7 shows the results from this analysis. We see that there is indeed a powerful negative interaction between ambivalence and accuracy of the interpretation of the evidence. While an accurate interpretation of the evidence produces greater discrepancy between the predicted and observed posteriors for univalent participants, the opposite is true for ambivalent respondents. This suggests that ambivalence plays an important role in moderating the conservatism bias, just as we had predicted.

Attitudinal Consequences of Belief Updating

The final topic that we should address concerns the effect of belief updating on attitudes toward capital punishment. During the experiment, the participants were asked twice to express their attitude toward capital punishment—"Do you favor or oppose capital punishment?" The responses were expressed on a 5-point scale, ranging from "strongly favor" (1) to "strongly oppose" (5), with a neutral point in the middle. In between these two attitudinal measures was the second stage of the experiment, which potentially produced a change in the beliefs about the effectiveness and fairness of capital punishment. The question is if this change had an impact on the participants' subsequent attitudes toward the death penalty.

We predict opinions about capital punishment at T2 from opinions at T1, as well as the logged values of the ratios of the priors to the posteriors for the fairness and effectiveness dimensions. The results are shown in Table 7.8 under the heading Model 1. As this table shows, belief change does have attitudinal ramifications. The log of the ratio of the prior to the posterior for beliefs about the effectiveness of capital punishment has a significant positive effect on T2 opinions about the death penalty. This means that if the prior exceeds the posterior—a person has become less sanguine about the effectiveness of capital punishment—opinions about the death penalty become less favorable compared to T1. On the other hand, if the prior falls short off the posterior—a person has become more optimistic about the effectiveness of capital punishment—opinions about the death penalty become more favorable compared to T1.

Past research suggests that ambivalence causes greater instability in people's opinions (Lavine 2001; Lavine, Johnston, & Steenbergen 2012). Thus, we expect the interaction between ambivalence and prior attitudes to be negative. The results of Model 2 corroborate this expectation. They suggest that ambivalent

TABLE 7.8 Attitudinal Effects of Belief Change

Predictors	Model 1	Model 2
Prior Attitude	4.921**	4.696**
	(.689)	(.705)
ln[Pr(H) / Pr(H|D)]:		
Effectiveness	.911**	.958**
Fairness	(.321)	(.347)
	−.088	−.375
	(.334)	(.300)
Ambivalence		.092*
		(.046)
Ambivalence × Prior Attitude		−.024⁺
		(.013)
Threshold 1	6.989**	5.727**
	(1.097)	(1.186)
Threshold 2	13.568**	12.638**
	(1.987)	(1.985)
Threshold 3	17.967**	17.091**
	(2.711)	(2.750)
Threshold 4	22.873**	22.016**
	(3.359)	(3.427)
Pseudo R^2	.711	.728

Notes: Table entries are ML ordered logit estimates with estimated standard errors in parentheses. $N = 86$.
⁺ $p < .10$, * $p < .05$, ** $p < .01$ (2-tailed).

citizens base their current opinions less on past positions, thus leaving more room for an effect of contemporary information such as is reflected in belief change. One indicator of this is to compare the probability for deviations from one's initial attitude in ambivalent and non-ambivalent participants. Assuming that the prior for effectiveness is 1.5 times higher than the posterior, maximally non-ambivalent participants, on the average, had a 0.191 predicted probability of changing opinions. The corresponding probability for maximally ambivalent participants was 0.441, more than twice as large. A similar picture emerges for participants whose prior was 67 percent of the value of the posterior. Maximally non-ambivalent participants in this group, on the average, had a 0.218 predicted probability of changing their opinion. The corresponding number for maximally ambivalent participants is 0.438.

The conclusion that we draw from these results is that belief change has important attitudinal implications. People's policy attitudes respond to changes in policy-relevant beliefs. At the same time, past attitudes form a powerful anchor for non-ambivalent participants, thus limiting the effect that belief updating can have. This is much less the case for ambivalent individuals, whose prior opinions constitute less of an anchor and who are therefore better able to incorporate current beliefs into policy opinions.

Conclusions

What conclusions can we draw from our findings? Focusing on the general patterns of belief change, we observe two biases. A confirmation bias causes decision makers to interpret evidence that contradicts prior beliefs as if it were neutral or even consistent with those beliefs. A conservatism bias causes decision makers to adjust their prior beliefs insufficiently in the light of new evidence. Interestingly, this second bias emerges as a second line of defense. That is, conservatism is most likely when the individual perceived the evidence as inconsistent with a prior belief. These biases have attitudinal ramifications, in that belief change or the lack thereof has an influence on subsequent attitudes toward an issue.

A second major finding is that ambivalence moderates the biases that we have observed. We find that strong prior beliefs are less likely to generate a confirmation bias when a person is conflicted about capital punishment. We also observed that the conflict by itself reduces the confirmation bias, at least when individuals are asked to evaluate the evidence. In addition, ambivalence moderates the conservatism bias, in that it suppresses this bias as a second line of defense. Not only do ambivalent individuals show less bias, they also root current attitudes less in past attitudes, thus leaving more room for belief change to have an effect.

These results are of both theoretical and normative significance. At a theoretical level, they shed light on both belief updating and ambivalence. While most political scientists would acknowledge that beliefs are not static, few empirical studies have, in fact, studied the character of belief change in detail. Following a long tradition of persuasion research, scholars are typically satisfied with studying attitudes before and after the introduction of a persuasive message, without asking how this message is interpreted and how it changes the beliefs that underlie the attitudes. Recent work by Lodge and Taber (2013) has begun to unpack this process. Here we relate the process to a normative benchmark of belief updating, which helps us pinpoint even more clearly the nature of the biases that may be triggered when individuals face a counter-attitudinal message.

Our research also contributes to the ambivalence literature. Few studies of ambivalence to date have focused on the role that ambivalence plays in processing political messages (but see Lavine et al., 2012). Based on a consideration of the distinctive information-processing motivation of ambivalent citizens, we show here that they should be less biased, both in terms of confirmation and conservatism. These results demonstrate the importance of ambivalence as a moderator of political behavior. They also show one pathway by which ambivalence can play this role, which has hitherto been neglected, namely change in the processing of information.

From a normative perspective, these results shed light on an important aspect of the deliberative potential of citizens, to wit their willingness/ability to accept evidence that challenges their convictions. The existence of the confirmation and conservatism biases gives some reason for pessimism. Counter-attitudinal messages frequently triggered defensive mechanisms that allowed existing beliefs to persevere. This individual-level conclusion is considerably more pessimistic than Gerber and Green's (1999) finding that, in the aggregate, American public opinion seems adaptive to new circumstances. Of course, we should keep in mind that biases at the individual level may cancel out in the aggregation process, which would produce exactly the kind of result reported by Gerber and Green.

The news is not all bad. Ambivalent individuals seem to approximate the normative ideal quite nicely. They seem open to new evidence and give it its due weight. At the aggregate level, these individuals may be responsible for whatever adaptation we observe, although this should be studied further.

While the evidence in this paper suggests definite patterns of belief updating, several caveats are in order. First, the small sample size necessitates that we treat the results as preliminary. Moreover, we should recognize that our results are limited to a single political issue, one on which public opinion is deeply divided. An interesting question is whether the patterns of belief updating observed here generalize to other issues, including those that stir up less controversy.

To obtain better insight in the causes of the confirmation bias, it will be important to see how individuals react to information that challenges their beliefs. How much counterarguing occurs? What is the nature of the counterarguments? What affective responses are elicited by counter-attitudinal messages? The answer to these questions may be particularly important in understanding the differences between ambivalent and non-ambivalent respondents.

Despite their limitations, the results so far are telling. They show not only that it is important to understand political belief change, but also to contrast it with a normative benchmark. In this manner, we can return to the old normative question—are citizens open-minded or closed-minded?

Notes

1. Bayes's theorem may cover many different belief statements but in this chapter, we limit ourselves to the simplest case of two opposing ideas.
2. We shall remain silent about the question of where these priors come from. They may themselves be rooted in misconceptions but we focus only on the *revision* of the priors.
3. Our use of confirmation bias is slightly different from the common definition, namely selective attention only to information that confirms one's prior beliefs (see Jonas, Schulz-Hardt, Frey, & Thelen, 2001).
4. Conservatism does not have a political meaning here. In principle, both ideological conservatives and liberals may show this bias. The vernacular is somewhat confusing in

the world of politics, but we have chosen to retain the "conservatism" label because it is widely used in psychology.
5. Current conceptions of ambivalence are rooted in the two-dimensional evaluative space model developed by Cacioppo, Gardner, and Berntson (1997). This model assumes that people's attitudes do not necessarily form a bipolar dimension such that an increase in the favorability of some object implies a corresponding decrease in the unfavorability of that object. Rather, the attitudinal space consists of two dimensions: intensity of likes and intensity of dislikes. When both dimensions are of high intensity, a person is said to be ambivalent.
6. Both dimensions are significant predictors of attitudes toward capital punishment. That is, prior beliefs about effectiveness and fairness are predictive of a person's attitude toward the death penalty.
7. Evidential strength was also manipulated. This manipulation did not work and will not be discussed further (details can be found in Steenbergen, 2001).
8. Note that $\log(k)$ is undefined if $=0$. This occurred occasionally in our study. In those cases, we added a small constant (0.001) to both $\Pr(D|H)$ and $\Pr(D|\bar{H})$.
9. Political knowledge is measured as a composite of 11 knowledge questions, which asked participants to identify the office of domestic and international political figures, to answer factual questions about the U.S. Constitution, and to answer various other factual items about politics. Wrong answers and don't knows were coded 0, whereas correct responses received a score of 1. High scale values, then, indicate a high level of political knowledge.
10. Comparable results were found when we performed a robust regression analysis or fitted a Tobit model to account for outliers and censoring, respectively.

References

Alvarez, R. Michael & Brehm, John. (1995). American ambivalence towards abortion policy: Development of a heteroskedastic probit model of competing values. *American Journal of Political Science*, 39, 1055–1082.

Alvarez, R. Michael & Brehm, John. (2002). *Hard choices, easy answers: Values, information, and American public opinion*. Chicago, IL: University of Chicago Press.

Baron, Jonathan. (1994). *Thinking and deciding*. Cambridge: Cambridge University Press.

Bartels, Larry M. (2002). Beyond the running tally: Partisan bias in political perceptions. *Political Behavior*, 24, 117–150.

Bassili, John N. (1996). Meta-judgmental versus operational indexes of psychological attributes: The case of measures of attitude strength. *Journal of Personality and Social Psychology*, 71, 637–653.

Cacioppo, John T., Gardner, Wendi L., & Berntson, Gary G. (1997). Beyond bipolar conceptualizations and measures: The case of attitudes and evaluative space. *Personality and Social Psychology Review*, 71, 3–25.

Chaiken, Shelly, Liberman, Akiva, & Eagly, Alice H. (1989). Heuristic and systematic information processing within and beyond the persuasion context. In James S. Uleman & John A. Bargh (Eds.), *Unintended thought* (pp. 212–252). New York: Guilford Press.

Dewey, John. (2004). *Democracy and education*. Mineola, NY: Dover.

Ditto, Peter H. & Lopez, David F. (1992). Motivated skepticism: Use of differential decision criteria for preferred and nonpreferred conclusions. *Journal of Personality and Social Psychology*, 63, 568–584.

Eberhardt, Frederick & Danks, David. (2011). Confirmation in the cognitive sciences: The problematic case of Bayesian models. *Minds & Machines*, 21, 389–410.

Edwards, Ward. (1954). The theory of decision making. *Psychological Bulletin*, 51, 380–417.
Edwards, Ward. (1968). Conservatism in human information processing. In Benjamin Kleinmuntz (Ed.), *Formal representation of human judgment* (pp. 17–52). New York: Wiley-Blackwell.
Entman, Robert M. (1989). *Democracy without citizens: Media and the decay of American politics*. Oxford: Oxford University Press.
Fischle, Mark. (2000). Mass response to the Lewinsky scandal: Motivated reasoning or Bayesian updating? *Political Psychology*, 21, 135–159.
Galston, William A. (1988). Liberal virtues. *American Political Science Review*, 82, 1277–1290.
Gerber, Alan & Green, Donald P. (1997). Rational learning and partisan attitudes. *American Journal of Political Science*, 42, 794–818.
Gerber, Alan & Green, Donald P. (1999). Misperceptions about perceptual bias. *Annual Review of Political Science*, 2, 189–210.
Gopnik, Alison. (2012). Scientific thinking in young children: Theoretical advances, empirical research, and policy implications. *Science*, 337, 1623–1627.
Habermas, Jürgen. (1996). *Die Einbeziehung des Andern: Studien zur politischen Theorie*. Frankfurt am Main: Suhrkamp.
Houston, David A. & Fazio, Russell H. (1989). Biased processing as a function of attitude accessibility: Making objective judgments subjectively. *Social Cognition*, 7, 51–66.
Huckfeldt, Robert & Sprague, John. (1998). *Sources of ambivalence in public opinion: The certainty and accessibility of abortion attitudes.* Paper presented at the Annual Meeting of the International Society of Political Psychology, Montreal.
Jonas, Eva, Schulz-Hardt, Stefan, Frey, Dieter, & Thelen, Norman. (2001). Confirmation bias in sequential information search after preliminary decisions: An expansion of dissonance theoretical research on selective exposure to information. *Journal of Personality and Social Psychology*, 80, 557–571.
Klein, William M. & Kunda, Ziva. (1992). Motivated person perception: Constructing justifications for desired beliefs. *Journal of Experimental Social Psychology*, 28, 145–168.
Koehler, Jonathan J. (1993). The influence of prior beliefs on scientific judgments of evidence quality. *Organizational Behavior and Human Decision Processes*, 56, 28–55.
Kruglanski, Arie W. & Freund, Tallie. (1983). The freezing and unfreezing of lay-inferences: Effects on impressional primacy, ethnic stereotyping, and numerical anchoring. *Journal of Experimental Social Psychology*, 19, 448–468.
Kunda, Ziva. (1987). Motivation and inference: Self-serving generation and evaluation of evidence. *Journal of Personality and Social Psychology*, 53, 636–647.
Kunda, Ziva. (1990). The case for motivated reasoning. *Psychological Bulletin*, 108, 480–498.
Lavine, Howard. (2001). The electoral consequences of ambivalence toward presidential candidates. *American Journal of Political Science*, 45, 915–929.
Lavine, Howard, Borgida, Eugene, & Sullivan, John L. (2000). On the relationship between attitude involvement and attitude accessibility: Toward a cognitive-motivational model of political information processing. *Political Psychology*, 21, 81–106.
Lavine, Howard, Huff, Joseph W., Wagner, Stephen H., & Sweeney, Donna. (1998). The moderating influence of attitude strength on the susceptibility to context effects in attitude surveys. *Journal of Personality and Social Psychology*, 75, 359–373.
Lavine, Howard, Johnston, Christopher, & Steenbergen, Marco R. (2012). *The ambivalent partisan: How critical loyalty promotes democracy*. Oxford: Oxford University Press.
Lodge, Milton & Taber, Charles S. (2005). The automaticity of affect for political leaders, groups and issues: An experimental test of the hot cognition hypothesis. *Political Psychology*, 26, 455–482.

Lodge, Milton & Taber, Charles S. (2013). *The rationalizing voter*. Cambridge: Cambridge University Press.

Lopes, Lola L. (1985). Averaging rules and adjustment processes in Bayesian inference. *Bulletin of the Psychonomic Society*, 23, 509–512.

Lord, Charles G., Ross, Lee, & Lepper, Mark R. (1979). Biased assimilation and attitude polarization: The effects of prior theories on subsequently considered evidence. *Journal of Personality and Social Psychology*, 37, 2098–2109.

Lu, Hongjing, Yuille, Alan L., Liljeholm, Mimi, Cheng, Patricia W., & Holyoak, Keith J. (2008). Bayesian generic priors for causal learning. *Psychological Review*, 115, 955–984.

Nisbett, Richard E. & Ross, Lee. (1980). *Human inference: Strategies and shortcomings of human judgment*. Englewood Cliffs, NJ: Prentice-Hall.

Nyhan, Brendan & Reifler, Jason. (2010). When corrections fail: The persistence of political misperceptions. *Political Behavior*, 32, 303–330.

Osherson, Daniel N. (1990). Judgment. In Daniel N. Osherson & Edward E. Smith (Eds.), *Thinking: An invitation to cognitive science* (Vol. 3, pp. 55–87). Cambridge, MA: MIT Press.

Peterson, Cameron R., Schneider, Robert J., & Miller, Allan J. (1965). Sample size and the revision of subjective probabilities. *Journal of Experimental Psychology*, 69, 522–527.

Petty, Richard E. & Cacioppo, John T. (1986). *Communication and persuasion: Central and peripheral routes to attitude change*. New York: Springer-Verlag.

Petty, Richard E., Ostrom, Thomas M., & Brock, Timothy C. (1981). Historical foundations of the cognitive response approach to attitudes and persuasion. In Richard E. Petty, Thomas M. Ostrom, & Timothy C. Brock (Eds.), *Cognitive responses in persuasion* (pp. 5–30). Hillsdale, NJ: Lawrence Erlbaum Associates.

Phillips, Lawrence D. & Edwards, Ward. (1966). Conservatism in a simple probability inference task. *Journal of Experimental Psychology*, 72, 346–354.

Pomerantz, Eva M., Chaiken, Shelly, & Tordesillas, Rosalind S. (1995). Attitude strength and resistance processes. *Journal of Personality and Social Psychology*, 69, 408–419.

Pyszczynski, Tom & Greenberg, Jeff. (1987). Toward an integration of cognitive and motivational perspectives on social inference: A biased hypothesis-testing model. *Advances in Experimental Social Psychology*, 20, 297–340.

Redlawsk, David P. (2002). Hot cognition or cool consideration? Testing the effects of motivated reasoning on political decision making. *Journal of Politics*, 64, 1021–1044.

Shanteau, James. (1972). Descriptive versus normative models of sequential inference judgment. *Journal of Experimental Psychology*, 93, 63–68.

Shanteau, James. (1975). Averaging versus multiplying combination rules of inference judgment. *Acta Psychologica*, 39, 83–89.

Slovic, Paul & Lichtenstein, Sarah. (1971). Comparison of Bayesian and regression approaches to the study of information processing in judgment. *Organizational Behavior and Human Performance*, 6, 649–744.

Sorrentino, Richard M. & Higgins, E. Tory. (1986). Motivation and cognition: Warming up to synergism. In Richard M. Sorrentino & E. Tory Higgins (Eds.), *Handbook of motivation and cognition* (Vol. 1, pp. 3–19). New York: Guilford Press.

Steenbergen, Marco R. (2001). *The Reverend Bayes meets J.Q. Public: Patterns of political belief updating in citizens*. Paper presented at the Annual Meeting of the International Society of Political Psychology, Guernavaca, Mexico.

Stein, Janice G. (1988). Building politics into psychology: The misperception of threat. *Political Psychology*, 9, 245–271.

Taber, Charles S. & Lodge, Milton. (2006). Motivated skepticism in the evaluation of political beliefs. *American Journal of Political Science*, 50, 755–769.

Tenenbaum, Joshua B., Kemp, Charles, Griffiths, Thomas L., & Goodman, Noah D. (2011). How to grow a mind: Statistics, structure, and abstraction. *Science*, 331, 1279–1285.

Thomson, Megan M., Zanna, Mark P., & Griffin, Dale W. (1995). Let's not be indifferent about (attitudinal) ambivalence. In R. Petty and J. Krosnick (Eds.), *Attitude Strength: Antecedents and Consequences* (pp. 361–386). Mahwah, NJ: Erlbaum.

Tourangeau, Roger, Rasinski, Kenneth A., Bradburn, Norman, & D'Andrade, Roy. (1989). Belief accessibility and context effects in attitude measurement. *Journal of Experimental Social Psychology*, 25, 401–421.

Tversky, Amos & Kahneman, Daniel. (1974). Judgment under uncertainty: Heuristics and biases. *Science*, 185, 1124–1130.

Von Neumann, John & Morgenstern, Oskar. (1944). *Theory of games and economic behavior*. Princeton, NJ: Princeton University Press.

8
MOTIVATED RESPONSES TO POLITICAL COMMUNICATIONS

Framing, Party Cues, and
Science Information

James N. Druckman, Thomas J. Leeper, and
Rune Slothuus

After an early foray into Soviet politics, Milton Lodge began a multi-decade effort to introduce political scientists to the theories, methods, and findings of social and cognitive psychologists. From early work on psychophysiology, through pioneering research on schemata, to more recent investigations of motivated thinking, Lodge and his collaborators shaped how a generation of political scientists think about human reasoning. Lodge's work is among the most psychologically sophisticated in political science, but it also is always distinctly political—attending to the political realities of over-time competition in an environment where citizens have low levels of information. The culmination of this work has been a landmark theoretical advance—"motivated reasoning."

In this chapter, we begin by outlining the evolution of Lodge's work on motivated reasoning. We then demonstrate how the theoretical framework he puts forth can be used to explain opinion or preference formation in response to political communications—that is, the typical context in which citizens, lacking information and being exposed to competing political messages, form political opinions. We focus on three distinct areas (which have not been a direct focus of Lodge's own work), including work on framing, partisan cues, and opinions about scientific issues. We conclude by accentuating how Lodge's approach is a model for integrating the realities of individual psychology with political competition.

From Online Processing to Motivated Reasoning[1]

Citizens' political preferences form the foundation for most conceptions of representative democracy (e.g., Dahl, 1971; Druckman, 2014; Erikson, MacKuen, & Stimson, 2002). It is thus not surprising that the question of how people form political preferences has been central to political science for nearly a century (e.g., Lippmann, 1922). For much of that time period, the dominant approaches focused on memory. The idea behind these memory-based models is that people base their evaluations on information that they retrieve from memory. For example, when called on to evaluate a candidate or issue, people canvas their memories for information on the candidate or issue and use what they find to form preferences (e.g., they recall that the candidate favors increased defense spending and that agrees with their belief so they support the candidate). Canvassing of memory can be a comprehensive incorporation of copious information (e.g., Enelow & Hinich, 1984) or, more realistically, can be based on whatever smaller amounts of information that happens to come to mind (Zaller, 1992). The key point is that memory of specific information is recalled and is the basis for opinions.

In the mid-1980s, Lodge and his colleagues launched a challenge to memory-based models by putting forward the online model of political processing. Building on research in psychology (Bassili, 1989; Hastie & Park, 1986), Lodge and colleagues acknowledged that cognitive limitations prevent exhaustive memory searches. But instead of just using whatever information happens to come to mind, the online model suggests that people form and maintain a running "evaluation counter" of certain objects (e.g., candidates). When an individual encounters new information about such objects, he or she immediately brings an affect-laden "evaluation counter" (i.e., running tally) into working memory, updates it given the new information, and then restores the counter to long-term memory.

An important aspect of this model is that, after updating the evaluation, the individual may forget the information that affected the evaluation. When asked to express their evaluation, people simply retrieve the evaluation counter without searching for the information on which it was based. Lodge, McGraw, and Stroh (1989, p. 401) explain that the result may be "that people can often tell you how much they like or dislike a book, movie, candidate, or policy [because they maintain a running evaluation] but not be able to recount the specific whys and wherefores for their overall evaluation." This is in sharp contrast to memory-based models where individuals do not maintain a running evaluation counter and instead base their evaluations on whatever information they happen to remember.

In a series of experiments, Lodge and his colleagues show that participants who engage in online processing base their evaluations on information that enters their evaluation counter (over time) more than the bits of information that happen to be available in memory at the time the evaluation is rendered (e.g., Lodge et al., 1989; Lodge, Steenbergen, & Brau, 1995; Lodge & McGraw, 1995).

For example, a pro-choice, tough on crime voter may receive campaign information that a candidate supports abortion rights and strict federal crime laws. As a result, the voter accesses and updates his or her online evaluation of the candidate in a favorable direction, and then quickly forgets the candidate's pro-choice and tough on crime stances (and restores the online evaluation in long-term memory). At a later point in time—when the voter needs to evaluate the candidate (e.g., cast a vote)—he or she simply retrieves the positive online evaluation and thus offers a favorable candidate evaluation, despite the fact that the voter may not recall the specific reasons for the positive evaluation (i.e., the voter may not remember the candidate's pro-choice or tough on crime stances). Thus, there may be no relationship between what the voter remembers and who the voter prefers, or the relationship may reflect *post hoc* rationalizations.

If people form their evaluations online, then we, as researchers, should not expect people to remember and report the reasons for their preferences. The online model (1) calls into question the use of recall questions to gauge opinion formation since people may forget the reasons for their opinions (also see Rahn, Krosnik, & Breuning, 1994), (2) suggests that the impact of campaigns cannot be assessed based on campaign information recalled, and (3) shows that citizens form more stable preferences that evolve over time rather than unstable preferences based on whatever comes to mind (see Druckman & Lupia, 2000; Lodge & Taber, 2000).

The online model has proven to be empirically successful across contexts, but it also left some questions unanswered such as how do people deal with different types of information and what information do they seek in the first place. These and other ambiguities presumably motivated Lodge and Charles Taber to develop a model of political motivated reasoning.[2] Again extending work from psychology (e.g., Kunda, 1990), Lodge and Taber put forth a model and provide extensive empirical data for motivated reasoning.

A starting point for this model is to consider the idealized, rational environment, where individuals integrate new information and update their prior opinions in an evenhanded and unbiased fashion. Absent substantial motivation to accurately process information, however, individuals often subconsciously interpret new information in light of their extant attitudes (Redlawsk, 2002). Lodge and Taber (2008, p. 33) explain that upon encountering new information, existing attitudes "come inescapably to mind, whether consciously recognized or not, and for better or worse these feelings guide subsequent thought." The result is *motivated reasoning*: the tendency to seek out information that confirms priors (i.e., a *confirmation bias*), view evidence consistent with prior opinions as stronger (i.e., a *prior attitude effect*), and spend more time counterarguing and dismissing evidence inconsistent with prior opinions, regardless of objective accuracy (i.e., a *disconfirmation bias*).[3] Each of these processes will lead to attitude polarization where individuals take more extreme positions in the direction of their preexisting attitude.

In their initial seminal study, Taber and Lodge (2006) invited participants to a single study session that focused on two partisan, contentious issues: affirmative action and gun control. The participants first reported their prior attitude and the strength of that attitude on one of the issues (e.g., affirmative action). After being encouraged to "view information in an evenhanded way so [as to] explain the issue to other [participants]," participants selected eight of 16 possible pro or con arguments about the issue (Taber & Lodge, 2006, p. 759; also see Taber, Cann, & Kucsova, 2009, p. 144). This tested for confirmation bias. Participants next reported their updated opinion on the issue and answered demographic questions.

In the next stage of the study, participants reported their opinions on the other issue (e.g., gun control), were again told to be "evenhanded," were asked to rate the strength of four pro and four con arguments, and then reported their updated opinions. This tested for the prior attitude effect and disconfirmation bias. Taber and Lodge report stark evidence that participants evaluated arguments that were consistent with their prior opinions as more compelling; spent more time counterarguing incongruent arguments; and chose to read arguments consistent, rather than inconsistent, with their prior opinions.

These dynamics led to attitude polarization: respondents developed more extreme opinions in the direction of their priors.[4] Lodge and Taber (2008, pp. 35–36) further explain that motivated reasoning entails the automatic "systematic biasing of judgments in favor of one's immediately accessible beliefs and feelings. . . . [It is] built into the basic architecture of information processing mechanisms of the brain."

Lodge and Taber spell out even more implications and dynamics of the model in their various papers and a seminal book (Lodge & Taber, 2000, 2013; Taber & Lodge, 2016). It is worth noting—a point to which we will return—that aside from prior opinion strength and sophistication, one's processing goal also moderates motivated reasoning (see Leeper & Slothuus, 2014). Importantly, though, Taber and Lodge (2006) recognize motivated reasoning is conditioned—specifically, sophisticated participants and those with stronger prior opinions registered the most significant effects (also see Kahan, Braman, Slovic, Gastil, & Cohen, 2009; Taber et al., 2009). In the case of the latter, people who feel passionate about their attitude are more apt to want to defend it via motivated reasoning. The former is the "sophistication effect": "the politically knowledgeable, because they possess greater ammunition with which to counterargue incongruent facts, figures, and arguments, will be more susceptible to motivated bias than will unsophisticates" (Taber & Lodge, 2006, p. 757).

Additionally, motivated reasoning requires that individuals have what is often called a directional or defensive processing goal such that they aim to uphold and maintain a desirable conclusion consistent with their standing attitude, even if it involves rejecting disconfirming information (Kunda, 1990). In some cases, individuals may have an "accuracy goal" such that they aim to form accurate opinions (or "correct" preferences; Taber & Lodge, 2006, p. 756), carefully attend to issue-relevant information, invest cognitive effort in reasoning, and process the information more deeply (Kunda, 1990, p. 485). The result is to form preferences with an eye towards what will be best in the future, rather than to simply defend prior beliefs. Even so, Taber and Lodge suggest directional goals are the norm (c.f., Druckman, 2012); they (2006, p. 767) conclude:

> despite our best efforts to promote the even-handed treatment of policy arguments in our studies, we find consistent evidence of directional partisan bias—the prior attitude effect [i.e., evaluations of arguments supporting prior opinions as more compelling than opposing arguments],

disconfirmation bias [i.e., extra effort devoted to counterarguing incongruent messages], and confirmation bias [i.e., seeking out consistent information].... Our participants may have tried to be evenhanded, but they found it impossible to be fair-minded.

When motivated reasoning occurs, individuals will miss out on relevant information and/or misinterpret information that may otherwise be helpful (Fazio & Olson, 2003, p. 149).

The review in this section makes clear that Lodge built a connected multi-decade research agenda that fundamentally altered how scholars understand preference formation. To us, no scholar has shaped research in this area to a greater extent. Importantly, Lodge did not simply import extant models from psychology (see Druckman, Kuklinski, & Sigelman, 2009). He drew on basic psychological insights to explain preference formation in *political contexts* (Druckman & Lupia, 2006). Three defining elements of politics are: ostensible low levels of citizen knowledge, competing coalitions or groups aimed at garnering support, and over-time campaigns to form such coalitions. Lodge's work, for example, shows low levels of reported political information may belie the data on which citizens actually draw in forming opinions (i.e., the online model). Even so, knowledge and sophistication matter as moderators of motivated reasoning. When it comes to time, Lodge was one of the first scholars to build time explicitly into micro-level studies of opinion formation by looking at preference formation over a 30-day period in his online reasoning experiments. And the focus on choosing between competing information streams and evaluating such flows differently via motivated reasoning goes a long way towards capturing the dynamics of coalition formation and coalition (e.g., party) polarization. For these reasons, it is not surprising Lodge's work has inspired a generation of related scholarship (e.g., Bartels, 2002; Gaines, Kuklinkski, Quirk, Peyton, & Verkuilen, 2007; Gerber & Huber, 2009, 2010; Groenendyk, 2013; Lavine, Johnston, & Steenbergen, 2012).

What we do in the remainder of this chapter is to present examples of how Lodge's work influenced our own work on communication and opinion formation across three distinct domains which Lodge himself did not explicitly investigate (or did so to a very limited extent). This includes scholarship on framing, party cues, and opinion formation about scientific issues, which all are important types of information citizens regularly encounter in an environment with competing messages over time. We show how motivated reasoning, in particular, explains processes in each of these domains, leading to a better understanding of *political* opinion formation.

Elite Influence Through Framing

Researchers studying elite-public interactions typically understand a citizen's attitude toward a policy or candidate as a weighted reflection of belief considerations relevant to that object. This "expectancy value" conceptualization of attitudes

(Eagly & Chaiken, 1993) characterizes an attitude A as sum of belief considerations, b, weighted by some measure of salience or importance, w, such that A = Σ b * w.[5] For citizens to be "responsive," they should update their attitudes in the face of any new considerations and weight those considerations according to their informativeness. The expectancy-value model highlights two mechanisms through which citizens might change their attitudes: belief change or belief reweighting. Beliefs might change, for example, in response to new information or a persuasive argument. Belief reweighting occurs when citizens temporarily or persistently adjust the *frame of reference* through which they consider an issue or candidate. This latter mechanism has received considerable attention in recent years and raises particular questions about the degree to which citizens form attitudes about public policy given only limited information provided by competing elite actors. We next describe some of these framing results and then discuss how framing studies can be interpreted from the perspective of motivated reasoning.

As an initial example of framing effects consider Chong and Druckman's (2007) study about attitudes toward a policy to restrict urban growth. The policy could be considered through at least two different frames (i.e., giving weight to distinct considerations when thinking about urban growth restrictions): one focused on the environmental benefits of the policy with respect to open space preservation, another about the economic costs. To study the effect of these alternative frames, Chong and Druckman randomly assigned some participants in a laboratory setting to read about the policy in a manner framed around environment concerns and another group of participants to read about the policy framed in terms of economic concerns. Unsurprisingly, they found that the environmental frame increased support for the policy (i.e., because they put greater weight on the environmental consequence of urban growth). Even with limited information, citizens could update their attitudes.

But beyond replicating this well-established finding of a "framing effect," Chong and Druckman went further in two respects. First, they included additional "weak" frames that highlighted non-compelling considerations (community building and the limited capacity of citizens to understand the issue). Second, they included additional experimental conditions where participants were presented with both frames together, that is by competing sides in the debate highlighting each of the different frames and thereby making multiple considerations salient. The findings regarding weak frames are important, but perhaps unsurprising: strong frames dominate weak frames when placed in competition and weak frames are ineffective on their own in changing attitudes. However, when strong rival frames are placed in competition, participants update their preferences, gravitating toward a middle position that reflects the balanced consideration of both frames. Prior values still mattered—with environmentalists holding more favorable views of the policy than those with stronger economic concerns—but participants were responsive to new information. That is, environmentalists did not simply reject the economic frame.

These findings, on their face, appear counter to the motivated reasoning model, in competitive environments, since the prior attitude effect posited by the model suggests prior attitudes/values should more strongly condition responses to frames. However, closer inspection suggests that Chong and Druckman's (2007) results leave many questions open when it comes to motivated reasoning and framing effects. First, if citizens are responsive to frames in the short-term, do these effects persist in the long-term or does motivated reasoning pull citizens back to their long-standing views? Second, while citizens are responsive to new information in an experimental context where information is randomly assigned to them, to what extent does citizens' capacity for information self-selection allow motivated selection of arguments that might prevent exposure to contrary views?

How do citizens respond to frames over the long term? Lodge and Taber's theory of motivated reasoning posits that strong attitudes should invite greater motivated reasoning, as citizens have a greater desire to defend those priors than they do to defend attitudes to which they are less committed. Their laboratory studies (Taber & Lodge, 2006) demonstrate this with individual differences in apparent confirmation bias across those with strong and weak attitudes. It is indeed possible that Chong and Druckman's (2007) result reflected the reality that most in their experiment probably had very weak prior attitudes about urban sprawl restrictions. Their study also was limited in ignoring over-time framing and information selection.

With these considerations in mind, Chong and Druckman (2010) undertook an over-time study about people's opinions on the Patriot Act. The authors (randomly) exposed individuals to a strong pro frame (i.e., battling terrorism is the primary consideration to weight) at what we will call Time 1. This was followed ten days later, at what we will call Time 2, by a strong con frame (i.e., civil liberty concern is the primary consideration to weight). Others received the con argument at Time 1 and the pro argument at Time 2.[6] Importantly, Chong and Druckman (2010) also randomly assigned people to engage in a task that either led them to form strong opinions after receiving the Time 1 frame or weak opinions after receiving the Time 1 frame. Even so, one might expect respondents, on average, to register similar opinions about the Act, since they all received the same mix of pro and con frames (this would be consistent with the aforementioned dual *simultaneous* strong frame study by Chong and Druckman (2007). This is not what Chong and Druckman find, however. They find instead that the opinions of those with weak priors dramatically reflected the last argument they heard; for example, they opposed the Patriot Act if they received a con frame (i.e., civil liberties) at Time 2 but supported the Act if they instead received the pro frame (i.e., terrorism) at Time 2. Participants formed opinions based on what came to mind, ostensibly in a memory-based fashion.

Importantly, those with strong priors did exactly the opposite: they formed opinions based on the Time 1 frame they received and then rejected the Time

2 frame. For example, they supported (opposed) the Act if they received the pro (con) argument at Time 1 and the con (pro) argument at Time 2. These individuals sought to protect their initial opinions, evaluated the second argument as ineffective and clung to what they had been induced to believe. These findings suggest that citizens with weak attitudes are highly responsive to new information, with framing effects moving their opinions potentially wildly over a two-week period. Those with strong attitudes, by contrast, display characteristic signs of disconfirmation biases (i.e., dismissing contrary frames). In short, once over-time competition—a reality of politics—is introduced, the motivated reasoning model explains behavior at least for those who form strong attitudes.

Adopting a similar experimental paradigm, Druckman and Leeper (2012) extend this result over an even longer period of time in which participants were also repeatedly exposed to either pro or con frames about the Patriot Act.[7] Yet the result was the same: even after repeated exposure to pro (con) frames, those with weakly formed attitudes were highly responsive to a final con (pro) frame. By contrast, those with strong attitudes resisted a final counter-attitudinal message.

Motivated reasoning is a powerful theory in competitive over-time framing situations. That people did not engage in motivated reasoning when they held weak attitudes—which again, we suspect was the case in the initial simultaneous frame Chong and Druckman (2007) study—is in fact consistent with the theory insofar as it suggests attitude strength increases the likelihood of motivated reasoning, as noted above. And in the over-time study, motivated reasoning clearly took place among those with strong attitudes. Moreover, the prior attitude effect was easily induced: participants encouraged to form strong views at Time 1 became resistant to new information at later points in time, even though the Time 1 information was simply a randomly chosen argument with no objective superiority over a counter-argument. The findings us present a perplexing normative dilemma since those most engaged in politics tend to have stronger attitudes, suggesting a trade-off between political engagement and deleterious effects of motivated reasoning.

The framing studies discussed so far all involve captive audiences who are fed information. What happens when people, in a low-information, competitive over-time environment, select information on their own? Do they choose information in ways suggests by motivated reasoning's confirmation bias such that they select only information consistent with their prior beliefs, ignoring alternative viewpoints?

These questions were addressed in a study by Druckman, Fein, and Leeper (2014). In an experiment carried out over the period of a month (with four sessions or one each week), the authors randomly assigned participants to receive either a pro message about health care policy at Time 1 and a con message at Time 4, or vice versa. At the intervening time periods (Times 2 and 3), they further randomly assigned participants to one of three conditions: a control condition with no exposure to issue-relevant information, a condition involving simple repetition of the Time 1 argument, or a third condition in which participants were given the choice of what information to receive from among an "information board" of pro and con arguments, and unrelated news. The question was whether the opportunity to self-select information would lead participants to seek out contrary arguments at Times 2 and 3, or whether they would reinforce the Time 1 argument, or instead avoid issue-relevant content entirely. Moreover, the study illuminated how this opportunity for information self-selection would impact their attitudes at Time 4. The result was striking: participants in the self-selection conditions closely resembled those in the repetition conditions. By inducing a particular opinion at Time 1, participants engaged in a confirmation bias a la motivated reasoning—seeking out frame-congruent information and Time 2 and 3—and displayed a prior attitude effect at Time 4, resisting the influence of a final opposing argument.

Rather than provide a route to open-minded consideration of diverse information, the opportunity for information choice actually invited further motivated reasoning via the confirmation bias. Leeper (2014) further shows that this motivated selection of information occurs even when the information environment is stacked against one's prior opinions. Varying the content of information in the "information board" to be heavily in favor of a health care proposal, heavily against the proposal, or evenly balanced, participants induced to hold strong views selected attitude-congruent information regardless of the balance of the environment. They further polarized in their views of the policy. Those induced to hold weaker opinions, by contrast, were responsive to the tilt of the information environment, updating their views accordingly. Recent work further shows that this kind of motivated reinforcement-seeking means that randomized experiments on information processing can generate misleading results when they fail to account for the role of information choice in the reasoning processes of those with strong and weak opinions (Leeper, 2017).

On balance, these findings regarding responses to framing suggest that motivated reasoning is ubiquitous, at least among the segment of the citizenry with strong opinions. The differences in motivated behavior across levels of attitude strength, however, suggests that there are likely to be wide degrees of variation in all aspects of motivated reasoning across individuals, across political issues, and over time. These limitations, unfortunately, are not well understood and merit further research. These findings also raise important questions about how motivated reasoning works in contexts involving competition and, in particular, the opportunity for information choice within competitive environments. Forced exposure to competitive arguments seems to moderate confirmation bias and the prior attitude effect, but under more realistic conditions of information self-selection, where motivated reasoning can affect both what information is received and how it is processed, competition enables rather than mitigates motivated reasoning.

These examples of how motivated reasoning theory explains framing effects accentuate the influence of theory in political contexts. Early accounts of framing effects treated them as pure memory-based processes such that a frame (e.g., civil liberties with regard to the Patriot Act) made certain considerations accessible in memory that, in turn, drove opinion formation (e.g., opposition to the Patriot Act) (e.g., Iyengar, 1990). Yet, as soon as the realities of over-time competition were introduced to framing studies, motivated reasoning emerged as a powerful explanation for observed effects—accounting for whether early or later frames won out and how people selected frames in the first place. That said, these studies also reveal that directional motivated reasoning occurs most clearly among those who hold strong attitudes. With this in mind, we now turn to a discussion of one of the strongest political beliefs: partisanship.

Party Cues and Motivated Reasoning

There is no doubt that when forming their opinions, citizens often rely on positions taken by political parties (e.g., they support a policy only if their party promotes it). Such party cues or endorsements are ubiquitous in news coverage of politics because the political parties are frequent promoters of policy proposals. Indeed, as we have noted, one of the distinctive features of politics is the competition between partisan elites to build coalitions and muster support for their policies. Consequently, citizens who pay attention to politics will routinely encounter party cues.

For a long time political scientists have been aware that party cues can shape citizens' policy preferences. An individual's party identification often raises "a perceptual screen through which the individual tends to see what is favorable to his partisan orientation" (Campbell, Converse, Miller, & Stokes, 1960, p. 133). Consistent with this idea, decades of research has shown that citizens who affiliate with a political party are more likely to support a policy if it is sponsored by their party than if it is sponsored by an opposing party. However, as noted by Leeper and Slothuus (2014, p. 134), despite that

> this impact of parties is fairly established, there is no scholarly agreement on how (i.e., through what psychological mechanisms) parties matter to citizens' political reasoning, and ... there is a surprising lack of empirical work trying to disentangling [sic] the various explanations.

Lodge's theory of motivated reasoning has helped to advance our understanding of how citizens respond to party cues and why party cues influence policy preferences. For political reasoning to be "motivated," a source of motivation is needed, and partisanship can provide just that. Partisanship is a fundamental and enduring political predisposition (Bisgaard & Slothuus, forthcoming; Campbell et al.,

1960; Green, Palmquist, & Schickler, 2002; Lavine, Johnston, & Steenbergen, 2012), probably more stable than core political values (Goren, 2005). Moreover, as demonstrated in Lodge's work, not only do many ordinary citizens affiliate with a political party, but party leaders and symbols associated with the political parties are highly affectively charged (e.g., Lodge & Taber, 2013, Chapter 5; Taber & Lodge, 2016; also see Iyengar, Lelkes, & Sood, 2012; Nicholson, 2012). Thus, partisanship can work as a preexisting attitude that motivates individuals to seek out, interpret, and assess new information, such as a policy proposal, in a way that is favorable to their own party and bolsters their affiliation with the party. This is direct extension of Lodge's work and is called partisan-motivated reasoning.[8]

The major theoretical alternative to partisan-motivated reasoning is using party cues as an informational shortcut to form opinions. Relying on partisan cues as shortcuts allows citizens to form policy opinions without paying attention to the content of the policy or the facts or arguments surrounding it. This way, parties can help citizens to prefer the policy they would have if they had more complete information (e.g., Lupia, 2006; Sniderman & Stiglitz, 2012). In other words, in this shortcut account, individuals simply do what their party tells them to do and they ignore the substantive information. This contrasts partisan-motivated reasoning where individuals do attend to the substantive information but in a partisan-biased fashion.

Both partisan-motivated reasoning and shortcuts are plausible, and non-exclusive, explanations of how party cues influence opinion. The shortcut mechanism resonates well with the political reality that most citizens possess limited policy information. The motivated reasoning explanation fits well with a competitive political environment where political groups strive to mobilize the loyalty of their supporters.

In an attempt to distinguish these two explanations, Slothuus and de Vreese (2010) created two experiments where they presented participants in Denmark with news articles about two different policy proposals and asked to what extent they opposed or supported the policies. The articles either emphasized the benefits of the policies (pro articles) or the disadvantages (con articles). Moreover, participants were either told that the policy was supported (in the pro articles) or opposed (in the con articles) by either the major left-of-center party or the major right-of-center party in Denmark. As would be expected from both the shortcut and the motivated reasoning accounts, the partisan source of the policy position pro or con mattered: participants—who were all partisans affiliating with one of the two parties—were more inclined to follow the party cue when it came from their party than when it came from the opposing party.

To directly test the differing accounts, Slothuus and de Vreese (2010) focused on two policy issues that varied in how salient they were to party competition. One was the basis for partisan conflict issue (welfare policy) and the other was a partisan consensus issue (international trade policy). The theory of party cues as an informational shortcut suggests party should have a larger effect on the consensus/low conflict trade issue because this is a less salient issue where citizens know little about the policy and so are likely to simply entirely delegate to their party (and not invest in substantive information processing). Motivated reasoning, in contrast, predicts citizens to be particularly motivated to use their partisanship when responding to party cues on the conflictual welfare issue. This is because party conflict, in contrast to consensus, signals that partisan values are at stake and emphasizes differences between the parties.[9]

The results of the experiments clearly support motivated reasoning: party cues mattered more on the conflict issue than on the consensus issue. As a result, partisans expressed stronger polarization in opinions on the conflict issue than on the consensus issue. Thus, when the parties are in conflict, citizens are more inclined to favor the policy position advocated by their party (i.e., akin to a prior attitude effect because partisans see their party as more persuasive). This result implies that the political environment (i.e., partisan conflict) can enhance the importance of a prior attitude (i.e., partisanship) effect which consequently leads citizens to respond more strongly to party cues. This study also speaks to how motivated reasoning helps explain partisan reasoning when parties compete, as they inherently do.

Another study of partisan competition looks at the prior attitude effect. Specifically, Druckman, Peterson, and Slothuus (2013) study support for the drilling for oil and gas off the U.S. Atlantic Coast and in the eastern Gulf of Mexico. Study participants randomly received two types of information. The first entailed a party endorsement with Democrats opposing drilling and Republicans supporting it. Respondents were also randomly exposed to information that suggested the parties were *highly polarized* (i.e., far apart) or *not particularly polarized* (i.e., not so far apart) on the issue. Second, respondents read an argument in favor of drilling and an argument opposed to drilling. The researchers randomly assigned whether each of the arguments was "objectively" strong/persuasive or weak; they confirmed by having individuals who were not in the main study rate the arguments as strong or weak. The respective pro and con strong arguments concerned economic benefits of drilling and dangers of drilling to workers and maritime life. The analogous weak arguments focused on technological developments from drilling and over-regulation due to drilling.[10]

The results reveal a strong prior attitude effect, anchored in partisanship. When told the parties are polarized, partisans *always* evaluated frames endorsed by their own party as more effective, regardless of the aforementioned "objective" strength. In other words, Democrats rated any con argument advocated by the Democratic party—including the weak regulation argument—as more effective than any pro argument, including the strong pro argument about the economy. Republicans did the opposite, always rating Republican pro arguments as stronger even when they were objectively weak (e.g., the technology argument). This is clear evidence of a prior attitude effect where partisanship as a preexisting attitude anchors evaluations. The results can also be read as indication of a disconfirmation bias as partisans always dismiss the argument advocated by the opposing party, although the results cannot tell how actively the experimental participants denigrate the out-party arguments.

Importantly, though, the authors show this bias disappears when respondents are told that the parties are not polarized: in that case, they always rate the objectively stronger arguments as more effective than the weak arguments, regardless of the party endorsements. For example, Democrats acknowledge that the Republication economic argument is stronger than the Democrat regulation argument. Thus, an antidote to the prior attitude effect lies in the information environment, and particularly, making clear that common rivals—such as the political parties—are not so far apart on the particular issue—that is, a possible political consensus might exist.

In another study exploring the nature of partisan competition on motivated reasoning, Bolsen, Druckman, and Cook (2014b) illuminate attitudes toward the U.S. Energy Independence and Security Act of 2007. This Act requires automakers to boost gas mileage for passenger cars, funds research and development for biofuels and solar and geothermal energy, and provides small business loans for energy efficiency improvements. The Act was supported by both parties at different points in the law-making process (e.g., was initially sponsored by a Democrat but signed into law by Republican President Bush).

Two factors varied in the experiment were which parties supported the Act and a prompt for respondents to justify their opinions. Specifically, respondents were randomly assigned to receive no endorsement, an endorsement stating the Act was being supported by Democrats, an endorsement stating the Act was being supported by Republicans, or an endorsement stating the Act was being supported by some, but not all, representatives of both parties (i.e., a "cross-partisan" frame).[11] In addition, some respondents were told they should view the policy from various perspectives and would have to later justify their policy views.[12]

The authors find that when individuals received their own party's endorsement (e.g., Republican respondents received the Republican endorsement) without the motivation prompt, they were strong motivated reasoners—they followed their party and increased support for the policy, relative to a control group that received no endorsement and the motivation prompt (i.e., the partisan groups polarized in their opinions, reflective of a prior attitude effect). They were also motivated reasoners in situations where they received an out-party endorsement frame (e.g., Republican respondents received the Democratic endorsement)—here they became less supportive (going against the out-party endorsement). Taken together, then, partisans supported or rejected *the identical policy* based only on the endorsement frame. However, when told that members of both parties supported the Act (i.e., the cross-partisan frame), respondents displayed careful analysis of the content of policy, mimicking the behavior of respondents who did not receive an endorsement but were encouraged to justify their responses.

The results show then that when there is cross-partisan competition, partisan-motivated reasoning wanes. Of course, this is often not an option given the realities of policy making. Even so, the same research shows that respondents who received the justification treatment displayed *no* evidence of partisan-motivated reasoning, *regardless* of what they were told about party support. For example, Democrats who were told only of Republican support or only of Democratic support analyzed the content of the policy and expressed views consistent with the content of the factual information (i.e., no attitude polarization occurred in response to the party cues). Partisan-motivated reasoning disappeared. Thus, not only does party competition moderate partisan-motivated reasoning but so does motivation to be accurate—a point, as explained above, recognized by Taber and Lodge in their own work.[13]

As discussed, another individual attribute that is thought to condition motivated reasoning—aside from accuracy motivation and strength of opinions—is individual-level knowledge or sophistication. In the aforementioned study, Slothuus and de Vreese (2010) investigate how political knowledge moderates partisan-motivated reasoning. Recall that the authors found great reliance on partisan cues on the conflictual welfare issue, in line with partisan-motivated reasoning theory. On this issue, they also report strong partisan effects among more knowledgeable respondents which is exactly what the theory predicts: sophistication or knowledge, as explained, increases motivated reasoning. This also is the opposite of what would be predicted by the information shortcut account as that would suggest low-knowledge individuals rely on party cues more to make up for their shortfall (see Slothuus, 2016 for another study showing greater attitude polarization among the more politically aware in response to party cues, consistent with the "sophistication effect").

A final limit to partisan-motivated reasoning that we will consider is the possibility individuals hold other beliefs or attitudes that will trump the effect of partisanship (e.g., Mullinix, 2016). Slothuus (2010) analyzed survey data collected over time in Denmark before and after the major left-of-center party, the Social Democrats, announced a reversal of their policy position on a major welfare policy issue. As in previous work, voters affiliating with the Social Democrats were more inclined to change their policy opinions according to the new party line. Moreover, those identifying strongly with the party were the most responsive to the changing party cue, consistent with Taber and Lodge's (2006, p. 757) "attitude strength effect." However, not all Social Democratic voters toed the party line, not even among the strong identifiers. Rather, they seemed to form policy opinions based in part on their own preexisting beliefs about the financial stress on public welfare budgets and hence were less responsive to the party cue. Slothuus's (2010) results suggest that *partisan*-motivated reasoning can be tempered when citizens hold other strong beliefs they turn to instead of relying on their party affiliation.

Citizens' partisanship has long been central to theories of opinion formation. What has been less clear is just how individuals use party cues when forming their opinions. Motivated reasoning theory has substantially advanced what we know about party effects.[14] It is fitting that the theory is particularly informative in competitive situations which often define political battles. As explained, Lodge did not simply introduce a psychological theory; instead, he used work in psychology to develop a *political* theory of reasoning. The theory applies most clearly when individuals are not hyper-motivated to form "accurate opinions," which may be the norm in political contexts. That said, that more knowledgeable people engage in partisan-motivated reasoning reveals the boundaries of the theory insofar as many citizens lack such knowledge. Our final set of examples come from a domain where knowledge is also in short supply: opinions about scientific issues.

Opinions About Scientific Issues[15]

A starting place to understanding opinion formation on scientific issues or technologies is the model of scientific literacy. This model treats citizens and consumers as rational thinkers who carefully integrate new information in expected ways (i.e., individuals are treated as Bayesians). The expectation is that knowledge facilitates accurate assessment of risks and benefits, and generally, increased knowledge "generates support for science and technology" (Gaskell, Bauer, Durant, & Allum, 1999, p. 386; Miller, 1998; Rodriguez, 2007; Sturgis & Allum, 2006). The reality, of course, is that citizens lack the motivation to obtain and process large amounts of information, and, as with politics, many scientific issues are contested over time, making it difficult for citizens to navigate the information environment (e.g., Nisbet & Mooney, 2007; Scheufele, 2006). Scheufele and Lewenstein (2005, p. 660) explain that "developing an in-depth understanding [of scientific issues/technologies] would require *significant* efforts on the part of ordinary citizens [and] the pay-offs ... may simply not be enough" (emphasis in original; also see Lee et al., 2005; Scheufele, 2006). As a result, in many cases, the application of motivated reasoning to such situations is spot on. We next make this point by offering several examples.

Our first example focuses on the confirmation bias where people seek out information consistent with their prior opinions. Yeo, Xenos, Brossard, and Scheufele (2015) study information seeking on nanotechnology—a technology that serves as a "good exemplar ... of scientific developments" (p. 177). The main part of their study offered participants the opportunity to choose one of nine news articles; the articles came from Fox News (a conservative outlet), MSNBC (a liberal outlet), or the Canadian Broadcasting Corporation. They find that, when provided with no prior information, individuals exhibit a strong confirmation bias: "conservatives were more likely to select Fox News, whereas liberals were more likely to select MSNBC" (183). This constitutes some of the only evidence of confirmation bias in the domain of science.

The authors do not stop there, however, as they also included an experimental condition such that respondents, prior to making a media choice, received an article that included cues, stating that a conservative think tank opposed the regulation of nanotechnology while a liberal think tank favored them. These ideological cues vitiated the confirmation bias—for these individuals, for example, "there is relatively little difference in the selection rate of MSNBC by liberals and conservatives" (p. 182). The authors thus add an important caveat to confirmation bias processes; when it comes to new issues, individuals appear to be first and foremost motivated to figure out where "their side stands" and this leads them to select ideologically consistent sources. However, once they learn ideological positions, they seek information from a much broader range of sources so as to learn more about the technology (e.g., become more scientifically literate).[16] In short, there seems to be, on scientific issues, a rule akin to lexicographical decision-making that prioritizes learning ideological positions first and foremost (Payne, Bettman, & Johnson, 1993, p. 26). This then moves Lodge's foundational motivated reasoning search along by showing search biases but also antidotes in the domain of science.

Science differs from politics, in part, because there is a potential for near consensus on certain issues/technologies. Consensus does not come easily, but when it does, motivated reasoning poses a particular challenge that individuals will not view evidence objectively but rather based on their prior attitudes (i.e., the prior attitude effect). An example comes from Druckman and Bolsen's (2011) two-wave study of new technologies. At one point in time, the authors measured respondents' support for genetically modified (GM) foods.

Then, about ten days later, respondents received three types of information about GM foods: positive information about how GM foods combat diseases, negative information about the possible negative long-term health consequences of GM foods, and neutral information about the economic consequences of GM foods. On its face, all of this information is potentially relevant. Indeed, when asked to assess the information, a distinct group of respondents—who were encouraged to think of all possible perspectives regarding GM food and told they would have to justify their assessments (thereby prompting an accuracy motivation)— judged all three to be relevant and valid.

Yet, Druckman and Bolsen (2011) report that, among the main set of respondents, the prior wave 1 opinions strongly conditioned treatment of the new information. Those previously supportive of GM foods dismissed the con information as invalid, rated the pro information as highly valid, and viewed the neutral information as being pro. Those opposed to GM foods did the opposite, invalidating the pro information, praising the con, and seeing the neutral as con (also see Kahan et al., 2009). The authors found virtually identical dynamics with the same design but on the topic of carbon nanotubes. This prior attitude effect can, at the aggregate level, result in a polarizing of opinions. Dietz (2013, p. 14083), in reference to scientific information, states,

> Once an initial impression is formed, people then tend to accumulate more and more evidence that is consistent with their prior beliefs. They may be skeptical or unaware of information incongruent with prior beliefs and values. Over time, this process of biased assimilation of information can lead to a set of beliefs that are strongly held, elaborate, and quite divergent from scientific consensus.

Put another way, scientific literacy fails because of a prior attitude effect.

Disconfirmation biases also influence scientific opinion formation, leading to the dismissal of evidence inconsistent with prior opinions even if that evidence has ostensible objective accuracy. This is a particularly critical process when it comes to science: even if a scientific consensus exists (e.g., near objective accuracy), citizens may dismiss it if their prior opinions are not to trust that consensus. This speaks to one of the most concerning aspects in science discourse, which is the politicization that occurs when an actor exploits "the inevitable uncertainties about aspects of science to cast doubt on the science overall . . . thereby magnifying doubts in the public mind" (Steketee, 2010, p. 2; see Jasanoff, 1987, p. 195; Oreskes & Conway, 2010; Pielke, 2007). The consequence is that "even when virtually all relevant observers have ultimately concluded that the accumulated evidence *could* be taken as sufficient to issue a solid scientific conclusion . . . arguments [continue] that the findings [are] not definitive" (Freudenburg, Gramling, & Davidson, 2008, p. 28, italics in original).[17]

The problem of politicization directly links to the credibility of information and motivated reasoning—when science is politicized, people become unclear on what to believe and thus scientific credibility declines and people tend to reject sound science (due to the prior belief that science is not credible). This phenomenon and the ostensible increase in politicization have led to tremendous concern among scientists—"politicization does not bode well for public decision-making on issues with substantial scientific content. We have not been very successful in efforts to counter ideological frames applied to science" (Dietz, 2013, p. 14085).

With such dynamics in mind, Bolsen, Druckman, and Cook (2014a, p. 5) explain that "frames that highlight politicization introduce uncertainty regarding whether one can trust science-based arguments." In one experiment, they told some respondents that,

> many have pointed to research that suggests alternative energy sources (e.g., nuclear energy) can dramatically improve the environment, relative to fossil fuels like coal and oil that release greenhouse gases and cause pollution. For example, unlike fossil fuels, wastes from nuclear energy are not released into the environment. A recent National Academy of Sciences (NAS)

publication states, "A general scientific and technical consensus exists that deep geologic disposal can provide predictable and effective long-term isolation of nuclear wastes."

When respondents received just this information (which did in fact come from an NAS report), support for nuclear energy increased. Yet, support for nuclear energy fell (i.e., the aforementioned evidence had no influence on opinions) when the information was *preceded* by a *politicization frame* that stated "it is increasingly difficult for non-experts to evaluate science—politicians and others often color scientific work and advocate selective science to favor their agendas." The results suggest that a politicization frame affected individuals' prior opinions about science, causing individuals not to know what to believe. This prior belief then generated a motivated reasoning disconfirmation bias such that they dismissed scientific evidence that was inconsistent with the politicization belief about a lack of consensus: they dismiss even ostensibly consensual scientific evidence due to their prior belief of politicization.

Bolsen and Druckman (2015) expand on this work, exploring techniques to mitigate politicization-driven disconfirmation bias. Focusing on the use of carbon nanotechnology and fracking, the authors demonstrate that warnings that state a scientific consensus exists and politicization should be dismissed—that come *prior* to politicization—or similar corrections that come *after* politicization dramatically stunt the impact of politicization (i.e., the questioning of science). Corrections are particularly effective when individuals are motivated to process information accurately. Thus, there is an antidote to a disconfirmation bias due to politicization. It is not clear in practice, however, how well these warnings and corrections work since the belief in consensus itself can be politically driven (Kahan, Jenkins-Smith, & Braman, 2011).

Taken together, these examples of motivated reasoning in the domain of science accentuate Lodge's contribution of extending work on the topic to areas where citizens lack information, there are contested claims (e.g., politicization), and over-time processes (e.g., formation of prior beliefs influence later attitudes and behaviors). We have offered only a few examples, but many others have imported the model to the domain of science (e.g., Hart, Nisbet, & Myers, 2015; Nisbet, Cooper, & Garrett, 2015; Stanovich, West, & Toplak, 2013). All of this work also invalidates the aforementioned scientific literacy model; as with politics, the model shows that one cannot simply assume straightforward processing of information. In their study of climate mitigation politics, Hart and Nisbet (2012, p. 715) conclude that, counter to the scientific literacy model,

> neither factual knowledge about global warming nor general scientific knowledge is associated with support for climate mitigation politics... [rather] motivated reasoning plays [a key role] in the interpretation and application of messages discussing scientific issues and calls into question

the traditional deficit model of science communication [i.e., scientific literacy model].

We have discussed ways to vitiate motivated reasoning when it comes to science—including ideological cues and consensus warnings or corrections—we imagine future work will continue to isolate such moderators. This next generation of work reflects the legacy of Lodge in establishing the model and considering conditions.

Conclusion

Lodge's work in political psychology is a model for how to integrate the workings of individual psychology with political context. As we have noted, opinion formation in the realm of politics takes place in an environment where citizens have low levels of information and where political parties and other elite actors compete over time to push frames, cues, and information intended to enlighten and persuade citizens. Citizens use their predispositions and prior attitudes to form political opinions, but a fundamental premise for understanding political opinion formation is that in most cases individuals' predispositions do not map onto political issues in any natural or straightforward way (see Leeper & Slothuus, 2014). Citizens need to rely on information from the political environment to form opinions and participate in politics. Lodge's work is superb in making the connections between psychological processes, predispositions, and context, hence offering a model for research that is both politically and psychologically sophisticated (see Druckman et al., 2009).

In this chapter, we have shown how Lodge's research program on motivated reasoning has inspired a variety of studies on how citizens form opinions in response to political communication. Our review of work in the three domains of elite framing, party competition, and science information made it clear that motivated reasoning could often help explain opinion formation in response to communication. However, we also pointed out that motivated reasoning seems highly conditional and can be reduced by differences in individuals' motivations and political sophistication and by mixes of information.

We close by pointing out two paths for further progress in research on motivated reasoning. First, we need to pinpoint more directly the psychological mechanisms underlying motivated reasoning. In our review of existing work, we often described results that clearly showed attitude polarization whereas the exact mechanisms accounting for this polarization were less clearly demonstrated. We did highlight some clear indications of a prior attitude effect, confirmation or disconfirmation biases but more work is needed to empirically show how citizens reason about political issues and to what extent reasoning is driven by the motivations we theorize.

Second, more systematic work is needed on how to generalize the conditions under which motivated reasoning occurs. For example, Druckman (2012) delineates a number of concerns about how the motivated thinking processes observed by Lodge and collaborators are limited to cases where partisan motivation is high. Highlighting the second component of motivated reasoning theory—accuracy motivation—should lead to distinct reasoning processes and potential outcomes. Leeper and Slothuus (2014) go further to suggest some clear cases where the effect of partisan/directional motivation might be constrained. Among these are cases where there are competing directional motivations (e.g., to defend one's party identification and to defend a particular policy prior), situations where social accountability drives a high degree of accuracy motivation (see, e.g., Lerner & Tetlock, 1999), and contexts where political realities run into such clear conflict with prior opinions that citizens are forced to respond (e.g., Bisgaard, 2015; Leeper & Slothuus, N.d.). We think these possibilities for contextual and situational constraint on directional motivation and its effects are important to study systematically to advance our understanding of political opinion formation.

Notes

1. Parts of this section are taken from Druckman and Lupia (2000), and Druckman (2012, 2015).
2. Lodge and Taber (2000, p. 186) initially introduced motivated reasoning as an extension to Lodge's work on online processing. While online reasoning is not necessary for motivated reasoning, it does increase the likelihood of it occurring. For further discussion, see Druckman et al. (2009) (also see Braman & Nelson, 2007; Goren, 2002).
3. In their 2006 article, Taber and Lodge employ the term "motivated skepticism"; we treat motivated reasoning as synonymous with "motivated skepticism" as well as "partisan perceptual screen" (Lavine et al., 2012). The idea of motivated reasoning has deep roots in psychological research of the 1950s and 1960s (see, for example, Festinger, 1957), and more contemporary research by Lord et al. (1979) and Kunda (1990) (for early political science applications, see Sears & Whitney, 1973).
4. This appears to contradict the ideal Bayesian reasoning (see Kim et al., 2010; Redlawsk, 2002 although also see Bullock, 2009 for a general treatment of Bayes).
5. This abstracted model of opinion formation is broadly consistent with a memory-based, online, or hybrid theory of information processing, as each belief element, b, might be cognitive or affective in nature and each weight, w, might reflect initial contributions to an online tally, weights imposed during memory retrieval, or both. The expectancy value calculation similarly imposes no restrictions on how weights should be determined or how beliefs should be acquired or evaluated.
6. Over the ten-day interval, no relevant information regarding the Patriot Act appeared in the news and respondents reported scant independent attempts to obtain information.
7. The experimental also exposed participants to arguments about a state-run casino in Illinois. The results for both issues are similar.
8. Taber and Lodge (2006) focus on prior issue attitudes, not partisanship, in their experiments on affirmative action and gun control, and while they did include the Democratic and Republican parties as sources of some of the arguments presented to study participants on the two issues, they did not explicitly analyze or isolate the partisan effects (e.g., if responses were moderated by party identification). Likewise, in other studies they focus on evaluations of candidates with an explicit party label, but not policy issues (e.g., Lodge & Taber, 2000, 2005, 2013).
9. Leeper and Slothuus (2014, p. 143) note, "the operation of motivated reasoning will look differently for individuals depending on what issues are at stake and how intensely they need to defend their prior attitudes or identities."

10. Some respondents, not described here, also received the arguments without a party endorsement. In those cases, the average respondents rated the strong arguments and weak arguments as such.
11. Another condition stated the Act was supported by both parties; the results of that condition suggest that respondents view such a consensus frame as being akin to an in-party frame.
12. Another justification condition described the environment as being highly partisan such that government is divided and fellow partisans rarely agree, and said that later the respondent would have to explain reasons for his/her partisan affiliation. This was similar to the polarized conditions in the previously discussed experiment, and the results in these conditions suggested strong partisan-motivated reasoning.
13. Taber and Lodge (2012, p. 249) maintain that "*defense of one's prior attitude is the general default* when reasoning about attitudinally contrary arguments, and it takes dramatic, focused intervention to deflect people off a well-grounded attitude" (italics in original). But Lodge does acknowledge such interventions do occur: "the model . . . does not claim that individuals never revise their initial attitudes or are unable to overcome their initial effects" (Kraft, Lodge, & Taber, 2015, p. 131; also see Leeper, 2012, Mullinix, 2016).
14. Given our focus on the effect of party cues, once received, on opinion formation, we did not offer an example of a partisan confirmation bias. Yet, there is a fair deal of evidence that such a bias frequently occurs. Indeed, Prior (2013, p. 111) explains, "Studies of selective exposure on television typically reach a . . . conclusion: Republicans and conservatives report more exposure to conservative outlets, whereas Democrats and liberals report greater exposure to liberal sources, so selective exposure in cable news viewing is common" (e.g., Iyengar & Hahn, 2009; Stroud, 2011, p. 34).
15. This is a domain where Lodge recently has worked; indeed, recently, Kraft et al. (2015, p. 130) state that the "theoretical mechanisms that the . . . model describes provide a strong framework to integrate the different findings related to political biases on public beliefs about science."
16. These findings are consistent with some other work that shows how variations in issue content, alternative cues, type of media, and the amount of choice condition confirmation biases (e.g., Arceneaux & Johnson, 2013; Iyengar, Hahn, Krosnick, & Walker, 2008; Messing & Westwood, 2013).
17. To cite an example—in response to the release of the *Climate Change Impacts in the United States* report that stated a scientific consensus exists that global climate change stems "primarily" from human activities (the report reflected the views of over 300 experts and was reviewed by numerous agencies including representatives from oil companies), Florida Senator Marco Rubio stated, "The climate is always changing. The question is, is manmade activity what's contributing most to it? I've seen reasonable debate on that principle" (Davenport, 2014, p. A15).

References

Arceneaux, Kevin & Johnson, Martin. (2013). *Changing minds or changing channels? Partisan news in an age of choice*. Chicago, IL: University of Chicago Press.

Bartels, Larry M. (2002). Beyond the running tally: Partisan bias in political perceptions. *Political Behavior*, 24(2), 117–150.

Bassili, John N. (1989). *On-line cognition in person perception*. Hillsdale, NJ: Lawrence Erlbaum.

Bisgaard, Martin. (2015). Bias will find a way: Economic perceptions, attributions of blame, and partisan-motivated reasoning during crisis. *Journal of Politics*, 77(3), 849–860.

Bisgaard, Martin & Slothuus, Rune. (Forthcoming). Partisan elites as culprits? How party cues shape partisan perceptual gaps. *American Journal of Political Science*.

Bolsen, Toby & Druckman, James N. (2015). Counteracting the politicization of science. *Journal of Communication*, 65, 745–769.

Bolsen, Toby, Druckman, James N., & Cook, Fay Lomax. (2014a). How frames can undermine support for scientific adaptations: Politicization and the status quo bias. *Public Opinion Quarterly*, 78, 1–26.

Bolsen, Toby, Druckman, James N., & Cook, Fay Lomax. (2014b). The influence of partisan motivated reasoning on public opinion. *Political Behavior*, 36, 235–262.

Braman, Eileen & Nelson, Thomas E. (2007). Mechanisms of motivated reasoning? *American Journal of Political Science*, 51(4), 940–956.

Bullock, John G. (2009). Partisan bias and the Bayesian ideal in the study of public opinion. *Journal of Politics*, 71(3), 1109–1124.

Bullock, John G. (2011). Elite influence on public opinion in an informed electorate. *American Political Science Review*, 105(3), 496–515.

Campbell, Angus, Converse, Philip E., Miller, Warren E., & Stokes, Donald E. (1960). *The American Voter*. Chicago, IL: University of Chicago Press.

Chong, Dennis & Druckman, James N. (2007). Framing public opinion in competitive democracies. *American Political Science Review*, 101(4), 637–655.

Chong, Dennis & Druckman, James N. (2010). Dynamic public opinion: Communication effects over time. *American Political Science Review*, 104(4), 663–680.

Dahl, Robert A. (1971). *Polyarchy*. Chicago, IL: University of Chicago Press.

Davenport, Coral. (2014). Miami finds itself ankle-deep in climate change debate. *New York Times*, May 7. Retrieved from www.nytimes.com/2014/05/08/us/florida-finds-itself-in-the-eye-of-the-storm-on-climate-change.html

Dietz, Thomas. (2013). Bringing values and deliberation to science communication. *Proceedings of the National Academy of Sciences*, 110(August), 14081–14087.

Druckman, James N. (2012). The politics of motivation. *Critical Review*, 24, 199–216.

Druckman, James N. (2014). Pathologies of studying public opinion, political communication, and democratic responsiveness. *Political Communication*, 31, 467–492.

Druckman, James N. (2015). Communicating policy-relevant science. American Political Science Association Task Force on Public Engagement. *PS: Political Science & Politics*, 48(Supp. S1), 58–69.

Druckman, James N. & Bolsen, Toby. (2011). Framing, motivated reasoning, and opinions about emergent technologies. *Journal of Communication*, 61(August), 659–688.

Druckman, James N., Fein, Jordan, & Leeper, Thomas J. (2014). A source of bias in public opinion stability. *American Political Science Review*, 106(2), 430–454.

Druckman, James N., Kuklinski, James H., & Sigelman, Lee. (2009). The unmet potential of interdisciplinary research: Political psychological approaches to voting and public opinion. *Political Behavior*, 31(4), 485–510.

Druckman, James N. & Leeper, Thomas J. (2012). Learning more from political communication experiments: Pretreatment and its effects. *American Journal of Political Science*, 56(4), 875–896.

Druckman, James N. & Lupia, Arthur. (2000). Preference formation. *Annual Review of Political Science*, 3, 1–24.

Druckman, James N. & Lupia, Arthur. (2006). Mind, will, and choice: Lessons from experiments in contextual variation. In Robert E. Goodin & Charles Tilly (Eds.), *The Oxford handbook of contextual political analysis* (pp. 97–113). Oxford: Oxford University Press.

Druckman, James N., Peterson, Erik, & Slothuus, Rune. (2013). How elite partisan polarization affects public opinion formation. *American Political Science Review*, 107(1), 57–79.

Eagly, Alice H. & Chaiken, Shelly. (1993). *The psychology of attitudes*. Orlando, FL: Harcourt Brace Jovanovich College Publishers.

Enelow, J. M. & Hinich, M. J. (1984). *The spatial theory of voting: An introduction*. New York: Cambridge University Press.

Erikson, Robert S., MacKuen, Michael B., & Stimson, James A. (2002). *The macro polity*. New York: Cambridge University Press.

Fazio, Russell H. & Olson, Michael A. (2003). Attitudes: Foundations, functions, and consequences. In M. A. Hogg & J. Cooper (Eds.), *The handbook of social psychology* (pp. 139–160). London: Sage.

Festinger, Leon. (1957). *A theory of cognitive dissonance*. Stanford, CA: Stanford University Press.

Freudenburg, William R., Gramling, Robert, & Davidson, Debra J. (2008). Scientific certainty argumentation methods (SCAMs): Science and the politics of doubt. *Sociological Inquiry*, 78, 2–38.

Gaines, Brian J., Kuklinski, James H., Quirk, Paul J., Peyton, Buddy, & Verkuilen, Jay. (2007). Same facts, different interpretations: Partisan motivation and opinion on Iraq. *Journal of Politics*, 69(4), 957–974.

Gaskell, George, Bauer, Martin W., Durant, John, & Allum, Nicholas C. (1999). Worlds apart? The reception of genetically modified foods in Europe and the U.S. *Science*, 285(5426), 384–387.

Gerber, Alan S. & Huber, Gregory A. (2009). Partisanship and economic behavior: Do partisan differences in economic forecasts predict real economic behavior? *American Political Science Review*, 103(3), 407–426.

Gerber, Alan S. & Huber, Gregory A. (2010). Partisanship, political control, and economic assessments. *American Journal of Political Science*, 54(1), 153–173.

Goren, Paul. (2002). Character weakness, partisan bias, and presidential evaluation. *American Journal of Political Science*, 46(3), 627–641.

Goren, Paul N. (2005). Party identification and core political values. *American Journal of Political Science*, 49(4), 882–897.

Green, Donald P., Palmquist, Bradley, & Schickler, Eric (2002). *Partisan hearts and minds*. New Haven, CT: Yale University Press.

Groenendyk, Eric W. (2013). *Competing motives in the partisan mind: How loyalty and responsiveness shape party identification and democracy*. New York: Oxford University Press.

Hart, P. Sol & Nisbet, Erik C. (2012). Boomerang effects in science communication how motivated reasoning and identity cues amplify opinion polarization about climate mitigation policies. *Communication Research*, 39(6), 701–723.

Hart, P. Sol, Nisbet, Erik C., & Myers, Teresa A. (2015). Public attention to science and political news and support for climate change mitigation. *Nature Climate Change*, 5(6), 541–545.

Hastie, Reid & Park, Bernadette. (1986). The relationship between memory and judgment depends on whether the judgment task is memory-based or on-line. *Psychology Review*, 93(3), 258–268.

Iyengar, Shanto. (1990). The accessibility bias in politics: Television news and public opinion. *International Journal of Public Opinion Research*, 2(1), 1–15.

Iyengar, Shanto & Hahn, Kyu. (2009). Red media, blue media: Evidence of ideological selectivity in media use. *Journal of Communication*, 59(1), 19–39.

Iyengar, Shanto, Hahn, Kyu S., Krosnick, Jon A., & Walker, John (2008). Selective exposure to campaign communication: The role of anticipated agreement and issue public membership. *Journal of Politics*, 70(1), 186–200.

Iyengar, Shanto, Lelkes, Yphtach, & Sood, Gaurav. (2012). Affect, not ideology: A social identity perspective on polarization. *Public Opinion Quarterly*, 76(3), 405–431.

Jasanoff, Sheila S. (1987). Contested boundaries in policy-relevant science. *Social Studies of Science*, 17(2), 195–230.

Kahan, Dan M., Braman, Donald, Slovic, Paul, Gastil, John, & Cohen, Geoffrey. (2009). Cultural cognition of the risks and benefits of nanotechnology. *Nature Nanotechnology*, 4, 87–90.

Kahan, Dan N., Jenkins-Smith, Hank, & Braman, Donald. (2011). Cultural cognition of scientific consensus. *Journal of Risk Research*, 14, 147–174.

Kim, Sung-youn, Taber, Charles S., & Lodge, Milton. (2010). A computational model of the citizen as motivated reasoner: Modeling the dynamics of the 2000 presidential election. *Political Behavior*, 32, 1–28.

Kraft, Patrick, Lodge, Milton, & Taber, Charles S. (2015). Why people "don't trust the evidence": Motivated reasoning and scientific beliefs. *The Annals of the American Academy of Political and Social Science*, 658(March), 121–135.

Kunda, Ziva. (1990). The case for motivated reasoning. *Psychological Bulletin*, 108(3), 480–498.

Lavine, Howard, Johnston, Christopher D., & Steenbergen, Marco R. (2012). *The ambivalent partisan*. New York: Oxford University Press.

Lee, Chul-Joo, Scheufele, Dietram A., & Lewenstein, Bruce V. (2005). Public attitudes toward emerging technologies: Examining the interactive effects of cognitions and affect on public attitudes toward nanotechnology. *Science Communication*, 27(2), 240–267.

Leeper, Thomas J. (2012). *Essays on political information and the dynamics of public opinion*. PhD Thesis, Northwestern University.

Leeper, Thomas J. (2014). The informational basis for mass polarization. *Public Opinion Quarterly*, 78(1), 27–46.

Leeper, Thomas J. (2017). How does treatment self-selection affect inferences about political communication? *Journal of Experimental Political Science*, 4(1), 21–33.

Leeper, Thomas J. & Slothuus, Rune. (2014). Political parties, motivated reasoning, and public opinion formation. *Advances in Political Psychology*, 32, 129–156.

Leeper, Thomas J. & Slothuus, Rune. (N.d.). *If only citizens had a cue: The process of opinion formation over time*. Working paper, Aarhus University.

Lerner, Jennifer S. & Tetlock, Philip E. (1999). Accounting for the effects of accountability. *Psychological Bulletin*, 125(2), 255–275.

Lippmann, Walter. (1922). *Public opinion*. New York: Harcourt, Brace and Company.

Lodge, Milton & McGraw, Kathleen M. (Eds.) (1995). *Political judgment: Structure and process*. Ann Arbor, MI: University of Michigan Press.

Lodge, Milton, McGraw, Kathleen M., & Stroh, Patrick K. (1989). An impression-driven model of candidate evaluation. *American Political Science Review*, 83(2), 399–419.

Lodge, Milton, Steenbergen, Marco R., & Brau, Shawn. (1995). The responsive voter: Campaign information and the dynamics of candidate evaluation. *American Political Science Review*, 89(2), 309–326.

Lodge, Milton & Taber, Charles S. (2000). Three steps toward a theory of motivated political reasoning. In Arthur Lupia, Mathew D. McCubbins, & Samuel L. Popkin (Eds.), *Elements of reason: Cognition, choice, and the bounds of rationality* (pp. 183–213). New York: Cambridge University Press.

Lodge, Milton & Taber, Charles S. (2005). The automaticity of affect for political leaders, groups, and issues: An experimental test of the hot cognition hypothesis. *Political Psychology*, 26(3), 455–482.

Lodge, Milton & Taber, Charles S. (2008). *The rationalizing voter: Unconscious thought in political information processing*. Unpublished paper, Stony Brook University.

Lodge, Milton & Taber, Charles S. (2013). *The rationalizing voter*. New York: Cambridge University Press.
Lord, Charles G., Ross, Lee, & Lepper, Mark R. (1979). Biased assimilation and attitude polarization: The effects of prior theories on subsequently considered evidence. *Journal of Personal and Social Psychology*, 37(11), 2098–2109.
Lupia, Arthur. (2006). How elitism undermines the study of voter competence. *Critical Review*, 18(1), 217–232.
Messing, Solomon & Westwood, Sean J. (2013). Selective exposure in the age of social media: Endorsements trump partisan source affiliation when selecting news online. *Communication Research*, 41(8), 1042–1063.
Miller, John D. (1998). The measurement of civic scientific literacy. *Public Understanding of Science*, 7, 203–223.
Mullinix, Kevin J. (2016). Partisanship and preference formation: Competing motivations, elite polarization, and issue importance. *Political Behavior*, 38(2), 383–411.
Nicholson, Stephen P. (2012). Polarizing cues. *American Journal of Political Science*, 56(2), 52–66.
Nisbet, Erik C., Cooper, Kathryn E., & Garrett, R. Kelly. (2015). The partisan brain: How dissonant science messages lead conservatives and liberals to (dis)trust science. *The ANNALS of the American Academy of Political and Social Science*, 658(1), 36–66.
Nisbet, Matthew C. & Mooney, Chris. (2007). Framing science. *Science*, 316, 56.
Oreskes, Naomi & Conway, Erik M. (2010). *Merchants of doubt: How a handful of scientists obscured the truth on issues from tobacco smoke to global warming*. New York: Bloomsbury Press.
Payne, John W., Bettman, James R., & Johnson, Eric J. (1993). *The adaptive decision maker*. New York: Cambridge University Press.
Pielke Jr., Roger S. (2007). *The honest broker: Making sense of science in policy and politics*. Cambridge: Cambridge University Press.
Prior, Markus. (2013). Media and political polarization. *Annual Review of Political Science*, 16, 101–127.
Rahn, Wendy M., Krosnik, Jon A., & Breuning, Marijke. (1994). Rationalization and derivation processes in survey studies of political candidate evaluation. *American Journal of Political Science*, 38, 582–600.
Redlawsk, David P. (2002). Hot cognition or cool consideration? Testing the effects of motivated reasoning on political decision making. *Journal of Politics*, 64(4), 1021–1044.
Rodriguez, Lulu. (2007). The impact of risk communication on the acceptance of irradiated food. *Science Communication*, 28(4), 476–500.
Scheufele, Dietram A. (2006). Five lessons in nano outreach. *Materials Today*, 9, 64.
Scheufele, Dietram A. & Lewenstein, Bruce V. (2005). The public and nanotechnology: How citizens make sense of emerging technologies. *Journal of Nanoparticle Research*, 7, 659–667.
Sears, David O. & Whitney, R. E. (1973). Political persuasion. In I. DeS. Pool, W. Schramm, F. W. Frey, N. Maccoby, & E. B. Parker (Eds.), *Handbook of communication* (pp. 253–289). Chicago, IL: Rand McNally.
Slothuus, Rune. (2010). When can political parties lead public opinion? Evidence from a natural experiment. *Political Communication*, 27(2), 158–177.
Slothuus, Rune. (2016). Assessing the influence of political parties on public opinion: The challenge from pretreatment effects. *Political Communication*, 33(2), 302–327.
Slothuus, Rune & de Vreese, Claes. (2010). Political parties, motivated reasoning, and issue framing effects. *Journal of Politics*, 72(3), 630–645.

Sniderman, Paul M. & Stiglitz, Edward H. (2012). *The reputational premium: A theory of party identification and policy reasoning.* Princeton: Princeton University Press.

Stanovich, Keith E., West, Richard F., & Toplak, Maggie E. (2013). Myside bias, rational thinking, and intelligence. *Current Directions in Psychological Science,* 22(4), 259–264.

Steketee, Mike. (2010). Some skeptics make it a habit to be wrong. *The Australian,* November 20. Retrieved from www.theaustralian.com.au/national-affairs/some-sceptics-make-it-a-habit-tobe-wrong/story-fn59niix-1225956414538?nk=88273c4b51f7681ad3c18 47e54436548

Stroud, Natalie J. (2011). *Niche news: The politics of news choice.* New York: Oxford University Press.

Sturgis, Patrick & Allum, Nick. (2006). *A literature review of research conducted on public interest, knowledge and attitudes to biomedical science: A report published by the Welcome Trust.* London: The Welcome Trust.

Taber, Charles S., Cann, Damon, & Kucsova, Simona. (2009). The motivated processing of political arguments. *Political Behavior,* 31(2), 137–155.

Taber, Charles S. & Lodge, Milton. (2006). Motivated skepticism in the evaluation of political beliefs. *American Journal of Political Science,* 50(3), 755–769.

Taber, Charles S. & Lodge, Milton. (2012). The scope and generality of automatic affective biases in political thinking: Reply to the symposium. *Critical Review,* 24(2), 247–268.

Taber, Charles S. & Lodge, Milton. (2016). The illusion of choice in democratic politics: The unconscious impact of motivated political reasoning. *Advances in Political Psychology,* 37, 61–85.

Yeo, Sara K., Xenos, Michael A., Brossard, Dominique, & Scheufele, Dietram A. (2015). Selecting our own science: How communication contexts and individual traits shape information seeking. *The ANNALS of the American Academy of Political and Social Science,* 658(1), 172–191.

Zaller, John. (1992). *The nature and origins of mass opinion.* New York: Cambridge University Press.

9
THE EFFECTS OF FIRST IMPRESSIONS ON SUBSEQUENT INFORMATION SEARCH AND EVALUATION

David P. Redlawsk and Douglas R. Pierce

The American Voter (Campbell, Converse, Miller, & Stokes, 1960) taught multiple generations of political scientists that voters, rather than being paragons of virtue, were instead ideologically innocent, unable to understand politics in ways that would allow them to exert effective control over those they elected to office. While only a small section of the book, the analyses by the authors of the "levels of conceptualization" (expanded upon by Converse, 1964) suggested that voters made choices that were mostly uninformed about campaigns, issues, candidates, or consequences of their votes. If voters must grasp the issues facing the country and act upon them to exercise control over their leaders, how could they do so when just one-tenth of all voters appeared to conceive of politics ideologically? Coming on top of other studies with similar findings (e.g., Berelson, Lazarsfeld, & McPhee, 1954) Campbell et al. (1960) confirmed what had often been assumed: voters were not very good at what they did. While scholars such as Key (1966), who suggested a "perverse and unorthodox argument . . . that voters are not fools" and Lane (1962), whose detailed interviews with surprisingly coherent voters suggested a common-man's ideology, may have believed otherwise, 30 years of voting research generally reinforced *The American Voter* view that most citizens fail to meet a (usually unclearly specified) democratic ideal.

Well-grounded in this negative view of voters through his undergraduate studies, the first author of this chapter was a new graduate student when he read a paper by Milton Lodge, Kathleen McGraw, and Patrick Stroh (1989) seeming to suggest voters might not be as incompetent as many believed. The basic claim was that political information processing occurs *online* as voters immediately extract the affective value of what they encounter and, once incorporated into an online running tally assessment, have no need to retain the underlying content. In fact, if people were what Fiske and Taylor (1984) called "cognitive misers," there would be no reason for voters to keep any content in long-term memory (or at least keep the links to access it) after it was factored into the online tally. One logical conclusion seemed to be that voters might not be so incompetent; instead, they could be taking much more into account than they were able to disgorge to political scientists with their after-the-fact survey questions relying on memory recall of complex political concepts. While this possibility led directly to Redlawsk's dissertation and early publications, the idea that American voters may be rehabilitated through online processing seems somewhat quaint today. Redlawsk (2001; Lau & Redlawsk, 2006) suggested, for example, that both online and memory processes are at play and if so, voters' inability to explain themselves may be more problematic than not.

Of course, Lodge's work has been broadly influential for reasons that go well beyond its setting the course for a long-term research agenda for one of us. In its first ten years, Lodge et al. (1989) garnered 113 citations according to Google Scholar. In the following ten years, another 309 citations were added, while in the most recent eight years (as of this writing) there are another 304. This paper has not only remained influential in its own right, but set the groundwork for a great deal of important work that has come after, including Lodge and Taber's capstone—2013's *The Rationalizing Voter*. As Lodge and his colleagues have developed the argument over the years, voters are not the potential paragons of political virtue that a beginning graduate student thought was implied by online processing. Instead, we now understand voters to be (potentially, under certain circumstances) motivated reasoners (Kunda, 1990; Lodge & Taber, 2000; Redlawsk, 2002; Redlawsk, Civettini, & Emmerson, 2010; Taber & Lodge, 2006) who, rather than using new information to accurately adjust any online evaluation, instead evaluate it in the service of maintaining priors.

So where do these priors come from? For a new candidate who emerges on the political scene, it must be from first impressions. That is, in learning about a candidate for the first time, the impression formed by that candidate through whatever means—based on party, or an initial TV/YouTube soundbite, or some other piece of information that becomes available—becomes the baseline and lens through which all additional information is considered. This leads to interesting questions about those first impressions themselves, some of which we attempt to address in this paper. We will look at first impressions from the perspective of information search and candidate evaluation, asking whether the initial encounters voters have with previously unknown candidates influence the nature of subsequent information search and evaluation. We suspect that they do, for a host of reasons. To examine this question we use the Dynamic Process Tracing Environment (DPTE) tool developed by Lau and Redlawsk (2001, 2006, 2013) to examine how what voters first learn about a candidate conditions what they do and learn next.[1]

Theoretical Background

Empirical investigations support the old canard that "first impressions matter." An edited volume by Ambady and Skowronski (2008) gives a sense of the breadth of the research, including sections on facial cues—so important to many first impressions—as well as environmental and behavioral cues, along with studies of the functionality of first impressions and the potential evolutionary bases of our tendency to make these snap judgments. The point is driven home that first impressions are ubiquitous. Research on first impressions goes back some 70 years or so; but even then, many thought the basic idea might simply be obvious. Kelley (1950, p. 431) wrote "that prior information or labels attached to a stimulus person make a difference in observers' first impressions is almost too obvious to require demonstration." Even so, he builds on Asch (1946) to show experimentally that providing labels as simple as "warm" or "cold" to describe a purported instructor students have not yet met can condition initial impressions once the instructor appears in classroom. In other words, knowing even basic information (for instance, party identification) about someone colors our first impressions.

But how important are those first impressions? Our parents certainly thought they mattered when they routinely reminded us that "you never get a second chance to make a first impression." And, to be sure, scholars have documented this "primacy" effect, in which information encountered first holds greater weight in evaluation than information acquired at a later time (Carney & Banaji, 2012). In fact, it is well established that initial reactions to a person have important implications for impression formation about the person (Anderson, 1965; Asch, 1946; Kelley, 1950; Tetlock, 1983).

Recent work in political science demonstrates that the impact of first impressions extends to candidate evaluations. One interesting set of studies performed by Todorov and his colleagues finds that subjects make split-second judgments about candidate traits after exposure to their pictures. These initial judgments have been found to be predictive of actual election outcomes (Mattes et al., 2010; Todorov, Mandisodza, Goren, & Hall, 2005; Willis & Todorov, 2006). Another relevant contribution comes from Holbrook, Krosnick, Visser, Gardner, and Cacioppo (2001) and their Asymmetric Nonlinear Model (ANM) of attitude formation. In contrast to some "rational" views of information processing in which comparable information is weighted equally, the ANM posits that people give disproportionate credence to information acquired early in the attitude formation process and that later information has a diminishing marginal effect on beliefs.

In fact, Lodge et al.'s (1989, 1995) early work on online processing provides some grounding for the importance of first impressions. Online processing presumes that evaluative context from information is extracted and processed, with an online tally maintained as a summary of the current evaluation. Depending on how one conceives of the tally, first impressions may anchor further evaluations (Lau & Redlawsk, 2006; Redlawsk, 2001). But more directly, the extensive literature on motivated reasoning (Kunda, 1990; Lodge & Taber, 2000; Redlawsk, 2002; Taber & Lodge, 2006) relies in great part on the idea that first impressions matter, and that in the realm of candidate evaluation voters are motivated to maintain those initial evaluations even in the face of counter-expectational information.

Online processing is one of the three pillars of this process, along with hot cognition and a "how-do-I-feel" heuristic (Lodge & Taber, 2000).

For example, Taber and Lodge (2006) find that prior attitudes have a significant effect on information seeking and appraisal. Subjects sought out more information that was congruent with their previously held attitudes and rated congruent arguments as more convincing than incongruent arguments. Redlawsk et al. (2010) documented how subjects who encountered incongruent information (defined in their study as information about the policy stands of the politician that deviated from the subject's professed position) about a candidate they favored initially *increased* their evaluations of the candidate, although the evaluations decreased as more incongruent information was encountered. Both these studies (and a host of others) support the notion that attitudes, once formed, are oftentimes resistant to new information. However, neither study expressly examined the impact of first impressions on information search and evaluations based on that search, which to us seems both important and understudied.

In this chapter, we seek to further our understanding of how first impressions affect political attitudes by considering the effect initial impressions of a candidate have on subsequent information search. That is, do negative or positive first impressions condition a subject's motivation to learn more about a candidate? Additionally, we consider whether a positive or negative first impression makes a person more likely to like or dislike the ensuing information encountered about a candidate. Our study contributes to the existing literature in several ways. First and foremost, our study design provides us with a case of "as if" randomization, which allows us to estimate the causal effects of first impressions on both the motivations to become informed about candidates and evaluations of later information. Furthermore, we test the extent to which first impressions persist even after a period of dedicated information search. Finally, we present a methodology that allows us to capture the real-time responses of participants to information, allowing for better measurement of affective reactions as they occur.

Hypotheses

We are unaware of any prior studies that have investigated direct effects of first impressions on information search and candidate evaluation, and thus in some respects our study is exploratory in its very nature. At the same time, we are guided by a set of hypotheses derived from the broader literature on first impressions. We begin by considering how first impressions influence final evaluations with Hypothesis 1:

> H1: First impressions will significantly affect subjects' evaluations of candidates, even after subsequent information search.

Simply put, we hypothesize that first impressions are "sticky" and will persist, even as subjects have the opportunity to learn more about the candidates. We do not necessarily mean this in the context of motivated reasoning, although it seems clear from prior work that first impressions condition the evaluation of new information. Instead, we suggest that the initial impression itself will remain "visible" in the overall final evaluation informed by subsequent information search.

Next, based on the ample evidence for negativity effects (Klein, 1991; Lau, 1982, 1985; Mattes & Redlawsk, 2014), we propose that:

> H2: Negative first impressions will have a greater impact on evaluations than positive first impressions, and
> H2a: It takes more positive information to counteract a negative first impression than it does negative information to counter a positive one (i.e., negative information is weighted more heavily than positive).

Furthermore, because people have a tendency to confirm their initial beliefs (Nickerson, 1998), we hypothesize that:

> H3: An initial negative (positive) impression about a candidate makes respondents more likely to judge future information about that candidate as negative (positive).

Our final hypothesis concerns the effect of a negative first impression on information acquisition. A common sense hypothesis would state that a negative first impression would decrease search, while a positive initial reaction would increase it. However, some research suggests that negative emotions (such as anxiety) lead people to become more vigilant and engage in more information-seeking behavior, while a positive response triggers a sense of complacency (Brader, 2005; Marcus, Neuman, & MacKuen, 2000; Redlawsk, 2006). Given this theoretical background, we hypothesize that:

> H4: Negative first impressions increase the motivation to learn more about a candidate while positive first impressions decrease the motivation

Data and Methods

We recruited 302 participants via Amazon's MTurk service (Berinsky, Huber, & Lenz, 2012). Subjects were invited to take part in a study on political decision-making using the Dynamic Processing Tracing Environment (DPTE) software (Lau & Redlawsk, 2006) and were paid a nominal fee for their time. The DPTE system presents users with a continuous stream of information and allows researchers to track the information search patterns of subjects engaged in evaluative and judgment tasks. Of these 302 subjects, we focus on a subset of 197 participants who were randomly assigned to a modified version of the dynamic information board software. These subjects were told that we were interested in how "people react and respond to information on the Internet" and were invited to register their impressions of the information as they encountered it. Subjects did so by clicking on buttons labeled "Share," "Like," and "Dislike" as they were reviewing the information (See Figures 9.1 and 9.2).[2] This functionality was designed to mimic the way in which online content frequently allows readers to provide their opinion on it as they read.

Our sample has an average age of 32.7, is 53% male, and 23% nonwhite. The modal respondent has a college degree and a self-reported income between $50,000 and $75,000. In political matters, the sample skews Democratic, with 62% of the respondents identifying as a Democrat (either leaning, weak, or strong) and

FIGURE 9.1   Dynamic Information Board. Subjects were able to choose which information about the candidates they wished to evaluate as well as to react to it by commenting, "liking," "disliking," or indicating they would "share" it.

The Effects of First Impressions   **157**

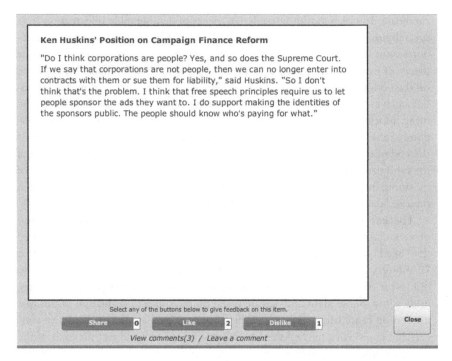

FIGURE 9.2   Dynamic Information Board Item Detail. After clicking on a headline, subjects saw more information about the topic and could react to the item by choosing one of the buttons along the bottom of the screen.

only 30% identifying as Republicans. On a seven-point scale of political ideology (0–6, with lower values indicating more liberal beliefs), the sample had a mean score of 3.21. On a four-point scale of political interest (1–4, with higher values indicating more interest), the sample had a mean score of 2.02; on a five-point scale of frequency of political discussion, the mean score was 3.27. Seventy-seven percent of the respondents indicated that they voted in the 2012 presidential election. While we make no claim that our sample is representative of any particular population, research indicates that MTurk subjects do not differ from more traditional samples drawn from the local community in their performance on similar decision-making tasks using the DPTE software (Paolacci & Chandler, 2014). We also have no theoretical reason to suspect that the psychological mechanisms detailed herein are idiosyncratic to MTurk participants.

Our decision-making study asked the participants to learn about and evaluate three hypothetical candidates competing in a party primary.[3] The candidates were designed to generally conform to mainstream liberal (or libertarian, in the case of the Republican candidate), moderate, and conservative viewpoints within their respective parties. We created 33 unique pieces of information about each candidate: 15 policy position stands, ten pieces of demographic information (e.g., age, religion, home state), and eight "general interest" items (e.g., personality anecdotes, scandals, family information). In total, subjects were exposed to 99 unique pieces of information during a 12-minute "primary." The information appeared on the computer screen in blocks of six "headlines" at a time; clicking on a headline, such as "Jones' Position on Entitlement Reform," allowed the subject to read more information on that topic.[4] Every 15 seconds, the items on the screen randomly refreshed, bringing up a new set of headlines for the subject to peruse. At the end of the information search stage, subjects were asked to indicate which of the candidates they would vote for and to evaluate the candidates on a number of measures, including feeling thermometers, competence, and the degree to which the candidates' policy stands were similar to the subject's.

The key independent variable in our study is the subject's first impression of a candidate, which we collected by examining whether a subject indicated she "liked" or "disliked" the first item encountered in the study. We found that 72 subjects liked the first item they encountered (positive first impression), 40 disliked it (negative first impression), and 85 registered no reaction (neutral first impression). Subsequent analyses are based on the subject's evaluation of this first impression candidate, whichever of the three options that may be. While we conceivably could have tracked the first impressions of each subject for each of the three candidates, we eschew this analytical strategy because it is possible that a subject's initial positive (negative) appraisal of one candidate may then condition how they feel about the next candidate they encounter. In fact, this would indeed be the case if we accept the assumption that the subject's first impression represents a case of "as if" randomization. We argue that since subjects knew practically nothing about the three candidates prior to selecting the first news item, whether they encountered a piece of information that they liked, disliked, or had no reaction to is entirely random. If that is the case, then we may plausibly contend that the effects detailed in this paper are causal ones.

Since our assumption of "as if" randomization is the linchpin of our argument, we must justify our claim empirically. We offer three pieces of evidence in support of our position. The first is the fact that since the candidates are hypothetical, subjects enter the information search stage of the study with no prior knowledge of any of the candidates.[5] This is important because if subjects had some way of divining the ideological positions of the candidates, they could effectively "self-select" into particular first impression groups; for example, a liberal subject might intentionally seek out an item about the conservative candidate in order to confirm his dislike for the candidate. Just before the study began, subjects did see an "introduction screen" with the candidates' names and pictures. Thus, it may be possible that this initial screen led subjects to form immediate impressions of a candidate which they then used to guide their first selections. However, there is no indication that any of the candidates were favored when it came to selecting the first piece of information to view. The percentage of subjects who first looked at an item about the moderate candidate is 34.5%; for the conservative candidate the percentage is 30.4% and for the liberal, 35.0%. None of these values is significantly different from 33.3% (p values of .720, .388, and .613, respectively for one sample t-tests), suggesting that subjects essentially picked a candidate at random to begin their search.

There is also no evidence that subjects of a particular ideological bent inferred from the initial pictures the ideology of the candidates. Self-identified liberal subjects were just as likely to first view an item about the conservative or moderate candidate as they were the liberal candidate, and this pattern holds for self-identified conservatives and moderates as well (a chi-square test of subject ideology versus candidate selection reveals no significant association; $\chi^2 = 3.587$, 4 df, $p < .465$). Furthermore, there is no evidence that subjects in any of the conditions were particularly discriminating about the first item to open. On average, participants in our study opened their first item 3.8 seconds after the study began and this time does not vary significantly by impression type ($F_{2, 194} = .317, p < .729$). Given that the items available are also randomized (by the software), it seems clear that the first item selected was indeed random.

Next, we consider whether a true counterfactual exists for our first impression groups. That is, in making our claim that first impressions are essentially random, we are assuming that any given subject could have a neutral, positive, or negative reaction to the first item encountered, regardless of what that item happened to be. This assumption could fail in one of two ways. First, we could have constructed candidates so unlikeable (or likeable) that it was highly improbable that our subjects would express the full range of reactions to items about that candidate. If this were so, then the counterfactual condition would not exist and our analysis would fail. To test this possibility, we looked at the subject's first impression (positive, negative, or neutral) by the target of the first contact (liberal, moderate, or conservative candidate). Table 9.1 presents *prima facie* evidence that each candidate engendered each of the possible affective responses. Furthermore, a chi-square test indicates that we cannot reject the null hypothesis (at $p < .069$) that first impression type is independent of the candidate selected (i.e., that the subject's selection of an item about a particular candidate is linked to the type of impression he or she indicates). Thus, each of the reactions was equally likely with any of the candidates. However, since the p value from this test is fairly close to the traditional .05 cutoff, we ran the analyses for each candidate separately and with results from one of the candidates removed. In each case, the general trends in the data that we report in the next section remain, although the magnitude of changes did vary by candidate.[6]

The second way our counterfactual assumption could fail is if the subjects in the positive, negative, and neutral groups differ from each other in some systematic way. For instance, perhaps the subjects in the positive first impression group are

TABLE 9.1 Impression Type by Candidate

Impression		Conservative	Moderate	Liberal	Total
Positive	Count	17	24	31	72
	Expected	21.9	24.9	25.2	
Negative	Count	19	11	10	40
	Expected	12.2	13.8	14.0	
Neutral	Count	24	33	28	85
	Expected	25.9	29.3	29.8	
Total		60	68	69	197

(Candidate spans Conservative, Moderate, Liberal columns.)

simply more optimistic in nature. Or, given that research has shown that political sophisticates tend to evince more affective reactions to political stimuli (Schreiber, 2007), perhaps those subjects in the neutral group were not as interested in politics. In order to assert that the subjects' first impressions represent a case of "as if" randomization, we must be able to demonstrate that, on average, the characteristics of each group are similar and the groups only differ in terms of the first impression type. We tested this claim using the Hansen and Bowers omnibus statistic (Hansen & Bowers, 2008). This summary statistic is based on the chi-square distribution and allows us to gauge whether two groups are essentially similar on a suite of pre-treatment variables. Based on five socio-economic variables (age, gender, education, income, and minority status) and five political variables (political interest, frequency of discussion, voted in the last election, liberalism, and partisan status), we can conclude that the positive first impression group and the neutral first impression group are balanced at $p < .820$ ($\chi^2 = 5.93$, 10 df). We can further conclude that members of the negative first impression and neutral first impression group are similar at $p < .087$ ($\chi^2 = 16.42$, 10 df), while those in the positive first impression and negative first impression groups are likely the same at $p < .218$ ($\chi^2 = 13.08$, 10 df).[7] At least in terms of observable, pre-treatment variables, there is no reason to suspect that the groups who experienced a positive, negative, or neutral first impression differ significantly from each other.

To summarize, there is little reason to contend that a subject's first response in our study is anything but random. The data strongly suggest that the first item opened was random, with each candidate having an equal chance of getting picked and scant evidence that the study participants spent much time deliberating before making their selection. Additionally, it seems that true counterfactuals exist for our impression groups, as each candidate was capable of generating the three types of reactions studied here, and there is no evidence that the subjects in any of the three groups differ in either socio-demographic characteristics or in their political behaviors and dispositions. We thus assert that our subsequent analyses are the product of an "as if" random process and should be interpreted as causal effects.

Results

First Impressions and Candidate Evaluations

We hypothesized that first impressions would have a significant impact on candidate evaluations, even after subjects had a chance to learn more about the politicians. Each of the dependent variables analyzed here were measured after the subjects had completed the information search portion of the study. Our first dependent variable of interest is the standard 101 (0–100 scale) point feeling thermometer, used to gauge how warm or cold a person feels towards an attitude object. To test the influence of first impressions on final feeling thermometer ratings, we ran a simple linear regression with feeling thermometer score for the first impression candidate (i.e., the very first candidate the subject encountered in our study) as the dependent variable and dummy variables for first impression type (either positive or negative, with neutral impressions serving as the baseline) as our main predictors. Based on the results presented in Table 9.2, we find that negative—but not positive—first impressions had a significant influence on feeling thermometer scores. In the neutral first impression group, the average feeling thermometer rating of the candidate was 58.2 (SD: 27.8), but this value dropped over 20 points in the negative first impression group. Ratings from subjects in the first impression group increased by 5.3 points, but this change was not significant.

Next, we examined the effect of first impressions on three additional evaluative measures. Using seven-point Likert scales, subjects rated how competent the candidates appeared, how similar the candidate's policy positions appeared to be to their own, and how likely they thought the candidate would be to win an actual primary election in their party. We used the mean of these three items to create a single evaluative scale and regressed impression type on this dependent variable.[8] Results appear in the second column of Table 9.2 and once again, we find

TABLE 9.2 Evaluation by Impression Type

	Feeling Thermometer Score	*Evaluative Scale*
(Intercept)	58.21★★★	4.53★★★
	(2.93)	(0.15)
Positive First Impression	5.29	0.29
	(4.33)	(0.22)
Negative First Impression	−20.81★★★	−0.99★★★
	(5.18)	(0.26)
R^2	0.11	0.11
Adj. R^2	0.11	0.10
Num. obs.	197	197
RMSE	27.02	1.35

Notes: ★★★$p < 0.001$, ★★$p < 0.01$, ★$p < 0.05$.

TABLE 9.3 Vote Propensity by Impression Type

	Vote Probability
(Intercept)	−0.45*
	(0.22)
Positive First Impression	0.18
	(0.33)
Negative First Impression	−1.49**
	(0.53)
AIC	248.11
BIC	257.96
Log Likelihood	−121.06
Deviance	242.11
Num. obs.	197

Notes: ***$p < 0.001$, **$p < 0.01$, *$p < 0.05$.

that negative first impressions significantly impacted evaluations of the candidate. Relative to the baseline score of 4.5, evaluations in the negative first impression group decreased by almost a full point. Evaluations in the positive impression group did increase, but not significantly so.

Finally, we looked at the effect of first impressions on the vote share of the candidates. Our dependent variable is a dichotomous indicator of whether the subject voted for the first candidate he or she encountered in our study, coded 1 if yes and 0 otherwise. For this analysis, we use a logit model, although our predictors remain the same. Translating the coefficients from the model in Table 9.3 into predicted vote probabilities, we find that subjects in the neutral first impression group had a 35.6% likelihood of voting for the politician they first encountered. However, those subjects who had an initial negative reaction to the first politician they met had a 13.4% chance of eventually voting for that candidate. For subjects in the positive first impression group, the probability of voting for the first candidate encountered increased 4.5 percentage points over the baseline, an increase that did not reach statistical significance.

First Impressions and Information Search

Here we take up the question of whether first impressions affect a subject's motivation to acquire information about a candidate. Based on affective intelligence theory, we hypothesized that a positive first impression would decrease search, while a negative one would increase it. To investigate this hypothesis we used the total pieces of information examined about the first impression candidate as our dependent variable, while impression type again served as our predictor variables. Contrary to what we had hypothesized, a negative first impression did not make our subjects any more motivated to acquire information about that particular politician. We do find, however, an effect for positive first impressions as shown in

Table 9.4. Relative to the baseline in the neutral impression condition, voters who reacted positively to the first item they read about a particular politician ended up looking at 3.2 more pieces of information about that candidate.

Next, we examined the dynamic reactions to the candidates as the subjects acquired more information; that is, did an initial negative (positive) reaction make the subjects more negative (positive) towards the candidate? To investigate this question, we created a count of the number of items subjects "liked" and "disliked" about the first impression candidate during the primary.[9] We then regressed these counts on impression group and added the total number of items accessed as a covariate (since likes and dislikes should naturally increase as a function of information). Our results appear in Table 9.5 and are supportive of our third hypothesis. In both the positive and negative first impression conditions, the tenor

TABLE 9.4 Candidate Information Search by Impression Type

	Total Pieces of Information Accessed
(Intercept)	16 92★★★
	(0.83)
Positive First Impression	3.21★★
	(1.22)
Negative First Impression	−0.02
	(1.46)
R^2	0.04
Adj. R^2	0.03
Num. obs.	197
RMSE	7.63

Notes: ★★★$p < 0.001$, ★★$p < 0.01$, ★$p < 0.05$.

TABLE 9.5 Liking and Disliking Information by Impression Type

	Total "Likes"	Total "Dislikes"
(Intercept)	−1.65	−0.98
	(0.85)	(0.66)
Items Accessed	0.25★★★	0.10★★
	(0.04)	(0.03)
Positive First Impression	3.23★★★	0.52
	(0.72)	(0.55)
Negative First Impression	0.22	5.08★★★
	(0.85)	(0.65)
R^2	0.28	0.28
Adj. R^2	0.27	0.26
Num. obs.	197	197
RMSE	4.41	3.40

Notes: ★★★$p < 0.001$, ★★$p < 0.01$, ★$p < 0.05$.

of the initial reaction influenced the propensity to evaluate future information. When holding total information searched at its mean, participants who had a positive first impression of a politician liked 3.2 more items than did subjects with a neutral first impression. Similarly, subjects who had a negative first impression disliked 5.1 more items overall than did subjects in the neutral first impression group. These results suggest that one way first impressions may persist is by conditioning reactions to subsequent information.

Overcoming First Impressions

Our final inquiry concerns the ability of subjects to overcome their initial first impressions with additional information search. As noted in the previous section, each of three groups liked or disliked some aspects of the candidates they encountered, as is true with most politicians. We would therefore like to know the extent to which subsequent positive reactions to a candidate can ameliorate an initial negative impression as well as whether initial positive reactions are similarly negated by negative reactions. In a theoretical model, Rabin and Schrag (1999) suggest that under some conditions first impressions may persist even after acquiring an infinite amount of new information. To examine this question empirically, we ran linear regressions with three independent variables. The first is simply a dummy variable coded 1 if the subject had a negative (or positive) first impression and 0 otherwise.[10] The other variables are a count of the number of liked (disliked) items and a count of the number of items the subject viewed but had no reaction to (neutral items). We regressed the candidate's feeling thermometer ratings on these variables to assess the ability of information search to counteract first impressions (Table 9.6).

Starting first with the effect of positive and neutral information on initially negative candidate impressions (column one in Table 9.6), we see that a negative first impression resulted in a 17.85 point decrease in candidate feeling thermometer ratings relative to those in the neutral first impression group. Each neutral item a subject viewed resulted in a small increase in feeling thermometer score, equivalent to roughly 1/25th of the magnitude of the negative first impression. This result is perhaps explicable in terms of the "mere exposure" effect, in which simple familiarity with an attitude object breeds more favorable impressions (Zajonc, 1968). Each positively rated item boosted feeling thermometer ratings by 2.3 points, or approximately one-eighth of deficit created by the negative first impression.

Turning to the impact of neutral and negative information on subjects with positive first impressions, we see a positive first impression results in a 7.44 point feeling thermometer increase, which is less than half of the decrease caused by a negative impression. Neutral items had no significant effect on feeling thermometer scores, but each negative item decreased the rating by 2.59 points. Importantly, our models suggest that it takes about three subsequent "dislikes" to erase the effects of a positive first impression on feeling thermometer ratings, while a

TABLE 9.6 Effect of Subsequent Information Search on Feeling Thermometer Scores

	Effect of "Likes"	Effect of "Dislikes"
(Intercept)	43.39★★★	60.59★★★
	(4.67)	(4.61)
Total "Liked" Information	2.30★★★	
	(0.38)	
Total "Disliked" Information		−2.59★★★
		(0.54)
Total Neutral Information	0.65★	−0.03
	(0.25)	(0.26)
Positive First Impression	−2.91	7.44
	(4.26)	(4.14)
Negative First Impression	−17.85★★★	−7.83
	(4.95)	(5.64)
R^2	0.26	0.21
Adj. R^2	0.24	0.20
Num, obs.	197	197
RMSE	24.85	25.62

Notes: ★★★$p < 0.001$, ★★$p < 0.01$, ★$p < 0.05$.

subject would have to like eight subsequent items in order to overcome the initial deficit caused by a negative first impression. In sum, these results confirm the disproportionate effect on evaluations of negative information in comparison to positive as well as suggest that negative first impressions are particularly difficult to eliminate.

Discussion

The results from our data provide support for a number of our hypotheses. First impressions—particularly negative ones—do matter. We find that candidates who got off on the wrong foot with our subjects created an "impression deficit" that was difficult to overcome. Our work also supports some of the conjectures of the Asymmetric Nonlinear Model of attitude formation (AMN; Holbrook et al., 2001). The ANM makes a number of theoretical claims about attitude formation, including that in the absence of any information there exists a positivity bias towards an attitude object, that negative information is weighted more heavily than positive information, and that earlier information, particularly the initial impression, is more integral to attitude formation than later information (2001, p. 932). Our data and design allow us to study dynamic processes during information search and impression formation and largely corroborates this theoretical approach. Assuming "as if" randomization, we find that an initial negative reaction to information about a candidate significantly decreases evaluations of that candidate along a variety of measures. We further find that negative first impressions are of a larger magnitude than positive ones and that impact of subsequent negative reactions is greater than that of positive ones, findings all consistent with previous work on negativity effects.

Our additional contribution to this literature comes from our examination of the effect of first impressions on subsequent information search and evaluation. Our data suggests that, contrary to some research arguing that negative information increases vigilance and attention, subjects who experienced a negative first impression were no more or less motivated to seek out information about a candidate than were subjects who had a neutral first response. Rather, our data indicates that it was positive first impressions that boosted information seeking. And while our results suggest that it may be possible to overcome first impressions via subsequent information search, our data also indicate that a valenced first impression increases the likelihood that additional information about that candidate will also be judged in a similar way. We conclude that the story our data tell is one of a desire to confirm initial impressions about candidates—whether positive or negative—from the very beginning of the attitude formation process.

Conclusion

At an "Author Meets Critics" panel for *The Rationalizing Voter*, the second author of this paper asked Milt Lodge and Chuck Taber how well their "John Q. Public" model of information processing (Lodge & Taber, 2013) comported with normative views of democratic decision-making. After all, in Lodge and Taber's model, political cognition is driven by affect and contains a significant automatic component. This suggests that positive or negative affect, even if incidental to the judgment task at hand, influences both the retrieval of relevant information as well as its evaluation. Subsequent information processing is therefore beholden to prior attitudes, even if those attitudes were formed under less than "rational" conditions. Lodge's response to the query was succinct: "Not well."

Although at that particular session the authors were reluctant to wholly abandon the classic view of reasoned political judgment, the possibility that our political views contain a substantial random element is no doubt one of the more fascinating—and perhaps troubling—implications of Lodge and Taber's work on political cognition. If incidental affect guides our reasoning process, then it follows that a chance negative or positive encounter with a political attitude object can have a lasting effect on our evaluations. Our results provide support for this position: of all the information available about our politicians, some voters just happened to pick something to which they would have a negative reaction, while others just as randomly chose information to which they would have a positive reaction. While the choice of any given news story about a politician to read seems largely inconsequential, we find that the initial selection influences not only subsequent information search and evaluations but also final attitudes and vote choices. On the backs of minor contingent events are political attitudes made, a startling possibility that we would not consider were it not for the path breaking work of Milton Lodge and his colleagues.

Notes

1. DPTE is available for any researcher to use at www.processtracing.org
2. Some of the subjects (n = 112) were also able to leave comments and read comments left by other subjects. All of the trends reported in this paper hold for both this group and the remaining group of subjects (n = 85), who only could "like," "dislike," or "share" the information. We therefore combined the two groups for the analyses.
3. Subjects registered for either the Democratic or the Republican primary. Trends in the data were the same for both groups, so we combine results here.
4. In our "live" experiment, subjects saw a picture of each of the three candidates to help them associate the information they encountered with the fictional politicians. To aid in the realism of the design, these candidate pictures were chosen from the official portraits of active members of state legislatures. However, to protect the privacy of these politicians, we have blurred the photos in Figure 9.1.
5. Additionally, the decision task involves a primary, so party cues are ineffectual.
6. In general, the strongest first impression effects were seen for the conservative candidate while the weakest were for the moderate.
7. Some readers may be concerned that the differences between the negative and neutral group approach statistical significance. This is largely due to members of the neutral group reporting higher incomes than those in the negative group. Removing the income variable results in a χ^2 value of 12.63 (9df, $p < .179$). Although it is conceivable that differences in income led some subjects to be more likely to dislike certain policies, some research suggest that objective material conditions have a much smaller impact on policy attitudes than often assumed (Doherty, Gerber, & Green, 2006; Sears, Lau, Tyler, & Allen, 1980). If we consider only the differences in political behaviors between the negative and neutral group, we would fail to reject the null that the groups are balanced at $p < .773$.
8. Alpha values for the scale varied by candidate; for Candidate One, alpha was .55, for Candidate Two, .71, and for Candidate Three, .68. The scale ran from 1 to 7, with a mean of 4.4 and a standard deviation of 1.2.
9. For subjects in the negative and positive first impression groups, we subtracted one from each of these counts; thus, our measure gives us the number of reactions subsequent to the initial one, whatever that may have been.
10. Some readers may question why we do not simply use a count of the disliked items instead of the dummy variable. Our main justification for using the dummy variable is theoretical; we argue that it is not the simple count of negative items that matters, but the fact that the first impression was negative. Simple bivariate correlations corroborate this claim. Among those subjects with a neutral first impression, the correlation between disliked items and feeling thermometer ratings is −.362; among those with a positive first impression, the correlations is −.481; and for the subjects in the negative first impression group, the correlation is −.572. Thus, the relationship between disliked items and evaluation is related to the nature of the first impression.

References

Ambady, Nalini & Skowronski, John Joseph. (Eds.) (2008). *First impressions*. New York: Guilford Press.

Anderson, Norman H. (1965). Primacy effects in personality impression formation using a generalized order effect paradigm. *Journal of Personality and Social Psychology*, 2(1), 1–9.

Asch, Solomon E. (1946). Forming impressions of personality. *The Journal of Abnormal and Social Psychology*, 41(3), 258–290.
Berelson, Bernard R., Lazarsfeld, Paul F., & McPhee, William N. (1954). *Voting: A study of opinion formation in a presidential election*. Chicago: University of Chicago Press.
Berinsky, Adam J., Huber, Gregory A., & Lenz, Gabriel S. (2012). Evaluating online labor markets for experimental research: Amazon.com's Mechanical Turk. *Political Analysis*, 20(3), 351–368.
Brader, Ted. (2005). Striking a responsive chord: How political ads motivate and persuade voters by appealing to emotions. *American Journal of Political Science*, 49(2), 388–405.
Campbell, Angus, Converse, Philip E., Miller, Warren E., & Stokes, Donald. (1960). *The American voter*. New York: John Wiley and Sons.
Carney, Dana R. & Banaji, Mahzarin R. (2012). First is best. *PloS One*, 7(6), e35088.
Converse, Philip E. (1964). The nature of belief systems in mass publics. In David E. Apter (Ed.), *Ideology and its discontents*. New York: Free Press.
Doherty, Daniel, Gerber, Alan S., & Green, Donald P. (2006). Personal income and attitudes toward redistribution: A study of lottery winners. *Political Psychology*, 27(3), 441–458.
Fiske, Susan T. & Taylor, Shelly E. (1984). *Social cognition*. Reading, MA: Addison-Wesley Pub. Co.
Hansen, Ben B. & Bowers, Jake. (2008). Covariate balance in simple, stratified and clustered comparative studies. *Statistical Science*, 23(2), 219–236.
Holbrook, Allyson L., Krosnick, Jon A., Visser, Penny S., Gardner, Wendi L., & Cacioppo, John T. (2001). Attitudes toward presidential candidates and political parties: Initial optimism, inertial first impressions, and a focus on flaws. *American Journal of Political Science*, 45(4), 930–950.
Kelley, Harold H. (1950). The warm-cold variable in first impressions of persons. *Journal of Personality*, 18(4), 431–439.
Klein, Jill. (1991). Negativity effects in impression formation: A test in the political arena. *Personality and Social Psychology Bulletin*, 4(17), 412–418.
Kunda, Ziva. (1990). The case for motivated reasoning. *Psychological Bulletin*, 108(3), 480–498.
Lane, Robert E. (1962). *Political ideology: Why the American common man believes what he does*. New York: The Free Press.
Lau, Richard R. (1982). Negativity in political perception. *Political Behavior*, 4(4), 353–377.
Lau, Richard R. (1985). Two explanations for negativity effects in political behavior. *American Journal of Political Science*, 29(1), 119–138.
Lau, Richard R. & Redlawsk, David P. (2001). An experimental study of information search, memory, and decision-making during a political campaign. In James H. Kuklinski (Ed.), *Citizens and politics: Perspectives from political psychology* (pp. 136–159). New York: Cambridge University Press.
Lau, Richard R. & Redlawsk, David P. (2006). *How voters decide: Information processing during election campaigns*. New York: Cambridge University Press.
Lau, Richard R. & Redlawsk, David P. (2013). Behavioral decision theory. In David O. Sears, Leonie Huddy, & Jack Levy (Eds.), *Oxford handbook of political psychology* (2nd ed., pp. 130–164). Oxford: Oxford University Press.
Lodge, Milton, McGraw, Kathleen, & Stroh, Patrick. (1989). An impression-driven model of candidate evaluation. *American Political Science Review*, 83(2), 399–419.
Lodge, Milton, Steenbergen, Marco, & Brau, Shawn. (1995). The responsive voter: Campaign information and the dynamics of candidate evaluation. *American Political Science Review*, 89(2), 309–326.

Lodge, Milton & Taber, Charles S. (2000). Three steps toward a theory of motivated political reasoning. In Arthur Lupia, Mathew D. McCubbins, & Samuel L. Popkin (Eds.), *Elements of reason: Cognition, choice, and the bounds of rationality* (pp. 183–213). New York: Cambridge University Press.

Lodge, Milton & Taber, Charles S. (2013). *The rationalizing voter.* New York: Cambridge University Press.

Marcus, George E., Neuman, W. Russell, & MacKuen, Michael. (2000). *Affective intelligence and political judgment.* Chicago, IL: University of Chicago Press.

Mattes, Kyle & Redlawsk, David P. (2014). *The positive case for negative campaigning.* Chicago, IL: University of Chicago Press.

Mattes, Kyle, Spezio, Michael, Kim, Hackjin, Todorov, Alexander, Adolphs, Ralph, & Alvarez, R. Michael. (2010). Predicting election outcomes from positive and negative trait assessments of candidate images. *Political Psychology*, 31(1), 41–58.

Nickerson, Raymond S. (1998). Confirmation bias: A ubiquitous phenomenon in many guises. *Review of General Psychology*, 2(2), 175.

Paolacci, Gabriele & Jesse Chandler. (2014). Inside the Turk: Understanding Mechanical Turk as a participant pool. *Current Directions in Psychological Science*, 23(3), 184–188.

Rabin, Matthew & Schrag, Joel L. (1999). First impressions matter: A model of confirmatory bias. *The Quarterly Journal of Economics*, 114(1), 37–82.

Redlawsk, David P. (2001). You must remember this: A test of the online model of voting. *Journal of Politics*, 63(1), 29–58.

Redlawsk, David P. (2002). Hot cognition or cool consideration: Testing the effects of motivated reasoning on political decision making. *Journal of Politics*, 64(4), 1021–1044.

Redlawsk, David P. (Ed.) (2006). *Feeling politics: Emotion in political information processing.* New York: Palgrave Macmillan.

Redlawsk, David P., Civettini, Andrew J. W., & Emmerson, Karen M. (2010). The affective tipping point: Do motivated reasoners ever "Get it"? *Political Psychology*, 31(4), 563–593.

Schreiber, Darren. (2007). Political cognition as social cognition: Are we all political sophisticates. In George E. Marcus, W. Russell Neuman, Michael MacKuen, & Ann N. Crigler (Eds.), *The affect effect: Dynamics of emotion in political thinking and behavior* (pp. 48–70). Chicago, IL: University of Chicago Press.

Sears, D. O., Lau, R. R., Tyler, T. R., & Allen Jr., H. M. (1980). Self-interest vs. symbolic politics in policy attitudes and presidential voting. *The American Political Science Review*, 74(3), 670–684.

Taber, Charles S. & Lodge, Milton. (2006). Motivated skepticism in the evaluation of political beliefs. *American Journal of Political Science*, 50(3), 755–769.

Tetlock, Philip E. (1983). Accountability and the perseverance of first impressions. *Social Psychology Quarterly*, 46(4), 285–292.

Todorov, A., Mandisodza, A. N., Goren, A., & Hall, C. C. (2005). Inferences of competence from faces predict election outcomes. *Science*, 308(5728), 1623–1626.

Willis, Janine & Todorov, Alexander. (2006). First impressions making up your mind after a 100-ms exposure to a face. *Psychological Science*, 17(7), 592–598.

Zajonc, Robert B. (1968). Attitudinal effects of mere exposure. *Journal of Personality and Social Psychology*, 9(2), 1.

10
RACIALLY MOTIVATED REASONING[1]

Stanley Feldman and Leonie Huddy

Milton Lodge's influence on the field of political psychology cannot be overestimated. He has inspired, educated, and nurtured numerous budding political psychologists. He has been a great colleague, mentor, and friend to many of us within the political psychology community. And he single-handedly created a vibrant community of political psychologists at Stony Brook University, our institutional home, improving immeasurably our intellectual lives. His willingness to attack conventional political science wisdom has paid enormous dividends and has had a lasting effect on the study of political behavior. One of Milton's key insights is that voters are very far from the well-informed rational decision makers embodied in democratic theory. Milton helped to crack open the black box of voter decision-making to reveal a process that fell far short of this democratic ideal: Voters' develop a lasting impression of political candidates based on exposure to information that they cannot recall (Lodge, McGraw, & Stroh 1989). They argue against contrary facts and arguments regardless of how well-reasoned and substantiated, a process most developed among the most sophisticated citizens (Taber & Lodge, 2006). And much political reasoning occurs outside conscious awareness, rendering voters susceptible to subtle cues of which they are unaware (Lodge & Taber, 2013).

Motivated Reasoning

We believe one of the most important and enduring ideas to emerge from Milton's impressive body of research concerns the process of motivated reasoning. When someone engages in motivated reasoning, they downgrade the quality of an argument that contradicts their view, scrutinize a contrary message to a far greater degree than one that is congenial in order to refute it, evaluate supportive arguments as stronger than contrary ones, and seek out information that confirms their view (Kunda, 1990; Taber & Lodge, 2006). This process generates attitude stability and maintains political beliefs. It also lends heat to political arguments because each interlocutor places greater weight on his or her own than the other's arguments and facts, and has given greater thought to flaws and problems with arguments on the other than his or her own side. Somewhat paradoxically, the most sophisticated and politically knowledgeable are most likely to engage in motivated reasoning, ensuring the presence of bias even in highly erudite political conversations (Taber & Lodge, 2006).

The basic process of motivated reasoning and its consequences are well established by now and its existence has been documented in defense of diverse attitudes, including climate change, energy policy, affirmative action, gun control, and Iraq's possession of WMD (Bolsen, Druckman, & Cook, 2014; Nyhan & Reifler, 2010; Taber & Lodge, 2006; Wood & Vedlitz, 2007). There has also been a spate of recent research demonstrating the conditions under which motivated reasoning is least and most likely to occur. Factors that mitigate motivated reasoning include social or financial pressures that increase the incentive towards accuracy (Bolsen, Druckman, & Cook, 2014; Prior, Sood, & Khanna, 2013), attitude ambivalence (Lavine, Johnston, & Steenbergen, 2012), and the presence of overwhelming disconfirming information (Redlawsk, Civiettini, & Emmerson, 2010; Parker-Stephen, 2013).

Research on the conditions that promote or inhibit motivated reasoning adds important insight into the nature and dynamics of public opinion. Despite Lodge and Taber's (2013) claim that the defense of one's attitudes is the basic default when confronted with contrary arguments and evidence, motivated reasoning is likely to vary with the underlying centrality and importance of an attitude. Central and important attitudes such as political ideology exhibit the greatest stability and as a consequence are likely to be maintained through the process of motivated reasoning. This helps to explain why much of the evidence for motivated reasoning has occurred in defense of partisanship, an early-learned, highly salient, and very stable political attitude (Leeper & Slothuus, 2014; Green, Palmquist, & Schickler, 2002; Sears & Funk, 1999). For example, Bolsen and colleagues (2014) found that Americans were more likely to support features of the 2007 Energy Independence Act when told it was sponsored by their party and more opposed to it when told it was supported by the other major party. In research by Claassen and Ensley (2016), American partisans were more outraged when told that the other major political party had engaged in dirty electoral tricks but were far less outraged when told their own party had engaged in such tactics. And following the global 2008 recession, Labour supporters in the UK were motivated to defend their party by downplaying the Labour government's responsibility for poor economic conditions (Bisgaard, 2015). These are just a few of the many studies documenting partisan-motivated reasoning (see also Cohen, 2003; Druckman, Peterson, & Slothuus, 2013; Lavine et al., 2012; Petersen, Skob, Serritzlew, & Ramsøy, 2013).

Partisanship is arguably one of the most stable political attitudes (Sears, 1983). But there is considerable variation across attitudes in their underlying stability and thus the degree to which they elicit motivated reasoning. Panel studies reveal far less stability in specific policy attitudes when compared to partisan identification, basic values such as egalitarianism, and group-related attitudes (Alwin, Cohen, & Newcomb, 1991; Converse & Markus, 1979; Jennings & Niemi, 1981; Sears, 1983). From our perspective, group-linked attitudes provide an especially fertile domain in which to study motivated reasoning. The motivation to establish and maintain positive distinctiveness for various identities grounded in race, ethnicity, and religion is well established (Huddy, 2013; Tajfel & Turner, 1979). It would therefore not be surprising to find that strongly held group identities and related attitudes elicit motived reasoning in response to threatening information that maligns one's group, places an outgroup in an overly favorable light, or some combination of the two. In fact, partisanship may be highly stable and elicit pervasive motivated reasoning precisely because it entails a strong social identity which arouses group defense when threatened (Huddy, Mason, & Aaroe, 2015).

Racial Motivated Reasoning

In this chapter, we zero in on racial attitudes which have been shown to be highly stable over time (Sears & Brown, 2013). We expect motivated reasoning to play a major role in their maintenance and defense, a proposition that has received relatively little prior attention (for an exception see Saucier & Miller, 2003). There are several distinct advantages to investigating the motivated defense of racial views which we believe will advance research on the general process of motivated reasoning and perhaps even more importantly help to shed light on the dynamics of American racial opinion.

First, evidence of racially motivated reasoning helps to underscore a divide in American society over the existence of racial discrimination and the extent to which its denial can be considered a form of racism. The denial of discrimination is a key component of contemporary racial attitudes such as racial resentment but one that has an unclear grounding in racism (Feldman & Huddy, 2005; Huddy & Feldman, 2009). Discrimination is difficult to document except in the most blatant of cases and is particularly hard to identity when manifested as institutional racism. As a consequence of this ambiguity, judgments about its existence are likely to reflect basic beliefs about the world. One possibility is that the denial of discrimination reflects a motivated defense of racial negativity and prejudice. Another is that it serves to defend ideologically conservative views that privilege individualism and the denial of group-based barriers to success. In a nutshell, the focus on motivated racial reasoning allows us to better understand the nature of beliefs about racial discrimination in American society.

Second, the existence and pervasiveness of racially motivated reasoning allows us to gauge how dispassionately white Americans evaluate evidence concerning the unfair treatment of blacks and whites in American society. Does a majority engage in this kind of biased reasoning? Or are most Americans reasonably even-handed in their assessment of potentially discriminatory events? Is there more biased reasoning among racially conservative than tolerant whites? Or do both sides engage in biased reasoning in defense of their beliefs, as one might expect from other motivated reasoning research? In other words, do those who hold positive views concerning blacks deny evidence of reverse discrimination against whites to the same degree that those who harbor negative racial views argue against evidence of discrimination against blacks?

Third, what are the consequences of motivated reasoning for the creation of a common understanding of race relations in the United States? Is it possible for Americans to agree on basic facts? Or does motivated reasoning make it difficult to find a common departure point for an ongoing discussion concerning race relations? We focus at some length on Americans' knowledge of past facts concerning historical racial discrimination in the United States. Our data reveal considerable ignorance about the past which is most pronounced among those with lower levels of education and political information. But we also find that historical ignorance is exacerbated by motivated racial reasoning.

Contention Concerning Racial Discrimination

There is an ongoing debate over the continued existence of racial discrimination which provides ideal fodder for racially motivated reasoning. As legal barriers to black participation in American society declined in the second half of the 20th century and blacks gained prominence in many aspects of American life, whites have increasingly questioned the existence of racial discrimination (Valentino & Brader, 2011). At the same time, black Americans continue to experience and perceive widespread discrimination, reflected in their experiences with law enforcement, sales clerks, and employers (Feagin, 2014). This racial schism in the perception of contemporary discrimination creates divergent views between blacks and whites, and among some whites, on the extensiveness of black opportunity and the reasons for persistent black poverty (Kinder & Winter, 2001; Schuman, Steeh, Bobo, & Krysan, 1997). These conflicting racial viewpoints raise pertinent questions about the extent to which perceived discrimination is a reflection of reality or a defense of existing racial attitudes.

Substantial differences in racial outcomes is the undeniable reality of contemporary life in the United States. When it comes to health outcomes, income, joblessness, college graduation rates, incarceration rates, and housing opportunities, blacks fare worse than whites, sometimes by a staggering margin (National Research Council, 2004). But as noted in the extensive report on the assessment of discrimination conducted by the National Research Council, "Differences in outcomes by race do not themselves provide direct evidence for the magnitude or even the presence of racial discrimination in any particular domain" (p. 48). Indeed, it is often exceedingly difficult to demonstrate the existence of discrimination in a given situation, even for social science researchers, because it depends on the ability to prove that a specific outcome, such as an employee being laid off, was due to race and not something else, such as poor performance. Moreover, discrimination can occur in different forms, some of which are subtler than others, making it even more difficult to prove that differential treatment was due to race (National Research Council, 2004).

This complexity has been largely ignored in research on the study of white Americans' racial attitudes. Indeed, the denial of racial discrimination is often included in popular measures of racial prejudice such as symbolic racism and racial resentment. For example, a question in the widely used racial resentment scale asks whether "generations of slavery and discrimination have created conditions that make it difficult for blacks to work their way out of the lower class" (Kinder & Sanders, 1996; Tarman & Sears, 2005). Another asks whether "government officials usually pay less attention to a request or complaint from a black person than from a white person" (Kinder & Sanders, 1996). And a question in the symbolic racism scale asks "How much discrimination against blacks do you feel there is in the United States today, limiting their chances to get ahead?" (Tarman & Sears, 2005; see also Henry & Sears, 2002). In essence, the rejection of continued racial discrimination is treated as racial prejudice in much political behavior research.

By examining the process of white motivated reasoning we get closer to understanding whether its denial is grounded in racial prejudice and the defense of racially negative views, reflects the defense of ideology, or simply reflects ignorance (Feldman & Huddy, 2005). Motivated reasoning is assessed by asking respondents to evaluate the strength or credibility of equally strong arguments or well-established facts. To the degree to which someone views congenial arguments and facts as stronger and more credible than those that contradict their position they are seen to engage in motivated reasoning. It is important to note that respondents are simply asked to rate the strength or credibility of different statements, facts, or events. In that sense, the questions are well removed from policy. They also avoid social desirability pressures by asking people to make a judgment that taps racial attitudes in a less-obvious fashion. More importantly, a measure of racially motivated reasoning helps to reveal the process by which racial beliefs are maintained.

Defending Negative and Positive Racial Attitudes

Part of the vitriol surrounding discussions of race in the United States derives from contention over the existence and origins of racial discrepancies in crime, poverty, and educational outcomes. Motivated reasoning undoubtedly exacerbates this situation, undermining dispassionate factual discussion. Racially negative whites may regard racial poverty and crime as caused by deficient black character and fail to see the pernicious influence of institutional racism. Conversely, racially positive whites may deny any black culpability for racial inequities and view poor outcomes among blacks as driven solely by institutional factors.

The study of racial attitudes has tended to focus on the negative side of the racial attitude dimension. But motivated reasoning is symmetrical and likely to exist among those with positive and negative racial views. By developing a measure of racially motivated reasoning, we are better able to judge the degree to which racially tolerant whites reason clearly about racial facts and arguments. This point may seem odd from a normative standpoint because it raises concerns about the inaccurate nature of positive racial attitudes. But that is not our point. Whites who hold positive racial views might arrive at the "right" conclusion via the wrong means. For example, affirmative action may mean that black students take college slots that would have been occupied by equally qualified white students. This fact has to be acknowledged in order to have a reasonable discussion about affirmative action programs, their purpose, rationale, and likely consequences.

In this study, we first develop a measure of racially motivated reasoning and assess its validity. Does it form a single dimension? Is it pervasive or relatively rare? Is it more common on one side of the racial or ideological divide than the other? And is it primarily grounded in the defense of racial attitudes such as negative racial stereotypes? Or is it also based on the defense of ideological principles? Second, what are the consequences of motivated reasoning for the acceptance of racial facts and evidence? Does racially motivated reasoning lead to the denial of past racial discrimination? And what other factors contribute to white ignorance concerning the nature of past race relations?

Data

We draw on data from the American Racial Opinion Survey (AROS) conducted as an RDD telephone interview of U.S. residents from October 23, 2003 until February 23, 2004, and then re-interviewed roughly eight weeks later (from February 4 till June 20, 2004). A total of 1,229 white, non-Hispanic, non-Asian respondents were interviewed in the first round; 868 second-wave interviews were completed (for a re-interview rate of 71%). The first wave also included 157 African Americans (not analyzed here). The survey was conducted by the Center for Survey Research at Stony Brook University.[2] The analyses reported here are confined to white respondents interviewed in wave 2. The second wave was designed to increase the survey's overall racial content without overburdening respondents with inordinate amounts of racial content in a single interview; it also allowed for some within-respondent experimental manipulations which are not discussed in the current paper.

The Motivated Reasoning Scale

We developed a motivated reasoning scale adapted from past measures. In one prior study, Saucier and Miller (2003) asked respondents to evaluate the strength of pro- and anti-black conclusions derived from a series of factual racial statements. Theory and research suggests that people will be more likely to endorse arguments that are consistent with their existing attitudes, and Saucier and Miller's measure had good measurement properties and reliably predicted racial attitudes and behaviors.

We draw on Saucier and Miller's work to develop a scale of motivated reasoning for use with a general population in a survey setting. Motivated reasoning depends on an individual arguing against a position or piece of evidence that it is at odds with their own. This can be detected, for example, by asking respondents to assess the strength of an argument. We adapted this format to assess the perceived *credibility* of research information concerning both racial and reverse discrimination. Information about racial bias was presented in a realistic format, as a newspaper story on the findings of a research study. To ensure that respondents felt comfortable agreeing with or arguing against such evidence, they were read the following statement:

> The news media often reports the results of research studies, some of which are controversial because of the way in which they are conducted. I am going to read you the findings from several different studies that have been in the news recently. Please tell me how CREDIBLE or BELIEVABLE you find each finding.

Respondents were read six "findings" in random order; three presented evidence of racial bias and three offered evidence of reverse discrimination. All six findings are shown in Table 10.1 along with the observed credibility distributions for the white sample. The motivated reasoning scale was asked only of whites re-interviewed in wave 2. The three findings that present "evidence" of black discrimination are shown first while the second three findings provide "evidence" of reverse discrimination against whites. The six items were presented in random order in the interview. As shown in Table 10.1, the modal response to each question was that the evidence was "somewhat credible." There is a significant amount of variation and responses ranged from "very credible" to "not at all credible" for each item.

With only one exception (discrimination against black patients) a majority of whites found all six pieces of evidence somewhat or very credible. This may not be terribly surprising given that all of the scenarios were based on stories that had appeared in the news. White respondents found evidence of racial discrimination in the workplace and among real estate agents most credible. On reverse discrimination, whites were most inclined to find evidence of differential college

TABLE 10.1 Racially Motivated Reasoning Scale

	Very Credible	Somewhat Credible	Not Very Credible	Not at all Credible	DK/NA
Item 1: A recent study found that when white and black job applicants with the same resume applied for exactly the same job, the white applicant was hired more often than the black applicant.	20.6%	50.4	17.1	6.7	5.3
Item 2: A recent investigation into racial bias in several big city hospitals found that black men who suffered a heart attack were treated more slowly than white men with the same condition and receive worse quality medical care.	11.3%	37.8	24.5	19.4	7.0
Item 3: A study conducted in several major suburban areas found that when black and white families with the same income and financial history approached local real estate agents the black families were shown homes that were in less desirable areas.	24.1%	46.7	14.9	8.9	5.5
Item 4: An analysis of students admitted to several state colleges in 2003 found that black students were more likely to be admitted than white students with the same test scores and grades.	14.9%	48.6	22.5	8.3	5.7
Item 5: Many city fire departments practice reverse discrimination against whites according to the findings of a recent poll in which a majority of white firefighters said they have been overlooked for a promotion in favor of someone who was black.	12.9%	43.8	26.0	8.9	8.4
Item 6: The government is biased against white contractors according to a recent study in which a majority of white building contractors said they had lost large government jobs to less qualified black-owned companies.	9.3%	42.7	29.0	10.5	8.4

Note: Sample size for these questions is 868. Data are from wave 2 re-interviews only.

admissions most credible. The mean inter-item correlation among the three black discrimination items is .36; the mean correlation for the three white discrimination items is .37.

Measurement Properties of the Motivated Reasoning Scale

We use respondents' credibility judgments as indicators of their tendency to engage in racially motivated reasoning. The items should therefore produce a single factor varying from those who strongly reject evidence of racial discrimination and accept evidence of reverse discrimination to those who believe stories about racial discrimination and reject evidence of reverse discrimination. We estimated the latent factor structure of the six motivated reasoning items using Mplus and begin by testing a simple two-factor model with one latent variable measuring belief in racial discrimination and the second tapping belief in reverse discrimination. Each latent variable has three indicators and each item loads on only one factor. If there is a generalized tendency toward racially motivated reasoning the two latent factors should be strongly negatively correlated. Those who deny the existence of racial discrimination should see reverse discrimination against whites, and vice versa.

The fit of the simple two-factor model is relatively good. The RMSEA[3] is .069, not quite at the .05 level of a very good fitting model but not far off. The comparative fit index (CFI) is .97 which is very good. Contrary to our expectations, however, the estimated correlation between the two factors is .18 (s.e. = .05). While the estimated correlation is only weakly positive, this model suggests that there is a *positive* relationship between the credibility of racial discrimination and reverse discrimination—exactly opposite to our prediction.

But this odd result is likely a consequence of a methods artifact in the six motivated reasoning questions, reflecting a strong response set or tendency to see all evidence presented by the news media as either credible or not credible. Each of the motivated reasoning questions should be a function of two factors—a belief in either racial discrimination or reverse discrimination and a tendency to see *any* news story as credible or not. We thus estimated a second model that included three latent variables: the same racial discrimination and reverse discrimination factors and a third factor to account for individual differences in whether or not someone rated news stories as credible regardless of content. To identify this model, we assume that each question loads equally on the credibility factor (all loadings constrained to be 1.0) and that there are no correlations between the credibility factor and the two discrimination factors.

The fit of this three-factor model is very good. The RMSEA decreases to .05, the value expected for a good fitting model. The CFI increased slightly to .99, very close to the maximum of 1.0. The addition of the credibility factor had a dramatic effect on the estimated correlation between the racial discrimination and reverse discrimination factors. The estimate is now −.80 (s.e. = .25). As predicted by motivated reasoning, there is a very strong tendency for beliefs about racial discrimination and reverse discrimination to go together negatively. Whites who reject evidence of racial discrimination are very likely to accept evidence of reverse discrimination. In turn, those who see evidence of racial discrimination strongly reject reverse discrimination.

The large negative correlation between the two discrimination factors (and a confidence interval that includes −1.0) suggests an even more parsimonious two-factor model in which all six motivated reasoning items load on a single motivated reasoning factor and on a second latent credibility factor. This model is completely consistent with the motivated reasoning argument. The single substantive latent variable ties together (inversely) beliefs about racial discrimination and reserve discrimination. This third two-factor model provides the best fit to these data. The RMSEA decreased to .046 with a CFI value of .99, both indicative of an excellent fit. One factor in the model taps beliefs about racial and reverse discrimination (motivated reasoning) and the other differences in the credibility of news stories. The two factors are uncorrelated. The existence of a single motivated reasoning factor indicates that whites who reject evidence of black discrimination are substantially more inclined to believe evidence of reverse discrimination, and vice versa.

The final standardized factor loadings for the two-factor model are shown in Figure 10.1. All of the six items load significantly on the motivated reasoning factor. The loadings vary from .28 to .56. Items 2 (racial bias in several big city

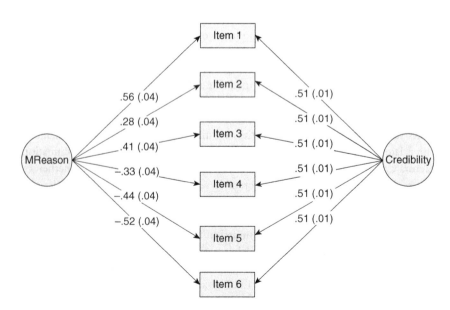

FIGURE 10.1 The Final Standardized Factor Loadings for the Two-Factor Model

hospitals) and 4 (admissions to state colleges) were somewhat less strongly related to the motivated reasoning factor than the other four items. The large loadings on the credibility factor shows that individual differences in finding *any* media report of a study credible accounts for a substantial amount of variance in these items.

Levels of Racial Motivated Reasoning Among White Americans

We first measured motivated reasoning by extracting factor scores on the substantive latent factor. In this approach, the inclusion of the second methods factor removes variance due to an individual's tendency to see all news story as credible or not. But there is a simpler way to calculate this score. The two-factor model assumed that all six motivated reasoning questions were equally affected by the credibility factor. Thus, an alternative way to extract a racial motivated reasoning score is to additively combine the three racial discrimination items and, separately, the three reverse discrimination items, and then subtract the reverse discrimination score from the racial discrimination score. This effectively cancels individual differences in the perceived credibility of all news items.

We constructed the motivated reasoning scale in this way. Both discrimination and reverse discrimination was coded so that 1 indicates high credibility and 0 indicates low. We then subtracted the racial discrimination subscale from the reverse discrimination subscale producing a measure that varies from -1 to $+1$. A score of $+1$ indicates that the respondent did not find any evidence of black discrimination credible but judged all evidence of reverse discrimination as very credible. A score of -1 indicates the reverse. The two methods for constructing a motivated reasoning score are correlated at .96 and are therefore virtually identical (and yield the same results in all analyses). We employ the second, more straightforward method of scale creation. By constructing the scale in this way, we remove ideological bias that would incline someone who is conservative to deny the existence of both discrimination and reverse discrimination. Someone who denies the existence of any kind of discrimination on ideological grounds is likely to score 0 on the scale, viewing all accounts of racially based treatment as non-credible.

We had raised a question at the outset about the degree of racial motivated reasoning among white Americans. The answer is somewhat reassuring. Figure 10.2 depicts the smoothed distribution of motivated reasoning which is very nearly normally distributed. The mean of the distribution is very close to zero indicating that, on average, white Americans are not systematically biased and are equally likely to believe some evidence of both racial and reverse discrimination. But there is also considerable variance in levels of motivated reasoning with some white Americans attaining scores of -1 and $+1$ in the sample. The 1st and 99th percentile of the motivated reasoning distribution are at $-.78$ and .67. In other words, some whites are very likely to accept evidence of racial discrimination

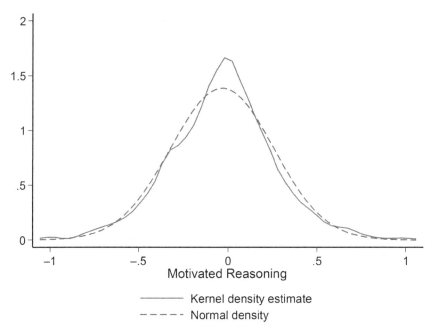

FIGURE 10.2 The Smoothed Distribution of Motivated Reasoning

while rejecting reverse discrimination whereas others fail to see racial discrimination but are quick to perceive reverse discrimination.

There is no evidence of asymmetry or skew in the distribution. This addresses another question we had raised at the outset as to whether or not motivated reasoning is more common on the conservative than liberal side of racial beliefs. The answer is that both sides—those who both deny and accept the existence of discrimination against blacks—engage in it equally when reasoning about racial discrimination.

Another way to demonstrate that white Americans are relatively evenhanded, on average, in how credible they view stories of racial and reverse discrimination is to examine levels of perceived discrimination in different domains of American life. Several questions in the survey tapped such perceptions. As seen in Figure 10.3, most white Americans believe whites are treated more fairly than blacks by the police, and have greater opportunity to live where they want. There is thus clear white acknowledgment of racial discrimination in both domains. In contrast, views are far more mixed concerning the existence of discrimination and reverse discrimination when it comes to gaining a college scholarship or government promotion. When asked about college scholarships or a government job promotion a substantial minority perceive black advantage. White views on racial discrimination are thus nuanced and reflect the tone of popular discussion

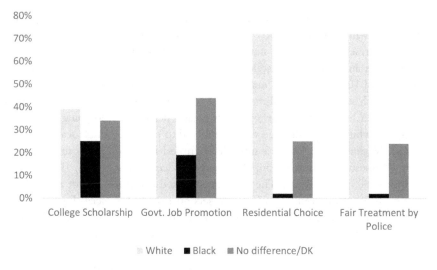

FIGURE 10.3 Most White Americans Believe Whites Are Treated More Fairly

about the different domains in which whites and blacks hold relative advantage in American society.

Racial or Ideological Motivated Reasoning?

To assess the validity of the racially motivated reasoning scale we examine its links to a set of racial and ideological beliefs. This sheds light on the racial nature of the denial of racial discrimination in the U.S. From one standpoint, it may seem obvious that motivated reasoning, especially the rejection of evidence for racial discrimination, has its origins in racial prejudice. But we have strong reasons to think there is also an ideological basis to such reasoning. Ideological conservatives tend to think in individual terms about economic success and may reject the notion that economic outcomes are influenced by group-based processes such as racial discrimination.

To assess the origins of motivated reasoning in racial beliefs we create two scales; the first assesses what we refer to as racial prejudice and combines racial stereotypes and negative views of black character. The second is a measure of overt racism.

Racial Prejudice

The scale is created by combining two subscales. The *racial stereotypes* subscale is created from six items which assess negative *racial stereotypes* in wave 2 of the survey. Respondents were asked, "On a scale of 1 to 10 where 1 represents lazy and 10 represents hard working where would you rate most blacks?" The question was repeated for "most whites." A second question asked respondents to place blacks and whites on a scale of 1 to 10, where 1 represents low moral standards and 10 represents high moral standards. A third question, asked respondents to place blacks and whites on a scale of 1 to 10, where 1 represents motivated to succeed and 10 represents not motivated to succeed. A difference score was created for each stereotype by subtracting the score given to blacks from that given to whites.[4] A higher score thus represents greater negative stereotyping of blacks relative to whites. Then all three were combined to create the single scale.

The *Negative Black Character* subscale is created from two items in batteries of racial questions adapted from the General Social Survey (GSS) (Huddy & Feldman, 2009; Hunt, 2007). The first battery asked about reasons for racial disparities in economic outcomes, and the second reasons for racial disparities in students' standardized test scores. The negative character scale was created from responses to "blacks just don't have the motivation or will power to perform well" and "blacks do not teach their children the values and skills which are required to be successful in school" as reasons for both racial differences in economic outcomes and student test scores. Racial stereotypes and negative black character were correlated at .32 and are combined into a single scale of racial prejudice.

Overt Racism was assessed with four questions drawn from the racial item batteries described above concerning the origins of racial disparities in economic outcomes and students' standardized test scores. Overt racism was based on the perceived importance of "racial differences in intelligence" and "fundamental genetic differences" as explanations for racial differences in standardized test scores and economic resources.

Ideology

The ideological origins of motivated reasoning were tested with four measures. First, respondents placed themselves on an *ideological self-placement* scale that ranged from very liberal to very conservative. A measure of *individualism* was constructed from six questions. The questions ask whether people who don't get ahead only have themselves to blame, if people who try hard often can't reach their goals, if a person who works hard has a good chance of succeeding, and whether people who work hard get what they want (α=.66). *Egalitarianism* was constructed from six items (gone too far in pushing equal rights, don't give everyone an equal chance, better if worried less about equality, ensure that everyone has an equal chance to succeed, fewer problems if people treated more equally, and would be better off if worry less about equality; α=.63). *Authoritarianism* was constructed from four questions that contrast authoritarian versus liberal child-rearing values.

Racially Based Motivated Reasoning

Several findings emerge from our analysis. First, there is clear evidence that racial prejudice leads to motivated racial reasoning, resulting in acceptance of reverse discrimination but not racial discrimination. We regressed the motivated reasoning scale on the racial and ideological variables and controlled for age, gender, and education. As seen in Table 10.2, racial prejudice increases the tendency to deny the credibility of stories about racial discrimination and increases acceptance of stories concerning reverse discrimination against whites. On the flip side, the least prejudiced were more likely to accept stories concerning racial discrimination and reject as non-credible those outlining reverse discrimination. This link is sizeable and significant as seen in Table 10.2. There is no evidence, however, that overt racism boosts motivated reasoning. Apparently, it is possible to express overt racism and view as credible instances of racial discrimination. Perhaps someone who is overtly racist regards racial discrimination as justified.

Second, Table 10.2 contains evidence that motivated reasoning has a strong foundation in the defense of ideological beliefs. The large, negative coefficient for egalitarianism suggests that strong egalitarians are most likely to deny the existence of reverse discrimination and accept racial discrimination, holding constant prejudice. Those who believe there is too much emphasis on equality in American society are far more likely to deny the existence of racial discrimination and accept reverse discrimination. Strong individualists are also more likely to deny the credibility of racial discrimination than reverse discrimination. The effect is not as large as for egalitarianism. But it is positive, sizeable, and significant. Authoritarians are also more likely to see as credible evidence of reverse discrimination against whites. There is no additional effect of ideological self-placement on motivated reasoning over and above the effects of the basic values of egalitarianism and individualism. Overall, the motivated denial of racial discrimination occurs in defense of racial beliefs *and* basic ideological values. This raises obvious concerns about equating the denial of racial discrimination with racism in contemporary

TABLE 10.2 Determinants of Motivated Reasoning

	Coefficient	*Std. Error*
Prejudice	**.34**	.09
Overt Racism	−.01	.04
Egalitarianism	**−.39**	.06
Individualism	**.19**	.06
Ideological Self-ID	.01	.03
Authoritarianism	**.07**	.02
Age (10 years)	−.005	.006
Gender (female)	−.03	.02
Education	**−.010**	.004
Constant	.14	.10

Notes: Coefficients in bold are more than twice the size of their standard error. The motivated reasoning scale ranges from −1 (racial discrimination is highly credible but reverse discrimination is not) to +1 (racial discrimination is not credible but reverse discrimination is highly credible). All other variables, with the exception of age, are coded on a 0 to 1 scale for ease of interpretation.

American society. The situation is more complex and at least partly colored by ideology. Finally, better educated individuals are less likely to see reverse discrimination as credible.

Historical Knowledge of Race Relations

We turn next to consider whether white Americans can agree on the basic contours of past race relations. We look at a number of factors that are likely to affect knowledge of black history. Our key focus is on the degree to which motivated reasoning leads to a motivated denial of past discrimination. We have demonstrated the diverse origins of racially motivated reasoning in both racial prejudice and political ideology. We now examine the direct effects of prejudice and ideology on historical knowledge and control for a number of additional factors that could influence views of past race relations, including education, age, and levels of contemporary political knowledge. Our goal is to determine the degree to which a motivated denial of past racial discrimination is grounded in prejudice and political ideology.

There are certain indisputable facts concerning the history of civil rights in the United States. Respondents in wave 2 were asked whether or not six different barriers had existed at the state or local level in the U.S. since 1950. Three of these had existed: (1) allowing storekeepers and restaurant owners to discriminate against black patrons by refusing to serve them, (2) concrete steps to prevent blacks from voting, and (3) allowing bus and train companies to discriminate against black patrons by making them sit in a separate section. Three had not existed: (1) legally allowing the ownership of slaves, (2) making it illegal for black children to attend school, and (3) making it illegal for blacks to hold political office. We create a scale to indicate the number of historical events (from 0 to 3) that were accurately identified. Our goal in including events that had not occurred was to increase the difficulty of the overall test. In our analysis, we focus primarily on knowledge of barriers that had existed in the past.

A majority of white Americans knew correctly that it had been legal in the recent past for storekeepers and restaurant owners (59%) and bus and train companies (61%) to discriminate against black patrons. Whites were less aware that state and local governments had taken steps to prevent blacks from voting (46%). These numbers are surprisingly low given ongoing discussions in the popular media and school classrooms on the civil rights era and the history of U.S. race relations. At best, 60% of whites were aware of these well-known occurrences. In light of recent attempts to enact voter identification laws that limit voting rights, it is particularly disturbing to see that less than a half of all white Americans are aware of past efforts to suppress black voter turnout.

There are multiple determinants of historical racial knowledge, suggesting it is a function of general knowledge, racial views, and ideology. We estimated an ordered probit model (shown in Table 10.4) to predict the number of correct answers to the three historical knowledge questions, using the same set of

TABLE 10.3 Frequencies for Historical Discrimination Items

	Yes	No	Don't know
As far as you know, since 1950 has there been any U.S. state or local government that allowed storekeepers and restaurant owners to discriminate against black patrons by refusing to serve them?	59.2%	33.4%	7.3%
As far as you know, has there been any state or local government since 1950 that took concrete steps to prevent legally entitled black citizens from voting in an election?	45.6	46.1	8.3
As far as you know, has there been any state or local government in the U.S. since 1950 that allowed bus and train companies to discriminate against black patrons by making them sit in a separate section?	61.3	33.0	5.5

TABLE 10.4 Determinants of Historical Knowledge

	Coefficient	Std Error
Knowledge and Demographics		
Political Knowledge	**1.00**	.19
Education	**.09**	.02
Age (10 years)	**.72**	.15
Age^2	**−.07**	.01
Gender (female)	**−.20**	.09
Motivated Reasoning	**−.38**	.16
Prejudice	−.20	.41
Overt Racism	**−.48**	.18
Egalitarianism	.13	.25
Individualism	−.25	.25
Ideological Self-ID	**−.30**	.14
Authoritarianism	**−.19**	.09
Threshold 1	2.14	
Threshold 2	2.63	
Threshold 3	3.38	

Notes: Coefficients in bold are more than twice the size of their standard error. The motivated reasoning scale ranges from −1 (racial discrimination is highly credible but reverse discrimination is not) to +1 (racial discrimination is not credible but reverse discrimination is highly credible). All other variables, with the exception of age, are coded on a 0 to 1 scale for ease of interpretation.

predictors as in the previous model (Table 10.2). In addition, we included a measure of political knowledge to estimate the extent to which incorrect historical knowledge of racial discrimination is simply a function of low levels of general political knowledge.[5] Finally, we include both age and age squared in order to estimate any nonlinear age effects on knowledge.

Not surprisingly, knowledge and greater educational attainment increased the ability to correctly identify past instances of discrimination. Thus, a significant amount of the variation in knowledge of past racial discrimination reflects general knowledge. We generated the predicted probability that someone would answer at least two of the three historical discrimination questions correctly. A college educated white person who got all four general knowledge questions correct had a probability of .77 of answering correctly two of the three questions. This probability drops dramatically to a low of .30 for a high school graduate who gave the wrong answer to all four political questions.

We had thought that those who lived through the civil rights era might be most knowledgeable about it. In support of this prediction, the effect of age is strongly nonlinear with the probability of correctly answering the historical knowledge questions increasing from age 18 to around 50. Those aged 50 at the time of the survey (in 2004) were 14 in 1968 and those under 50 would have thus been young children or not born at the height of the civil rights movement in the late 1960s. This supports the notion that having been very young or born after the civil rights era weakened knowledge of it. But results were somewhat more complex than that because after the age of 60, knowledge of historical discrimination declines significantly even though such individuals had lived through the events associated with civil rights. This was less expected, although the pattern is consistent with an impressionable years model of political socialization in which memory for events should be strongest among those who were in their teens and early 20s at the time they occurred (Sears & Brown, 2013). The predicted probability of answering at least two of the questions correctly across the range of age is shown in Figure 10.4.

There is also evidence in Table 10.4 of the motivated denial of historical facts. Those who found evidence of contemporary racial discrimination less credible were more likely to also deny past racial discrimination. Conversely, whites who viewed an account of current discrimination as credible were more likely to correctly perceive past discrimination. The predicted probability of answering at least two of the historical discrimination questions correctly decreased from .68 to .58 as the motivated reasoning measure ranged from the 1st (discrimination credible) to 99th percentile (reverse discrimination credible). Thus, whites who are reluctant to accept evidence of contemporary racial discrimination are also likely to not "know" historical facts about discrimination. This might occur because whites who are motivated to accept discrimination are willing to see it everywhere. But that is not what we found. When we analyzed knowledge of the three discriminatory events that had not occurred in the past, there was no greater tendency for whites who scored low on the motivated reasoning measure to answer these any differently than those who scored high.

The prejudice variable is not significant in the model shown in Table 10.4 but overt racism is. Whites who believe racial inequities are grounded in fundamental racial differences in ability held less accurate knowledge of historical

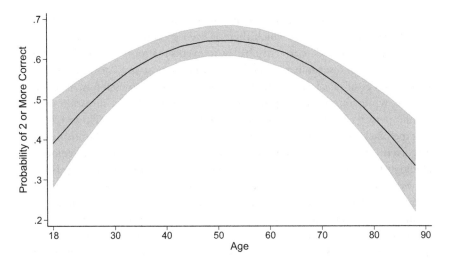

FIGURE 10.4 The Predicted Probability of Answering at Least Two of the Questions Correctly Across the Range of Age

discrimination. The effect size is comparable to that for motivated reasoning. Taken jointly, the motivated reasoning measure and racism have a substantial effect on the probability of answering at least two of the questions correctly. At the 1st percentile of both (reject reverse discrimination and score low on overt racism) the probability is .72 and this drops to .38 at the 99th percentile (reject discrimination and score high on overt racism) of both measures. Ideology also colors awareness of past discrimination. Conservatives and those high in authoritarianism were also less likely to correctly identify instances of historical discrimination.

Conclusion

Our findings underscore the minefield presented by any discussion of current or past instances of racial discrimination in the U.S. It should be relatively easy for white Americans to acknowledge the country's unjust past from slavery through Jim Crow to current instances of racial profiling and police brutality. But things are not so simple. For starters, racial prejudice, political ideology, and plain ignorance present obstacles to the acceptance of well-established facts concerning the history of recent American race relations. A majority of white Americans know that some states had practiced racial segregation in public transportation and public accommodations but fewer (under 50%) knew that some states had tried to prevent blacks from voting. Ignorance about past voter suppression complicates current discussion and understanding of the legal status of voter ID laws and other state-based efforts to suppress black and Latino voter turnout.

Things are similarly fraught when it comes to an understanding of contemporary discrimination around which there is even greater contestation. Education and knowledge provide corrective ballast to events that occurred in the past. But current forms of discrimination are less clear in the post-Jim Crow era. And current instances of racial discrimination are more difficult to establish. As a consequence, white acceptance of plausible instances of racial discrimination depend on the person's level of racial prejudice and political ideology. Those who stereotype blacks as lazy or lacking willpower are very willing to dismiss instances of current discrimination. But the rejection of discrimination is also colored by ideology. Individualists who believe people need to pull themselves up by their proverbial bootstraps and get ahead on their own deny instances of current discrimination. This rejection of racial discrimination is also stronger among non-egalitarian whites for whom societal equality is not a major concern. The denial of racial discrimination is thus fueled by a defense of racial beliefs and a conservative political outlook. In the absence of clear-cut evidence of racial discrimination, some whites remain skeptical of its existence.

The good news is that the tendency to reject evidence of racial discrimination is not the response of the majority. Most whites in our study rated as credible the instances of racial discrimination with which they were presented. And this open-minded response is likely enhanced by solid evidence. This is borne out by our finding that a majority of whites in the survey believe that blacks are discriminated against in housing and by the police. In both cases, there has been substantial credible evidence presented to support such claims. Recent live recording of police encounters with black motorists undoubtedly further strengthens awareness of racial discrimination in the criminal justice system. Thus, even politically conservative whites who harbor negative racial views may find it difficult to reject such clear-cut evidence.

From our vantage point, unambiguous evidence of racial discrimination in other domains, beyond housing and the criminal justice system, has the potential to convince white Americans that racial discrimination remains an important societal issue (Huddy & Feldman, 2009). And this matters because we find that the acceptance or denial of racial discrimination plays a powerful role in shaping support for ameliorative racial policies such as affirmative action, school spending, and residential integration. It thus becomes important to cast a clearer light on current racial inequities in American society. For example, clear evidence that more is spent on white than black children in some school districts, racial differences in children's access to libraries and other educational resources, and documented evidence on racial differences in bank lending practices would help to dispel the idea that racial disparities are a thing of the past. But this evidence needs to be clear-cut, frequently cited, and indisputable in order to get through to white Americans and alter their attitudes.

In this manuscript, we have demonstrated the ability of a motivated reasoning framework to shed light on the nature and complexity of white racial attitudes. In so doing, we are adding to the very rich research literature on political reasoning initiated by Milton Lodge and his colleagues. We find that the motivated denial of racial discrimination is consequential. But it is also complicated, grounded in both racial prejudice and political ideology. In going forward, it would be useful to replicate this study examining attitudes towards other types of discrimination linked to gender, ethnicity, or religion. A study along these lines would help to identify the ideologically motivated denial of group-based discrimination writ large. We believe the concept of motivated reasoning has the power to transform research on the study of white racial attitudes. In the Lodge tradition, we attack well-worn shibboleths, in this case the singularly prejudicial nature of a denial of discrimination. And in so doing we hope to effect change in the way in which racial attitudes are studied.

Notes

1. This research was supported by Grants SES-030318800 and SES-0555068 from the National Science Foundation and a presidential award from the Russell Sage Foundation.
2. The cooperation rate was 44% (AAPOR COOP3; www.aapor.org).
3. Root mean squared error of approximation.
4. There were a small number of cases where blacks were rated more highly than whites on a trait. Recoding those cases to zero (no negative stereotyping) increased the correlations among the three stereotype measures.
5. There were four questions in the general political knowledge scale: What job or political office does Dick Cheney now hold? How long is the term of office for a United States Senator? As far as you know, what job or political office does William Rehnquist now hold? As far as you know, how many times can an individual be elected President?

References

Alwin, D. F., Cohen, R. L., & Newcomb, T. M. (1991). *Aging, personality and social change: Attitude persistence and change over the life-span.* Madison, WI: University of Wisconsin Press.

Bisgaard, M. (2015). Bias will find a way: Economic perceptions, attributions of blame, and partisan-motivated reasoning during crisis. *The Journal of Politics,* 77(3), 849–860.

Bolsen, Toby, Druckman, James N., & Cook, Fay Lomax. (2014). The influence of partisan motivated reasoning on public opinion. *Political Behavior,* 36(2), 235–262.

Claassen, R. L. & Ensley, M. J. (2016). Motivated reasoning and yard-sign-stealing partisans: Mine is a likable rogue, yours is a degenerate criminal. *Political Behavior,* 38(2), 1–19.

Cohen, Geoffrey. (2003). Party over policy: The dominating impact of group influence on political beliefs. *Journal of Personality and Social Psychology,* 85, 808–822.

Converse, P. E. & Markus, G. B. (1979). Plus ça change. . . : The new CPS election study panel. *American Political Science Review,* 73, 32–49.

Druckman, J. N., Peterson, E., & Slothuus, R. (2013). How elite partisan polarization affects public opinion formation. *American Political Science Review,* 107(1), 57–79.

Feagin, J. R. (2014). *Racist America: Roots, current realities, and future reparations.* New York: Routledge.

Feldman, Stanley & Huddy, Leonie. (2005). Racial resentment and white opposition to race-conscious programs: principles or prejudice? *American Journal of Political Science,* 49(1), 168–183.

Green, Donald, Palmquist, Bradley, & Schickler, Eric. (2002). *Partisan hearts and minds: Political parties and the social identity of voters*. New Haven, CT: Yale University Press.

Henry, P. J. & Sears, D. O. (2002). The symbolic racism 2000 scale. *Political Psychology*, 23(2), 253–283.

Huddy, Leonie. (2013). From group identity to political commitment and cohesion. In Leonie Huddy, David O. Sears, & Robert Jervis (Eds.), *Oxford handbook of political psychology* (pp. 737–773). New York: Oxford University Press.

Huddy, Leonie & Feldman, Stanley. (2009). On assessing the political effects of racial prejudice. *Annual Review of Political Science*, 12, 423–447.

Huddy, Leonie, Mason, Lilly, & Aaroe, Lene. (2015). Expressive partisanship: Campaign involvement, political emotion, and partisan identity. *American Political Science Review*, 109(1), 1–17.

Hunt, Matthew O. (2007). African American, Hispanic and White beliefs about Black/White inequality, 1977–2004. *American Sociological Review*, 72, 390–415.

Jennings, M. K. & Niemi, R. G. (1981). *Generations and politics*. Princeton, NJ: Princeton University Press.

Kinder, D. R. & Winter, N. (2001). Exploring the racial divide: Blacks, whites, and opinion on national policy. *American Journal of Political Science*, 45(2), 439–456.

Kinder, Donald R. & Sanders, Lynn M. (1996). *Divided by color: Racial politics and democratic ideals*. Chicago, IL: University of Chicago Press.

Kunda, Ziva. (1990). The case for motivated reasoning. *Psychological Bulletin*, 108, 480–449.

Lavine, Howard, Johnston, Christopher, & Steenbergen, Marco. (2012). *The ambivalent partisan: How critical loyalty promotes democracy*. Oxford: Oxford University Press.

Leeper, T. J. & Slothuus, R. (2014). Political parties, motivated reasoning, and public opinion formation. *Political Psychology*, 35(S1), 129–156.

Lodge, Milton, McGraw, Kathleen, & Stroh, Patrick. (1989). An impression-driven model of candidate evaluation. *American Political Science Review*, 83, 399–419.

Lodge, Milton & Taber, Charles S. (2013). *The rationalizing voter*. Cambridge: Cambridge University Press.

National Research Council. (2004). *Measuring racial discrimination*. Washington, DC: The National Academies Press.

Nyhan, B. & Reifler, J. (2010). When corrections fail: The persistence of political misperceptions. *Political Behavior*, 32, 303–330.

Parker-Stephen, E. (2013). Tides of disagreement: How reality facilitates (and inhibits) partisan public opinion. *The Journal of Politics*, 75(4), 1077–1088.

Petersen, M. B., Skov, M., Serritzlew, S., & Ramsøy, T. (2013). Motivated reasoning and political parties: Evidence for increased processing in the face of party cues. *Political Behavior*, 35(4), 831–854.

Prior, M., Sood, G, & Khanna, K. (2013). *You cannot be serious: Do partisans believe what they say? (PDF)—Semantic Scholar. (n.d.).* Retrieved August 1, 2016, from www.semanticscholar.org/paper/You-Cannot-Be-Serious-Do-Partisans-Believe-What-Prior-Sood/1d108a1ffe4ce2058b7c6565cad76542952302b8/pdf

Redlawsk, D. P., Civettini, A. J., & Emmerson, K. M. (2010). The affective tipping point: Do motivated reasoners ever "get it"? *Political Psychology*, 31, 563–593.

Saucier, D. A. & Miller, C. T. (2003). The persuasiveness of racial arguments as a subtle measure of racism. *Personality and Social Psychology Bulletin*, 29(10), 1303–1315.

Schuman, H., Steeh, C., Bobo, L., & Krysan, M. (1997). *Racial attitudes in America: Trends and interpretations* (Revised ed.). Cambridge, MA: Harvard University Press.

Sears, D. O. (1983). The persistence of early political predispositions: The roles of attitude object and life stage. In L. Wheeler & P. Shaver (Eds.), *Review of personality and social psychology* (Vol. 4, pp. 79–116). Beverly Hills, CA: Sage.

Sears, D. O. & Brown, C. (2013). Childhood and adult political development. In L. Huddy, D. O. Sears, & R. Jervis (Eds.), *Oxford handbook of political psychology* (pp. 59–95). New York: Oxford University Press.

Sears, D. O. & Funk, C. L. (1999). Evidence of the long-term persistence of adults' political predispositions. *Journal of Politics*, 61, 1–28.

Taber, Charles S. & Lodge, Milton. (2006). Motivated skepticism in the evaluation of political beliefs. *American Journal of Political Science*, 50, 755–769.

Tajfel, Henri & Turner, John. (1979). An integrative theory of intergroup conflict. In W. G. Austin & S. Worchel (Eds.), *The social psychology of intergroup relations* (pp. 33–47). Monterey, CA: Brooks/Cole.

Tarman, C. & Sears, D. O. (2005). The conceptualization and measurement of symbolic racism. *The Journal of Politics*, 67(3), 731–761.

Valentino, Nicholas A. & Brader, Ted. (2011). The sword's other edge: Perceptions of discrimination and racial policy opinion after Obama. *Public Opinion Quarterly*, 75(2), 201–226. doi:10.1093/poq/nfr010

Wood, B. D. & Vedlitz, A. (2007). Issue definition, information processing, and the politics of global warming. *American Journal of Political Science*, 51(3), 552–568.

11
ALL IN THE EYE OF THE BEHOLDER

Asymmetry in Ideological Accountability[1]

Gaurav Sood[2] and Shanto Iyengar[3]

It is well established that American political leaders are ideologically polarized (Aldrich, 1995; Stonecash, Brewer, & Mariani, 2003; McCarty, Poole, & Rosenthal, 2006). It is also well corroborated that polarization harms the body politic; polarization causes "gridlock" in legislatures (Jones, 2001; Binder, 2005; McCarty et al., 2006), impedes the work of judicial and administrative bodies (Binder 2005; McCarty et al., 2006), and reduces trust in government (Hetherington, 2005). Worryingly, the polarization of American legislatures continues apace (Shor & McCarty, 2011).

The worry turns to puzzlement when we juxtapose three observations. First, over the last four decades, elected representatives of both major parties have become more ideologically extreme (Aldrich, 1995; Stonecash et al., 2003; McCarty et al., 2006). Second, there has been far less centrifugal movement among the rank and file; the median voter remains moderate on many of the issues (DiMaggio, Evans, & Bryson, 1996; Evans, 2003; Fiorina, Abrams, & Pope, 2005, 2008; Hill & Tausanovitch, 2014). Third, supporters of the two parties still express strong affection for their party (Iyengar, Sood, & Lelkes, 2012) and its leaders (as we show later), while expressing hostility towards the opposing party and its leaders.[4]

In this chapter we offer an explanation for the paradox of unabated partisan support despite increased ideological divergence within parties between followers and leaders. Either due to biases in information provided by trusted sources, e.g., communiqués from co-partisan elites, invention of partisan congenial facts, or biases in processing of information, partisans' perceptions of parties' and party leaders' policy positions are strikingly distorted. For instance, despite the increasingly stark differences between elite and mass preferences, the distance between partisans' ideological self-placements and where they place their own party has remained stable over the past four decades.

There is more to the explanation than biases in information exposure and wishful thinking. Partisans appear to use the information they learn in a manner inconsistent with the dominant spatial model (more spatially proximal candidates get more support); when provided information about candidates' policy positions, partisans approve of co-partisan candidates with more extreme (and more distal) positions no less than, and occasionally more than, co-partisan candidates with more moderate (and more proximate) positions. We begin by examining the relationship between representatives' actual ideology (estimated via roll-call votes or campaign contributions) and their popularity among partisans. To assess the relationship, we use a very large collection of state-level polls that ask about approval of elected officials, and combine it with estimates of officials' ideology. We find that the most ideologically extreme representatives draw nearly as much support from co-partisans as the more moderate representatives. On the other hand, notably fewer partisans support more extreme out-party representatives than their more moderate out-party counterparts.

Next, we investigate whether asymmetric changes in approval are founded in asymmetries in the spatial calculus used by voters to judge candidates. Jointly scaling respondents' and congressional officials' positions using data from the 2006 Cooperative Congressional Election Study (CCES), we find this asymmetry is partly a consequence of the different spatial calculus that partisans use to judge co-partisan and opposing party representatives. We find that independents are most sensitive to spatial distance, and that partisans are far more sensitive to ideological position of elected officials of the opposing party than their own party.

To explain this differential discounting of actual ideological distance, we first consider the role of perceptions by examining perceptual bias with data from the 2006 CCES, comparing perceptions of senators' votes with their actual voting record. We find that co-partisan senators are perceived as more moderate than their actual record, with bias greater in perceptions of co-partisan senators' voting records than out-party senators' voting records. Last, we explore how partisans judge politicians when information about policy positions is provided to them. Even when given information about candidate policy positions, partisans approve of co-partisan candidates with more extreme positions no less than—and sometimes more than—co-partisan candidates with more moderate positions. All in all, these results paint a sobering picture of voters' ability to hold elected officials of their own party accountable for their ideological positions.

Partisan Affect, Perceptual Asymmetries, and Motivated Processing

That most people attach themselves to political parties for policy-based reasons is an appealing, even obvious, theory. But empirical evidence for the theory has always been scant. One of the earliest challenges to the theory came from Campbell, Converse, Miller, & Stokes (1960), who discovered that only a few people reasoned about politics in ideological terms, and theorized that partisan identification is primarily affective.[5] This more "primal" view of partisanship has since been validated by considerable work on the underpinnings of partisan identity (Green, Palmquist, & Schickler, 2004; Greenstein, 1965; Jennings, Stoker, & Bowers, 2009). The claim that the bond between voters and parties is primarily affective is buttressed by extensive evidence showing that partisans know little about the policy positions of party elites (Campbell et al., 1960; Delli Carpini, 1996; Luskin, 2002; Bawn et al., 2012).[6] Evidence of mass ignorance led researchers to investigate how citizens fend in the absence of information. The ensuing studies suggested that people use what little information they have (or what information is made available to them) to infer information they do not have (Brady & Sniderman, 1985; Conover & Feldman, 1989; Feldman & Conover, 1983; Popkin, 1991; Lau & Redlawsk, 2001). For instance, on learning that a candidate is a woman, some voters infer that the candidate supports social welfare programs (McDermott, 1997; Lawless, 2004).

Perhaps a more widespread heuristic is the use of affect to derive politicians' positions on issues. People (dis)like some groups instinctively, and use that "information" to infer policy positions of group members (Brady & Sniderman, 1985; Achen & Bartels, 2006).[7] The "likability heuristic"—those you like appear ideologically closer to you than those you dislike—is especially relevant in the current era of strong partisan affect (Iyengar et al., 2012; Iyengar & Westwood, 2015).[8] The implications of the heuristic are straightforward—uninformed partisans will believe that representatives of their party are ideologically close and representatives of the opposing party, distant.

To this point we have discussed how partisans cope in the absence of information. But affect-based reasoning can intercede, even when information is made available. For instance, a large proportion of Republicans believe that President Obama is a Muslim (Hollander, 2010) although reliable evidence to the contrary is widely available. The tendency to reject uncongenial information—where congeniality is defined on the basis of group affiliation—is well established (Lord, Ross, & Lepper, 1979; Kunda, 1987). Seminal work by Lodge and his collaborators has documented the pervasive use of confirmatory bias and motivated skepticism (toward disconfirmatory messages) in information processing; both heuristics allow partisans to protect their sense of identity from short-term threats (Taber & Lodge, 2006; Kim, Taber, & Lodge, 2010; Lodge & Taber, 2013).[9]

Aside from biases in exposure and processing stemming from partisan affect, institution level processes also likely contribute to distorted perceptions of candidates' policy positions. During election campaigns, many ideologically extreme politicians present themselves as centrists and their opponents as extremists (Henderson, 2013). Famously, George W. Bush, one of the most ideologically extreme of recent presidents ran as a "uniter, not a divider." This combined with the fact that ads are most effective at persuading voters who share the partisanship of the sponsoring candidate (Ansolabehere & Iyengar, 1995) suggests that campaigns likely contribute to distorted perceptions of candidates' positions. Changes in the market for broadcast news, most notably, the success of Fox News and the emergence of MSNBC as the cable network on the left, mean that there are news outlets that deliver biased rhetoric. And while the number of partisans who limit their exposure to partisan channels remains small, a fair number are exposed to some partisan information regularly via their online social networks.

Due to all these reasons, we expect ideological differences to matter less to partisans than to independents. We further expect partisans to be more sensitive to the actual ideological distance of representatives of the opposing party than representatives of their own party.

Asymmetry in the Ideology-Affect Relationship

We begin by showing that the relationship between a representative's ideology and approval depends on the match between representative and respondent. While approval among co-partisans is nearly unrelated to representatives' ideology, with more extreme representatives enjoying nearly as much support among co-partisans as their more moderate counterparts, more extreme representatives have much lower approval ratings among supporters of the opposing party than more moderate representatives. In the next section, we show that these differential patterns of approval among in- and out-partisans are in part due to differential accounting of actual ideological proximity by partisans.

Data and Measures

The data come from a series of monthly state-level polls conducted by SurveyUSA between 2005 and 2011. SurveyUSA uses Random Digit Dialing and automated interviewing for its polls. All the polls we use have a sample size of at least 600 respondents. In all, we have 1,873 polls, covering all fifty states, with approximately 1.08 million respondents rating over a 100 U.S. senators. Polls asked respondents about their opinion about officials from their own states. The approval question was typically worded as follows—"Do you approve or disapprove of the job Senator [NAME] is doing?"[10] We merged these approval data with DW-Nominate estimates of ideology (McCarty et al., 2006). We also present analyses with Campaign Finance-based estimates of ideology (CF-Scores) (Bonica, 2013).

Analytical Strategy

To assess the relationship between ideology and support among different partisan groups, we modeled the support that an elected representative enjoys among different partisan groups within a state as a function of representatives' ideology, office held, and the match between representatives' and respondent's party affiliation. To this model, we made three amendments. First, given that a Democrat from Massachusetts is not the same as a Democrat from Texas (a Democrat from Texas is likely to be more conservative than one from Massachusetts and thus expected to like conservative politicians more and liberal ones less), we added state fixed effects to make within state comparisons.[11] Second, since we have data on the same representative at multiple time points, we added random effects for representatives. And third, to account for polls that contributed more than one observation to our data set, we clustered standard errors by polls. Letting i index polls, j index representatives, and s index states, our model takes the form:

$$y_{ij} \sim N\left(X_j \beta + \alpha_i + \gamma_j + \delta_s; \sigma_e^2\right)$$
$$\alpha_i \sim N\left(0, \sigma_\alpha^2\right)$$
$$\gamma_j \sim N\left(0, \sigma_\gamma^2\right)$$

In all, we modeled approval, y, as a function of ideology (X); α captures idiosyncratic variation across senators, γ the dependence between observations, and δ the state fixed effects. To ease interpretation, we rescale all our measures to lie between 0 and 1. For approval, going from 0 to 1 means going from 0% approval to 100% approval. For DW-Nominate and CF-Score, the 0 to 1 range means going from the most liberal representative (DW-Nominate = −.512; CF-Score = −1.124) to the most conservative representative (DW-Nominate = .900; CF-Score = .977) in our sample.

Results

In several national polls conducted between December 2008 and August 2010, Sarah Palin's support never once slipped below 69% among Republicans. Typically, it was higher than 75%. As we will see below, such robust support for ideologically extreme party leaders is typical. The most conservative Republican senators (in roughly the top decile of ideology in their own party, with DW-Nominate scores of over .8) enjoyed an average approval rating of over 65% among Republicans. On the other side of the aisle, the most liberal Democratic senators (with DW-Nominate scores of less than −.4), enjoyed approval from more than 68% of Democrats on average.

We start by plotting the locally smoothed relationship between ideological extremity[12] and approval separately for in-party and out-party representatives. Figure 11.1 shows that approval of co-partisan senators is only weakly related to their ideology. However, the relationship between approval and ideology is much stronger when the senators are of the opposing party.

For ease of exposition, we split the analyses by party of the elected official and respondent.[13] Beginning with Republicans' evaluations of Republican senators, more extreme Republican senators elicit somewhat lower approval ratings

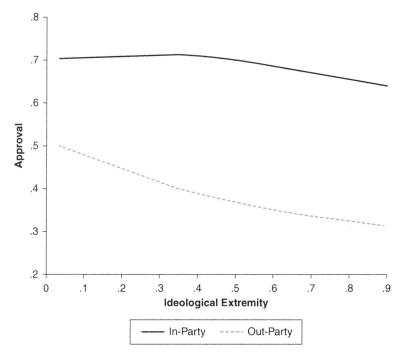

FIGURE 11.1 Relationship Between Ideology and Approval by Whether or Not Respondent and Representative's Party Match

($b = -.18, p = .14$; see Table 11.1). In particular, moving from the most liberal Republican senator in our data ($-.05$ on DW-Nominate) to the most conservative (.90 on DW-Nominate), changes approval among Republicans by only about 13%. Democrats' evaluations of the same Republican senators, however, respond strongly to ideology ($b = -.65, p < .001$), a more than three-fold increase in responsiveness.

As expected, Republicans evaluate more liberal Democratic senators more harshly ($b = 1.09, p < .001$).[14] But when Democrats rate the same senators, they are far less responsive to ideology ($b = .37, p > .10$); ratings of the most conservative senator ($-.05$ on DW-Nominate) are merely 12% higher than those of the most liberal senator ($-.512$ on DW-Nominate). Given these sizable differences in how partisans respond to in- and out-party senators, the hypothesis that coefficients are equal is easily rejected; the chances of the two coefficients being equal are literally less than one in a million.[15] (The results look substantively the same when we substitute CF-Scores for DW-Nominate estimates of ideology. These results are presented in Table 11.A1 of Appendix A.[16])

It is well known that evaluations of incumbents are increasingly polarized (see Jacobson, 2006).[17] Scholars typically attribute the increased polarization in

TABLE 11.1 Approval of Senator as a Function of Ideology (DW-Nominate)

| | Republican Senators | | Democratic Senators | |
	Republicans	Democrats	Republicans	Democrats
Intercept	.87***	.91***	.16***	.62***
DW-Nominate	−.18	−.65***	1.09***	.37
n	920	920	953	953
r^2	.59	.69	.69	.46

Notes: ***$p < .001$. Estimated separately for Republican and Democratic senators, further split by party of the respondent, with fixed effects for states. Fixed effects for states are not reported.

approval ratings to shifts in elite ideology (see Jacobson, 2006; Fiorina, et al., 2008). Our results suggest that this account is at best only half accurate. There is a penalty for ideological extremity, but it is generally limited to officials of the opposing party.

Asymmetric Discounting of Actual Ideological Differences

A modest relationship between approval and ideological extremity for co-partisan officials does not necessarily mean that partisans account for ideological distance differently depending on the party of the representative. The weakness in the relationship can, for instance, be a consequence of lower approval among partisan moderates being offset by greater approval among partisan extremists.

To assess the extent to which partisans' responses to ideological proximity vary by party of the elected official, we estimated the relationship between approval and ideological distance between the representative and the voter. If partisans are evenhanded in their evaluations of party leaders, the relationship between ideological distance and approval should not depend on the party of the representative. If, however, our theory holds, actual ideological distance to leaders of one's own party should matter less to approval than distance to leaders of the opposing party.

We used data from the 2006 CCES. (Appendix B provides details about sampling.) The survey included questions on several key roll-call votes by senators including votes on (1) the ban on partial-birth abortion, (2) federal funding of stem-cell research, (3) extending lower tax rates for capital gains, (4) ratifying the Central America Free Trade Agreement (CAFTA), (5) immigration reform, (6) withdrawing troops from Iraq, (7) raising the minimum wage. (See also Ansolabehere and Jones [2010] who use a similar list of votes.) In addition to assessing respondents' beliefs about the votes of their senators, the survey asked respondents how they would have voted on each of the issues. We recoded the votes attributed to senators and the respondents' votes so that in each case 1 indicated support for the conservative position and 0 indicated the opposite.

We jointly scaled the votes by senators and respondents using a two-parameter latent trait model (Lord et al., 1968). We modeled the probability of respondent i supporting policy j as a function of x_i, the respondent's unobserved ideological position, y_j, the policy "discrimination parameter" tracking how strongly the respondent's ideological positions are related to the probabilities of supporting the policy, and α_j, the policy "difficulty parameter" or the general level of support enjoyed by a policy,

$$P(y_{ij} = 1) = \Theta(\gamma_j x_i - \alpha_j)$$

Θ is the cumulative distribution function of the standard normal. Scaling the votes using the 2-PN latent trait model yields estimates of ideology that are strongly correlated with alternate measures of ideology. For instance, senators' positions recovered from these votes correlate with their DW-Nominate scores at .92. Similarly, scaling a survey respondent's positions on the votes yields a measure that correlates with the 7-point party identification question at .70.

Respondent partisan self-identification was assessed using the conventional party identification question. We pooled independents that leaned toward a party with self-identified partisans. Approval of senators was measured on a 4-point scale going from "strongly disapprove" (coded as 0) to "strongly approve" (coded as 1). Our measure of spatial ideological distance between senators and respondents is simply the absolute distance between the senator's and respondent's position on the vote-based ideology scale. We rescale it to lie between 0 (no difference between positions) to 1 (all positions are different).

We assess asymmetry in the relationship between ideological distance and approval by comparing the relationship across independents, partisans assessing out-party senators, and partisans assessing in-party senators. We start by plotting a locally smoothed estimate of the relationship between ideological distance and affect (see Figure 11.2a). As is clear from the plot, a linear relationship approximates the relationship well. We thus next move to regressing senatorial approval on the absolute distance between the policy positions of senators and respondents. Since each respondent assessed two senators, we cluster standard errors by respondent.

Our expectation is that vis-à-vis independents, the relationship between ideological distance and approval will be weaker among partisans. In line with the theory and results above, we further expect the relationship to be still more attenuated when respondents are evaluating senators of their own party.

Simply because the senator belongs to the same party as the respondent, he or she gets a large bump in their approval. Conditional on actual ideological

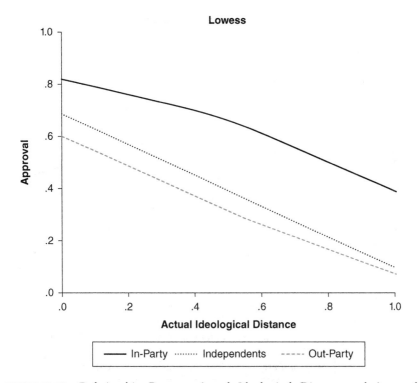

FIGURE 11.2A Relationship Between Actual Ideological Distance and Approval Among Independents, Partisans Evaluating Opposing Party Senators, and Partisans Evaluating Co-Partisan Senators

disagreement, senators' approval is on average 13% higher among co-partisans than among independents, and 23% higher among co-partisans than among opposing partisans (see Table 11.2; see also Figure 11.2B). (See Table 11.C1 in Appendix C for results from a model that includes a broad set of covariates. The results are nearly identical to the results presented in Table 11.2.)

Actual ideological disagreement expectedly increases disapproval among all subgroups. However, there are striking differences in the strength of the relationship. The relationship is strongest among independents ($b = -.54, p < .001$), somewhat weaker when the respondent belongs to a different party than the senator ($b = -.48, p < .001$; $\text{Diff.}_{\text{Ind.-Out-party}} = .06, p < .05$), and appreciably weaker when partisanship of the respondent is the same as the senator's ($b = -.34, p < .001$, $\text{Diff.}_{\text{Ind.-In-party}} = .20, p < .01$).[18]

To get a sense of the effect of these differences, we simulated how approval ratings would have looked like had partisans used the same spatial calculus as independents—mean approval of co-partisan representatives would have been

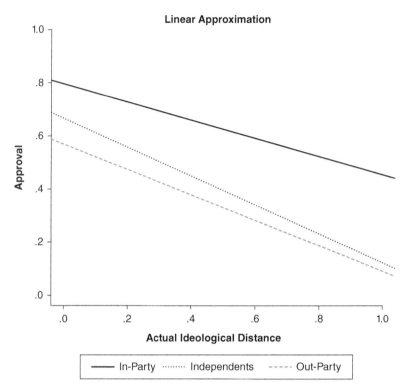

FIGURE 11.2B Relationship Between Actual Ideological Distance and Approval Among Independents, Partisans Evaluating Opposing Party Senators, and Partisans Evaluating Co-Partisan Senators

TABLE 11.2 Approval of Candidate as a Function of Actual Ideological Distance

	In-Party	Out-Party	Independents
Intercept	.80★★★	.57★★★	.67★★★
Absolute Distance	−.34★★★	−.48★★★	−.54★★★
n	15,118	13,054	3,255
r^2	.05	.16	.18

Notes: ★★★$p < .001$. Estimated separately among independents, partisans evaluating opposing party senators, and partisans evaluating co-partisan senators.

nearly 20 points lower, and mean approval of opposing party representatives approximately 6 points higher, on average.

Perhaps still more pertinent to our finding of high approval ratings of co-partisan extremists is the fact that partisans are less likely to account for ideological differences with their own party's elites if those elites are more ideologically extreme than them (to the right of Republicans, or to the left of Democrats) ($b = -.27, p < .001$)

than when they are more moderate than them (to the left of Republicans, or to the right of Democrats) ($b = -.37, p < .001; b_{\text{Diff.}} = .10, p_{\text{Diff.}} < .01$).

In all, partisans react less strongly to ideological differences with their representatives than independents, with partisans being particularly averse to penalizing ideologically distant representatives of their party. Additionally, partisans react less strongly to ideological differences with elites from their own party who are more extreme than them, than to differences with co-partisan elites who are more moderate than them.

Explaining the Partisan Asymmetry

To this point, we have focused on documenting the asymmetry in the relationship between ideology and partisan affect. But what explains this asymmetry? We have two conjectures—bias in perceptions of ideology of the representatives and the parties, and differences in how partisans use information to judge approval. Both biases are best understood as caused by partisan affect, or mechanisms related to the sense of partisan identity. We first provide evidence of biases in perceptions, and then document differential weighting of information.

Bias in Perceptions of Senators' Positions

Moving from parties to placements of elected representatives, we again turn to CCES 2006 and the questions on senators' voting behavior. A majority of the partisan respondents were either uninformed or misinformed about the position of their senators on each of the votes. We jointly scaled respondents' positions, respondents' beliefs about senators' positions using a two-parameter latent trait model, assuming the data were missing at random.

To motivate our discussion of perceptual errors, we assessed the relationship between approval and perceived ideological distance. Expectedly, partisans appear to react far more strongly to perceived ideological differences than to actual ideological differences. (See Table 11.D1 in Appendix D.) Moreover, the relationship is much more symmetric. While undoubtedly some of the strength of relationship between approval and perceived differences is a consequence of approval causing perceived distance, endogeneity concerns are likely less severe given proximity measures were built indirectly from positions on separate lists of items, and not via semantic self- and candidate-placement scales that follow each other. Either way, the structure of the boost in coefficients between actual and perceived ideological distance—far greater for in-partisans than out-partisans—strongly hints at the asymmetry we note above.

Different kinds of errors can weaken correlations between actual ideological distance and approval. The first possibility is that perceptions of co-partisan senators' positions carry more random error than perceptions of opposing party senators' positions. We find little evidence for it (see Section D2, Appendix D), though we find some differences in how the error is distributed, with error more strongly correlated with ideology of in-partisan representatives than out-partisan representatives (see Section D2, Appendix D).

The key conjecture about errors in perceptions, however, is about directional error. Consistent with the bias in perceptions of positions of parties that we find in the previous section, we find that on average Democrats thought Republican senators were more right wing than Republicans, and Republicans thought Democratic senators were more liberal than Democrats (see Figure 11.3).

More consequentially, the bias in ratings of co-partisan senators was considerably higher than ratings of opposing party partisans. Democrats understated the extremity of Democratic senators by a considerable margin (Mean Diff.$_{\text{perceived-true}}$ = .42). Meanwhile, the bias in Democrats' perceptions of the Republican senators was considerably smaller (Mean Diff.$_{\text{perceived-true}}$ = −.09). Conversely, Republicans understated the extremity of Republican senators (Mean Diff.$_{\text{perceived-true}}$ = −.27), and the extent of error in their perceptions of Democratic senators was somewhat lower (Mean Diff.$_{\text{perceived-true}}$ = .24). Thus, the magnitude of the average directional error in perceptions of co-partisan senators' positions exceeded the error in perceptions of opposing party senators' positions.

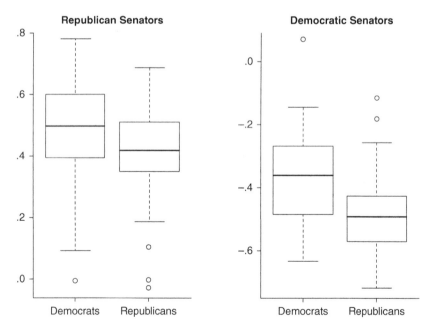

FIGURE 11.3 Perceived Ideological Location of Democratic and Republican Senators by Party of Respondent

These differences in the structure of error in perceptions of in- and out-party candidates have consequences for correlations. The correlation between DW-Nominate scores and perceived ideology of in-party senators is about .69, about 7% lower than the same correlation for opposing party senators ($r = .75$; $p_{Diff.} < .05$).

Last, we assess consequences of perceptual errors. We expect the greatest errors in perceptions of co-partisan senators' positions to be among respondents furthest away from their own party (so the greater the error, the lower the approval). Conversely, we expect the greatest errors in perception of opposing party senators' positions to be among respondents closest to the opposing party (the greater the error, the higher the approval). To assess this claim, we regressed approval on absolute distance between perceived and actual positions. Expectedly, the errors are positively correlated with approval for opposing partisans, and negatively correlated with approval for in-party elites (see Table 11.4). Further, and in line with expectations, there was no relation between errors made by independents and approval. However, as the low r-squares suggest, errors do not explain much of the variance in approval, though taken jointly, they go some ways toward explaining the asymmetry.

In all, we find—(1) greater bias in perceptions of in-party candidates than opposing party candidates, (2) greater bias (and greater error) in perceptions of co-partisan candidates who are more extreme than the respondent, than co-partisan candidates more moderate than the respondent, and 3) that these errors matter modestly, partly explaining the asymmetry we observe in the relationship between actual ideology and approval.

Impact of Provision of Information on Approval

As we have acknowledged, the relationship between perceptual errors and approval is likely endogenous no doubt, errors in perceptions affect approval, but approval also likely causes perceptions. So how would representatives fare if their policy positions were made known to partisans? To understand how partisans account for

TABLE 11.3 Approval of Candidate as a Function of Absolute Distance Between Perceived Policy Positions and Actual Policy Positions

	In-Party	Out-Party	Independents
Intercept	.78★★★	.20★★★	.44★★★
Error	−.30★★★	.43★★★	.04
n	15,118	13,054	3,255
r^2	.03	.04	.00

Notes: ★★★$p < .001$. Estimated separately among independents, co-partisan senators, and opposing party senators.

known differences, we report results from an experiment in which we attributed policy positions to hypothetical candidates at random. The experiment allows us to estimate the effects of policy information on candidate evaluations. When voters are made aware of candidates' positions, to what extent do they factor policy distance into their evaluations of the candidates? As we discuss below, we find that partisans approve of more distant (and more ideologically extreme) co-partisan candidates no less than more proximate (and more moderate) co-partisan candidates.

Research Design

We conducted the survey experiment in early 2013 on a sample drawn from the online opt-in panel maintained by YouGov. (See Appendix B for details about sampling.) The experiment was limited to self-identified or leaning partisans ($n = 954$). The experiment manipulated positions of hypothetical candidates on a social welfare issue (government spending), and a moral issue (abortion). We first asked respondents to place themselves on a scale that ranged from 1 (most conservative) to 7 (most liberal) and then presented them with the position of a hypothetical Democrat (or Republican) candidate on the same scale. To increase ecological validity of our experiment, we only randomized over partisan-consistent positions. So the Democratic candidate could only be at 5 or 7 and the Republican candidate could only be at 1 or 3 on both the issues. After presenting the respondents with candidate positions, we asked respondents to evaluate the candidate on the basis of their policy position. Respondents rated the candidates on a 5-point scale that ranged from strongly approve to strongly disapprove; we recoded these ratings to lie between 0 and 1 with higher values indicating greater approval. (For exact wording of each of the questions and a screenshot of one of the treatment conditions, see Appendix E.)

Results

On the 7-point government services scale, on average, Democrats placed themselves at 4.9 while Republicans placed themselves at 2.2. The corresponding figures on abortion were 5.5 and 3.1. The means for either policy did not differ significantly across conditions. Thus, on both issues, the average Democrat was considerably closer to the Democratic representative with the more moderate position (5) than to the Democratic representative with the more extreme position (7), and the average Republican was much closer to the Republican representative with the more moderate position (3) than to the Republican representative with the more extreme position (1). In such situations, the commonly used symmetric spatial utility model predicts greater support for the representative with the more moderate position. However, in two of the four cases, the representative with the more extreme position enjoyed greater support from co-partisans than the representative with the more moderate position (see Table 11.4). Democrats' mean approval rating of the Democratic candidate who held the most liberal position on abortion was .74, comfortably higher than the average rating of .60 received by the Democratic candidate with the more moderate position ($p < .01$). Similarly, Republicans' ratings of the Republican candidate with the most conservative position on government services were considerably higher than for the candidate with the more moderate position (Mean Diff. = .10, $p < .05$). In the other two cases, the difference in support for extreme and moderate representatives was statistically indistinguishable from 0. Thus, even when given information, partisans are disinclined to penalize more distal and more extreme co-partisans.

On the flip side, partisans consistently responded to the position of opposing partisan candidates in expected ways: opposing party candidates with more extreme positions drew far less support than more moderate candidates. In all four cases, the out-party representative with the more extreme position received less support. The average decline in support across the four cases was roughly .12 ($p < .05$).

Finally, we present some suggestive analysis that sheds additional light on why increases in ideological extremity do not erode support among co-partisans. We think it likely that partisans who hold more extreme views often also care more about ideology. The striking finding that partisans sometimes support the co-partisan candidate with the more extreme, and on average, more distant position may thus be a consequence of partisans with more extreme positions being more responsive to ideological distance than partisans with more moderate positions. To assess this possibility, one can regress approval on self-placement, distance to the candidate, and the interaction between self-placement and distance. However,

TABLE 11.4 Approval of Candidate by Candidate Position on the Issues[+]

	Democratic Candidate			*Republican Candidate*		
	7	5	Diff.	3	1	Diff.
Gov. Services						
Democrat	.61	.65	−.04	.33	.19	.14★
n	129	128		121	128	
Republican	.10	.27	−.17★	.70	.80	−.10★
n	97	111		106	134	
Abortion						
Democrat	.74	.60	.14★	.25	.16	−.09★
n	142	125		127	112	
Republican	.23	.33	.10★	.60	.62	−.02
n	126	108		109	105	

Notes: ★$p < .05$; [+]Independents were not interviewed in the study.

given candidates were only allowed to take certain positions, distance to the candidate and self-placement can be perfectly correlated. For instance, Democrats most distant to the most liberal Democratic candidate also have the most conservative position. Given this limitation of the design, we opted for something simpler. We compared how approval ratings of the two Democratic candidates by Democrats with the most liberal position (7) differed from ratings by more moderate Democrats (who placed themselves at "5") (i.e., comparing a distance of 0 and 2 points away from the candidate). We replicated the analysis for Republicans, comparing ratings of the two Republican candidates by Republicans with the most conservative position (1) and Republicans who placed themselves at 3 (again 0 and 2 points away from the candidate).

In each of the four cases, more extreme partisans approved of the co-partisan candidate with the same position as theirs considerably more than the more moderate partisans, with average ratings of around .9 versus .7 ($p < .01$). Moreover, the drop in approval in response to increasing policy distance by two points was always considerably sharper among the more extreme partisans (an average decline of .3) than among more moderate partisans (an average decline of .1) (Mean Diff. = .2, $p < .01$). In all, the evidence suggests that extremist partisans' greater sensitivity to ideological distance partly explains why more moderate partisan representatives, closer to the party mean, generally fare no better than considerably more extreme representatives.

Discussion

Elected representatives are far more ideologically extreme than their supporters (Bafumi & Herron, 2010). This state of affairs has been termed a "disconnect" (Fiorina & Abrams, 2012). Our evidence suggests that the term is a misnomer. On average, partisans believe that their party is as close to their own ideological position as it was before the start of the current divergence between the parties. Partisans also feel warmly towards their own parties (Iyengar et al., 2012) and approval of co-partisan leaders bears little relationship with their ideological extremity. Thus, the chances of entry of a more moderate third party look remote. In fact, some of our evidence suggests that if there is an opening for new entrants, it is further to the extremes, as indicated by the recent rise of the Tea Party movement.

Our findings also potentially help explain the conundrum of polarized ratings of ideologically extreme elites by less-than-extreme voters. It appears that low approval ratings of opposing party elites are to a large degree indeed a consequence of the "positions they take" (Jacobson, 2006), but high approval ratings of the same elites among co-partisans are likely a result of motivated reasoning (or elite miscommunication). It is likely that this basic asymmetry also helps explain the over-time pattern in partisan affect—near constant warm feelings toward the in-party and steadily cooler feelings toward the opposing party.

In discovering this asymmetry in partisan perceptual bias, our study also contributes to our understanding of the nature of partisan bias. To date, partisan bias has been assumed to be symmetric, i.e., equal bias in perceptions of policy positions of co-partisan and opposing party leaders. Our study documents that bias is greater in perceptions of the positions of the in-party, and its leaders. This finding converges with some other findings on perceptual bias. For instance, over the course of the campaign, partisans' perceptions of their proximity to the in-party candidate show little change, while the perceived distance between their position and that of the out-party candidate increases sharply (Sood & Iyengar, 2012).

In many other ways, the evidence we present here is consistent with the more standard account of partisanship. For instance, we find that partisans are less responsive to ideological distance from partisan representatives than independents. This finding is consistent with evidence from other scholars who find that independents are more likely to vote for the spatially proximate candidate than partisans (Jessee, 2012; Shor & Rogowski, 2012). Other studies that have manipulated positions of hypothetical candidates have also found evidence of partisan bias in voting decisions (Sniderman & Stiglitz, 2012; Rogowski, 2014).

Sniderman and Stiglitz (2012), however, offer a different explanation for the bias, arguing that voters take both the candidate's and party's position into account when evaluating a candidate. This may well be true though the data underlying the claim merely suggest that those who know the parties' policy reputations choose between candidates as if they were taking account of party positions. We think it more plausible that attenuation of the weight informed partisans put on ideological disagreements with candidates is more due to "unprincipled" reasons.

At any rate, even if informed partisans account for policy reputations, the heuristic may still be normatively unappealing. For it is not clear to us whether partisans should average across party reputations and candidate positions when judging candidates. In a legislative system lacking mechanisms to ensure party discipline, with a tradition of sincere voting (so much so that the most frequently used ideology estimates of representatives are based on how they vote in Congress), and no tradition of coalition politics, it is far from clear why people should vote for anyone other than the spatially proximate candidate. There are reasons to prefer the more distant candidate of one's own party than the more spatially proximate candidate only if one expects some dilution in ideology due to coalition politics. If representatives vote their ideological positions, voters should choose the representative closest to them in the ideological space.

All of this is not to say that the average voter has a utility function that is spatially symmetric. Indeed, our data are not consistent with that hypothesis. Instead, many of our results are consistent with a directional model of voting (Rabinowitz & Macdonald, 1989). In line with Rabinowitz and Macdonald (1989), we find that candidates have a wide berth in choosing their position on issues, and "that candidates can compete successfully by taking extreme stands on issues" (Rabinowitz & Macdonald, 1989, p. 111). Neither is it to say that all voters have the same utility function. Parallel to the finding among legislators by Carroll, Lewis, Lo, Poole, and Rosenthal (2013), data from the experiment strongly suggests that more extreme partisans are more sensitive to ideological differences.

There are psychological theories of persuasion that bear on the partisan asymmetry documented in this paper. In particular, our findings bear a striking resemblance to the classic "assimilation-contrast" model of attitude change developed by Hovland and his colleagues in the 1950s (Hovland, Harvey, & Sherif, 1957; Sherif & Hovland, 1961). When voters have strong attachments to political parties, the model predicts a "boomerang" effect whereby the position attributed to a disliked party perceived as ideologically distant is pushed even further away from the receiver's position (the contrast effect). For instance, a Democrat who encounters a Republican campaign ad on government spending enlarges the discrepancy between herself and the Republican on the issue. On the other hand, when the initial discrepancy between the party and receiver is relatively small, and the party is held in high regard—the case of intra-party communication—the receiver shrinks any difference and assimilates the party's position to her own. (For evidence of assimilation and contrast effects in voter perceptions, see Merrill, Grofman, & Adams, 2001). In the current era of ill will across the party divide, this model provides a parsimonious account of the polarizing effects of campaign communication.

In closing, we note that our findings have pessimistic implications for the prospect of representation based on ideological proximity between candidates and voters. Party elites enjoy considerable leeway to stake out positions at odds with the preferences of their supporters. And, given the extent to which partisans dislike each other (Iyengar et al., 2012; Iyengar & Westwood, 2015), candidates have weak incentives to take positions that appeal to the supporters of the other party.

Finally, partisan asymmetry in candidate evaluation is also likely to have an impact on mass polarization. Democrats witnessing Republican voters' adulation of Sarah Palin in 2008 may have concluded that ordinary Republicans were just as right wing as their standard bearer. Thus, the failure of voters to penalize—and the propensity of activists to reward—ideologically extreme candidates from their own party gives partisans on the other side good reason to (mistakenly) infer that opposing partisans are just as extreme as their leaders.

Notes

1. Replication data and scripts are at: https://github.com/soodoku/in-n-out
2. Gaurav is a scientist. He can be reached at gsood07@gmail.com
3. Shanto is Professor of Political Science at Stanford University. He can be reached at: siyengar@stanford.edu

4. While it is possible that ideological sorting of rank-and-file partisans (see e.g., Levendusky, 2009) explains some of the rise in partisan animus, and continued warmth toward one's own party, as Mason (2014) shows, once you control for partisan identification, difference between sorted and unsorted partisans on "thermometer bias," "anger at outgroup candidate," and "activism" is statistically indistinguishable (see Figure 5, Mason, 2014).
5. Though see also Berelson, Lazarsfeld, and McPhee (pp. 310–311, 1954), who summarize some of their findings thus: political preferences have "their origin in ethnic, sectional, class, and family traditions," and are "characterized more by faith than by conviction and by wishful expectation rather than careful prediction of consequences."
6. Ignorance about parties' positions need not mean that partisan affiliation is unprincipled. See Achen (2002) for a theoretical sketch of one such scenario.
7. See also Bartels (2002) and Sood and Iyengar (2012) who show that partisans learn (or infer or invent) in a motivated manner over the course of election campaigns.
8. While we anticipate increased use of the heuristic during periods of strong affective polarization, we make no claims about its reliability in getting voters to correct positions (see Luskin 2002).
9. See also Bartels (2014); Druckman and Bolsen (2011); Druckman, Peterson, and Slothuus (2013); Harrison (2012); Petersen, Skov, Serritzlew, and Ramsøy (2013).
10. A very small set of polls—fifteen to be precise—offered more expansive response options, going from strongly approve to strongly disapprove. We dichotomized these ratings, coding neutral and over as "approve" and somewhat or strongly disapprove as "disapprove." Removing this polls or dichotomizing using an alternate scheme: counting only "approve" and "strongly approve" as approval makes little difference to our results.
11. Given respondents from Texas were asked to assess only Texas senators, not Massachusetts senators, the state-to-state variance is potentially already covered by the endogeneity of election winning. However, we opt for a conservative specification as the main specification given the size of the data, efficiency is not a concern, but bias is. We try out other specifications in Section A3 of Appendix A, including introducing state-level estimates of ideology of Republicans and Democrats.
12. We coded ideological extremity as follows: We took the absolute value of DW-Nominate scores, folded the scores by party, and rescaled them to lie between 0 (most moderate) and 1 (most extreme).
13. These analyses drop states that have only one representative of a party, and where the ideology of the representative doesn't change across different Congresses. Section A2 in Appendix A presents estimates from a model that pools Republicans and Democrats, using a more complete set of data.
14. The positive coefficient stems from the fact that bigger ideology scores imply more conservative Democrats. And these more conservative senators elicit more support from Republicans.
15. Since we expect intercepts to vary only by "in" and "out" party, and not depend on whether the "in" or "out" party is Democratic or Republican, we also analyzed the data after splitting by "in" and "out" party. These results are presented in Table 11.A2 of Appendix A.
16. Redoing analyses using item response theory based measures of ideology by Clinton, Jackman, and Rivers (2004) also produce results that are substantively the same. These results are available from the authors upon request.
17. For recent data on polarization in evaluation of presidential performance, see www.gallup.com/poll/152222/obama-ratings-historically-polarized.aspx, and Pew: www.pewresearch.org/2009/04/02/partisan-gap-in-obama-job-approval-widest-in-modern-era/

18. We replicated this analysis using a simple average across votes. Results are substantively similar, which suggests roughly equal weighting across issues.

References

Achen, Christopher H. (2002). Parental socialization and rational party identification. *Political Behavior*, 24(2), 151–170.

Achen, Christopher H. & Bartels, Larry M. (2006). *It feels like we are thinking: The rationalizing voter and electoral democracy*. In Annual Meeting of the American Political Science Association, Philadelphia.

Aldrich, John H. (1995). *Why parties? The origin and transformation of party politics in America*. Vol. 15. Cambridge: Cambridge University Press.

Ansolabehere, Stephen & Edward Jones, Philip. (2010). Constituents' responses to congressional roll-call voting. *American Journal of Political Science*, 54(3), 583–597.

Ansolabehere, Stephen & Iyengar, Shanto. (1995). *Going negative*. New York: Simon and Schuster.

Ansolabehere, Stephen & Schaffner, Brian F. (2011). *Re-examining the validity of different survey modes for measuring public opinion in the US: Findings from a 2010 multi-mode comparison*. In AAPOR Annual Conference, Phoenix AZ, pp. 12–15.

Bafumi, Joseph & Herron, Michael C. (2010). Leapfrog representation and extremism: A study of American voters and their members in Congress. *American Political Science Review*, 104(3), 519–542.

Bartels, Larry M. (2002). Beyond the running tally: Partisan bias in political perceptions. *Political Behavior*, 24(2), 117–150.

Bartels, Larry M. (2014). Remembering to forget: A note on the duration of campaign advertising effects. *Political Communication*, 31(4), 532–544.

Bawn, Kathleen, Cohen, Martin, Karol, David, Masket, Seth, Noel, Hans, & Zaller, John. (2012). A theory of political parties: Groups, policy demands and nominations in American politics. *Perspectives on Politics*, 10(3), 571–597.

Berelson, Bernard, Lazarsfeld, Paul Felix, & McPhee, William N. (1954). *Voting: A study of opinion formation in a presidential campaign*. Chicago: University of Chicago Press.

Binder, Sarah A. (2005). Elections, parties, and governance. In Paul Quirk & Sarah Binder (Eds.), *Institutions of American democracy: The legislative branch* (pp. 148–170). New York: OUP.

Bonica, Adam. (2013). Ideology and interests in the political marketplace. *American Journal of Political Science*, 57, 294–311.

Brady, Henry E. & Sniderman, Paul M. (1985). Attitude attribution: A group basis for political reasoning. *The American Political Science Review*, 1061–1078.

Campbell, Angus, Converse, Philip E., Miller, Warren E., & Stokes, Donald E. (1960). *The American voter*. New York: Wiley-Blackwell.

Carroll, Royce, Lewis, Jeffrey B., Lo, James, Poole, Keith T., & Rosenthal, Howard. (2013). The structure of utility in spatial models of voting. *American Journal of Political Science*, 57(4), 1008–1028.

Clinton, Joshua, Jackman, Simon, & Rivers, Douglas. (2004). The statistical analysis of roll call data. *American Political Science Review*, 98(2), 355–370.

Conover, Pamela Johnston & Feldman, Stanley. (1989). Candidate perception in an ambiguous world: Campaigns, cues, and inference processes. *American Journal of Political Science*, 912–940.

Delli Carpini, Michael X. (1996). *What Americans know about politics and why it matters.* New Haven, CT: Yale University Press.

DiMaggio, Paul, Evans, John, & Bryson, Bethany. (1996). Have American's social attitudes become more polarized? *American Journal of Sociology*, 690–755.

Druckman, James N. & Bolsen, Toby. (2011). Framing, motivated reasoning, and opinions about emergent technologies. *Journal of Communication*, 61(4), 659–688.

Druckman, James N., Peterson, Erik, & Slothuus, Rune. (2013). How elite partisan polarization affects public opinion formation. *American Political Science Review*, 107(1), 57–79.

Evans, John H. (2003). Have Americans' attitudes become more polarized? An update*. *Social Science Quarterly*, 84(1), 71–90.

Feldman, Stanley & Conover, Pamela. (1983). Candidates, issues and voters: The role of inference in political perception. *The Journal of Politics*, 45(4), 810–839.

Fiorina, Morris P. & Abrams, Samuel J. (2012). *Disconnect: The breakdown of representation in American politics.* Vol. 11. Norman, OK: University of Oklahoma Press.

Fiorina, Morris P., Abrams, Samuel J., & Pope, Jeremy C. (2005). *Culture war? The myth of a polarized America.* New York: Pearson Longman.

Fiorina, Morris P., Abrams, Samuel A., & Pope, Jeremy C. (2008). Polarization in the American public: Misconceptions and misreadings. *The Journal of Politics*, 70(2), 556–560.

Green, Donald, Palmquist, Bradley, & Schickler, Eric. (2004). *Partisan hearts and minds: Political parties and the social identities of voters.* New Haven, CT: Yale University Press.

Greenstein, Fred. (1965). *Children and politics.* New Haven, CT: Yale University Press.

Harrison, Brian F. (2012). *Bully partisan or partisan bully?* Presented at the Annual Meeting of the American Political Science Association, Washington, DC.

Henderson, John. (2013). *Issue distancing in congressional elections.* Working Paper.

Hetherington, Marc J. (2005). *Why trust matters: Declining political trust and the demise of American liberalism.* Princeton, NJ: Princeton University Press.

Hill, Seth & Tausanovitch, Chris. (2014). *Non-polarization in the American public.* Working Paper.

Hollander, Barry A. (2010). Persistence in the perception of Barack Obama as a Muslim in the 2008 presidential campaign. *Journal of Media and Religion*, 9(2), 55–66.

Hovland, Carl I., Harvey, O. J., & Sherif, Muzafer. (1957). Assimilation and contrast effects in reactions to communication and attitude change. *The Journal of Abnormal and Social Psychology*, 55(2), 244.

Iyengar, Shanto, Sood, Gaurav, & Lelkes, Yphtach. (2012). Affect, not ideology a social identity perspective on polarization. *Public Opinion Quarterly*, 76(3), 405–431.

Iyengar, Shanto & Westwood, Sean. (2015). Fear and loathing across party lines: New evidence on group polarization. *American Journal of Political Science*, 59(3), 690–707.

Jacobson, Gary C. (2006). The polls: Polarized opinion in the states: Partisan differences in approval ratings of governors, senators, and George W. Bush. *Presidential Studies Quarterly*, 36(4), 732–757.

Jennings, M. Kent, Stoker, Laura, & Bowers, Jake. (2009). Politics across generations: Family transmission reexamined. *The Journal of Politics*, 71(3), 782–799.

Jessee, Stephen A. (2012). *Ideology and spatial voting in American elections.* Cambridge: Cambridge University Press.

Jones, David R. (2001). Party polarization and legislative gridlock. *Political Research Quarterly*, 54(1), 125–141.

Kim, Sung-youn, Taber, Charles S., & Lodge, Milton. (2010). A computational model of the citizen as motivated reasoner: Modeling the dynamics of the 2000 presidential election. *Political Behavior*, 32(1), 1–28.

Kunda, Ziva. (1987). Motivated inference: Self-serving generation and evaluation of causal theories. *Journal of Personality and Social Psychology*, 53(4), 636.

Lau, Richard R. & Redlawsk, David P. (2001). Advantages and disadvantages of cognitive heuristics in political decision making. *American Journal of Political Science*, 951–971.

Lawless, Jennifer L. (2004). Women, war, and winning elections: Gender stereotyping in the post-September 11th era. *Political Research Quarterly*, 57(3), 479–490.

Levendusky, Matthew. (2009). *The partisan sort: How liberals became Democrats and conservatives became Republicans*. Chicago, IL: University of Chicago Press.

Lodge, Milton & Taber, Charles S. (2013). *The rationalizing voter*. Cambridge: Cambridge University Press.

Lord, Charles G., Ross, Lee, & Lepper, Mark R. (1979). Biased assimilation and attitude polarization: The effects of prior theories on subsequently considered evidence. *Journal of Personality and Social Psychology*, 37(11), 2098.

Lord, Frederic M., Novick, Melvin R., & Birnbaum, Allan. (1968). *Statistical theories of mental test scores*. Boston, MA: Addison-Wesley.

Luskin, Robert C. (2002). From denial to extenuation (and finally beyond): Political sophistication and citizen performance. *Thinking about Political Psychology*, 281–301.

Mason, Lilliana. (2014). "I disrespectfully agree": The differential effects of partisan sorting on social and issue polarization. *American Journal of Political Science*, 59(1), 128–145.

McCarty, Nolan M., Poole, Keith T., & Rosenthal, Howard. (2006). *Polarized America: The dance of ideology and unequal riches*. Cambridge, MA: MIT Press.

McDermott, Monika L. (1997). Voting cues in low-information elections: Candidate gender as a social information variable in contemporary United States elections. *American Journal of Political Science*, 270–283.

Merrill, Samuel, Grofman, Bernard, & Adams, James. (2001). Assimilation and contrast effects in voter projections of party locations: Evidence from Norway, France, and the USA. *European Journal of Political Research*, 40(2), 199–221.

Petersen, Michael Bang, Skov, Martin, Serritzlew, Søren, & Ramsøy, Thomas. (2013). Motivated reasoning and political parties: Evidence for increased processing in the face of party cues. *Political Behavior*, 1–24.

Popkin, Samuel L. (1991). *The reasoning voter: Communication and persuasion in presidential campaigns*. Chicago, IL: University of Chicago Press.

Rabinowitz, George & Macdonald, Stuart Elaine. (1989). A directional theory of issue voting. *The American Political Science Review*, 93–121.

Rivers, Douglas. (2007). Sampling for web surveys. In Joint Statistical Meetings.

Rivers, Douglas & Bailey, Delia. (2009). Inference from matched samples in the 2008 US national elections. *Proceedings of the Joint Statistical Meetings*, 627–639.

Rogowski, Jon. (2014). *Voter decision-making with polarized choices*. Working Paper.

Sherif, Muzafer & Hovland, Carl I. (1961). *Social judgment: Assimilation and contrast effects in communication and attitude change*. New Haven, CT: Yale University Press.

Shor, Boris & McCarty, Nolan. (2011). The ideological mapping of American legislatures. *American Political Science Review*, 105(3), 530–551.

Shor, Boris & Rogowski, Jon C. (2012). *Congressional voting by spatial reasoning, 2000–2010*. Working Paper.

Sniderman, Paul M. & Stiglitz, Edward H. (2012). *The reputational premium: A theory of party identification and policy reasoning*. Princeton, NJ: Princeton University Press.

Sood, Gaurav & Iyengar, Shanto. (2012). *Coming to dislike your opponents: The polarizing impact of political campaigns*. In the Annual Meeting of the American Political Science Association, Washington, DC.

Stonecash, Jeffrey M., Brewer, Mark D., & Mariani, Mack D. (2003). *Diverging parties: Social change, realignment, and party polarization*. Boulder, CO: Westview Press.

Taber, Charles S. & Lodge, Milton. (2006). Motivated skepticism in the evaluation of political beliefs. *American Journal of Political Science*, 50(3), 755–769.

Tausanovitch, Chris & Warshaw, Christopher. (2013). Measuring constituent policy preferences in Congress, state legislatures and cities. *The Journal of Politics*, 75(2), 330–342.

APPENDIX A

Relationship Between Ideology of Representatives and Approval

A1: Impact of Ideology on Senatorial Approval Using CF-Scores

We re-estimated the relationship between affect and ideology using CF-Scores. Expectedly, substituting CF-Scores for DW-Nominate made little difference to our substantive results. Republicans' ratings of Republican senators hardly respond to senators' ideology ($b = -.00$; see Table 11.A1). Meanwhile Democrats' ratings of the same senators are much more responsive to their ideology ($b = -.39$). The reverse pattern holds for Democratic senators. Their ratings by Democrats move much more modestly to changes in their ideology ($b = .12$) than their ratings by Republicans ($b = .42$).

TABLE 11.A1 Approval of Senators as a Function of Ideology (CF-Scores)

	Republican Senators		Democratic Senators	
	Republicans	Democrats	Republicans	Democrats
Intercept	.75★★★	.73★★★	.25★★★	.66★★★
DW-Nominate	−.00	−.39★★★	.42★★★	.12
n	920	920	953	953
r^2	.60	.67	.71	.46

Notes: ★★★$p < .001$. Estimated separately for Republican and Democratic senators, further split by party of the respondent, with fixed effects for states. Fixed effects for states are not reported.

TABLE 11.A2 Approval of Senators as a Function of Ideological Extremity (DW-Nominate)

	Own Party Senators	Opposing Party Senators
Intercept	.76	.59
Extremity (DW-Nominate)	−.02	−.27★★★
n	1,457	1,457
Pseudo r^2	.44	.58

Notes: ★★★$p < .001$. Estimated separately where respondent and senator party match, and where they don't, with fixed effects for states. Fixed effects for states are not reported.

A2: Relationship Between Ideology and Affect by Whether or Not Representative and Respondent Ideology Match

To estimate the impact of ideology on approval of senators that belong to the respondent's party, and senators that belong to the main opposing party, we split ideology data by party and rescaled it to lie between 0 (most moderate senator in our data for the party) to 1 (most extreme senator in our data for the party). The asymmetry is clear. Respondents' approval of senators of their own party is mostly linearly unassociated with extremity ($b = -.02$, see Table 11.A2 but also Table 11.A3). The reaction to extremity of senators of the opposing party is considerably sharper ($b = -.27, p < .001$). Aside from differences in slopes is a sharp difference in intercepts, best interpreted as credit given to senators for simply belonging to respondents' party.

A3: Alternate Specifications

We model the support an elected representative enjoys among different partisan groups within a state as a function of representatives' ideology, her position, and whether or not representatives' party matches that of the partisan group. Since our data come from state-level polls, we must account for inter-state differences in kinds of partisans that can affect relationship between ideology and approval. For instance, if there is positive correlation between "state ideology" and the (state-level) representative's ideology, as is likely, estimate of the relationship between ideological extremity and approval is liable to be biased towards zero. In light of these concerns, the most conservative model—our main model in the paper—allows for only within-state comparisons.

However, one can also model cross-state differences. This modeling strategy should produce unbiased estimates of differences in how partisan groups react as

TABLE 11.A3 Approval of Senators as a Function of Ideology (DW-Nominate) With Random Effects of States

	Republican Senators		Democratic Senators	
	Republicans	Democrats	Republicans	Democrats
Intercept	.31*	.91***	.64***	.73***
DW-Nominate	−.03	−.53***	1.03***	.09
Rep. Ideology	.38*		−.34*	
Dem. Ideology		.17		.03
n	916	916	953	953
r^2	.77	.80	.83	.76

Notes: ***$p < .001$, *$p < .05$.

long as ideology of partisan groups moves in tandem across states. To that end, one can estimate a model that controls for state-level ideology. A still more conservative model—in that it requires even fewer assumptions controls for ideology of Democrats and Republicans separately. We estimate this model using measures of state party ideology from Tausanovitch and Warshaw (2013). Results from this model are presented below. Aside from this model, we also estimated other models in which we control for year fixed effects, gender of the elected representative, and years in position. Our results are robust to these modifications as well. Results from these latter specifications are available from authors upon request.

APPENDIX B

Details About YouGov Sampling Methodology

The YouGov sampling methodology is as follows. YouGov first draws a random sample from a large high quality RDD sample (designated as the target sample), and then recruit a sample from their online panel that matches the target sample on designated attributes. The end result is a roughly "representative" sample (Rivers, 2007; Rivers & Bailey, 2009; Ansolabehere & Schaffner, 2011).

For our survey experiment, YouGov used the 2007 American Community Study (ACS) as the sampling frame to which it added data on party identification, ideology, and political interest from the 2008 Pew Religious Life Survey using matching. The target sample was selected by stratifying on age, race, gender, education using simple random sampling within strata. Next, YouGov used nearest neighbor matching to find respondents from the online panel that most closely resembled the characteristics of the target sample on gender, age, race, education, party identification, ideology, and political interest. This yielded the final matched sample to which the questionnaire was administered. Imperfections in matching were addressed by post-stratification weights.

APPENDIX C

Relationship Between Approval and Ideological Distance

We here present results from models that utilize all the data. Model 1 in Table 11.C1 is a complete data version of the subgroup models presented in Table 11.2 of the main text. As one can see, the coefficients in Model 1 (Table 11.C1) are almost the same as those in Table 11.2. Furthermore, adding a broad set of exogenous covariates has little effect on the coefficients of interest (see Model 2 in Table 11.C1). In particular, we added age, education in five categories (base category: college graduates), gender (female = 1), race coded in five categories (base category: Asian), and marital status coded in four categories (base category: married). For each variable, we coded missing responses as a separate category.

TABLE 11.C1 Relationship Between Approval and Ideology

	Model 1	Model 2
Intercept	.67***	.67***
	(.01)	(.02)
In-Party	.23***	.23***
	(.01)	(.01)
Out-Party	−.09***	−.10***
	(.01)	(.01)
Abs. Diff.	−.54***	−.54***
	(.01)	(.01)
Abs. Diff.*In-Party	.14***	.13***
	(.01)	(.01)
Abs. Diff.*Out-Party	.06***	.06***
	(.01)	(.01)
Age		.00***
		(.00)

	Model 1	Model 2
Educ.: HS or Less		−.01*
		(.00)
Educ.: Missing		.02
		(.03)
Educ.: Post-Grad		.01
		(.00)
Educ.: Some College		−.00
		(.00)
Female		.03***
		(.00)
Race: Black		−.00
		(.01)
Race: Hispanic		−.02
		(.01)
Race: Other		−.07***
		(.02)
Race: White		−.04**
		(.01)
Marital: Missing		.02**
		(.01)
Marital: Other		.01*
		(.00)
Marital: Single		.01***
		(.00)
AIC	17601.04	17365.23
BIC	17673.43	17555.25
Log Likelihood	−8792.52	−8661.61
Num. obs.	62849	62849
Num. groups: a1	2	2
Var: a1 (Intercept)	0.00	0.00
Var: Residual	0.08	0.08

Notes: ***$p < 0.001$, **$p < 0.01$, *$p < 0.05$.

APPENDIX D

Perceptual Bias in Placement of Senators

D1: Relationship Between Approval and Perceived Distance

Regressing approval on perceived distance yielded coefficients that were uniformly healthier than coefficients obtained when we regressed approval on actual ideological distance. Expectedly, the difference between coefficients for actual distance and perceived distance were substantially greater for in-party representatives (a 28-point difference), than out-party (3 points) or independents (9 points). Note too that now the in-party representative furthest away from the respondent nets on average a paltry 18 points, versus a hefty 46 points (see Table 11.3 in the main manuscript).

D2: Structure of Random Error in Perceptions of Senators' Ideology

Greater random error in perceptions of in-party candidates vis-à-vis out-party candidates may explain why association between actual ideological distance and

TABLE 11.D1 Approval of Candidate as a Function of Perceived Ideological Distance

	In-Party	Out-Party	Independents
Intercept	.83★★★	.52★★★	.63★★★
Error	−.62★★★	−.51★★★	−.63★★★
n	15,118	13,054	3,255
r^2	.12	.21	.18

Note: Estimated Separately Among Independents, Partisans Evaluating Opposing Party Senators, and Partisans Evaluating Co-Partisan Senators.

approval is weaker when partisans assess in-party candidates versus out-party candidates. However, we find little evidence of greater absolute error in perceptions of co-partisan senators vis-à-vis perceptions of opposing senators (Mean Absolute Error$_{\text{In-party}}$ = .192, Mean Absolute Error$_{\text{Out-party}}$ = .186).

While the mean absolute error may be the same across perceptions of in- and out-party representatives, it may be the case that error is more heavily correlated with ideology of co-partisan representatives than among opposing party representatives. If so is the case, it will also help explain our initial set of results which suggest that ideological accountability is especially weak for the most extreme of the representatives. We find that absolute error in respondents' beliefs about co-partisan senators' positions was more than twice as strongly correlated with senators' ideological extremity ($r = .14$), than respondents' beliefs about out-party senators ($r = .06$; $p_{\text{Diff.}} < .05$). The positive correlation between extremity and ideology in perception of in-party candidates naturally shows up in perceptions of candidates more extreme than the respondent. We find 25% greater error in perceptions of in-party candidates who are more extreme than the respondent (Mean Absolute Error = .21) than perceptions of in-party candidates more moderate than the respondent (Mean Absolute Error = .15, $p < .05$).

APPENDIX E

Details About Experimental Manipulations

Government Spending

Some people think the government should provide fewer services even in areas such as health and education in order to reduce spending. Suppose these people are at one end of a scale, at point 1. Other people feel it is important for the government to provide many more services even if it means an increase in spending. Suppose these people are at the other end, at point 7. And, of course, some other people have opinions somewhere in between, at points 2, 3, 4, 5, or 6.

Where would you place yourself on this scale or haven't you thought much about this?

Abortion

Next we would like to know about your position on the issue of abortion. Some people believe that by law, abortion should never be permitted. Suppose these people are at one end of a scale, at point 1. Others feel that by law, a woman should always be able to obtain an abortion as a matter of personal choice.

Suppose these people are at the other end, at point 7. And, of course, some other people have opinions somewhere in between, at points 2, 3, 4, 5, or 6.

Where would you place yourself on this scale or haven't you thought much about this?

On this scale below, we have represented the position of an unnamed Republican political leader on government services and spending.

↓

Government should provide many fewer services; Reduce spending a lot | 1 – 2 – 3 – 4 – 5 – 6 – 7 | Government should provide many more services; Increase spending a lot

If you had to decide on this basis, how strongly would you of approve or disapprove of this Republican political leader?

○ Strongly Approve
○ Approve
○ Neither Approve nor Disapprove
○ Disapprove
○ Strongly Disapprove

FIGURE 11.E4   Screenshot of the Survey Experiment

12

(WORKING TOWARD) AFFECTIVE TRANSFER IN THE REAL WORLD

Tessa M. Ditonto and Richard R. Lau

In *The Rationalizing Voter* (2013), Lodge and Taber demonstrate the influence of unconscious thinking on political behavior. Their *John Q. Public* (*JQP*) model of voter decision-making challenges conventional models that place conscious information processing and deliberation at the center of how voters make decisions in the political realm. Rather than "rational" decision-making, *JQP* posits that political behavior is actually the result of numerous unconscious, automatic cognitive and affective processes. In this model, conscious consideration is little more than post hoc rationalization of these processes, and it is these largely unnoticed forces that drive voters and their decisions.

Central to *JQP* is the concept of *affect transfer*, or the notion that affective primes can transfer positive or negative feelings to a target of thought, whether those primes are related to the target or not. In other words, evaluations of a particular person, policy, or other political target can be influenced by a completely irrelevant, affectively charged word or image. Moreover, the primes need not be consciously perceived, but can be delivered subliminally via a very brief exposure preceding the target itself.

The implications of these findings are dramatic and suggest that voters may ultimately be making decisions based on arbitrary factors and/or intentional attempts at manipulation by campaigns and interest groups (such as the infamous "RATS" attack ad against Gore produced by the RNC in 2000). However, Lodge and Taber's evidence for affect transfer comes from experiments conducted in a highly controlled laboratory setting and in which very particular protocols were followed.

This chapter seeks to shed some light on the extent to which affect transfer may occur in the political world under less rigid conditions. In particular, we are interested in whether evaluations of fictitious political candidates are influenced by the presentation of subliminal affective primes under several different conditions: 1) when they are presented outside of the lab (and conducted on the personal computers of MTurk workers); 2) when they are presented without the rigid protocol followed by Lodge and Taber; and 3) when subjects are exposed to fewer primes over the course of the experiment than in Lodge and Taber's studies. We think it is important to determine whether affect transfer holds under these conditions since they more closely resemble the ways in which actual campaigns may seek to use subliminal priming to influence voters, and in which other kinds of primes may be encountered in an actual election. Because of this, we argue that the results of our studies move us closer to understanding the effects of affect transfer in the "real world."

To preview our results, we find that under these less rigid conditions, affect transfer does seem to occur more often than we would expect from chance. We conducted four separate tests of the affect transfer hypothesis and varied the number of primes per candidate that subjects were exposed to, the number of candidates evaluated at one time, and the type of prime (text or image) shown to subjects. Across all variations, we find that affect transfer does seem to occur for some candidates in some studies but not others. Specifically, we find that effects seem to be stronger when subjects are exposed to more than one prime per candidate, when images are used as primes rather than words, and when candidates are evaluated individually and immediately following exposure to the primes.

Unconscious Processing and the Importance of Affect

Our understanding of human cognition has changed drastically over the past several decades. Dual-process models of information processing that view automatic, affect-driven reasoning as central to how we make decisions have challenged political scientists' reliance on rationality and deliberation to explain political behavior. In these models, fast and reflexive *System 1* processing comprises the bulk of our information processing (Kahneman, 2011), while slow and effortful *System 2* processing is employed only in certain circumstances, and only after earlier automatic processing takes place. As well as being fast and automatic, *System 1* processing is also often implicit. That is, it takes place outside of conscious awareness. This means that much of our cognition (as much as 98%) happens "below the surface," mostly without our knowledge (see Lodge and Taber, 2013 for a comprehensive overview of this literature).

The consequences of the ubiquity of unconscious processing are manifold, and both psychologists and political scientists have found that implicit cues and attitudes affect many different aspects of life, including personal and political. For example, implicit racial attitudes influence various social and political behaviors (Dovidio, Kawakami, & Gaertner, 2002; Greenwald & Nosek, 2009; Greenwald, Poehlman, Uhlmann, & Banaji, 2009; Lambert, Payne, Ramsey, & Shaffer, 2005; Nosek & Smyth, 2007; Payne, Krosnick, Pacek, Lelkes, Akhtar, & Tompson, 2010;

Ziegert & Hanges, 2005), facial expressions and voice frequencies of news broadcasters can influence viewers' judgments of particular people or issues (Babad, 1999, 2005; Friedman, DiMatteo, & Mertz, 1980; Gregory & Gallagher, 2002; Mullen et al., 1986), non-political events such as shark attacks (Achen & Bartels, 2006) and the performance of local sports teams (Healy, Malhotra, & Mo, 2010) can influence election outcomes, and a person's physical appearance—whether attractiveness (e.g., Eagly, Ashmore, Makhijini, & Longo, 1991; Feingold, 1992; Langlois et al., 2000), facial dominance (Little, Burriss, Jones, & Roberts, 2007; Mueller & Mazur, 1996), or competence (see Todorov, Oliviola, Dotsch, & Mende-Siedlecki, 2015)—affect all sorts of social and political judgments made about him or her.

While much of the research on implicit cues considers incidental primes that occur without intention, advertisers in both the political and commercial realms have also been utilizing "subliminal advertising," or the strategic placement of unconscious primes, to manipulate viewers' behaviors and attitudes for decades. Evidence that the use of such cues works has been mixed—particularly since the most prominent of these studies, reported by the marketer James Vicary in 1957, turned out to be a hoax.[1] But a fair amount of more recent evidence suggests that subliminal messages do in fact have an effect on viewers (e.g., Karremans, Stroebe, & Claus, 2006). Perhaps the most famous example of this effect in the world of political advertising comes from an RNC TV ad against Al Gore in the 2000 election that flashed the word "RATS" (as part of the larger word "bureaucrats") at the end of the ad. Whether or not this was intended to be a negative subliminal prime for viewers, Weinberger and Westen (2008) found that associating a similar "RATS" prime with other candidates did lead to more negative evaluations of those candidates.

Further, much of what is processed via *System 1* is affective in nature. That is, *System 1* often deals in positive or negative feelings about a target. In fact, much evidence suggests that, contrary to classical ideas about rational thought, affect actually precedes cognition, and in fact cognition may be impossible without affect. Indeed, *hot cognition* suggests that every concept, event, or object stored in long-term memory is associated with an affective "tag" or a positive/negative/ambivalent feeling about that thing (Abelson, 1963; Bargh, 1997; Fazio, Sanbonmatsu, Powell, & Kardes, 1986; Lodge & Taber, 2005; Sears, 2001). When concepts are activated and moved from long-term memory to working memory, it is actually these affective tags that come first, before any cognitive component of the memory. This tendency for feelings to precede cognition is known as *affective primacy* (Zajonc, 1980, 2000). One of the important implications of affective primacy is that this initial affect can influence thoughts and feelings that occur later in the decision stream without a person's conscious awareness.

One consequence of the influence of affect encountered early in a decision stream is what Lodge and Taber refer to as *affective contagion*, or the ability of early affect to influence the types of considerations an individual will entertain when forming judgments about a person, object or issue, such that negative affect facilitates negatively charged considerations and positive affect leads to more positive considerations (Erisen, Lodge, & Taber, 2014; Lodge & Taber, 2013; Taber and Lodge, 2014). This affect can be intrinsic, i.e., stemming from the individual's previous associations with the target being considered, or it can be incidental, such as that produced by the implicit primes mentioned above. Indeed, previous studies have found that unrelated implicit primes influence the conscious deliberation about political issues, groups, and leaders (Lodge & Taber, 2013; Taber and Lodge, 2014).

Additionally, the *affect transfer* hypothesis states that previous affective states, whether they are relevant to a particular decision task or not, and whether they are experienced implicitly or explicitly, can transfer positive or negative feelings directly to a current target of thought, essentially "skipping" the process of conscious deliberation altogether. According to Lodge and Taber, this is a form of classical conditioning operating below conscious awareness in which one's current affective state becomes associated with the target in question. A good example of this is the "sunny day effect" in which everything seems better, happier, etc. on a beautiful day (Lodge & Taber, 2013).

In *The Rationalizing Voter*, Lodge and Taber test the ability of implicit affective primes to influence evaluations of political candidates via affect transfer and find that, even controlling for similarity on issue positions, these primes impact judgments made about fictitious candidates. In these studies, candidates paired with positive primes were evaluated more favorably than those paired with negative primes. Further, these effects were stronger among political sophisticates and among subjects who were asked to stop and think about the candidates before making a final judgment. While these last two findings stand in contrast to expectations based on traditional models of voter decision-making, they are in line with hypotheses stemming from *JQP* since, according to Lodge and Taber's theory, sophisticates and those with an opportunity to deliberate will have a greater number of opportunities for primed affect to enter the decision stream via affectively charged associations. Sophisticates simply have a larger number of associations in LTM from which to pull—all of which should be affectively charged, and subjects asked to deliberate will bring more associated concepts to mind than those who are not given the opportunity to do so.

Method and Hypotheses

Lodge and Taber's findings related to affect transfer are the result of a series of carefully designed and controlled laboratory experiments in which subjects were asked to learn about a fictitious political candidate in part by reading a series of 20 substantively uncontroversial statements about the candidate, each of which was immediately preceded by an affectively charged, preconscious prime (or a no-prime control condition). The primes used were text based (words) with either a clear positive or negative connotation (for example, "love," "joy," "happy," "death," "sad," and "torture"). Each prime was presented for 39 ms (well below the threshold for conscious awareness) and was preceded by a 13 ms forward mask of random letters, and followed by another 13 ms backward mask of random letters. After reading all 20 sentences, subjects provided a summary evaluation of the candidate.

This chapter seeks to determine whether the affect transfer from implicit primes to a political target occurs under less rigid experimental conditions. This is an important step in beginning to understand whether the types of implicit cues that might be encountered in the "real world" could have the same effect as those presented in the lab. In particular, we test the affect transfer hypothesis in a series of experiments that differ from Lodge and Taber's procedure in three important ways. First, we use samples recruited from Amazon's Mechanical Turk, which are both more diverse than the student samples used by Lodge and Taber, and are recruited online and asked to take the studies at home on their own computers, rather than in a laboratory setting. We believe that this latter difference is particularly important, as subjects in a lab are able (and probably more willing) to participate in a study with relatively little distraction. Our subjects, on the other hand, could have had other websites, email, music, or any number of other distractions up on their computer at the same time that they were completing our studies—not to mention children, pets, phone calls, co-workers, and other distractions in their immediate environment. Second, the implicit primes in our studies are embedded in a video about a candidate or series of candidates (depending on the study). They are still preconscious (lasting for one frame, or 33 ms), but are embedded immediately prior to (and in some studies, immediately after) the target image. Another important difference is that approximately half of our studies used image-based primes, rather than words. Specific details about these primes will be discussed below. Finally, subjects in our studies viewed far fewer primes than those in Lodge and Taber's experiments. Whereas their subjects saw 20 implicit primes, ours saw between one and three per candidate, depending on the study.

Though clearly still experimental in nature, we contend that our designs likely provide a closer approximation of the ways in which voters might actually encounter implicit affective primes in an election, whether through subliminal messaging in political advertisements or other incidental types of primes. Voters in the real world are likely to experience affective primes in setting rife with distraction, such as on their own computers or televisions at home or work, than they are in quiet, sterile environment like a lab. Deliberate use of subliminal primes, to the extent that they are used, is also likely to occur in a political advertisement, so our use of video provides a test of their effectiveness in such instances. Last, subjects are probably far more likely to encounter a single prime or a small number of affectively congruent primes in an actual election than they are to encounter 20 similarly valenced primes related to a particular target, so we seek to test the extent of affect transfer with a much smaller number of primes.

Despite the differences between our studies and those conducted by Lodge and Taber, we assume that *JQP* is an accurate model of political cognition and expect to find similar effects of affect transfer. In particular, we hypothesize that candidates paired with a positive prime (or a series of positive primes) will be evaluated more favorably than candidates presented without primes, and that candidates paired with negative primes will be evaluated less favorably than neutral candidates (without primes) and even more negatively than those associated with positive primes. Further, because sophisticates have a broader and deeper knowledge store with regard to politics, we expect that sophisticated subjects will be more strongly affected by the primes than their less sophisticated counterparts.[2]

Study 1

Citizen exposure to politicians in the real world almost always occurs via brief 10-second clips of the politician saying something in a speech or answering a question during a press conference, as shown on the nightly television news and/or repeated on some political blog such as the Huffington Post or RedState. Our first study was designed to answer a basic feasibility question: If we insert subliminal primes into such short video clips, is it possible to observe any measurable effects of the primes on evaluations of the person in the video clip?

Method

Subjects were recruited (via Amazon's Mechanical Turk) for a brief online study of first impression formation. After logging onto the experiment's web page and viewing an online informed consent page, subjects read:

> We are developing an experiment about how people make vote decisions. We are ultimately going to present subjects with a lot of different types of information about these candidates, but today we need you to help us determine the first impressions people are likely to form about these candidates based just on their name, their current office, and their picture.
>
> The experiment is going to be about a presidential election, and as in the case of our real presidential election, our campaign is going to begin with primary elections in each major party. We have developed very brief videos to introduce our voters to the candidates. We are considering a number of different hypothetical figures to run in our experimental campaigns, but the computer is going to randomly select one video about three Democratic candidates for you to see, and one video about three Republican candidates. After each video, you will be asked to provide your first impression of the three candidates that were introduced to you in that video.

Subjects were then randomly assigned to see either a video describing the three Democratic candidates followed by a video describing the three Republican candidates, or vice versa. Each video started with the iconic red, white, and blue Democratic donkey (Republican elephant) on the screen, while an announcer is saying "The Democratic (Republican) candidates for president include," and then the picture of each of the three candidates appears on the screen for 3–4 seconds while the announcer says the candidate's name, state, and current position. The candidates for each party included a white male, a white female, and a nonwhite male. The Democrats were "Congressman Jim Davis from New York," "Senator Ed Ramirez of California," and "Governor Susan Turner from Illinois." The Republicans included "Governor Lou Baker of Georgia" (an African American), "former Governor Michael Harris from Florida," and "Senator Debra Johnson from South Dakota." Each video lasted about 12 seconds.

Seven different videos were created for each party. A random draw determined the order of the candidates for each party: Ramirez—Turner—Davis for the Democrats; Harris—Baker—Johnson for the Republicans. One of the videos presented the pictures of the candidates without any subliminal primes. The remaining six videos presented the three party candidates with every possible combination of one candidate with a positive implicit prime and one candidate with a negative implicit prime. The primes were inserted for a single frame (33 ms) immediately before the candidate's picture appeared. As primes, we used universally recognized positive and negative images provided by International Affective Picture System (IAPS)—a smiling baby, kittens, a snarling dog, a snake about to strike (see Bradley & Lang, 2007; Lang, Bradley, & Cuthbert, 2008).

Immediately after watching the video introducing each party's candidates, subjects were asked to evaluate the three candidates in the same order in which they appeared in the video. Subjects rated how competent each candidate appeared to be, and how favorably they evaluated them on a 100-point feeling thermometer.

Subjects

Three hundred seventy-five subjects were recruited from Amazon's Mechanical Turk for a 5-minute study of first impressions. All five of our studies employed "workers" from this same source. They were paid 75 cents for their time. Subject characteristics from all five studies are listed in Table 12.A1 in the Appendix, but our subjects were very much like prior published samples using Mechanical Turk subjects: about 60% male, 80% white, 35 years old, on average, with about 15 years of education. Approximately 45% were Democrats, 16% were Republican, with the remainder independents (for comparisons, see Berinsky, Huber, & Lenz, 2012; Buhrmester, Kwang, & Gosling, 2011; Mason & Suri, 2012; Paolacci, Chandler, & Ipeirotis, 2010; Shapiro, Chandler, & Mueller, 2013).

Results

As the competence and feeling thermometer evaluations of each candidate were highly correlated, we formed summary evaluations of each candidate by averaging together the two ratings. To control for inter-subject incommensurability (that is, systematic differences across subjects in how positively they tend to rate anyone), we subtracted the average rating of the three Democrats from the rating of each individual Democrat candidate, and subtracted the average rating of the three Republicans from the rating of each individual Republican candidate.[3]

As a first cut, Table 12.1 shows the mean ratings of each candidate in the positive and negative treatment conditions, restricted to in-party partisans (that is, strong and weak party identifiers, and leaning independents). The straightforward hot cognition hypothesis is that each candidate should be evaluated more positively when his or her picture was preceded by a positive prime, compared to when it was paired with a negative prime. As can be seen in the first column of Table 12.1, there is support for the hot cognition hypothesis in three of six preliminary tests. This is a promising start.

We then conducted more sophisticated multivariate analysis where the summary evaluation of each candidate was regressed on separate indicators of the strength of Democratic and Republican party identification, dummy variables

TABLE 12.1 Ratings of In-Party Candidates, by Partisans

	Study 1	*Study 2*	*Study 3$_I$*	*Study 3$_W$*	*Study 4*
Democrats:					
Davis,					
Positive Prime	6.81*	.13	−2.21	1.41	−1.50
Negative Prime	1.50	.04	−1.04	.76	−1.74
Ramirez,					
Positive Prime	−7.52	−.17	−2.30	−1.99*	−5.58**
Negative Prime	−4.91	−.07	−2.76	−4.31	1.43
Turner,					
Positive Prime	0.67	.15	2.06	3.37	1.76*
Negative Prime	3.26	.06	4.26	2.78	6.24
Republicans:					
Baker,					
Positive Prime	1.15***	−.07	−.45	−5.51	−2.00
Negative Prime	−13.61	−.03	2.79	−5.53	−2.43
Harris,					
Positive Prime	9.32	.05	5.04*	6.63	3.59
Negative Prime	8.50	.09	1.10	6.05	.69
Johnson,					
Positive Prime	2.34*	−.05	.69	−.28	3.70
Negative Prime	−7.57	.02	4.91	1.31	6.19

Notes: *$p < .05$ **$p < .01$ ***$p < .001$.

representing the positive and negative prime conditions, and multiplicative interactions between strength of in-party identification and the positive prime condition, and strength of out-party identification and the negative prime condition (along with a set of demographic controls). These multivariate analyses were conducted on the full sample, so that the comparison group in every instance is the evaluation of the candidate in the no-prime control condition, by pure (independent-) independents. Lodge and Taber predict the first interaction should be positive and significant, while the second interaction should be negative and significant. As seen in the first column of Table 12.2, this hypothesis is confirmed in only two of 12 instances, just for the Republican candidate Debra Johnson. This is a much less promising result.

Each of these first two analyses involves between-groups comparisons. To provide the most powerful test of the Lodge–Taber hot cognition hypothesis, we also conducted repeated measures ANOVAs restricted to in-party partisans, where the between-subjects factors were the specific candidate receiving the positive prime and a dichotomized measure of political sophistication, and the repeated measure is the evaluation of the candidates paired with the positive and negative implicit primes. We have no hypotheses about why the implicit primes should have stronger effects on some candidates rather than others (although clearly they did), but hot cognition predicts a main effect of the repeated measure, either by itself or interacting with political sophistication, with stronger effects expected for more politically sophisticated subjects.

Among Democrats, neither the hypothesized main effect of the repeated measure, nor its interaction with political sophistication, was significant. Instead, we observed a very powerful three-way interaction ($p < .001$) between candidate, political sophistication, and the repeated measure. Essentially we observed the differences we expected for Davis (although primarily among novices rather than experts), not at all for Ramirez, and for Turner but only among experts.

The results were stronger among Republican partisans. Here we do see the predicted main effect of the repeated measure ($p < .01$), with the Republican candidate receiving the positive prime being evaluated about 11 points higher than the Republican candidate paired with the negative prime. One again, however, there is an unexpected three-way interaction between candidate, political sophistication, and the repeated measure. Both Baker and Harris are evaluated more positively by experts than novices in the positive prime condition than in the negative prime condition (as predicted), but it is just the opposite for evaluations of Debra Johnson.

Discussion

In sum, Study 1 provides mixed support for the Lodge–Taber affect transfer hypothesis. At best, we observed the hypothesized differences only half of the time. On the one hand, this is much greater support than would be expected by

TABLE 12.2 Multivariate Analysis of Candidate Evaluation, Interactions With Party Identification

	Study 1 B S.E.	Study 2 B S.E.	Study 3₁ B S.E.	Study 3_w B S.E.	Study 4 B S.E.
Jim Davis					
Dem. PID	1.71 (2.55)	.28 (.21)	1.65 (2.40)	−.19 (2.48)	10.64★★ (4.03)
Rep. PID	12.59★★★ (3.87)		10.24★★★ (3.00)	−2.13 (2.91)	8.91 (4.91)
Pos. Prime	.95 (2.40)	−.05 (.18)	−2.94 (1.62)	.53 (1.48)	3.59 (2.51)
Neg. Prime	−1.50 (1.96)	.13 (.07)	.59 (1.32)	1.40 (1.23)	1.16 (1.74)
Pos. x Dem. PID	3.93 (4.81)	.32 (.23)	2.26 (2.63)	1.06 (2.27)	−5.09 (3.97)
Neg. x Rep. PID	−2.39 (5.99)		−8.37★ (3.78)	2.07 (3.20)	9.04 (5.15)
					7.11 (4.80)
Ed Ramirez					
Dem. PID	−1.37 (2.56)	−.25 (.19)	−1.48 (2.64)	−1.50 (2.40)	5.66 (5.49)
Rep. PID	−9.99★★ (3.67)		−.89 (2.93)	4.78 (2.83)	.47 (2.62)
Pos. Prime	−3.86 (2.35)	−.08 (.17)	−3.09 (1.65)	−4.03★★ (1.46)	5.31★ (2.14)
Neg. Prime	−4.63★ (1.99)	.13★ (.06)	−2.54 (1.32)	−1.04 (1.12)	−4.25 (4.24)
Pos. x Dem. PID	−1.69 (4.31)	.15 (.22)	2.08 (2.52)	6.31★★ (2.16)	−9.57 (5.40)
Neg. x Rep. PID	12.22 (6.38)		1.44 (4.08)	−4.03 (3.10)	
Susan Turner					
Dem. PID	.13 (2.33)	−.30 (.18)	−1.24 (2.58)	.10 (2.49)	−16.85★★★ (4.10)
Rep. PID	−7.35★ (3.22)		−5.60 (3.38)	−5.08 (2.89)	−12.77★★ (4.81)
Pos. Prime	−1.87 (2.06)	−.19 (.17)	.07 (1.70)	1.75 (1.44)	−4.08 (2.31)
Neg. Prime	−2.28 (1.83)	−.03 (.06)	.06 (1.23)	−.81 (1.21)	3.01 (1.81)
Pos. x Dem. PID	−1.87 (3.75)	.31 (.22)	−1.32 (2.68)	−2.49 (2.20)	6.19 (3.76)
Neg. x Rep. PID	11.55 (6.46)		−2.42 (3.45)	8.03★★ (3.08)	−7.00 (5.01)
Lou Baker					
Rep. PID	−.27 (2.91)	−.16 (.16)	−7.98★★ (3.21)	−1.99 (2.80)	−9.06 (5.25)
Dem. PID	3.61 (2.05)		11.61★★★ (2.90)	7.25★★ (2.56)	.53 (4.51)

Pos. Prime	−.58 (1.62)	−.25** (.09)	−4.79*** (1.49)	−1.32 (1.38)	1.17 (1.95)
Neg. Prime	−7.13*** (1.86)	−.12 (.07)	8.30*** (1.85)	−2.61 (1.47)	−3.86 (2.57)
Pos. x Rep. PID	1.55 (5.90)	.22 (.16)	17.68*** (3.65)	3.94 (3.12)	−3.04 (5.32)
Neg. x Dem. PID	.52 (3.57)		−21.90*** (3.00)	4.69* (2.29)	1.79 (4.16)
Michael Harris					
Rep. PID	15.06*** (3.31)	.44** (.18)	−2.37 (3.46)	9.17** (3.01)	7.76 (5.34)
Dem. PID	−8.22*** (2.30)		−2.51 (2.78)	−9.75*** (2.66)	.41 (4.38)
Pos. Prime	2.24 (1.81)	−.03 (.10)	−2.71* (1.37)	−1.87 (1.27)	.09 (2.00)
Neg. Prime	−1.48 (2.16)	−.09 (.08)	4.92** (1.82)	−3.16 (1.66)	4.29* (2.74)
Pos. x Rep. PID	−7.67 (5.59)	.02 (.18)	15.30*** (3.34)	1.37 (3.33)	12.76* (5.91)
Neg. x Dem. PID	3.37 (3.95)		−13.00*** (2.76)	5.94* (2.52)	−7.56 (4.35)
Debra Johnson					
Rep. PID	−17.69*** (3.66)	−.40** (.16)	−2.53 (2.88)	−9.28*** (2.55)	−2.15 (3.84)
Dem. PID	6.07* (2.59)		5.68* (2.59)	−1.20 (2.20)	−1.40 (3.38)
Pos. Prime	−2.85 (2.07)	−.07 (.09)	−2.68* (1.29)	1.11 (1.04)	−.51 (1.51)
Neg. Prime	1.80 (2.43)	.03 (.07)	2.10 (1.56)	.45 (1.29)	−.86 (1.97)
Pos. x Rep. PID	20.03** (6.75)	.05 (.17)	4.09 (3.83)	−.19 (2.77)	−5.14 (4.40)
Neg. x Dem. PID	−8.71* (4.37)		−9.25*** (2.74)	.07 (2.05)	1.32 (2.98)

Notes: *p < .05 **p < .01 ***p < .001.
All analyses included controls for gender, age, race, and political sophistication.

chance. But on the other hand, this is much weaker support than Lodge and Taber report from their studies. As a basic feasibility test of this new format for delivering implicit primes, however, we were sufficiently encouraged to continue this line of investigation.

We thought of several immediate possibilities as to why our results were weaker than Lodge and Taber's. The first was that there was a poor match between our treatment and the measurement of candidate evaluation. Our treatment was a video describing three hypothetical candidates competing for a party's presidential nomination, one of whom is paired with a positive implicit prime, and one of whom is paired with a negative implicit prime. But then we asked subjects to evaluate each of those candidates on two absolute scales, rather than rating them relative to each other. A primary election campaign is essentially a comparative battle about which of several competing candidates is liked best by party members. Perhaps we would see stronger results if subjects were making comparative rather than absolute judgments about the different candidates.

A second possibility is that our treatment was too weak to work. Our videos provided only a single pairing of the treated candidates with a positive or negative implicit prime. Lodge and Taber's procedures provided up to *20* pairings of implicit affective primes with a targeted candidate. Twenty pairings seemed a bit much to us—at least we were not imagining videos that were long enough to provide that many opportunities to deliver an implicit prime. But we could imagine delivering two or three primes about a targeted candidate during a short video.

A third possibility is that the IAPS images we used as positive and negative primes are not as effective as the positive and negative words that Lodge and Taber employed as their affective primes. Our intuitions were that images would provide stronger implicit primes than words, but intuition is not always right. A fourth possibility is that our sample in Study 1 was too small to reliably detect significant effects. Had our results always been in the expected direction, just not always statistically different, we would have jumped on this possibility . . . but that was not the case. Still, larger samples are always better than smaller samples.

And of course a fifth possibility is that we are just wrong, and that these affect transfer effects require highly controlled experimental settings to occur, and therefore they are unlikely to generalize to more realistic settings. We systematically explore each of these possibilities in a series of follow-up studies.

Study 2

Each of our follow-up studies employed experimental procedures similar to those employed in Study 1, and we will provide much briefer descriptions from here on out, concentrating simply on the differences between the current study and the one(s) preceding it. Study 2 utilized the same videos as Study 1, but with a somewhat different procedure. Study 2 (and all remaining studies) began with subjects answering a few basic demographic questions, including the standard measure of party identification, which allowed us to treat self-proclaimed Democrats and Republicans differently.[4] Democrats in Study 2 first saw a "practice" video describing the three Republican candidates, none of whom were associated with any implicit primes. They were not asked to evaluate any of the candidates from the practice video. But then they were randomly assigned to view one of the six treatment videos from Study 1 describing the three Democratic candidates. Republican subjects followed just the opposite procedure, first viewing a "practice" control video describing the three Democratic candidates, and then viewing one of the six treatment videos from Study 1 describing the three Republican candidates, one of whom was associated with a positive implicit prime, and one of whom was associated with a negative implicit prime.

The major change in Study 2 was how the in-party (treatment) candidates were evaluated. Rather than rating them one at a time, as in Study 1, in Study 2 subjects were asked to make a series of explicitly comparative judgments. They were first asked which of the three in-party candidates appeared to be the most *competent*, and then which of the three appeared to be the least competent. The two questions allowed for a complete ranking of the three in-party candidates according to their apparent competence.[5] Then subjects were asked which of the three in-party candidates appeared to be the most *likable*, followed by selecting the one who appeared to be the least likable. Again, these two questions gave us a complete ranking of the three in-party candidates according to their relative likability. Ratings of the relative attractiveness of the three candidates came next, followed by finally asking subjects, if they had to choose today, which of these three candidates they would vote for. These rankings resulted in highly reliable evaluations of the different candidates, so they were averaged together to form summary evaluations of the three in-party candidates.

Results and Discussion

Unfortunately, as can be seen in the second column of Tables 12.1 and 12.2, the results of Study 2 were considerably less promising than those of Study 1. While in Study 1 partisans rated in-party candidates associated with a positive prime significantly more highly than when they were associated with a negative prime, in Study 2 this *never* happened (and this is with three times as many subjects in Study 2 as there were in Study 1). And while the hypothesized Positive Prime X Party ID interaction was always positive, as expected, it was larger than its standard error only half the time, and never significantly so.[6]

All told, then, Study 2 was a disappointment. It is apparently asking too much of subjects—or perhaps, asking too much of implicit primes—that the differential effects of experiencing a positive or negative implicit prime will persist across viewing three separate targets, all of whom must be evaluated.

Study 3

Our third study made three important changes to our basic procedures. First, rather than showing a single video including all three candidates from a particular party, we cut them up so that the candidates could be presented one at a time, followed immediately by an evaluation of that particular candidate. Second, whenever a candidate was in a treatment condition, their picture was both *preceded and followed* by a one-frame (33 ms) affective prime. Hence we effectively doubled the strength of the implicit affect manipulation. Third, after running the study employing IAPS images as the affective primes (as had been the case in Studies 1 and 2), we repeated the study with the exact same design, except that we replaced the image primes with the type of word primes that Lodge and Taber (2013) employed in their book.[7] Because these data were gathered several months apart, we report their findings separately, as Studies 3_I (with image primes) and 3_W (word primes).

Results and Discussion

The simple mean ratings of the different candidates by party members who had evaluated the candidate in either the positive or negative prime conditions, are shown in the third and fourth columns of Table 12.1. While the candidates are rated higher in the positive prime than the negative prime condition more often than not in Study 3, the differences are not very large, and only twice (of 12 comparisons) are they significantly higher.

The more telling multivariate analyses are reported in the third and fourth columns of Table 12.2, and here the hypothesized results are more often observed. The key predictions are a positive in-party ID X Positive Prime interaction, and a negative out-party ID X Negative Prime interaction. The predicted (positive) positive prime interaction is observed in nine of 12 instances, three significantly; the predicted (negative) negative prime interaction is observed only half of the time, but four of those instances were statistically significant. If we compare image primes (Study 3_I) to word primes (Study 3_W), the image primes work much better. Of the 12 hypothesized positive and negative interaction terms, ten have their predicted sign when IAPS images provided the primes (six significantly), but only six of 12 have the predicted sign when words are used as the implicit primes.

So, lessons from Study 3: Image primes work better than word primes, two primes work better than one prime, and priming effects are easier to detect if the targeted candidate is evaluated immediately after the primes are presented.[8]

Study 4

Because Lodge and Taber employed word primes consistently throughout their book, we wanted to try one more study using simple words as our implicit primes. Moreover, because we have been pretesting stimuli for an eventual mock election study experiment in the studies presented in this chapter, and that eventual experimental design dictates that we have to introduce all three party candidates in a single video, we wanted to go back to presenting the three party candidates together in a single video. To not go against all of the lessons of Study 3, however, we determined to try to make the implicit affect effect even stronger by associating a third implicit prime with our targeted candidates.[9]

Hence we created a new set of videos for the final study, this time varying the candidate order within party. The videos were lengthened slightly, always starting with the red, white, and blue party mascot (Democratic donkey or Republican elephant); but then followed by a one-frame (33 ms) positive/negative word prime, the candidate's picture for 3 seconds, another single frame positive/negative prime, and then the interstate road sign (with the state map) associated with the candidate's home state, a third one-frame positive/negative word prime, and then the presidential seal as a 2-second mask between candidates. The remaining two candidates were presented with similar procedures. To reduce the total number of videos we needed to produce, however, the first candidate presented in any video was always associated with three positive (or negative) primes, the second candidate was always the no-prime control candidate, and the third was always associated with three negative (or positive) primes.

We wanted to try one further manipulation in this final study. About 10% of our subjects across studies evaluated *all* of the mock candidates negatively—that is, below the neutral point, on average, in the various rating scales employed. We wondered if this apparent negativity toward politicians was suppressing the hypothesized affective priming effects. We therefore created one set of videos describing the six candidates exactly as they had been in previous studies—as governors, senators, and congressmen running for president. But the other half of the videos, employing the exact same images and primes, described the six people as high school principals applying for the job of principal of a brand new high school being built in Little Rock, Arkansas, or Columbus, Ohio. Our final hypothesis is that these people will be evaluated more positively when they are presented as high school principals than as politicians, and further that the observed priming effects would be stronger in the principals condition than in the politicians condition.

We tried a third new procedure for having the three candidates evaluated after the experimental video introducing them. We went back to having the candidate evaluated individually (as in Studies 1 and 3) in the order they were presented, rather than explicitly in comparison to each other (as in Study 2). But to help subjects remember which candidate was which, each rating scale employed in Study 4 included the candidate's picture.

Results and Discussion

For comparability with previous studies, the data presented in the final column of Tables 12.1 and 12.2 come only from the half of the subjects in the presidential election condition. These results, although based on only about 300 subjects, look pretty much like those of Study 2—that is, more random than consistent with the affective priming hypotheses. Moreover, we found no support for our hypotheses about principal–politician differences. One of the candidates (Turner) was rated significantly more positively as a principal than as a politician, while another one (Davis) was rated significantly more positively as a politician than as a principal. And there were no interactions between the implicit affect manipulation, and the principal-politician manipulation. Bottom line on Study 4: Ignoring the lessons of Study 3 was not a good idea.

Pushing a Little Harder: Social Identities vs. Party Identification

Thus far we have been exploring the effects of implicit affective primes on the evaluations of Democratic and Republican political candidates. As such, the primary social identifications that we have considered to interact with the primes have been partisan—Democratic or Republican party identifications. But Lodge and Taber (2013) conducted several studies where they found that other social identifications—race or gender, produced even stronger effects. Two of our six candidates (Davis and Harris) were white males, but two others were nonwhite males (Ramirez, a Latino male, and Baker, an African American male), and two others were white females (Turner and Johnson).

Table 12.3 presents alternative specifications of our basic multivariate analyses for the two nonwhite male candidates and the two female candidates, where the positive and negative primes are interacted not with party ID, but with dummy variables representing the candidates' race/ethnicity (for the two nonwhite males), or their gender, for the two female candidates. In this final set of analyses, the main effects of the two primes represent the effects of the primes among non-group members, while the interaction terms represent the differences between the effects of the primes on group members, relative to non-group members.[10] The most promising results here occur for the two nonwhite males, Ramirez and Baker, in Study 3, where both of the Latino (Black) X Positive Prime interactions are positive and statistically significant. We saw no evidence that the affective primes associated with either of our female candidates worked any better among female subjects, however.

General Discussion and Conclusion

Affect transfer seems to be taking place more than we would expect from chance in several of our study designs. Clearly, however, our results are not as strong as Lodge and Taber's (2013), and certain design choices led to better results than others. A few conclusions can be drawn. First, image primes seemed to work better in our studies than did word primes. This could be because our primes were

TABLE 12.3 Multivariate Analysis of Candidate Evaluation, Interactions With Ethnicity, Race, and Gender

	Study 1 B S.E.	Study 2 B S.E.	Study 3₁ B S.E.	Study 3_w B S.E.	Study 4 B S.E.
Ed Ramirez	−1.37 (2.56)	.33 (.17)	1.07 (3.50)	2.00 (3.19)	9.78★★★(2.66)
Latino					
Pos. Prime	−3.86 (2.35)	.04 (.06)	−3.31★★ (1.33)	−2.00 (1.15)	−.78 (1.24)
Neg. Prime	−4.63★ (1.99)	.15★ (.06)	−2.15 (1.25)	−1.35 (1.06)	.82 (1.25)
Pos. x Latino	−1.69 (4.31)	−.27 (.24)	12.42★★ (4.39)	8.03★ (4.11)	−11.80★★ (4.29)
Neg. x Latino	12.22 (6.38)	−.34 (.25)	.14 (4.31)	−3.62 (4.12)	−1.78 (4.22)
Lou Baker	.86 (4.72)	.05 (.32)	.64 (4.18)	−.46 (3.55)	−13.27★★★(3.93)
Black					
Pos. Prime	−.16 (1.50)	−.18★★ (.07)	−2.41 (1.46)	−1.02 (1.29)	−.80 (1.14)
Neg. Prime	−6.98★★★(1.49)	−.12 (.07)	−.72 (1.40)	−.11 (2.65)	.02 (1.19)
Pos. x Black	−11.91 (9.95)	.31 (.39)	9.31★★ (5.10)	8.38★★ (4.72)	20.42★★★ (5.15)
Neg. x Black	1.25 (8.27)	−.06 (.38)	−1.92 (6.11)	7.29 (4.62)	11.75★ (5.38)
Susan Turner	5.00★ (2.13)	.35★★★ (.09)	4.93★★ (1.60)	6.98★★★ (1.52)	3.77★ (1.75)
Female					
Pos. Prime	−2.14 (2.04)	.04 (.08)	−.40 (1.48)	.70 (1.39)	4.88★★ (1.60)
Neg. Prime	1.06 (2.10)	.09 (.08)	−.04 (1.42)	1.40 (1.41)	3.30★ (1.55)
Pos. x Female	−1.71 (3.26)	−.01 (.13)	−.66 (2.34)	−.05 (2.08)	−5.61★ (2.40)
Neg. x Female	−6.08★ (3.60)	−.31★★ (.12)	−.69 (2.23)	−2.22 (2.12)	−.49 (2.37)
Debra Johnson	−.25 (2.36)	.13 (.10)	−3.85★ (1.59)	−1.69 (1.38)	.03 (1.73)
Female					
Pos. Prime	1.20 (2.27)	−.04 (.09)	−2.22 (1.52)	.20 (1.23)	−.33 (1.58)
Neg. Prime	−.23 (2.38)	.01 (.09)	−2.98★ (1.44)	−.42 (1.23)	−1.50 (1.56)
Pos. x Female	−4.41 (4.19)	−.05 (.15)	.47 (2.37)	2.40 (1.89)	.89 (2.30)
Neg. x Female	−2.04 (3.75)	.05 (.14)	3.89 (2.25)	2.14 (1.96)	2.46 (2.34)

Notes: ★p < .05 ★★p < .01 ★★★p < .001.
All analyses included controls for gender, age, race, party identification, and political sophistication.

embedded in videos, and preceded other images, rather than text. Perhaps images were more easily processed by subjects than words were given the overall context. It is also possible that the size of the primes made a difference. The images were inherently larger than the words and took up more of the screen, so larger primes may also be more easily processed.

Second, more primes seem to have a larger effect than fewer (two worked better than one in Study 3). This is not surprising, given that seeing more primes with the same affect serves to reinforce the association. A large part of why Lodge and Taber's findings are so much stronger than ours likely has to do with the fact that our subjects were exposed to so many fewer primes. On the other hand, simply adding a third prime (in Study 4) did not improve our results. It appears that the other changes we made in Study 4 (using word primes instead of images and presenting all candidates together in one video) trumped the inclusion of an additional prime per candidate.

Third, asking subjects to evaluate a candidate immediately after the prime(s) and target are presented maximizes the chances of detecting the predicted effect. Combining all candidates and the associated primes into one video seriously weakened the effects of the primes. This suggests that distraction (being asked to consider other candidates) and/or elapsed time may lessen the effects of affect transfer, in general.

Fourth, while Lodge and Taber found consistent effects of political sophistication such that sophisticates were more influenced by implicit primes than their less sophisticated counterparts, we found very little support for this hypothesis. Sophistication often interacted with the candidate and the repeated measure, such that the priming hypothesis worked better among sophisticated voters for some candidates, but worse among others. We could see no consistent pattern across studies.

Finally, politically salient identities still seem to play a major role in candidate evaluation, as Lodge and Taber find as well. It is when we interact the prime conditions with partisanship that we find our most compelling results in general, and we also find some limited evidence that racial and ethnic identity may interact with the primes for black and Latino subjects when they see black and Latino candidates, respectively, such that positive primes are particularly effective. It seems that voters may be more susceptible to incidental primes when they are motivated to feel a particular way about a candidate in the first place.

Clearly, there is much work still to be done on the effects of affect transfer in the "real world." It is obvious that implicit affective primes have some influence on some subjects in some circumstances. Political psychologists should continue to parse the conditions in which implicit primes can impact voter behavior, ideally by testing the affect transfer hypothesis in an increasingly diverse range of experimental study designs. Lodge and Taber (2013) have convincingly demonstrated that unconscious processes have an important role to play in voter decision-making, and we must continue to examine the extent to which those processes determine our behaviors, if political scientists are to gain a better understanding of phenomena such as political attitude formation, candidate evaluations, and ultimate vote choices.

Notes

1. See, e.g. Pedro De Bruyckere "Subliminal Advertising, Does It Work?" https://theeconomyofmeaning.com/2012/09/13/subliminal-advertising-does-it-work/.
2. Our studies do not test for any moderating effects of deliberation.
3. In each of the studies described in this chapter, a handful of subjects—never more than 2%—mentioned that they thought they might have seen a picture flashing during one or the other of the videos. We eliminated those subjects from the analyses reported here, but the results change little if they are included. A more troubling factor was the tendency of some (politically correct?) subjects—about 10–12% across the different studies—to refuse to make first impressions—or rather, to rate every candidate identically, presumably because there was so little discriminating information provided. This would not be a bad practice in general, but it does undermine the power of our experimental manipulations to produce differences in candidate evaluations. To compensate for this political correctness, we weighted our data by the within-subject standard deviation of candidate evaluations (adding a small number to those subjects with a standard deviation of 0) so that the more "discriminating" subjects counted more in the analysis.
4. "Pure" independents were randomly assigned to either the Democratic condition or the Republican condition.
5. Overall, subjects in Study 2 made over 2700 such comparative evaluations. In only four instances (twice for Democrats, and twice for Republicans) was the same candidate chosen as the most and least competent (or attractive or likable). We take this as a very strong indication of how carefully these subjects were reporting their evaluations.
6. Because treatment videos with the positive and negative primes were only shown to in-party partisans in Study 2, it is not possible to test the (out-)Party ID X Negative Prime interaction.
7. "Happy," "Love," "Miracle," and "Sunshine" were used as positive word primes; "Cancer," "Hate," "Torture," and "Vomit" were the negative word primes.
8. Study 3 presented the opportunity for one additional design change. While the candidates in Studies 1 and 2 were always presented to subjects in the same order (Ramirez—Turner—Davis for the Democrats; Harris—Baker—Johnson for Republicans), creating separate videos for each candidate made it much easier to vary the order of candidates. We always alternated between presenting Democratic and Republican candidates to subjects; and always presented one of the candidates from each party with positive primes, one with negative primes, and one with no primes; but within that basic structure, randomized the actual order of presentation of the six candidates. Hence "order" was entered as an additional factor in the analyses of Study 3. Order proved to have significant effects only once, however, and as we had no theoretical reason to expect order effects in the strength of affective priming, we interpreted this one positive result as a chance finding, and give it no further attention.
9. The three positive word primes used in the final study were "Good," "Smile," and "Love." The three negative word primes were "Bad," "Vomit," and "Hate."
10. It seems clear that the interaction between the positive prime and group membership should be positive: implicit primes could give group members an excuse, a reason, to rate their fellow group member more positively than they might otherwise have rated them. It is not so obvious to us whether we would expect the interaction between group membership and negative primes to be positive or negative, however.

References

Abelson, Robert. (1963). Computer simulation of "hot" cognition. In Silvan Tomkins & Samuel Messick (Eds.), *Computer simulation of personality, frontier of psychological theory* (pp. 277–298). New York: John Wiley and Sons, Inc.

Achen, Christopher & Bartels, Larry. (2006). *It feels like we're thinking: The rationalizing voter and electoral democracy*. Paper presented at the annual meeting of the American Political Science Association, Philadelphia, PA, August 31–September 3.

Babad, Elisha. (1999). Preferential treatment in television interviewing: Evidence from nonverbal behavior. *Political Communication*, 16(3), 337–358.

Babad, Elisha. (2005). The psychological price of mass media bias. *Journal of Experimental Psychology: Applied II*, 4, 245–255.

Bargh, John. (1997). The automaticity of everyday life. In Robert Wyer (Ed.), *Advances in social cognition* (pp. 1–61). Mahwah, NJ: Erlbaum.

Berinsky, Adam J., Huber, Gregory A., & Lenz, Gabriel S. (2012). Evaluating online labor markets for experimental research: Amazon.com's Mechanical Turk. *Political Analysis*, 20(3), 351–368.

Bradley, M. M. & Lang, P. J. (2007). The international affective picture system (IAPS) in the study of emotion and attention. In J. A. Coan & J. J. B. Allen (Eds.), *Handbook of emotion elicitation and assessment* (pp. 29–46). Oxford: Oxford University Press.

Buhrmester, Michael, Kwang, Tracy, & Gosling, Samuel D. (2011). Amazon's Mechanical Turk: A new source of inexpensive, yet high-quality, data? *Perspectives on Psychological Science*, 6(1), 3–5.

Dovidio, J., Kawakami, K., & Gaertner, S. (2002). Implicit prejudice and interracial interaction. *Journal of Personality and Social Psychology*, 82, 62–68.

Eagly, Alice, Ashmore, Richard, Makhijini, Mona, & Longo, Laura. (1991). What is beautiful is good, but. . . : A meta-analytic review of the research on the physical attractiveness stereotype. *Psychological Bulletin*, 110(1), 109–128.

Erisen, Cengiz, Lodge, Milton, & Taber, Charles S. (2014). Affective contagion in effortful political thinking. *Political Psychology*, 35(2), 187–206.

Fazio, Russell, Sanbonmatsu, David, Powell, Martha, & Kardes, Frank. (1986). On the automatic activation of attitudes. *Journal of Personality and Social Psychology*, 50(2), 229–238.

Feingold, Alan. (1992). Gender differences in mate selection preferences: A test of the parental investment model. *Psychological Bulletin*, 112(1), 125–139.

Friedman, Howard M., DiMatteo, Robin, & Mertz, Timothy. (1980). Nonverbal communication on television news. *Personality and Social Psychology Bulletin*, 6(3), 427–435.

Greenwald, Anthony & Nosek, Brian. (2009). Attitudinal disassociation: What does it mean? In Richard Petty, Russell Fazio, & Pablo Brinol (Eds.), *Attitudes: Insights from the new implicit measures* (pp. 65–118). New York: Psychology Press.

Greenwald, Anthony, Poehlman, Andrew, Uhlmann, Eric, & Banaji, Mahzarin. (2009). Understanding and using the implicit association test: III. Meta-analysis of predictive validity. *Journal of Personality and Social Psychology*, 97(1), 17–41.

Gregory, Stanford & Gallagher, Timothy. (2002). Spectral analysis of candidates' nonverbal vocal communication: Predicting U.S. presidential election outcomes. *Social Psychology Quarterly*, 65(3), 298–308.

Healy, Andrew, Malhotra, Neil, & Mo, Cecilia Hyunjung. (2010). Irrelevant events affect voters' evaluations of government performance. *Proceedings from the National Academy of Sciences of the United States of America*, 107(29), 12804–12809.

Kahneman, Daniel. (2011). *Thinking, fast and slow*. New York: Farrar, Straus and Giroux.

Karremans, Johan, Stroebe, Wolfgang, & Claus, Jasper. (2006). Beyond Vicary's fantasies: The impact of subliminal priming and brand choice. *Journal of Experimental Social Psychology*, 42(6), 792–798.

Lambert, A. J., Payne, B. K., Ramsey, S., & Shaffer, L. M., (2005). On the predictive validity of implicit attitude measures: The moderating effect of perceived group variability. *Journal of Experimental Social Psychology*, 41(2), 114–128.

Lang, P. J., Bradley, M. M., & Cuthbert, B. N. (2008). *International affective picture system (IAPs): Affective ratings of pictures and instruction manual.* Technical Report A-8. University of Florida, Gainesville, FL.

Langlois, Judith, Kalakanis, Lisa, Rubenstein, Adam, Larson, Andrea, Hallam, Monica, & Smoot, Monica. (2000). Maxims or myths of beauty? A meta-analytic and theoretical review. *Psychological Bulletin*, 126(3), 390–423.

Little, Anthony, Burriss, Robert, Jones, Benedict, & Roberts, Craig. (2007). Facial appearance affects voting decision. *Evolution and Human Behavior*, 28(1), 18–27.

Lodge, Milton & Taber, Charles S. (2005). The automaticity of affect for political leaders, groups, and issues: An experimental test of the hot cognition hypothesis. *Political Psychology*, 26(3), 455–482.

Lodge, Milton & Taber, Charles S. (2013). *The rationalizing voter.* New York: Cambridge University Press.

Mason, Winter A. & Suri, Siddharth. (2012). Conducting behavioral research on Amazon's Mechanical Turk. *Behavior Research Methods*, 44(1), 1–23.

Mueller, Ulrich & Mazur, Allan. (1996). Facial dominance in West Point cadets predicts military ranks 20+ years later. *Social Forces*, 74(3), 823–850.

Mullen, Brian, Futrell, David, Stairs, Debbie, Tice, Dianne, Baumeister, Roy, Dawson, Kathryn, Riordan, Catherine, Radloff, Christine, Goethals, George, Kennedy, John, & Rosenfeld, Paul. (1986). Newscasters' facial expressions and voting behavior of viewers: Can a smile elect a president? *Journal of Personality and Social Psychology*, 51(2), 291–295.

Nosek, Brian & Smyth, Frederick. (2007). A multi-trait multi-method validation of the implicit association test: Implicit and explicit attitudes are related but distinct constructs. *Journal of Experimental Psychology*, 54(1), 14–29.

Paolacci, Gabriele, Chandler, Jesse, & Ipeirotis, Panagiotis. (2010). Running experiments on Amazon Mechanical Turk. *Judgment and Decision Making*, 5(5), 411–419.

Payne, K., Krosnick, J., Pasek, J., Lelkes, Y., Akhtar, O., & Thompson, T. (2010). Implicit and explicit prejudice in the 2008 American presidential election. *Journal of Experimental Social Psychology*, 46(2), 367–374.

Sears, David O. (2001). The role of affect in symbolic politics. In J.H. Kuklinski (Ed.), *Citizens and politics: Perspectives from political psychology* (pp. 14–40). New York: Cambridge University Press.

Shapiro, Danielle N., Chandler, Jesse, & Mueller, Pam A. (2013). Using Mechanical Turk to study clinical populations. *Clinical Psychological Science*, 1(2), 213–220.

Taber, Charles S. and Lodge, Milton. (2014). Motivated skepticism revisited:
The scope and generality of automatic affective biases in political thinking. *Critical Review*, 24 (2): 157–184.

Todorov, Alexander, Oliviola, Christopher Y., Dotsch, Ron, & Mende-Siedlecki, Peter. (2015). Social attributions from faces: Determinants, consequences, accuracy, and functional significance. *Annual Review of Psychology*, 66, 519–545.

Weinberger, Joel & Westen, Drew. (2008). RATS, we should have used Clinton: Subliminal priming in political campaigns. *Political Psychology*, 29(5), 631–651.

Zajonc, Robert. (1980). Feeling and thinking: Preferences need no inferences. *American Psychologist*, 35(2), 117–123.
Zajonc, Robert. (2000). Feeling and thinking: Closing the debate over the independence of affect. In Joseph Forgas (Ed.), *Feeling and thinking: The role of affect in social cognition* (pp. 31–58). Cambridge: Cambridge University Press.
Ziegert, Jonathan C. & Hanges, Paul J. (2005). Employment discrimination: The role of implicit attitudes, motivation, and a climate for racial bias. *Journal of Applied Psychology*, 90(3), 553–562.

APPENDIX

TABLE 12.A1 (MTurk) Subject Characteristics

	Pretest 1	Pretest 2	Pretest 3_I	Pretest 3_W	Pretest 4
% Female	35.1%	41.0%	39.0%	40.4%	42.4%
% White	83.4%	79.1%	75.4%	76.4%	80.0%
% Black	4.7%	5.9%	5.9%	6.1%	5.5%
% Latino	7.4%	6.2%	7.8%	7.4%	6.6%
Mean Yrs Education	14.6	14.6	14.8	14.7	14.9
Mean Age	34.4	35.3	34.2	33.3	36.3
% Democrat	36.4%	46.3%	45.9%	46.7%	46.2%
% Republican	11.2%	15.9%	15.2%	16.0%	18.6%
% Independent	52.4%	37.8%	38.9%	37.2%	35.0%
N	375	912	841	1023	644

INDEX

accuracy motivation 5, 14, 21–23, 70, 72–73, 76, 104, 106, 128, 138, 140, 144, 172
activation 5, 7, 16, 19–20, 22
actual ideological differences 196, 198, 201–206
affective contagion 18, 25, 71, 73, 231, 248
affective primacy 231
affect transfer 7, 23, 229–234, 237, 240, 244, 246
ambivalence 7, 37, 70, 73–74, 100, 104–106, 110, 113–120
American National Election Studies (ANES) 67
American Racial Opinion Survey (AROS) 176
American Voter, The 12, 30, 151
assimilation-contrast model 212
attitudes 6–8, 12, 15–21, 31–32, 37–38, 40, 42, 65, 69, 71–76, 81, 83–84, 103–106, 111, 117–119, 121, 127, 129–134, 137–138, 140, 142–145, 154, 166–167, 172–173, 175–177, 190–191, 230–231
attitudinal consequences of belief updating 117
attitudinal effects of belief change 118
authoritarianism 8, 185, 187, 189
automaticity 3, 8, 11, 14–18, 25–26, 50, 60, 63, 105, 122, 148, 248–249

Bargh, John 18
Bassili, John 50

Bayesian model 20–21, 59–60, 61, 99–100, 121
bias 5, 7, 14–17, 20–22, 38–39, 55–57, 61, 66, 69–75, 81–84, 100, 102–106, 113, 115–117, 119–120, 127–129, 131–135, 137–145, 165, 172, 174, 177, 180–181, 195–198, 205–207, 211, 213
black-box models 12, 26

candidate evaluation 37, 56, 70, 153, 161–162, 208, 247
capital punishment 100–102, 106–112, 117, 119, 121
CF-Scores 198, 200, 218
citizen competence 5, 65–66, 69–70, 73, 78–79
Clinton, Hillary 49
closed-minded cognition 81–82, 97
cognitive misers 151
cognitive structure versus process 34
common-man's ideology 151
computational experiments 12, 26–27
Conover, Pam 33
conscious thinking 18, 20, 229
conservatism bias 102–103, 105–106, 115, 117, 119
Cooperative Congressional Election Study (CCES) 196, 201, 205

Davies, Caitlin 66, 68, 70, 72, 74, 76, 78, 80
De Bruyckere, Pedro 247
democratic citizen 3, 5, 65
determinants of motivated reasoning 185

directional motivation 5, 15, 22, 70, 72–73, 81–84, 128, 134, 144, 206
Ditonto, Tessa M. 230, 232, 234, 236, 240, 242, 244, 246, 248, 250
dogmatic expert 87
Dolan, Tom 42
Druckman, James N. 43–44, 125–126, 128, 130, 132, 134, 136, 138, 140, 142, 144, 146, 148, 150
dual-process theories 19, 22, 104, 230
DW-Nominate 198–202, 207, 213, 218–220
dynamic information board 23, 156–157
Dynamic Process Tracing Environment (DPTE) 152, 155, 157, 167

earned dogmatism 86–87, 89–95, 97
ease of retrieval 89, 97
effectiveness of capital punishment 108–109, 112, 117
effortful processing 13, 69, 75, 230
egalitarianism 173, 185, 187
elite rhetoric 31, 39, 77
emotion 6, 21, 91, 155

"fact-free" politics 100
Feldman, Stanley 7, 30, 33, 171–172, 174, 176, 180, 182, 184, 186, 188, 190, 192
Fenno's *Home Style* 40
first impressions 151–167
Fischle, Mark 38

General Social Survey (GSS) 56, 184
Griffin-type measure 110

Haidt, Jonathan 6
Hamill, Ruth 33
Handbook of Political Psychology 14, 27, 44, 168, 192–193
heuristic processing 83
high-expertise 90–93, 95
high information rationality 14, 17
hot cognition 8, 14–17, 20, 23, 26, 38, 61, 63, 70–73, 76, 97, 104, 122–123, 148–149, 154, 169, 231, 236–237, 249
Huckfeldt, Robert 7, 48, 50, 52, 54, 56, 58, 60, 62, 64
Huddy, Leonie 2, 7, 27, 30, 44–45, 168, 171–172, 174, 176, 180, 182, 184, 186, 188, 190, 192–193

IAPS images 240, 242
ideological self-placement 184–185, 195
ideology-affect relationship 198
individualism 173, 185, 187

information-processing motivation 104, 119
information search 151–152, 154–156, 161–167
in-party candidates 208, 224–225, 236, 241
issue-relevant values 68
Iyengar, Shanto 7, 39, 196, 198, 200, 202, 204, 206, 208, 210, 212, 214, 216, 220

Jerit, Jennifer 7, 65–66, 68, 70, 72, 74, 76, 78, 80
John Q. Public (JQP) 18–21, 166, 229, 232, 234
Jones, Jeff 38
judgement processes 3–4, 6, 15, 18, 22, 34–35, 37–41, 53, 56, 59, 65, 74, 82–84, 89, 105, 128, 153, 156, 166, 175, 179, 231–232, 241

Kuklinski, James H. 11, 33–34
Kunda, Ziva 5, 14, 50

Lau, Richard R. 43, 229–230, 232, 234, 236, 240, 242, 244, 246, 248, 250
Lavine, Howard 2, 4, 6–8, 14, 29, 99–100, 102, 104, 106, 108, 110, 112, 114, 116, 118, 120, 122, 124
Leeper, Thomas J. 125
Levine, Jeff 50
long-term memory (LTM) 20–21, 35, 60, 126, 231–232
low-expertise 90–92

magnitude scaling 32, 43
McGraw, Kathleen M. 29–30, 32, 34, 36, 38, 40, 42–46
memory-based processing model 14, 17, 20, 23, 34–38, 42–43, 69–70, 77, 109, 126, 131, 134, 147
Miller, Art 33
Monica Lewinsky scandal 102
motivated reasoning 5, 7, 11, 14–16, 20, 21–23, 31, 36, 60, 65–66, 69, 72–74, 83–84, 125–144, 153, 155, 172–191, 21

National Academy of Sciences (NAS) 141–142, 146, 248
National Annenberg Election Study (NAES) 20
Negative Black Character subscale 184
negative prime condition 237, 242

online processing model 11, 15, 17, 31, 34–38, 42, 65, 69, 125–129, 144, 152–154

open-mindedness 7, 81–82, 83–94, 97
Ottati, Victor 7, 30, 81–82, 84, 86, 88, 90, 92, 94–96
overt racism 183–185, 187–189

paradox of the dysfunctional citizen 17
Parker-Stephen, Evan 72–76, 79, 172, 192
partisan-motivated reasoning 76, 135, 138–139, 145, 172, 191
partisanship 49, 52, 56, 86, 95, 134–136, 138–139, 144, 172–173, 197, 203, 211, 246
Party Cues 68, 125, 129, 134–136, 138–139, 145, 167, 192, 216
party identification 17, 64, 134, 144, 147, 150, 153, 202, 214, 217, 221, 236–239, 241, 244–245
perceived policy positions 207
Pierce, Douglas R. 152, 154, 156, 158, 160, 162, 164, 166, 168
Pinney, Neil 34
POLI model of U.S. foreign policy 12
political cognition 11–13, 17, 19, 32–34, 43, 48–50, 55, 58–59, 61–62, 65–66, 71, 81, 95, 166, 169, 234
political expertise 7, 54, 71, 77–78, 81–87, 89–91, 93–97
political judgments 4, 6, 27, 40, 82–84, 231
political knowledge 33–34, 57, 62, 65–67, 69–73, 75–77, 79, 82–91, 94–95, 109, 113, 116, 121, 138, 186–187, 191
political novice 82, 87–88, 93
political preferences 49, 57–58, 125, 213
political psychology 1–3, 9, 11, 14, 16, 25–27, 30–33, 37, 41–45, 47, 55, 75, 78–80, 96, 106, 122–123, 143, 148, 150, 168–169, 171, 192–193, 216, 248–249
political sophistication 36–37, 66–69, 73, 75, 114, 128–129, 138, 143, 237, 246
political thinking 12, 18–19, 25, 27, 77, 150, 169, 248–249
posterior beliefs 100, 107–108, 111, 115
post hoc rationalizations 127
preconscious processes 54
Price, Erika 7
primacy of affect 16, 18, 231
priming 16–17, 230, 242–244, 246–247

racially motivated reasoning 7, 173–179, 181, 183, 185–187, 189, 191, 193
racial prejudice 175, 183–186, 189–192

randomization 154, 158, 160, 165
rationalization 6–7, 45, 74, 127, 149, 229
Rationalizing Voter, The 3, 7, 9, 11, 18, 26, 44, 70–73, 96, 123, 148, 152, 192, 214, 216, 229, 232, 248
Redlawsk, David P. 151–152, 154, 156, 158, 160, 162, 164, 166, 168
Righteous Mind, The 8

schema theory 12, 30, 33–34, 125
selective attention 92, 120
selective exposure 6, 145
self-perceptions of political expertise 84–85, 90, 94
short-term memory (STM) 18, 20, 60–61, 126, 231
simple act of voting model 75
Slothuus, Rune 7
social identity 173, 215, 244
social roles 82, 84–87, 91–93
Sood, Gaurav 7, 196, 198, 200, 202, 204, 206, 208, 210, 212, 214, 216, 220
Sprague, John 48–50, 61
Steenbergen, Marco 7, 12, 18, 34, 100–124
Stenner, Karen 38
stereotypes 83, 176, 183–184
St. Louis study 50, 55, 57–58
subliminal advertising 231, 247
Sumaktoyo, Nathanael 7
sustained disagreement 57
systematic processing 69, 83, 105

Taber, Charles S. 5–8, 29–31, 36, 38, 41–42, 49, 59–60, 70, 72, 100, 102, 104, 113, 119, 127–128, 131, 138, 144, 152, 154, 166, 172, 229–234, 237, 240, 242, 244–246
Trump, Donald 16, 49
Two-Factor Model 179–181

unconscious thinking 6, 18–22, 24, 75, 229–232, 246

validity-seeking goals 104

Wilson, Chase 7, 81
working memory (WM) 18, 20, 126, 231

YouGov sampling methodology 221

Zaller, John 4
Zinnes, Dina 11